A SERIOUS PROPOSAL TO THE LADIES

A SERIOUS PROPOSAL TO THE LADIES

PARTS I AND II

Mary Astell

edited by Patricia Springborg

broadview literary texts

National Library of Canada Cataloguing in Publication Data

Astell, Mary, 1668-1731
A serious proposal to the ladies. Parts I and II

(Broadview literary texts)
Includes bibliographical references.
ISBN 1-55111-306-6

1. Feminism—Early works to 1800.
2. Women—Education—Early works to 1800.
I. Springborg, Patricia II. Title. III. Series.

HQ1596.A87 2001 305.42 C2001-903585-3

Broadview Press Ltd. is an independent, international publishing house, incorporated in 1985

North America
Post Office Box 1243, Peterborough, Ontario, Canada K9J 7H5
3576 California Road, Orchard Park, NY 14127
Tel: (705) 743-8990; Fax: (705) 743-8353;
e-mail: customerservice@broadviewpress.com

United Kingdom
Thomas Lyster, Ltd.,
Units 3 & 4a, Ormskirk Industrial Park, Burscough Rd, Ormskirk,
Lancashire L39 2YW Tel: (1695) 575112; Fax: (1695) 570120;
E-Mail: books@tlyster.co.uk

Australia
St. Clair Press, P.O. Box 287, Rozelle, NSW 2039
Tel: (02) 818-1942; Fax: (02) 418-1923

www.broadviewpress.com

Broadview Press gratefully acknowledges the financial support of the Book Publishing Industry Development Program, Ministry of Canadian Heritage, Government of Canada.

Typesetting and assembly: True to Type Inc., Mississauga, Canada.
PRINTED IN CANADA

Contents

Acknowledgments

Let me begin with grateful thanks to all those individuals and institutions who by their inspiration and assistance made this edition possible. I wish to thank those who contributed materially, either by supplying answers to textual puzzles, or by assisting with its processing, especially the late Christine Ambrose, Dick Ashcraft, the late Bruce Cochrane, Conal Condren, Ros Conyngham, Kathy Dempsey, Jim Farr, Bridget Frost, Mark Goldie, Philip Hamburger, Bridget Hill, Isobel Horton, Ann Kelly, Kathleen Lesko, Shareen Matthews, John McCrystal, Carole Pateman, John Pocock, Maria Robertson, Lois Schwoerer, Quentin Skinner, Johann and Margaret Sommerville, Patricia Stablein, and Steven Zwicker.

The Vice-Chancellor's Publication Fund of the University of Sydney and the Research Council of Australia, through ARC Small Grant F10.26994 93/94/95, covered research expenses specific to this project, for which I am greatly indebted. To the Librarian of Fisher Library, University of Sydney; the State Library of New South Wales, in particular Sue Thomas; the State Library of Victoria; the Rare Book Librarian of the Library of Congress; Georgiana Ziegler, Betsy Walsh and the unfailingly helpful staff of the Folger Shakespeare Library; and Gesine Bottomley and her staff at the Wissenschaftskolleg zu Berlin my grateful thanks. I owe enormous responsibility to those institutions which provided financial support for full-time research, 1993-95 and 2000-01: The University of Sydney; The Folger Institute; The Woodrow Wilson International Center for Scholars; the Brookings Institution, Washington, D.C.; the John D. and Catherine T. MacArthur Foundation for a Research and Writing Grant which the Brookings Institution administered (1993-5); and the Wissenschaftskolleg zu Berlin (2000-01). To my programme directors at these institutions, Lena Orlin at the Folger Institute; Jim Morris, Michael Lacey and Ann Sheffield, at the Woodrow Wilson Center; John Steinbruner at Brookings and Kate Early at the MacArthur Foundation, and Wolf Lepenies, Rektor of the Wissenschaftskolleg zu Berlin and his staff, I am truly thankful for support and understanding as I juggled my projects. Bridget Frost, my editor at Pickering and Chatto, Barbara Conolly, Eugene Benson, and Betsy Struthers at Broadview Press have also shown unflagging enthusiasm and exemplary patience. To those who offered assistance on points of information and by reading drafts of my material, I owe special thanks: Professors Quentin

Skinner, Christ's College, and Mark Goldie, Vice-Master, Churchill College, Cambridge; John Pocock, of the Johns Hopkins University; Johann Sommerville, of the University of Wisconsin, and Margaret Sommerville; Kathleen Lesko and Patricia Stablein, Scholars-in-Residence at the Folger Shakespeare Library; Ann Kelly, of Howard University, Washington, DC; and Steven Zwicker of Washington University, St. Louis, Missouri, and the late Bruce Cochrane of the University of Canterbury, New Zealand.

Besides a general debt to individuals and institutions, I owe acknowledgment of specific tasks. Immense thanks to Maria Robertson, Ros Conyngham, Isobel Horton, and Shareen Matthews of the Department of Government, University of Sydney, and to Christine Ambrose and Kathy Dempsey, senior research assistants, who entered the text, checked and rechecked it.

This edition is dedicated to the memory of Christine Ambrose who sadly died while it was still in press, and without whose thoughtful work it would not have been possible.

Introduction

The Woman, the Work, and the Context

Mary Astell's *Serious Proposal to the Ladies for the Advancement of their True and Greatest Interest*, first published in 1694, is one of the most important and neglected in a long series of works advocating the establishment of academies for women. Republished in 1695, its reception was sufficiently controversial to cause Astell to respond with a lengthy sequel, *A Serious Proposal, Part II* (1697). Of all Astell's works, this one has the most complicated textual history. It was the cause of her great notoriety, only increased by the publication of *Reflections upon Marriage* in 1700. For her pains Astell was pilloried on the stage, lampooned in the press, and publicly debated by some of the greatest wits of the land.

Such public attention could hardly have been anticipated by the young woman who, departing poverty and obscurity, arrived in London in her early twenties from Newcastle-upon-Tyne. Born into a declining Northern gentry family in 1666, Catholic on her mother's side, Astell gave the lie to most received wisdom about the prospects of an academic career for girls in her era. Once in London, Astell entered a circle of high-church Anglican, aristocratic and Tory women, eventually settling in the house of Lady Catherine Jones, to whom works marking both the beginning and the culmination of her career are dedicated.[1] Friendly with her Chelsea neighbour, Elizabeth Elstob, Anglo-Saxon scholar and correspondent of George Ballard and the learned Bishop Francis Atterbury,[2] Astell had access to London intellectual circles and a fine library to equip herself for a career as one of the most theologically serious and philosophically competent theorists of her age.[3]

---

1 *Letters Concerning the Love of God* (1695) and *The Christian Religion as Profess'd by a Daughter of the Church* (1705).

2 Both Ballard and Atterbury leave accounts of her, the former (Ballard, *Memoirs of Several Ladies of Great Britain*), constituting an important source for the contemporary reception of her work.

3 Because her works were published anonymously they were not always taken for the work of a woman.

Showing customary North of England spiritedness, Astell introduced herself to High Church circles by presenting her religious poems *Dedicated to the most Reverend Father in God William by Divine Providence Lord Archbishop of Canterbury*, to the man himself, William Sancroft, possibly to request from him financial support for her endeavours.[1] Astell, perhaps already engaged in the religious controversy occasioned by the famous *Essay Concerning Human Understanding* (1689) of John Locke (1632-1704), then initiated a correspondence with John Norris (1657-1711), Rector of Bemerton. Begun in 1693, and published at Norris's instigation in 1695 as *Letters Concerning the Love of God*, the Astell-Norris Correspondence debated the relative autonomy of human motivation and cognition. Astell challenged Norris to accept the corollary of his argument that if God was the author of our pleasure, he was equally the author of our pain, twin motivational principles of Lockean sensationalist psychology. Commended by Norris for her remarkable philosophical acuity, Astell here already demonstrated a talent on which both her detractors and defenders were to comment. The theme she set in her opening letter described, in Cartesian language, what was to become a life-long programme:

> Sir, though some morose Gentlemen would perhaps remit me to the Distaff or the Kitchin, or at least to the Glass and the Needle, the proper Employments as they fancy of a Woman's Life; yet expecting better things from the more Equitable and ingenious Mr. Norris, who is not so narro-Soul'd as to confine Learning to his own Sex, or to envy it in ours, I presume to beg his Attention a little to the Impertinence of a Woman's Pen .... For though I can't pretend to a Multitude of Books, Variety of Languages, the Advantages of Academical Education or any Helps but what my own Curiosity affords; yet, *Thinking* is a Stock that no Rational Creature can want.[2]

The Astell-Norris correspondence, published in 1695 between the first and second parts of *A Serious Proposal to the Ladies*, undoubtedly prepared the reception of the more philosophically controversial *Part II*. The latter laid the ground in turn for Astell's notorious *Reflections upon Marriage* of 1700, which was to run through five editions in her lifetime. To the third edition (1706), she

---

1 Rawlinson MSS poet. 154:50, Oxford: The Bodleian Library; excerpted in Bridget Hill, *The First English Feminist*, 183-84, and printed in full in Ruth Perry, *The Celebrated Mary Astell*, 400-54.

2 Astell, *Letters Concerning the Love of God, between the Author of the Proposal to the Ladies and Mr. John Norris*, 1695 edn, 1-2.

added a controversial preface, expanding her argument to include one of the earliest critiques of Locke's *Two Treatises of Government* (1690). In 1704, on the strength of an already established name as the sworn enemy of Whigs, and probably commissioned by her printer, Richard Wilkin, Astell published three Tory pamphlets: *Moderation truly Stated*, *A Fair Way with the Dissenters*, and *An Impartial Enquiry*. All three addressed issues of religious toleration surrounding the Occasional Conformity debate, the latter entering the Tory canon as a classic statement of the historiography of civil war as a function of Dissent.[1] And in 1705 Astell's systematic defense of the Church of England, her magnum opus, *The Christian Religion as Profess'd by a Daughter of the Church*, appeared, in which she has her final say on the epistemology of Locke as the foundation of non-conformity.

Astell's last major published work, *Bart'lemy Fair, or an Enquiry after Wit in which due Respect is had to a Letter Concerning Enthusiasm* (1709), addressed a work directed against the Cambridge Platonists[2] in particular and religious enthusiasts in general. Astell believed it to be the work of Jonathan Swift, but the *Letter Concerning Enthusiasm* in question was in fact written by John Locke's protégé, Anthony Ashley Cooper (1671-1713), the third Earl of Shaftesbury. Astell dispatched it with customary alacrity, confronting the "triviality" of the eighteenth-century culture of the "Wits," who saw theological seriousness as a species of Enthusiasm. After 1709 Astell continued to support Tory causes. She was specifically acknowledged for her research assistance in the preface to Dr. John Walker's massive study, *The Sufferings of the Clergy* (1714), a Tory counterpart to Dr. Calamy's *Abridgement of the Life of Mr Baxter* for the non-conformists.[3] And in 1724 she supplied a Preface to Lady Mary Wortley Montagu's (1689-1762) *Letters from the East*, which were not published in fact until 1763.

---

1 See Mark Goldie, *Tory Political Thought 1689-1714*, 46, 206.

2 The Cambridge Platonists, who included Ralph Cudworth, father of Astell's interlocutor Damaris Masham, and John Norris, her correspondent in the *Letters concerning the Love of God*, flourished at Cambridge between 1633 and 1688. Although educated as Puritans, they reacted against prevailing doctrinal rigidity on ritual, church government, and dogma. Because of their toleration of religious diversity, they were also referred to as "lattitude men," and even condemned as Unitarians or atheists.

3 Hill, *The First English Feminist*, 48.

The Genre

Astell's project, set out in the first part of *A Serious Proposal* (1694), was to establish a religious community for "Ladies of Quality,"[1] funded by the dowries they brought with them and monies earned by founding a school. As such the proposal fell into a class of proposals for women's education in England of which it was to become the most famous. Earlier, Juan Luis Vives of Valencia (1492-1540), author of *De Institutione Christianae Feminae* (1523), translated as *Instruction of a Christian Maid*, during a five-year stay in England had promoted the education of women, writing a specific course of studies for Princess, later Queen Mary I, entitled *Satellitium*.[2] The exiled Thomas Becon (1512-67) had demanded in his *Catechism* that "schools for women and children be erected and set up in every Christian Commonwealth" by public authority, in imitation of the "monasteries of solitary women whom we heretofore call nuns."[3] More immediately, George Hickes (1642-1715), former chaplain to Charles II, a High Church Bishop who refused to swear allegiance to William and Mary, and suffragan to the non-juring[4] Archbishop Sancroft of Astell's acquaintance, had in a 1684 sermon called for the endowment of "colleges for the Education of young Women, much like unto those in the Universities for the Education of young Men."[5] Hickes, the rather free translator of Fénelon's

---

1. *A Serious Proposal* (1694 edn, 145; 2002 edn 102. Henceforth pages to both editions will be cited.). Richard Allestree's proposals, even more pointedly, were directed to "Women of Quality that converse among those who call themselves the *Wits* of the *Age*." Allestree lamented that women "are excluded out of the Scheme of Education ... as below the regard of Persons of Quality" (*The Ladies Calling*, 1705 edn, part 1, sect. 5, 106, and part 2, sect. 2, 219).
2. These works are reprinted in Watson, *Vives and the Renascence Education of Women* (1912). See Paula L. Barbour's Introduction to the Augustan Reprint edition, v-vi.
3. *The Catechism of Thomas Becon*, ed. Rev. John Ayre (Cambridge, Parker Society, 1844), 376- 77, cited in Bridget Hill, "A Refuge from Men: The Idea of a Protestant Nunnery," 110.
4. The term non-jurors refers to those Churchmen who refused to take the oaths of allegiance to William and Mary after the Revolution of 1688, because they had previously taken similar oaths to James II. Archbishop Sancroft, five bishops, and around 400 clergy refused to swear, and were deprived of their posts for doing so.
5. George Hickes, *Sermons on Several Subjects*, 2 vols (London, 1713), vol. I, 397, cited by Hill, "A Refuge for Men," 114.

De L'Education des Filles,[1] was an influential contemporary who knew and possibly influenced Astell.[2] While we have no direct evidence that Astell had read Fénelon, despite striking similarities, the renown of the Maison de Saint Louis at Saint-Cyr, a school for noblewomen founded in 1686 by Louis XIV's mistress and later wife, with which Fénelon was closely associated, suggests a possible model for *A Serious Proposal*.[3] Richard Allestree, whose popular *The Ladies Calling* of 1673 Astell cites, in his chapter "Of Virgins," wished that the Church of England might have reformed women's monasteries, rather than abolishing them, raising the possibility of "Nuns who are not profess'd" as a constructive path now open and perhaps, in his estimate, the highest form of the Ladies' Calling.[4]

The same year the irrepressible Bathsua Makin, author of *An Essay to Revive the Antient Education of Gentlewomen* (1673), provided a model in tune with Astell's proposal. Makin was tutor to Princess Elizabeth, daughter of Charles I, around 1641. The Princess succeeded in mastering Greek, Latin, French, German, Italian, Hebrew, and Arabic before she died in 1650, languages in which Makin herself had facility, despite her condemnation of foreign tongues as a medium educated males employed to assert their superiority.[5] Makin's project was to establish in the Tottenham Cross girls' school a boarding school that would turn out women properly equipped to perform their domestic roles. Her work followed closely the program of her correspondent, the famous scholar from the University of Utrecht, Anna Marie van Schurman, whose *De Ingenii Muliebris* was translated into English as *The Learned Maid* in 1659. Makin also espoused the educational theo-

---

1 Hickes's translation of Fénelon's *De L'Education des Filles*, was published as *Instructions for the Education of a Daughter* (London, 1699).

2 See Hickes's letter to Dr. Charlett of 9 December 1704, commending her intolerance of non-conformity or occasional-conformity. See Ballard MSS 62:85 (1985 edn, 386), cited Perry, *Celebrated Mary Astell*, 100, 488 n. 9.

3 The founder of the Saint Cyr school, Françoise d'Aubigné, Marquise de Maintenon, the nature of its charter, and relations with Fénelon are the subject of Lougee's *Les Paradis des Femmes* (1976), part 4, "Saint-Cyr: The Counterinstitution."

4 Richard Allestree (1619-1681), *The Ladies Calling* (1705 edn, 257).

5 Astell, and Judith Drake, whose *An Essay In Defence of the Female Sex* (1696), was taken for a work by Astell, employed the same argument. Drake's work is excerpted in Appendix A below, 237-66.

ries of John Amos Commenius, who in his *Great Didactic* of 1632 had argued for the education of girls and modernizing the curriculum to make this possible.

Astell shares with Makin a desire to abandon the tyrannies of custom and William Lily's *Grammar.*[1] The language of Makin's programme, and injunctions to "reform these Exorbitancies," to abandon "Toyes and Trifles," and to see the men who denied their intellectual potential for what they were, "debauched Sots" who care only for their "Lusts and Pleasure," have their echo in Astell.[2] Like Astell she supports traditional authority, warning her readers that "God hath made Man the Head" and that "To ask to much is the way to be denied all."[3] That Astell does not mention her predecessor by name may be due to the earlier woman's Puritanism and political sympathies on the Parliament side. Worse yet, Makin had addressed her *Essay* to Lady Mary, Duchess of York, daughter of James II, who in 1689 was to become Queen Mary II, as wife of William of Orange, while Astell's friends numbered among the Jacobites and non-jurors who refused to swear allegiance to this perceived imposter.

Astell's *Proposal* thus fell into the class of ideas whose time had come. But for every George Wheler who gave unqualified acknowledgment to Astell's influence in *A Protestant Monastery* of 1698, there were ten who stole her ideas without acknowledgment and then satirized her to cover their tracks.[4] Gilbert Burnet (1643-

1 Makin's opening remarks on custom anticipate the remarks by William Wotton, repeated by Astell in the first part of *A Serious Proposal* (1694, 78-79/79-80). See Makin's *Antient Education of Gentlewomen*, sig. A2:

> Custom, when it is inveterate, hath a mighty influence: it hath the force of Nature it self. The Barbarous custom to breed Women low, is grown general amongst us, and hath prevailed so far, that it is verily believed (especially among a sort of debauched Sots) that Women are not endued with such Reason, as Men; nor capable of improvement by Education, as they are. It is lookt upon as a monstrous thing, to pretend to the contrary. A Learned Woman is thought to be a Comet, that does Mischief, when ever it appears.

2 Astell, *A Serious Proposal* (1694, 13/55). See Bathsua Makin, *An Essay to Revive the Antient Education of Gentlewomen* (1673), sig. A2v. See Paula L. Barbour's Introduction to the Augustan Reprint edition, iii-xi.

3 Ibid., 4.

4 George Wheler, *The Protestant Nunnery* (London, 1698), cited in Hill, "A Refuge from Men," 115.

1715), bishop of Salisbury, while persuading against support of Astell's project as being too monastic, himself proposed for women "something like Monasteries without Vows which would be a glorious design."[1] Daniel Defoe (1661?-1731), although expressing admiration for Astell's proposal, argued against it on account of women's incorrigible levity, substituting his own proposal for an "Academy for Women" (1697) which differed in no significant aspects from hers.[2] Richard Steele (1672-1729), Irish essayist, dramatist and politician, lampooned Astell in the *Tatler* as the founder of an "order of Platonick Ladies ... who ... gave out, that their Virginity was to be their State of Life during their Mortal condition, and therefore resolv'd to join their Fortunes and erect a Nunnery."[3]

Even the stage did not spare her. Susanna Centlivre (c. 1667-1723) in her play, *The Basset Table* (1706), has Valeria, "that little She-Philosopher," doubtless modelled on Astell, "founding a College for the Study of Philosophy where none but Women should be admitted."[4] And as late as 1847 Lilia, of Alfred, Lord

---

1 Gilbert Burnet, *History of his Own Time, II*, 653.

2 Daniel Defoe, *An Essay upon Projects* (1697) in *The Earlier Life and Chief Earlier Works of Daniel Defoe*, 145-46. See Appendix B below, 267-75, esp. 268.

3 See Astell's Forward to the second edition of *Bartley Fair*, 1722 (A2a), on how Swift put Steele up to the satire of her *A Serious Proposal*, 1694 in *Tatler*, No. 32, from White's Chocolate-house, June 22, 1709, "a little after the Enquiry [*Bartley Fair*] appear'd." See also *Tatler*, No. 63, 1-3 September, 1709, both reproduced below as Appendices C, 277-85, and D, 287-90, Ruth Perry, in *The Celebrated Mary Astell* (229-30, 516 n.81), and Bridget Hill, in "A Refuge from Men" (118, ns 47 and 48), ascribe authorship of the *Tatler* pieces to Swift, but the revised *Tatler* does not, and Astell clearly believes them to be the work of Steele:

> ... But tho' the *Enquirer* had offended the *Tatler*, and his great Friends, on whom he so liberally bestows his Panegyrics, by turning their Ridicule very justly upon themselves; what had any of her Acquaintances done to provoke him? Who does he point at? For she knows of none who ever attempted to *erect a Nunnery*, or declar'd *That Virginity was to be their State of Life*....

4 *The Works of the Celebrated Mrs. Centlivre*, 3 vols (London 1761), vol. 1, 210, 218, cited in Hill, "A Refuge from Men," 120. Susanna Centlivre, a gentlewoman whose family fled to Ireland at the Restoration, may have disliked Astell's politics, *Basset Table* having been written after the publication of Astell's royalist political pamphlets of 1704. The widow of two husbands, Centlivre had raised herself from obscurity by writing plays, was a friend of Richard Steele, and in 1706 married Queen Anne's chief cook, Joseph Centlivre (*Encyclopaedia Britannica*, 11th edn, vol. 5, 674).

Tennyson's *The Princess*, dreams of a women's college cut off from male society, over whose gates the inscription would read, "Let no man enter on pain of death" — the proposal so famously lampooned in Gilbert and Sullivan's *Princess Ida*, which satirized Astell as well.[1]

In 1752 at the end of her life, Lady Mary Wortley Montagu, early travel writer and Astell's friend, confessed to her daughter a life-long attraction to the proposal to found an "English monastery" for ladies, to which she would have elected herself "Lady abbess."[2] Lady Montagu's letter to her daughter chiefly concerned criticisms of Samuel Richardson's novel *Sir Charles Grandison*, the only redeeming feature of which in her estimate was his proposal to found Protestant nunneries, "in which single women, of small or no fortunes might live with all manner of freedom," in every English county.[3] Lady Montague was not the only one to deal rather roughly with Richardson,[4] whose friend and admirer of Astell, Sarah Chapone, may have advised him to read the author of

1 *The Works of Alfred, Lord Tennyson* (London, 1905), 167, 176, cited by Hill, "A Refuge from Men," 107.

2 *Works of Lady Mary Wortley Montagu*, vol. 4, 184, letter to the Countess of Bute, 20 October 1752, cited by Bridget Hill, "A Refuge from Men," 120. Mary Wortley Montagu, who had spurned a marriage proposal from Pope, was married to the English Ambassador to Constantinople, Edward Montagu, and cousin of Charles Montagu, Lord Halifax, First Lord of the Treasury in George I's ministry. Her *Letters from the East*, important for English perceptions of Russia and the "barbarous" North and well as East, chronicle journeys made alone for unstated reasons in 1639. Astell's preface was written in 1724, but the Letters were not published until 1763.

3 *The Works of Samuel Richardson*, 19 vols (London, 1811), vol XVI, 155-56, cited Hill, "A Refuge from Men," 121. See also the authoritative modern edition of Richardson's *History of Sir Charles Grandison*, 3 vols, ed. Jocelyn Harris, vol. 2, 255-56 and notes.

4 But she did it more than once, see her letter of 19 May 1756 to Lady Bute, where she remarks that "Books are so far from giving Instruction, they fill the Head with a set of wrong Notions from whence spring the Tribes of Clarissas, Harriets, etc.," *The Complete Letters of Lady Mary Wortley Montagu*, vol. 3, 40, cited by Flynn, *Samuel Richardson*, 59.

A Serious Proposal,[1] and whose *Clarissa* some claim to have been modelled on Astell.[2]

Astell, Masham, and Locke

If *A Serious Proposal, Parts I and II,* together with *Reflections upon Marriage,* are the best known of Astell's works and the most often noted by her contemporaries, they have so far escaped serious commentary. The works stand to one another in an organic relationship, the central argument of Astell's work on marriage already foreshadowed in her proposal for a woman's place of academic retirement. But an important and undisclosed hiatus divides the first from the second parts of *A Serious Proposal.* Into that gap stepped Lady Damaris Masham. As a consequence Astell's project changed course. What began as a fairly conventional proposal for a women's academy ended as a full-scale philosophical defense of women's intellectual equality and Cartesian epistemology that would support it. The peculiar history of this development is worth telling.

Ironically, when Astell's proposal was first published in 1694 it was taken for the work of Damaris Masham (1658-1708), Locke's companion, as typical of the daughter of the Cambridge Platonist Ralph Cudworth (1617-88). So far from this being the case, Astell's proposal, together with the Astell-Norris correspondence, attracted a fierce response from Lady Masham in her *Discourse Concerning the Love of God* of 1695. Astell responded to her critics in general, and Masham in particular, although not by name, with *A Serious Proposal, Part II.* The chain of contingencies set in motion by these exchanges resulted in a curiously cerebral *ménage à trois,* in which Astell proved to be the spiritual daughter of Ralph Cudworth and Masham the Platonist consort of John Locke. Masham had challenged the fundamental premise of the Astell-Norris *Letters Con-*

---

1 Sara Chapone, mid-eighteenth century "bluestocking," advised George Ballard to read the Astell-Norris correspondence, for instance. See letter to George Ballard dated 12 March 1742, Ballard MSS 43:132, cited by Perry, *The Celebrated Mary Astell,* 488, n. 8.

2 See Upham's "A Parallel Case for Richardson's *Clarissa,*" *Modern Language Notes,* 103-05. It is notable, however, that standard works on Richardson, including the authoritative biography by Eaves and Kimpel, and Tom Keymer's study of *"Clarissa" and the Eighteenth Century Reader,* do not even include Astell in the index.

cerning the Love of God, that the individual's dependence on her divine maker extended to cognition itself. Unmediated dependence on God, as the disposition of the knowing subject, entailed withdrawal from the world and denial of human sociability, leading to the nunnery as a logical consequence, Masham claimed.[1] Masham targeted the thesis under discussion in the Astell-Norris letters that "we see all things in God," made famous by Nicolas Malebranche (1638-1715), and promulgated by John Norris, who later published a full-scale exposition of Malebranche's philosophy and refutation of Locke, in his *Essay Towards the Theory of the Idea and Intelligible World* of 1701.

It was not only the substance of Masham's challenge to which Astell responded in *A Serious Proposal, Part II*, a work enormously wide-ranging in its capacity to syncretize contemporary philosophical debate, but also the demeaning mode in which it was cast. Masham had implied that Astell, as demonstrated in her correspondence with Norris, was no more than his acolyte:[2]

> These Opinions of Mr. *N.* seem also to indanger the introducing, especially amongst those whose Imaginations are stronger than their Reason, a Devout way of talking; which having no sober, and intelligible sense under it, will either inevitably by degrees beget an Insensibility to Religion, in those themselves who use it, as well as others; By thus accustoming them to handle Holy things without Fear; or else will turn to as wild an Enthusiasm as any that has been yet seen; and which can End in nothing but Monasteries, and Hermitages; with all those sottish and Wicked Superstitions which have accompanied them where-ever they have been in use.

Astell took Masham's *Discourse* to be the work of Locke — or at least pretended to, there being various unkind asides in her subsequent works to suggest she knew Masham's authorship quite well. The peculiar intimacy of Masham and Locke — peculiar because its degree of Platonism has never been established — was public knowledge by 1697. One John Edwards (1637-1716), son of the infamous and scurrilous Calvinist Thomas Edwards, author of *Gangraena* (1646), whom Astell elsewhere quotes,[3] seems to have made

1 Masham, *Discourse Concerning the Love of God*, 1696 edn, 120.

2 Ibid., 120.

3 In *Moderation truly stated* (1704, 53 to 60 ff.), Astell takes up the "Dissenters Arguments against Schism and Toleration," deferring to "what has been writ upon this Subject by much better Pens." The texts to which she refers, as indicated in the marginal notes, include Edward Stillingfleet's *The Mischief of Separation* (1680) and the *Unreasonableness of Separation* (1681); Thomas Edward's [*The Second Part of Gangraena ... or*]

it his life's work to expose Locke, with a series of books and even some scurrilous letters that impugned the man not only on technical grounds — attacking Locke's *Reasonableness of Christianity*, his Socinianism and his *Some Thoughts Concerning Education* — but also for his private life. In 1697 Edwards published his *Brief Vindication of the Fundamental Articles of Christian Faith*, in which he referred to Locke as "a lewd disclaimer," a "raving tutor and reformer," a "profligate scribe," a "hater of women," and "the governor of the seraglio at Oates" — the residence at which Locke resided with the Masham family.[1] Whether Astell knew of Edwards' specific allegations or not, she gives hints that she knows the Masham set-up. For reasons of propriety perhaps, given Locke's association with William III's circle, and his notorious reticence about his work, Astell waited until Locke's death in 1704 to publish her open rebuttal, *The Christian Religion* (1705), dedicated to refuting Masham's *Discourse*, along with Locke's *Reasonableness of Christianity, Essay on Human Understanding* and *Two Treatises of Government* as if they were all by the same hand.

But one has only to look closely at *A Serious Proposal, Part II* to see the lineaments of her mature arguments, along with the works that occasioned them, already there. Something of a revolution in her thought — hitherto unremarked — takes place between Parts I and II. Astell takes seriously Masham's claim that to deny the relative autonomy of individual cognition is gratuitous Platonist quietism.[2] To deny the Creator who made us the power to endow us with independent cognition is both to deny God essential attributes and to ignore New Testament exhortations to take responsibility for our own salvation. The consequence of "seeing all things in God" is a form of solipsism that allows the self as the only object of real knowledge, thus denying humans the ability to participate in

---

Further Discovery (1646), his *Antapologia* (1644), and his *Epistle Dedicated to the Lords and Commons before his Gangraena* (1646).

1 See Maurice Cranston, *John Locke: A Biography* (New York, Macmillan, 1957), 430-31; and Sheryl O'Donnell, "Mr. Locke and the Ladies: the Indelible Words on the *Tabula Rasa*," *Studies in Eighteenth Century Culture*, vol. 8 (1979), 151-64, esp. 154.

2 Quietism is a form of religious mysticism involving passive contemplation and withdrawal from the world (*OED*).

understanding and in implementing a programme for a Christian life. It logically leads to the nunnery.

In *A Serious Proposal, Part II,* Astell appears to concede Masham's first charge and tries to address the second. She declares the proposition of Malebranche endorsed by John Norris, that "we see all things in God," if not true, at least pious.[1] And she denies that her house of retirement for women was ever intended as other than a primarily academic establishment. Her struggle to accommodate Masham's challenges has a happy outcome. Astell had fortuitously to hand an institution for which her proposal was the perfect fit, the Port Royal School, founded by a famous woman early in the thirteenth century, reformed by another late in the sixteenth, and specifically designated as a place of retirement for women who were not required to take religious vows in order to live there.[2]

---

1 *A Serious Proposal, Part II,* 1697 edn, 118/166. In *The Christian Religion,* however, Astell returns to the question, as seeming to vindicate Malebranche again.

2 Port Royal, a famous Cistercian abbey established south-west of Paris in 1204 by Mahaut de Garlande, wife of Mathieu de Montmorenci-Marli, was singled out in 1223 by Pope Honorius III as a place of retreat for women who wished to withdraw from the world without taking the perpetual vows of a religious order. Its modern history commences in 1598 with the appointment of Angélique Arnauld, sister of the famous Jansenist philosopher Antoine Arnaud. Angélique Arnauld made the contact to Jean Duvergier, Abbot of Sain Cyran, and chief apostle of Jansenism, herself, a movement with which her family and her convent became inextricably associated. In 1648 the abbey set up a school for the sons of Jansenist parents, but doctrinal skirmishing with the papacy consumed the next two decades, concluding in 1669 with the "Peace of Clement IX," who lifted the interdict on the school and admitted all Jansenists to grace. The convent split along lines that had developed over a long time into a conformist branch in the Faubourg St. Jacques, and a Jansenist branch at Port Royal des Champs. The protection of Mme de Longueville, Louis XIV's cousin, gave the convent a decade of peace, but between her death in 1679 and the forcible removal of the Jansenists from Port Royal by the police in 1709, the king, enlisting papal support, exerted relentless pressure against them, eventually destroying their buildings and even their cemetery. (See *Encyclopaedia Britannica,* vol. 12, 130.) It is hardly surprising that Port Royal should have been both a model and a warning for Astell's project.

Moreover Port Royal was a philosophical academy under whose roof the greatest French philosophers of the age had been schooled.[1] Conceding that "Education is a beaten subject and has been accounted by better pens" than hers,[2] Astell disavows any intention of laying out a curriculum, which she is happy to leave to those who "have a more exact Knowlege of Human Nature, a greater Experience of the World, and of those differences which arise from Constitution, Age, Education, receiv'd Opinions, outward Fortune, Custom and Conversation, than I can pretend to"[3] — deference paid to Locke in heavy sarcasm.

Under the sting of criticism Astell turned a fairly conventional proposal for the education of women in *A Serious Proposal, Part I* into a major philosophical edifice in Part II. Education as such was no longer her project, but rather those deep background philosophical and theological assumptions which deny women the capacity for improvement of the mind. Following this line of attack, she entered a metaphysical thicket far above the plane of educational theory, joining the company of René Descartes (1596-1650), Nicolas Malebranche (1638-1715), Antoine Arnauld (1612-94), Pierre Nicole (1625-95), and Locke himself, in a full-scale debate over the consequences of the Cartesian *cogito*. *A Serious Proposal, Part II* contains one of the most brilliant disquisitions of the age on Descartes' clear and distinct ideas and the possibility of moral certitude,[4] the very topics which had occasioned Locke's *Essay Concerning Human Understanding* (1689), to the reception of which Astell's corpus belongs. Locke's *Reasonableness of Christianity* (1695) and his First and possibly Second Letters to Edward Stillingfleet, Bishop of Worcester (1696-97), which focused on Descartes' notion of clear and distinct ideas and their implications for the Christian doctrine of

---

1 Port Royal was the nursery of such famous Jansenist philosophers and pietists as Antoine Arnauld, Pierre Nicole and Blaise Pascal (1623-62), to whose philosophical tenets Astell is committed.

2 *A Serious Proposal II*, 1697 edn, 277/228.

3 Ibid., 278/229.

4 Chapter 8 of Antoine Arnauld's *Art of Thinking* is entitled, "Of the Clearness and Distinctness of Ideas."

the Trinity, are works which Astell specifically addresses in *A Serious Proposal, Part II.*[1]

Appealing to the Jansenist[2] philosophers of the Port Royal school, Arnauld, Nicole and Pascal, who were so influential on Locke, Astell not only succeeds in improving the rigour of her model by abandoning Malebranche and endorsing the Port Royal logic of his critics, notably Arnauld, but she can then hold Locke accountable to his own acknowledged sources. The task of *A Serious Proposal, Part II* was less to elaborate the specifications for an academy set out in Part I than to provide it with sound epistemic, moral, and Christian footings. This involved Astell in laying out the foundations of her metaphysics, ethics, philosophy of education, and religion systematically, a programme which she completed in *The Christian Religion* of 1705.

---

1 Locke's first letter to Stillingfleet (Locke, *Works*, 1823 edn, vol. 4, 1-96) is dated January 7, 1696/7; his second (*Works*, 1823 edn, vol. 4, 97-184) is dated June 29, 1696; and his third (*Works*, 1823 edn, vol. 4, 191-498) is dated May 4, 1698. Locke used the epistolary style for his *Letters on Toleration* and even his *Essay Concerning Human Understanding*, which is in the first person, as women writers of the period did, to indicate that his works were intended for a popular and not just an academic audience. Astell replied to Locke's third letter to the Bishop of Worcester, which deals with "Certainty by Reason, Certainty by Ideas, and Certainty by Faith; the Resurrection of the Body; the Immateriality of the Soul" and Christology in general, in *The Christian Religion* of 1705. But there is internal evidence in *A Serious Proposal, Part II* to suggest that she is familiar with the arguments of the first and second letters to Stillingfleet, specifically concerned with "a late Discourse of his Lordship's in Vindication of the Trinity," at that early date, and that she is refuting them there. It is in fact a more wide-ranging and extensive rebuttal than that of 1705, which focuses exclusively on Locke's rather injudicious remarks about the possibility of "thinking matter."

2 Jansenism was a philosophical movement named after its founder Cornelius Jansen (1585-1638). Basically, Jansen argued that without a special grace from God it is impossible to perform his commandments, and that the operation of grace is irresistible. Hence, man is the victim of either a natural or supernatural determinism, which is only limited by the fact that it is not violently coercive. Such theological pessimism was expressed in the general harshness and moral rigour of the movement, the unifying characteristic of which was antagonism to the Jesuits. (F.L. Cross and E.A. Livingstone, eds, *The Oxford Dictionary of the Christian Church*, 2nd edn, Oxford University Press, London, 1974.)

The brilliance of her exposition is attested by the number of times it was pirated. Some 147 pages of chapter three, sections 1-5 of the 1697 edition of *A Serious Proposal, Part II,* were excerpted without acknowledgment in *The Ladies Library* of 1714,[1] a work widely circulated, which went through eight impressions up to 1772 and was translated into French and Dutch.[2] Richard Steele was until recently believed to be the compiler of *The Ladies Library*.[3] Astell herself, in the 1722 Preface to *Bart'lemy Fair*, attributed the plagiarism to Steele, having a bone to pick with him for having satirized her in the *Tatler*.[4] But *The Ladies' Library*, according to the title page, "published by Mr. R[ichard] Steele," who

---

1 Notes to the text of *A Serious Proposal II* below indicate the passages excerpted.

2 See E.J.F. and D.B., "George Berkeley and *The Ladies Library*," *Berkeley Newsletter* (Dublin), no. 4 (December 1980), 5-13. These authors note that Steele has been given credit for a greater role in the work than he claims for himself: "I am only her [the Lady's] Gentlemn-Usher," he wrote in the preface. G.A. Aitken, in "Steele's 'Ladies' Library,'" *The Athenaeum*, no. 2958 (July 5, 1884), 16-17, earlier attributed to Astell sections excerpted from *A Serious Proposal, Part I* (1690 edn), in *The Ladies Library*, vol. 1, 438-524. Greg Hollingshead, in "Sources for the *Ladies' Library*," *Berkeley Newsletter*, no. 11 (1989-90), 1-9, esp. 1, attributes some 17,000 words of Astell's *A Serious Proposal, Part II*, (1697 edn 68-189/144-97, ch. 3, sections 1-5, except for the last 3 paragraphs), comprising §§ 7-96 of the section on "Ignorance" of *The Ladies Library*, vol. 2. Astell's work appears alongside *The Ladies Calling* (*LL* 1.32-48, 240-58; 2.38-57, 87- 106, 184-205, 347-75, 377-85; 3.22-53, 292-303, 332-42). Fénelon's *Education of a Daughter* (*LL* 2.270-346) was also included, as well as Locke's *Some Thoughts Concerning Education*. (See E.J.F. and D.B., "George Berkeley and *The Ladies Library*," 6).

3 Ruth Perry, in *The Celebrated Mary Astell*, 100, still believes Steele to be the author. However, authoritative scholarship suggests otherwise.

4 Astell, in *Bart'lemy Fair* (1722 edn, Preface, A2a), remarks of Steele, with customary acerbic wit:

> The harmless Satyr does not bite; and tho' it shew'd its teeth against the *Proposal to the Ladies*, our honest *Compilator* has made an honourable Amends to the Author, (I know not what he has to the Bookseller) by transcribing above an hundred Pages into his *Ladies Library*, *verbatim*; except in a few Places, which if the Reader takes the Trouble to compare, perhaps he will find improv'd.

supplied a preface, and "written by a Lady," was in fact compiled by Bishop George Berkeley.[1] Berkeley's great contribution to philosophy was his critique of the materialism of Hobbes and Locke, which he believed, like Astell, to be a negative consequence of Cartesian dualism.[2] Accepting ideas in Locke's sense as the immediate objects of mind in the cognition process, Berkeley insisted that ideas were not outside the mind, but constituted the world of reality in the mind. Moreover, ideas were required as a translation language, to interpret experience given by sensation.

The Ladies Library, one of a number of works devoted to self-improvement that included *The Ladies Calling*, *The Gentleman's Calling*, cited by Astell, and *The Gentleman's Library* (2nd edn, 1722), was referred to by the author of the latter as "having been read in most counties, though it was swell'd out into three volumes and sold at a pretty handsome price."[3] Astell's pirated work appears in volume 1 alongside *The Ladies Calling* (1693 edn), which she often quotes, as well as Fénelon's *Education of a Daughter*, in Hickes's translation, and her nemesis Locke's *Some Thoughts Concerning Education*.

Astell's Critique of Locke's Epistemology

In *A Serious Proposal, Part II*, Astell addresses challenges raised by Masham and Locke to her specific *Proposal* and to her general system of beliefs. The first, most fundamental, and most successfully

---

1 George Berkeley (1685-1753), Bishop of Cloyne, in Ireland, philosopher and polymath, as a young man in Dublin formed a society of "new philosophy" with some friends to study the works of Descartes, Hobbes, Locke, Malebranche, Leibnitz, and Newton. His early works were compared with those of Norris and Malebranche, but moving to England in 1713, he became associated with "the wits" Steele, Addison, and Pope (*DNB*).

2 Descartes made a radical separation between the mental and material realms in his famous mind/body distinction.

3 See E.J.F. and D.B., "George Berkeley and *The Ladies Library*," 6. It is noteworthy that *The Ladies Library* (vol. 3, paras 285-334, of "Religion") also reproduces Pierre Nicole's *Moral Essays*, vol. 2, Pt. 2, "The True Idea's [*sic*] of Things," in the 1677-80 English translation. (See Hollingshead, 2, who incorrectly cites Pierre Nicole as the translator, rather than co-author, of the 1677-80 English edition.)

disposed of, is the challenge to any notion of improving the condition of women raised by Locke's sensationalist psychology and philosophy of environmental conditioning. She was not the first to criticize Locke's psychology for its fatalism and profaneness. Indeed John Norris, in remarks on Locke's *Essay Concerning Human Understanding*, appended to his *Discourses Upon the Beatitudes*, had as early as 1690 raised some of the topics Astell pursues. In particular, Norris had claimed that Locke's empiricism can account only for perceptions relating to the body and not higher order metaphysical notions of truth, justice, order, and good, which are products of the mind. Locke's dualism, he argued, ruling out criteria to validate necessary as opposed to contingent truths, is therefore self-refuting.

Locke considered Norris's remarks sufficiently devastating to provide a written rebuttal, published posthumously, of which Astell could not have been aware, called "Remarks upon some of Mr. Norris' Books, Wherein he asserts P. Malebranche's Opinion of our seeing all things in God."[1] Signed by him and dated at Oates, the Masham home, in the year 1693, Locke's thirty-five numbered remarks deal summarily with the arguments of Malebranche as expressed by Norris.[2] They are a useful guide to Locke's own difficulty with the problem of ideas and the reasons for his reluctance to develop further explanation of perception and its modes.

Locke's entire system, from the *Essay Concerning Human Understanding*, his tract on education, through *Reasonableness of Christianity* to his *Two Treatises of Government*, was devoted to proving the democracy of experience and the transparency of reason after Descartes. Not only are all humans susceptible to the same sense impressions which the mind combines to produce ideas, but they are in principle equally susceptible to reason, whose accessibility is guaranteed by the cognitive apparatuses with which we have been endowed, and sanctioned in the egalitarianism of the Christian life as set out in Scripture.

---

1 Locke, *Works*, 1823 edn, vol. 10, 248.

2 See John Norris, *Cursory Reflections upon a Book called, An Essay Concerning Human Understanding* ... appended to *Christian Blessedness, or Discourses upon the Beatitudes of our Lord and Saviour Jesus Christ* (London, 1690), and Norris's earlier *Reason and Religion; or the Grounds and Measures of Devotion* (London, 1689).

But what would seem to be democratic and egalitarian foundations for the emancipation of the poor and the downtrodden, as well as for women, Astell correctly perceives to be a bulwark for the status quo. If in fact the reception of ideas is largely dependent on environmental conditions, what Locke trumpets as Reason amounts to no more than custom. And if the reasonableness of Christianity sanctions this, then everything is left as it was. As long as the human psyche is environmentally conditioned, self-improvement is theoretically impossible and women are condemned to the tyranny of custom and convention, their jailors hitherto. A theory of environmental conditioning would cut the ground right from under Astell's project for a women's academy. But Astell claimed to see through to the very foundations of Locke's system, arrived at expeditiously, like that of Hobbes on which it is based, as a strategy against religious sedition and the independency of popery and puritanism.

Astell's refutation of empiricism as sanctioning custom, that aggregate of material conditions which chains women to their posts, comprises one of the most important tasks of *A Serious Proposal, Part II*. Her case against custom foreshadows in general the arguments of *Reflections upon Marriage*, an attack on eighteenth-century morals and mores that demean marriage and reduce it from a sacrament to a form of slavery. It also casts specific light on Astell's famous rhetorical question: "*If all Men are born free*, how is it that all Women are born slaves? as they must be if the being subjected to the *inconstant, uncertain, unknown arbitrary Will* of Men, be the *perfect Condition of Slavery?*"[1] Astell's addendum gives the question away, putting it in the same class as Allestree's claim that marriage is "a Bargain and Compact, a Tyranny perhaps on the Man's part and a Slavery on the Woman's."[2] Her claim about the subordination of women, properly framed, would read: "only if men are born free can women be born slaves." But of course neither can be either. For Astell denies the very premise of Locke's *tabula rasa*, the slate wiped clean of hereditable obligations for persons, on three counts. First — and here Astell embraces the argument for sociability from Aristotle and Cicero through to the Church Fathers, which Masham claims she had denied — individuals are born into

Refutation of Locke's tabula rasa.

1 Astell, *Reflections upon Marriage*, 1706 edn, xi.

2 Richard Allestree, *The Ladies Calling*, part 2, sect. 3, "Of Wives," [1673] 1705 edn, 181.

families, countries, villages, towns and cities, entering a world of pre-existent conditions to which they must conform. Second, if these obligations are not hereditable, however, women would be as unencumbered as men. Locke's rejection of hereditable obligations as regards one's person, but retention of hereditable obligations as regards one's property, was standard Scholastic doctrine. It disenfranchised women who, as legal minors, could not own property and are therefore dependent on men as mere chattels. More grievously, in Locke's system, where property represents the objectification of personality through work, to deny women property rights was to deny them the means to express their personality as public persons and, thus, effectively to deny them the ownership of their own selves he was committed to uphold.

Astell cut a swathe through natural rights, like Filmer denying the possibility of such freedoms in an imperfectly and hierarchically ordered world.[1] Notions of natural right served further to obscure the fact that women's servitude is the product of obdurate custom — customs perpetuated by those very men who would claim for themselves the highest degree of enlightenment, who think it "Honourable to break a Vow that ought to be Kept, and Dishonourable to get loose from an Engagement that ought to be broken." "What do they think of Greatness who support their Pomp at the Expence of the Groans and Tears of many Injur'd Families?,"[2] Astell reproaches, a cry echoed in her famous Preface to *Reflections upon Marriage* of 1706: "is it not then partial in Men to the last degree, to contend for, and practise that Arbitrary Dominion in their Families, which they abhor and exclaim against in the State?"[3]

A tissue of systemic ironies surrounds Astell's famous question about female slavery. It frames a paradox which goes to the heart of Locke's doctrine and her own project. She sometimes appears to be seduced by her own rhetoric as when, for instance, she suggests a master/slave analogue for the relations between God and his subjects:

> For had we indeed that Esteem for GOD and Intire, Conformity to his Will, which is at once both the Duty and Perfection of all Rational Beings, we shou'd not complain of his Exercise of that Power, which a Prince or even an Ordinary Master has a Right to; which is, to set his Servants about

---

1 Sir Robert Filmer, *Patriarcha* (1680), ed. Johann P. Sommerville (Cambridge, Cambridge University Press, 1991).

2 Astell, *A Serious Proposal, Part II*, 1697 edn, 129/170.

3 Astell, *Reflections upon Marriage*, 1706 edn, x.

> such work as he thinks them fittest for. If we allow that GOD Governs the Universe, can we so much as imagine that it is not Govern'd with the Greatest Justice and Equity, Order and Proportion? Is not every one of us plac'd in such Circumstances as Infinite Wisdom discerns to be most suitable, so that nothing is wanting but a careful observation whither they lead us, and how we may best improve them? What reason then to complain of the Management of the world? and indeed except in the Morals of Mankind which are visibly and grossly deprav'd, I see not why we shou'd so much as wish for any alteration.[1]

But if this would seem to be a quietist argument, discouraging a program of social change, Astell here sanctions custom on grounds other than Locke. It is not because humans are subject to environmental conditioning that nothing changes, or nothing should be changed. It is because, although in principle capable of self-improvement and governing the will, humans give constant witness to the fallen state of human nature, from which Christ alone has the power to redeem them. Astell's religiosity fits in a coherent system. The theodicy paradox, according to which God is author of both good and evil, enjoins humans to strive for a perfection that the power of evil more or less guarantees they will never attain. These are all consequences of divine design, but they have little to do with Reason as we conceive it.

Astell's epistemic assault on Lockean rationalism, sensationalist psychology, and environmentalism allows her to deliver a moral diatribe against women who succumb to custom too easily. *A Serious Proposal, Part II* begins in chapter one with an exhortation to women to abandon frivolity and get theologically serious. It is up to them to abandon the "Yoke of impertinent Customs" and claim liberty back for themselves.[2] As rational creatures they can free themselves from the Shades of irrational mechanism. What appears to be an inconsistency here is rather a paradox. To deny that men (or women) are born free is not to deny the case for liberty. Freedom Astell understands classically as the capacity to embrace a principle of conduct and follow it. The false deduction of natural rights theorists from the fact of existence to a right to freedom — a violation of the is/ought distinction that passes for Reason — far from liberating individuals, chains them to custom by virtue of the irrational mechanistic psychology imported to explain how material conditions impede freedom's exercise.

---

1 Astell, *A Serious Proposal, Part II*, 1697 edn, 273-74/227.

2 Ibid., 6/120.

Staying with freedom of the will as true freedom — and here Astell follows classical models since Aristotle on voluntary and involuntary conduct — she resorts to moral pathologies to explain not only corruption of the will but miscarriages of perception. And here her philosophy follows both Plato and the Stoics, for whom all thinking involves a degree of assent and for whom a disciplined will is a precondition to knowledge. Moral corruption is all-pervasive. Disease of the passions stands in the way of the proofs of Christianity, because the heart not the head, she argues, is the seat of atheism.

Astell, Descartes, and the Port Royal School

In chapter two of *A Serious Proposal, Part II*, Astell is not only able to knock down Locke's theory of environmental conditioning as self-refuting, but sets a superior argument in its place. To this end she invokes the distinction between true and false forms of self-love or interest-seeking made famous by Pierre Nicole of the Port Royal school. She acknowledge the passions as an appetitive and motivating force, essential to maintenance of animal spirits, preservative of the body. And here again she follows Plato. It is, of course, supremely ironic that she should turn against Locke the notion of true and false self-love, *amour-de-soi* and *amour propre*, set out in Pierre Nicole's *Essais de Morale*, the first four volumes of which reached an English audience from 1677 to 1680, translated by a Gentleman of Quality who was very likely Locke.[1] The distinction between true and false forms of self-love opens a space for human control of the passions, while allowing that malignant passions account for the corruption of the will. It allows Astell to hold out hopes of human self-improvement, while accounting for why this hope is so seldom realized.

Astell refutes Locke as Plato, in the *Republic*, refuted Thrasymachus: to read human behaviour as strictly interest-governed is to

---

1 Locke is believed to have undertaken the translation at the instruction of his patron, Anthony Ashley Cooper (1621-83), first Earl of Shaftesbury. Although it is claimed by Harry M. Bracken in the *Encyclopedia of Philosophy* (London, Macmillan, 1967, vol. 5, 502) that Locke's translations were not published until the nineteenth century, the translations of the 1680s by "A Gentleman of Quality," the pseudonym used elsewhere by Locke and/or Shaftesbury, bear his stamp.

invalidate one's own. Locke, like Thrasymachus, exempts himself by authorial *hubris*, which leads Astell to attack self-proclaimed authorities in general. Distinguishing between rational and genealogical argument she remarks that, "tho properly speaking all Truth is Antient, as being from Eternity in the Divine Ideas,"[1] the genealogy of authority is no substitute for reason: "our Forefathers were Men of like Passions with us, and are therefore not to be Credited on the score of Authority but of Reason."[2] Only the Church is exempted from Astell's wholesale attack on customary authority, on the grounds that ministers function as divinely appointed guides[3] — once again the language of Platonism and of Descartes, who embraced the insight of Protestantism that the tabernacle of the human heart was the shrine of Reason and Truth.

That the work of Descartes should, in the seventeenth century, have been associated with manuals for self-improvement is not inappropriate. The epistemology of Descartes cast a long shadow over his century because of the consequences of the Cartesian *cogito* for individual autonomy. Astell employed Descartes brilliantly for her cause, drawing the consequence of women's right to education from a notion of individual autonomy that nevertheless fell short of denying the individual believer the right to divide the Church by private opinion. If the work of Descartes, like that of Antoine Arnauld and Pierre Nicole, had been aimed at scholastic education and the Jesuit stranglehold on theology, it was equally aimed at Calvinist casuists, who imported scholastic arguments to challenge the Catholic Church, and in so doing questioned the very possibility of truth. Descartes' earliest work, his unfinished *Regulae ad Directionem Ingenium*, or *Rules for the Direction of the Mind*, written around 1628 but unpublished until 1701, represented a method for the arrival at certain knowledge in response to the sceptic Chandoux, who believed that science was at best founded on probabilities.[4] Descartes' *Discourse on Method* (1637), prefacing three treatises on mathematics and physics, had been followed by

---

1 *A Serious Proposal, Part II*, 1697 edn, 50/137.

2 Ibid., 47/136.

3 Ibid., 54/139.

4 See Bernard Williams's excellent essay on Descartes in *The Encyclopedia of Philosophy* (London: Macmillan, 1967, vol. 5), 344-54, esp. 344-45. Chandoux, both a philosopher and chemist, about whom little now is known, was executed in 1631 as a counterfeiter. (Pierre Larousse, *Grand Dictionnaire Universel*.)

his *Meditations on First Philosophy* (1641), published together with six sets of *Objections*, among them those of Thomas Hobbes, Antoine Arnauld, and Pierre Gassendi. The sceptical response of the English philosophers, Hobbes, Locke, and later Hume, to the Cartesian project was of great importance in the history of philosophy. Among those anxious to refine the Cartesian method for certain knowledge, Malebranche and Arnauld were important friendly critics. Some of Arnauld's criticisms still stand, in particular his charge in *Quatrième Objection*, 1641, that the proof of the *cogito* involves circularity — affirming the truth of God's existence in terms of a prior certainty that "whatever we clearly and evidently perceive is true."[1] If Descartes distinguishes between our ideas and ideas in the mind of God, on what grounds do our ideas conclusively demonstrate mind to be incorporeal, Arnauld asked. Arnauld questioned the basis on which Descartes arrived at a categorial distinction between mind and body, and here Locke followed him.

But Arnauld was a constructive critic and it was in the spirit of Descartes' *Regulae* that he and Nicole set out in *The Art of Thinking* (1662) known as *The Port Royal Logic*, on which Astell's system is based, to improve on the Cartesian method for establishing certain truth. Having countered Descartes on one side of the mind/body problem, they faced Malebranche on the other. If Descartes' solution involved crediting human thinking with the power of certitude *a priori*, Malebranche subsumed all human cognition in the mind of God. Arnauld, in *True and False Ideas* (1683), published his rebuttal to the famous thesis of Malebranche's *Search for Truth* (1674), that "we see all things in God," reclaiming relative cognitive autonomy for individuals. Arnauld showed Cartesian sensitivity in accounting for the element of representation in human cognition — something that Malebranche, in subsuming all ideas under the perfect (Platonist) ideas of God, denied. At the same time he was unwilling to determine the logical status of those representations, whether as emanations of divine ideas, or as a reflection of the power of material objects and processes. Arnauld rejected Malebranche's Platonism as redundant — representations obviated the necessity for ideas — a step that not even Locke was prepared to take. To this Malebranche issued the countercharge that Arnauld

1 See Harry M. Bracken in the *Encyclopedia of Philosophy* (London: Macmillan, 1967, vol. 1), 165-67, esp. 165.

was in grave danger of the Pyrrhonic scepticism[1] he was devoted to refuting: the problem of knowing that our perceptions are true. For although we can perceive external objects, ideas of truth and falsity involve more than perceptions — they require ideas and the ability to compare ideas by means of criteria. The debate devolved to a discussion over "mental substance" in which Malebranche stalwartly maintained a distinction between mind and body that ruled out perceptions as containing ideas, and in which Arnauld charged Malebranche with redundancy for endowing Descartes' "triangle in the mind" with ontological integrity.

This set of problems, and its consequences for individual piety, constituted the field of modern philosophy of mind and ethics. It is a discourse in which Locke and Stillingfleet, Astell and Masham, are intimately involved, arguing and rehearsing arguments in the language of "triangles," substance — the Indian "I-know-not-what" of Locke's *Essay* — algebra, and optics, to which Descartes gave currency, and which is still the language of modern philosophy of mind. For there is no denying the profundity with which Locke challenged Descartes. The deep-seatedness of his scepticism is nowhere more evident than in the correspondence between Locke and Stillingfleet, the first two installments of which Astell gives every indication of having read. The opening salvo of *A Serious Proposal, Part II*, delivered as part of an ongoing controversy about the Trinity, puts Astell with Stillingfleet on the theological implications of Lockean doubt.

Descartes had formulated his proposition that perception entails existence as one of the proofs for the existence of God. But by opening up a divide between thought and existence, in the categorial mind/body distinction, Descartes cut away the very proof of God that he sought. Perception entails existence, but certainty is established by Reason. And Reason, according to Descartes, inhabits a noncorporeal realm. In various imaginative ways Locke, in the correspondence with Stillingfleet, explored the ramifications of this conclusion from Descartes' theorem, which he accepts, and which calls into question the very notion of clear and distinct ideas that Descartes was at pains to establish.[2]

---

1 The doctrine of the impossibility of certain knowledge associated with Pyrrho of Elis (*c.* 300 BC), the founder of Scepticism.

2 *Mr. Locke's Letter to the Bishop of Worcester*, 1823 edn, 49.

Astell, Stillingfleet, and Locke on Ideas and Extension

Astell turns Locke's scepticism against him, as a sign of *hubris* disguised as humility. She charges him with the sceptic's dilemma: if we take his word about the impossibility of certitude, how are we to take what he says seriously at all? Moreover, she detects a fundamental contradiction in Locke's entire program, which asserts the Reasonableness of Religion and the transparency of belief on the one hand, and the intractability of things in themselves to clear and distinct ideas on the other. Astell turns against Locke the *ad hominem* argument that, denying the rest of mankind access to certain truth, he then makes them dependent upon his own word, dependent on "*My* Discovery, *My* Hypothesis, the Strength and Clearness of *My* Reasonings, rather than the Truth,"[1] typical of "every little warm Disputer and Pretender to Reason, whose Life is perhaps a continual contradiction to it."[2] Thus, once again, by appearing in his ordinary language philosophy to favour the man in the street, for whom he crafts images of the burghers of Harlem or Amsterdam and the citizens of Bristol or London, Locke in fact disenfranchises him.

Astell stands by the principle that "Truth in general is the Object of the Understanding, but all Truths are not equally Evident, because of the Limitation of the Humane Mind, which tho' it can gradually take in many Truths, yet cannot any more than our sight attend to many things at once."[3] She follows Descartes, whom Locke in turn followed, on the computational function of the mind. Those ideas not evident to us by intuition or introspection are relational, arrived at by the comparison of ideas we already hold or by searching for an independent criterion. Simple ideas are not false, but the way in which we compound them may be.[4] Not

---

1 *A Serious Proposal, Part II*, 91-92/155.

2 Ibid., 74/148.

3 Ibid., 71/146, §1.

4 Ibid., 124-25/168-69:

> For that Idea which represents a thing so Clearly, that by an Attent and Simple View we may discern its Properties and Modifications, at least so far as they can be Known, is never false; all our Certainty and Evidence depends on it, if we Know not Truly what is thus represented to our Minds we know nothing. Thus the Idea of Equality between 2 and 2 is so evident that it is impossible to doubt of it, no Arguments could convince us of the Contrary, nor be able to persuade us that the same may be found between 2 and 3.

all ideas are given to us by God immediately, and uncertainty enters whenever a standard of comparison must be sought. Astell refers for a specific instance to the debate between Locke and Stillingfleet over the nature of the Trinity, "of late very much controverted tho to little purpose, because we take a wrong method, and wou'd make that the Object of Science which is properly the Object of Faith...".[1]

Astell challenges Locke on the impossibility of forming an idea of God for whom there is no standard of comparison. Accepting his fundamental axiom that all knowledge is propositional, Astell goes on to hold Locke to account by his own stipulation that the comparison of ideas requires a measure or standard. "All the Commerce and Intercourse of the World is manag'd by Equivalents, conversation as well as Traffick,"[2] she declares, generalizing this principle in a marvellously Lockean way.[3] But knowledge of the infinite is something by definition beyond the structures of human cognition. Beyond the limits of human understanding lies not darkness, but greater light, and Astell invokes Platonist ecstatic metaphor to characterize God who "has folded up his own Nature, not in Darkness, but in an adorable and inaccessible Light."[4] In the language of

---

1 Ibid., 72/147.

2 Ibid., 138.

3 In fact the phraseology is directed at Masham, who in *Discourse Concerning the Love of God* (1696 edn, 121) had convicted Astell's project of denying human sociability, making "it impossible to live in the daily Commerce and Conversation of the World, and love God as we ought to do."

4 *A Serious Proposal, Part II,* 74/148. See also 235-36/212, Astell's Platonist hymn to the Divinity that continues the metaphor of veiled light:

> Let then these little things be drawn aside, these Clouds that hide the most adorable Face of GOD from us, these Mud-walls that enclose our Earthly Tabernacle and will not suffer us to be pierc'd with the Beams of his Glory, and wounded, not to Death but Life, with the Arrows of his Love and Beauty. In him we find that infinite Good which alone can satisfie us, and which is not to be found elsewhere. Somewhat in which we lose our selves with Wonder, Love and Pleasure! Somewhat too inefiable to be nam'd, too Charming, too Delightful not to be eternally desir'd! And were we not sunk into Sense, and buried alive in a crowd of Material Beings, it might seem impossible to think of any thing but Him. For whether we consider the Infinite Perfection of his Nature, or the Interest we have in, and our entire dependance on him. Whether we consider him as Maker and Governor of all things, as filling all places, intimately

optics to which Descartes, Locke, and Masham resort, Astell introduces the Stoic notion of assent. A strictly optical theory of cognition omits the will, but all human understanding involves a degree of assent. Thus even in the very structures of cognition a disciplined will is a condition of truth. In the realm of prejudice, passion and darkened eye-sight, "tho' Truth be exceeding bright, yet ... it requires no little Pains and Application of Mind to find her out."[1]

The logical impossibility of finding an equivalent for the Infinite causes Astell to conclude that Faith, Knowledge, and Opinion do not concern different modes of knowing so much as different degrees of evidence. "Men of dry Reason and a moderate Genius, I suppose will think Nature has done very well in allotting to each Sense its proper employment."[2] But they forget that the senses were made to tend the body, and not as "Testimony in our Enquiries after Truth," precisely because they elide their own distinction between certain knowledge produced by logical deduction and the unreflected immediacy of sensation.[3]

> In this enumeration of the several ways of Knowing, I have not reckon'd the Senses, in regard that we're more properly said to be *Conscious* of than to *Know* such things as we perceive by Sensation. And also because that Light which we suppose to be let into our Ideas by our Senses is indeed very dim and fallacious, and not to be relied on till it has past the Test of Reason; neither do I think there's any Mode of Knowlege which mayn't be reduc'd to those already mentioned.[4]

Astell's Refutation of Materialism and Assertion of Idealism

Astell's critique of Locke's sensationalist psychology is devastating. She has him caught every which way. If sensations are cognitively prior, as he claims, then he is in no position to claim for himself a privileged position in expounding truth. But if truth is a function of propositional logic, as he also maintains, he cannot claim the priority of sensational knowledge, which must be submitted to the

---

acquainted with all Events, as Righteous in all his ways, and holy in all his works. Whether we contemplate his Almighty Power; or what seems more suitable to our Faculties and Condition, the Spotless Purity of his Nature, which guided by Infallable Wisdom always Chuses what Best.

1 Ibid., 121-22/167.

2 Ibid., 83/152.

3 Ibid., 115/164.

4 Ibid., 78-79/150.

criterion of reason. He overstates the importance of sense-data and understates the role of prudential or customary knowledge. It is not due to false sensations that women are enslaved, Astell insists, but to the tyranny of false opinion. Ironically, she once again turns against Locke, the proponent of plain speech and first philosopher of common language, the charge that "Many times our Ideas are thought to be false when the fault is really in our language."[1] She is very Aristotelian in according prudential knowledge such an important role. For if lack of prudence accounts for our vices, its practice perfects our virtues. Like Aristotle she understands virtue to be the yield of good attitudes and habits productive of good character.

To this degree Astell accepts Aristotle's revision of Plato — that having the right ideas is not sufficient, it is the capacity to convert theory into practice that is the mark of good character. The realm of ethics is thus a prudential realm. Moreover, it is a realm in which all have an equal capacity to excel. Locke, in *The Reasonableness of Christianity*, had made the case that Neoplatonism was excessively esoteric, arguing from the impossibility of making "the Day-Labourers and Tradesmen, the Spinsters and Dairy Maids ... perfect Mathematicians," an equal impossibility of perfecting them "in *Ethicks*."[2] In *A Serious Proposal, Part II*, Astell wilfully misreads Locke, accusing him of a category mistake in inferring an ethical incapacity from a lack of theoretical knowledge. Then she charges him with merciless insensitivity: "a Mechanic who must work for daily bread for his Family, wou'd be wickedly Employ'd shou'd he suffer 'em to starve whilest he's solving Mathematical Problems."[3] In *The Christian Religion* of 1705, she clinches her case declaring that her theology comprised only "*plain Propositions and short Reasonings about things familiar to our Minds, as* need not *amaze* any part of Mankind, no not the *Day Labourer and Tradesmen, the Spinsters and Dairy Maids*, who may very easily *comprehend* what a Woman cou'd write."[4]

---

1 Ibid., 132/171.

2 Locke, the *Reasonableness of Christianity*, 1695 edn, 279.

3 *A Serious Proposal, Part II*, 202-03/200. Richard Allestree in *The Ladies Calling*, part 2, sect. 1, "Of Virgins" (1705 edn, 164), had declared that "the Laws both of God and Man have provided for the meanest Mechanick."

4 *The Christian Religion*, 1705, 402-03. Note that by the use of italics Astell indicates the deliberate quotation from Locke.

The full argument is foreshadowed in *A Serious Proposal, Part II.* There Astell treads a fine line, rejecting the plainness of Locke's necessary knowledge as ruling out improvement of the mind, upon which salvation, "the Grand Business that Women as well as Men have to do in this World," is conditional.[1] To this work of preparation an appropriate level of knowledge is requisite. Astell opts for a Platonist solution that is wholly Christian, a division of labour based on the distribution of talents — the very principle, ironically, on which Locke's Aristotelian economics in the *Two Treatises of Government* is founded. Astell makes an appeal to individualism against those very individualists, Hobbes and Locke, whose pragmatism she is confronting. She claims to "see no reason why there may not be as great a variety in Minds as there is in Faces."[2] This being the case, she asks, "Why shou'd not every individual Understanding be in a more especial manner fitted for and employ'd in the disquisition of some particular Truth and Beauty?"[3] If "Variety gives Beauty to the Material World ... why not to the Intellectual?"[4]

But while Astell's attack on Locke is strong, her defense of her own position is weaker than it appears. For those areas in which evidence in the nature of things is relatively lacking, faith is said to make up the deficit — a poor basis for certitude in the technical philosophical sense, which was Locke's very reason for scepticism. Astell's moral certainty is arrived at as a compound of faith and science and she is able to maintain the Platonist principle that no one is willingly ignorant. The notion of clear, as opposed to distinct, ideas,[5] allows her to distinguish between those intangibles of which we can form certain ideas — the triangle and other mathematical and theoretical entities — and those for which we cannot, chiefly the nature of God and the Christian mysteries:

> For that Idea which represents a thing so Clearly, that by an Attent and Simple View we may discern its Properties and Modifications, at least so far as they can be Known, is never false; all our Certainty and Evidence depends on it.[6]

---

1 *A Serious Proposal, Part II,* 1697 edn, 203/200.

2 Ibid., 87/153.

3 Ibid., 89/154.

4 Ibid., 87-88/153.

5 Ibid., 134-35/172-73, following Arnauld's *Art of Thinking,* ch. 8, "Of the Clearness and Distinctness of Ideas."

6 Ibid., 124-25/168-69.

In these discussions Astell, like Descartes and Locke, uses mathematical examples such as "the Idea of Equality between 2 and 2," so evident she claims "that it is impossible to doubt of it" and "no Arguments could convince us of the Contrary."[1] Turning to Descartes' own definition, she argues that whatever may be said to be "Distinct ... is so clear, Particular, and Different from all other things that it contains not any thing in it self which appears not manifestly to him who considers it as he ought."[2] If distinctness is a function of the discreteness or singularity of an idea, as Descartes argued, then complex ideas like the concept of God are not likely to be clear. This Locke had already conceded to Stillingfleet. Astell argues to the contrary, and not very convincingly, that clear ideas entail distinctness, but that distinctness does not entail clearness, thus yielding the conclusion that "we may have a Clear, but not a Distinct and Perfect Idea of God and of our own Souls."[3]

It is easy to see that a reticence to reduce the psychological to the physiological, a category mistake of which she convicts Locke, is what drives Astell. And yet she is loath to admit scepticism in any form. She thus concludes concerning minds that "their Existence and some of their Properties and Attributes may be Certainly and Indubitably Known" but that we cannot know their nature distinctly, "for Reasons too long to be mentioned"; or "of God because he is Infinite."[4] In fact Astell could have clinched her case by arguing that we cannot have a clear idea of mind because it, too, is complex. But this she does not do.

There are other indications that Astell's position has not fully matured. Proceeding from her (unproven) assumption that we know enough about the structure of mind to adopt rules for its improvement, she turns to *The Port Royal Logic* for an exposition of what these are. Her exposition of the syllogism,[5] following Arnauld

---

1 Ibid. See Locke's first letter to Stillingfleet, 1823 edn, 52-53, where he contests Descartes' notion of clear and distinct ideas with reference to his claims in *An Essay Concerning Human Understanding*, bk 4, ch. 10, §7.

2 Astell, *A Serious Proposal, Part II*, 1697 edn, 134-35/172, citing *Les Principes de la Philosophie de M. Des Cartes*, Part 1, §45.

3 Ibid., 135/173.

4 Ibid.

5 The syllogism is a classical form of logical proof that involves the deduction of a conclusion (third term) from a principle (first term), applied to circumstances (second term). It was made famous by Aristotle.

and Nicole,[1] leads her into strange territory, however. The example she gives endorses Locke's hypothesis that the mind is "thinking matter," of which she was later to give such a brilliant demolition in *The Christian Religion*, once again wilfully misreading his argument. Taking as her example the question "Whether a Rich Man is Happy," Astell pleads Cartesian dualism and the inconvertiblity of the two terms, riches and happiness, as a reason for denying the derivation of a proper conclusion, therefore disqualifying the proposition "the rich man is happy" as a valid syllogism:

> Now if we compare the Idea of Riches with that which we have of Man, we shall find in the former nothing but what's Material, External and Adventitious, but our Idea of the latter represents to us somewhat that Thinks, and so is of an Immaterial and more noble Nature....[2]

So far so good. If one accepts Descartes' principle of the inconvertibility of mind and matter, then material goods do not yield spiritual goods. But Astell then proceeds to remark that:

> by Consequence the less Noble cannot be the Good of the more, nor a Body or an Extended Substance, the Proper Good of the Mind, a Spiritual or Thinking Substance, So that upon the whole matter we find, that we cannot affirm a Man is Happy because he is Rich, neither can we deny it....[3]

While her conclusion that body, extended substance, cannot be the good of the mind or spirit is impeccable, her reading of Locke leads her by a semantic lapse to endorse a principle that she later trumps in spades. In *A Christian Religion*, Astell makes a categorial distinction between material substance and immaterial nature. The latter, having no parts, is incorruptible and immortal, and therefore does not qualify as extension or substance at all.[4] This is a distinction as categorial as that between the triangle and the circle, she maintains, its acceptance a precondition for thinking as such.[5] Those who would allow "thinking matter" to fudge the mind/body divide are led to the ineluctable conclusion that "if a body can think, thought must be the essence of body," which is to make of God himself a principle of extension![6] But God is pure spirit, the

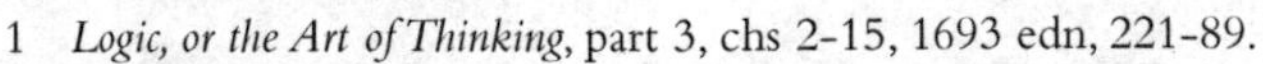

1 *Logic, or the Art of Thinking*, part 3, chs 2-15, 1693 edn, 221-89.

2 *A Serious Proposal, Part II*, 1697 edn, 160-61/183.

3 Ibid., 161/183.

4 *The Christian Religion*, §257, §258, §259, 1705 edn, 247-50.

5 Ibid., §259, 249-50.

6 Ibid., §261, §262, 250-52.

only cause and principle of our love as a stream of affectivity, and thought is a divine mode set over against body and extension. Astell brings her theology full circle, back to the point at which she began in *Letters Concerning the Love of God* in defence of Malebranche.

Conclusion

Mary Astell, as a religious writer, promoter of women's causes, and a commissioned High Church Tory pamphleteer, poses problems for commentators, who struggle to make a comprehensible account of her views. To compound the difficulties, the period leading up to and following the Revolution of 1688 is undergoing its own historiographic revolution as the Whig interpretation is challenged by a more balanced view. Astell's contribution to modern philosophy of mind, albeit on the losing side in the contest between the Cambridge Platonists and the Lockean empiricists, has gone unacknowledged for too long. If the ultimate triumph of the Whig view of history has served to make Tory views of her day implausible, explorations of soul and spirit undertaken by the Cambridge Platonists have been similarly eclipsed by modern physiology of mind. But without the rough-house of these debates in which Astell participated, analytic philosophy might never have gained the ascendancy it enjoys. And Astell in turn, without the stimulus of Masham"s refutation of Malebranche's principle of "seeing all things in God," might never have felt compelled to perfect her model along Port Royal lines. It is symptomatic that she should close *A Serious Proposal, Part II* by revisiting Masham's charge that her project merely imitated foreign monasteries, which Astell vehemently denies, asserting the calling of the single lady to be a mission of reform. "They must either be very Ignorant or very Malicious who pretend that we wou'd imitate Foreign Monastries," she says, "it is altogether beside the purpose, to say 'tis too Recluse, or prejudicial to an Active Life; 'tis as far from that as a Ladys Practising at home is from being a hindrance to her dancing at court."[1] Retirement, so far from being a withdrawal from the world, is a preparation for work in it, for "the whole World is a single Lady's Family, her opportunities of doing good are not lessen'd but

---

1 *A Serious Proposal, Part II* (1697 edn), 284-85/232.

encreas'd by her being unconfin'd." To such women is reserved in a special way, "the Glory of Reforming this Prophane and Profligate Age."[1]

1 *A Serious Proposal, Part II* (1697 edn), 211/203.

Mary Astell: A Brief Chronology

1666 Born on 12 November at Newcastle-upon-Tyne.

1672 Charles II's Declaration of Indulgence for Protestant Dissenters.

1673 Declaration of Indulgence revoked and the Test Act, banning Catholics from holding office, passed.

1678 Sancroft becomes Archbishop of Canterbury.
Astell's father dies.

1679 Exclusion Bill to exclude James II from the throne debated.

1681 Oxford Parliament meets.
Oxford Parliament dissolved.

1683 Rye House Plot.

1685 Charles II dies and is replaced by James II.
James II's Parliament.

1686 Astell moves to London, living mainly in Chelsea.

1687 James II's Declaration of Indulgence for liberty and conscience.

1688 James II dissolves Parliament.
Birth of a son to James, a possible Catholic heir.
Invasion of Prince William of Orange and his wife Mary, James's own daughter.
James flees to France.

1689 Convention Parliament meets and offers the Crown jointly to William and Mary.
Coronation of King William III and Queen Mary II.
Nine Years War against France begins.
Bill of Rights, regulating the English succession, nominates Mary's sister Anne and her children as the next in line.
Toleration Act, allowing freedom of worship for Protestant dissenters, passed.
Astell presents "A Collection of Poems" to Archbishop Sancroft.

1690 Secession of non-jurors from the Church of England.

1693 Astell begins her correspondence with John Norris.

1694 Queen Mary II dies childless.
Astell's *A Serious Proposal to the Ladies, for the Advancement of Their True and Greatest Interest. By a Lover of her Sex* first published.

1695 Astell's mother dies.
The letters written between Astell and John Norris from 1693 are published as *Letters Concerning the Love of God Between the Author of the Proposal to the Ladies and Mr. John Norris, wherein his Discourse shewing That it ought to be entire and exclusive of all other Loves is further clear and justified.*
Second edition, corrected, of Astell's *A Serious Proposal to the Ladies* published.

1696 The Fenwick conspiracy, a plan by James II and King Louis XIV of France to assassinate King William, uncovered.
Third edition, corrected, of Astell's *A Serious Proposal to the Ladies*, published.

1697 Astell's *A Serious Proposal to the Ladies, Part II: wherein a method is offer'd for the improvement of their minds* published. It was dedicated to the Princess of Denmark who later became Queen Anne.
Astell's *A Serious Proposal to the Ladies, for the Advancement of Their True and Greatest Interest,* in two parts, published anonymously as "By a Lover of her Sex."

1700 Queen Anne's only child, William, dies.
Astell's *Some Reflections upon Marriage, Occasion'd by the Duke and Dutchess of Mazarine's Case; which is also consider'd* published anonymously. (No copies of a second edition have been found, although one is believed to have been published in 1703 or 1704.)

1701 The Act of Settlement establishes the Dowager Electress Sophia of Hanover, a grand-daughter of James I, as next in line after Anne.
James II dies in exile.
Louis XIV of France nominates the son of James II, James III, known as the Old Pretender, as heir.

1702 King William III dies unexpectedly in an accident.
Queen Anne, daughter of James II and the last of the Stuarts, succeeds him.

1704 The following works by Astell are published: *Moderation Truly Stated: Or a Review of a Late Pamphlet entitul'd Moderation a Vertue. With a Prefatory Discourse to Dr. D'Avenant concerning his late Essays on Peace and War*;
A Fair Way with the Dissenters and their Patrons. Not writ by Mr. L—y, or any other Furious Jacobite whether Clergyman or Layman; but by a very moderate person and dutiful subject to the Queen;
An Impartial Enquiry into the Causes of Civil War in this Kingdom in an examination of Dr. Kennet's Sermon, Jan. 31, 1703-4 and Vindication of the Royal Martyr.

1705 An octavo volume of Astell's entitled *The Christian Religion as Profess'd by a Daughter of the Church of England* published anonymously.
A second edition of Astell's *Some Reflections Upon Marriage....*, "corrected by the author with some few things added," published.

1706 Astell engaged in controversy with Atterbury.
Third edition of Astell's *Some Reflections upon Marriage...* published under the title of *Reflections upon Marriage*, "To which is added a preface in answer to some objections."

1707 The first Parliament of Great Britain meets.

1709 Astell's *Bart'lemy Fair or an Enquiry after Wit in which due Respect is had to a Letter Concerning Enthusiasm. To my Lord XXX by Mr. Wotton*, published.

1711 Occasional Conformity Act passed.

1714 The Electress Sophia dies.
Queen Anne dies and is succeeded by the Lutheran King George I, Sophia's next descendant in line.

1715 First Parliament of George I.

1719 Occasional Conformity Act repealed.

1722 Atterbury's plot to launch an armed invasion of Britain on behalf of the Old Pretender discovered.
Atterbury exiled and Robert Walpole seals his position as the King's number one minister, a position he holds for 20 years.
Astell's *An Enquiry after Wit wherein the Trifling Arguing and Impious Raillery of the Late Earl of Shaftesbury in his letter con-*

cerning Enthusiasm and other Profane Writers are fully answered, and justly exposed, published as a second edition to *Bart'lemy Fair...*

1727 George I dies and is succeeded by his son George II.

1730 Three of Astell's works are republished: a fourth edition of *Reflections upon Marriage* "with additions" in London and a fifth edition of the same in Dublin; a third edition of *Letters Concerning the Love of God...*; and a third edition of *The Christian Religion as Profess'd by a Daughter of the Church of England*.

1731 Astell dies of breast cancer on 9 May.

A Note on the Text

This edition is based on the text of the first editions of *A Serious Proposal*, Part I (1694) [Wing A4063], and Part II (1697) [Wing C40654] held in the Folger Shakespeare Library, Washington DC, and reproduces these texts exactly with the following exceptions. The "Contents of the Second Part," which precedes the separate title page of the 1697 edition of *A Serious Proposal, Part II,* has been placed after it, and the dedicatory preface in italics to Princess Ann of Denmark has been rendered in Roman, with italics for emphases. (In the body of the text italics indicate quotation or paraphrase, for which sources are indicated in the notes wherever possible.) Long and short "s" are both printed as "s." The ampersand "&" is replaced with "and" or "et" (as in "Etc."). *A Serious Proposal,* Part I, is written in a more archaizing style than its sequel, and the stylistic annotations on the latter are correspondingly sparser. Significant amendments in the 1695 edition (Wing A4063) and 1701 edition (Folger Library, PR3316.A655.S3.Cage) of Part I have been noted, but not minor variations of spelling, punctuation, or changes in persons or tenses, which do not affect the meaning.

Care has been taken in the notes to clearly distinguish Astell's marginal notes from the Editor's comment. *A Serious Proposal Parts I and II* are cross-referenced to the pagination of this edition as well as to the original 1694 and 1697 editions. Similarly for *Reflections Upon Marriage* (1700), *A Fair Way with the Dissenters* (1704), and *An Impartial Enquiry* (1704), which are cross-referenced with the following format: 1704/1996, to the 1996 edition, edited by Springborg, *Mary Astell: Political Writings* (Cambridge, Cambridge University Press). Astell's other works lack modern editions and are cross-referenced to the original editions.

A Serious

PROPOSAL

To the

Ladies,

For the Advancement of their true and greatest Interest.

By a Lover of Her SEX.

LONDON,

Printed for R. Wilkin at the *King's Head* in St. *Paul's Church-Yard.* 1694.

A Serious
PROPOSAL
To The
LADIES

LADIES,

Since the Profitable Adventures that have gone abroad in the World, have met with so great Encouragement, tho' the highest advantage they can propose, is an uncertain Lot for such matters as Opinion (not real worth)[1] gives a value to; things which if obtain'd, are as flitting and fickle as that Chance which is to dispose of them. I therefore persuade my self, you will not be less kind to a Proposition that comes attended with more certain and substantial Gain; whose only design is to improve your Charms and heighten your Value, by suffering you no longer to be cheap and contemptible. Its aim is to fix that Beauty, to make it lasting and permanent, which Nature with all the helps of Art cannot secure: and to place it out of the reach of Sickness and Old Age, by transferring it from a corruptible Body to an immortal Mind. An obliging Design, which wou'd procure them *inward* Beauty, to whom Nature has unkindly denied the *outward*; and not permit those Ladies who have comely Bodies, to tarnish their Glory with deformed Souls. Wou'd have you all be Wits,[2] or what is better Wise. Raise you above the Vulgar by something more truely illustrious, than a sounding Title or a great Estate. Wou'd excite in you a generous Emulation to excel in the best things, and not in such Trifles as every mean person who has but Money enough, may purchase as well as you. Not suffer you to take up with the low  thought of distinguishing your selves by any thing that is not truly valuable; and procure you such Ornaments as all the Treasures of the *Indies* are not able to purchase.[3] Wou'd help you to surpass the Men as much in Vertue and Ingenuity, as you do in Beauty; that you may not only be as lovely, but as wise as Angels. Exalt and Establish your Fame, more than the best wrought *Poems*, and loud-

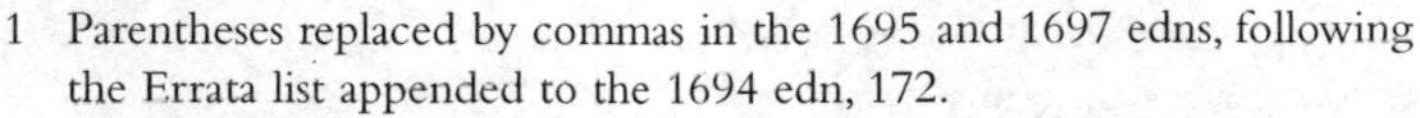

1 Parentheses replaced by commas in the 1695 and 1697 edns, following the Errata list appended to the 1694 edn, 172.

2 Learned, clever or intellectual person (arch.) (*OED*).

3 The example and phraseology of Richard Allestree (1619-1681) in *The Ladies Calling* [1673], part 1, §5 (1705 edn, 100).

est *Panegyricks*, by ennobling your Minds with such Graces as really deserve it. And instead of the Fustian[1] Complements and Fulsome Flatteries of your Admirers, obtain for you the Plaudit of Good Men and Angels, and the approbation of him who cannot err. In a word, render you the Glory and Blessing of the present Age, and the Admiration and Pattern of the next.

And sure, I shall not need many words to persuade you to close with this Proposal. The very offer is a sufficient inducement; nor does it need the set-off's of *Rhetorick* to recommend it, were I capable, which yet I am not, of applying them with the greatest force. Since you cannot be so unkind to your selves, as to refuse your *real* Interest, I only entreat you to be so wise as to examine wherein it consists; for nothing is of worser consequence than to be deceiv'd in a matter of so great concern. 'Tis as little beneath your Grandeur as your Prudence, to examine curiously what is in this case offer'd you; and to take care that cheating Hucksters don't impose upon you with deceitful Ware. This is a Matter infinitely more worthy your Debates, than what Colours are most agreeable, or whats the Dress becomes you best? Your *Glass* will not do you half so much service as a serious reflection on your own Minds; which will discover Irregularities more worthy your Correction, and keep you from being either too much elated or depress'd by the representations of the other. 'Twill not be near so advantageous to consult with your Dancing-master as with your own Thoughts, how you may with greatest exactness tread in the Paths of Vertue, which has certainly the most attractive *Air*, and Wisdom the most graceful and becoming *Meen*:[2] Let these attend you and your Carriage will be always well compos'd, and ev'ry thing you do will carry its Charm with it. No solicitude in the adornation of your

---

1 Fustian, formerly a kind of coarse cloth made of cotton and flax, named for *Fustat*, old Cairo, where it was manufactured; (*fig.*) inflated or turgid speech (*OED*). It is worth noting that Astell quickly begins her proposal in the realm of discourse, poetry, and rhetoric, where she sees the role models for frivolous women to lie. It is through education, principally reading, that the reform of women is to be carried out; it is indeed reform, rather than emancipation in the usual sense.

2 "Meen" is changed in the 1695 edn, 8 and the 1701 edn, 7, to "*Mien*," the English poetic form of French *mine*, expression, aspect of countenance, look, appearance (*OED*).

selves is discommended,[1] provided you employ your care about that which is really your *self*, and do not neglect that particle of Divinity within you, which must survive, and may (if you please) be happy and perfect when it's unsuitable and much inferiour Companion is mouldring into Dust. Neither will any pleasure be denied you, who are only desir'd not to catch at the Shadow and let the Substance go. You may be as ambitious as you please, so you aspire to the best *things*; and contend with your Neighbours as much as you can, that they may not out-do you in any commendable Quality. Let it never be said, that they to whom pre-eminence is so very agreeable, can be tamely content that others shou'd surpass them in *this*, and precede them in a *better* World! Remember, I pray you, the famous Women of former Ages, the *Orinda's*[2] of late, and the more Modern *D'acier*[3] and

---

1 Dissuaded, the opposite of commended (*OED*).

2 Katherine Philips (1631-64), who wrote under the pseudonym Orinda. Her first works, published in 1661, gained her fame as a poet, but she died of smallpox at the height of her career.

3 Anne Lefèvre Dacier (1654-1720), a French scholar and classics translator. Born in Saumur, the daughter of Tannequy Lefèvre, the renowned classical scholar, she married her father's most prominent student, André Dacier (1651-1722), in 1683. Moving to Paris on her father's death in 1672, she, with her future husband, became an editor of the Delphin series of classical authors, editing translations of Callimachus, Florus, Dictys, Cretensis, Aurelius Victor, and Eutropius. In 1681 she published a prose version of Anacreon and Sappho, followed by a translation of Terence and plays of Plautus and Aristophanes. In 1684 Mme Dacier and her husband retired to Castres to study theology and in 1985 announced their conversion to Catholicism, for which they were awarded a pension by the king. In 1699 Anne Dacier published her translation of the *Iliad*, and one of the *Odyssey* in 1708, sparking a controversy over Homer, to which A. Houdart de la Motte contributed an abridged and expurgated Homer, along with his *Discours sur Homère* (1714), and to which Anne Dacier responded with her *Des causes de la corruption du goût* (1714). The French debate between the ancients and the moderns, to which they so brilliantly contributed, engaged Jean Terrasson, who published his *Dissertation critique sur l'Iliade* (1715), drawing in the science and philosophy of Descartes to demonstrate the superiority of the moderns. Père C. Buffier's *Homère en arbitrage*, conciliated and brought together the parties, including M. de Valincourt, Mme Dacier, and La Motte, to celebrate the genius of Homer at supper on 5 April, 1716 and to drink to his health (*Encyclopaedia Britannica*, 11th edn., 1910-11, vol. 7, 727).

others,[1] and blush to think how much is now, and will hereafter be said of them, when you your selves (as great a Figure as you make) must be buried in silence and forgetfulness! Shall your Emulation fail *there only* where 'tis commendable? Why are you so preposterously humble, as not to contend for one of the highest Mansions in the Court of Heav'n? Believe me, Ladies, this is the only *Place* worth contending for, you are neither better nor worse in your selves for going before, or coming after *now*, but you are really so much the better, by how much the higher your station is in an Orb of Glory. How can you be content to be in the World like Tulips in a Garden, to make a fine *shew* and be good for nothing; have all your Glories set in the Grave, or perhaps much sooner? What your own sentiments are, I know not, but I cannot without pity and resentment reflect, that those Glorious Temples on which your kind Creator has bestow'd such exquisite workmanship, shou'd enshrine no better than *Egyptian* Deities;[2] be like a tarnish'd Sepulchre, which for all its glittering, has nothing within but Emptiness or Putrefaction! What a pity it is, that whilst your Beauty casts a lustre round about,[3] your Souls which are infinitely more bright and radiant, (of which if you had but a clear Idea,[4] as lovely as it is, and as much as you now value it, you wou'd then despise and neglect the mean *Case* that encloses it) shou'd be suffer'd to overrun with Weeds, lye fallow and neglected, unadorn'd with any Grace! Altho' the Beauty of the mind is necessary to secure those

1 The 1695 edn, 9, and the 1701 edn, 8, substitute "more Modern Heroins" for the 1694 edn's "the more modern *D'acier* and others." Dacier appears later in *A Serious Proposal, Part I* (1697 edn, 51) in Astell's list of French authors.

2 Astell's image of woman's body as a tarnished sepulchre for Egyptian deities is biblical, referring to the worshippers of the golden images (Daniel, 3, 7-14) and the golden calves (2 Kings, 10, 29). It also reflects familiarity with the burgeoning literature on ancient Egyptian religion among the antiquarians, Deists, and advocates for primitive Christianity, Thomas Hobbes (1588-1679), John Locke (1632-1704), John Toland (1670-1727), William Whiston (1667-1752) and others, to whom she is opposed.

3 The 1695 and 1701 edns substitute for "round about" the words "all around you."

4 Astell's "clear Idea" presages the "clear and distinct ideas" of Descartes, which she gives extended discussion in *A Serious Proposal, Part II* (1697 edn, ch. 3, §4, "A Natural Logic," 119-44).

Conquests which your Eyes have gain'd; and Time that mortal Enemy to handsome Faces, has no influence on a lovely Soul, but to better and improve it. For shame let's abandon that *Old*,[1] and therefore one wou'd think, unfashionable employment of pursuing Butter flies and Trifles! No longer drudge on in the dull beaten road of Vanity and Folly, which so many have gone before us; but dare to break the enchanted Circle that custom has plac'd us in,[2] and scorn the Vulgar way of imitating all the Impertinencies[3] of our Neighbours. Let us learn to pride ourselves in something more excellent than the invention of a Fashion:[4] And not entertain such a degrading thought of our own *worth*, as to imagine that our Souls were given us only for the service of our Bodies, and that the best improvement we can make of these, is to attract the eyes of men. We value *them* too much, and our *selves* too little, if we place any part of our worth[5] in their Opinion; and do not think our selves capable of Nobler Things than the pitiful Conquest of some

1 A satirical reference to the battle between the ancients and moderns and especially to William Wotton (1666-1727), who took the side of the moderns, and whose *Reflections on Antique and Modern Learning* (1694) Astell later cites in this work (see below 79-80). Astell's *Bart'lemy Fair* (1609), is published under Wotton's name, in order to engage Swift.

2 This apparently innocent mention of the tyranny of custom is developed in *A Serious Proposal, Part II* into a full blown critique of Lockean empiricism as an apparently radical epistemology that in fact leaves everything as it is. Astell follows Descartes in believing that human beings have in principle equal access to the facts of existence, which are available through thought and reflection. But customary attitudes and values stand in the way of women's intellectual and spiritual accomplishment. Astell engages in consciousness raising in the first part of *A Serious Proposal*, persuading women to break the chains of custom that bind them.

3 Astell consistently uses "impertinent" and "impertinency" to mean inappropriate in the sense of irrelevant or absurd rather than insolent or impolite, a seventeenth- and eighteenth-century usage (*OED*).

4 Astell's analysis of fashion and dress as gilded chains that keep women in subjection follows that of Fénelon, author of *De l'Education des filles* (1687), who argues elsewhere that "Through luxury the nobles are being ruined in order to enrich the merchants. By this luxury the manners of the entire nation are corrupted. This luxury is more pernicious than the profit from fashion is useful." (Fénelon, "Plans de gouvernement," in *Oeuvres complètes de Fénelon*, ed. J.E.A. Gosselin, 10 vols. Paris, 1848-52, vol. 3, 436, cited by Lougee, *Les Paradis des Femmes*, 179, n. 19).

5 In the 1695 and 1701 edns "desert" is substituted for "worth."

worthless heart. She who has opportunities of making an interest in Heaven, of obtaining the love and admiration of GOD and Angels, is too prodigal of her Time, and injurious to her Charms, to throw them away on vain insignificant men.[1] She need not make her self so cheap, as to descend to Court their Applauses; for at the greater distance she keeps, and the more she is above them, the more effectually she secures their esteem and wonder. Be so generous then Ladies, as to do nothing unworthy of you; so true to your Interest, as not to lessen your Empire and depreciate your Charms.[2] Let not your Thoughts be wholly busied in observing what respect is paid you, but a part of them at least, in studying to deserve it. And after all, remember that Goodness is the truest Greatness, to be wise for your selves the greatest Wit, and *that* Beauty the most desirable which will endure to Eternity.

Pardon me the seeming rudeness of this Proposal, which goes upon a supposition that there is something amiss in you, which it is intended to amend. My design is not to expose, but to rectify your Failures. To be exempt from mistake, is a privilege few can pretend to, the greatest is to be past Conviction, and too obstinate to reform. Even the *Men*, as exact as they wou'd seem, and as much as they divert themselves with our Miscarriages, are very often guilty of greater faults, and such as considering the advantages they enjoy, are much more inexcusable. But I will not pretend to correct their Errors, who either are, or at least *think* themselves too wise to receive Instruction from a Womans Pen. My earnest desire is, That you Ladies, would be as perfect and happy as 'tis possible to be in this imperfect state; for I Love you too well to endure a spot upon your Beauties, if I can by any means remove and wipe it off.

---

1 Astell's scathing opinion of men as husbands is often read as proto-feminist talk, but in fact the focus of her attack is on the mores that permit the degradation of marriage, a degradation in which women, as slaves of custom, collude.

2 Astell's early satirical use of the language of "Interest" and "Empire" points toward the sustained critique she mounts against Charles Davenant (1656-1714), author of *Essays upon Peace at Home and War Abroad* (1704), which Astell attacks in the long Preface hastily appended to her first pamphlet of the same year, *Moderation truly Stated*. She extends her critique to other Whigs, especially Locke, Daniel Defoe (1661?-1731), and White Kennett (1660-1728), in her subsequent political pamphlets of 1704, *A Fair Way With the Dissenters and their Patrons*, and *An Impartial Enquiry*. (Citations are given both to the 1704 and 1996 edns, ed. Springborg.)

I would have you live up to the dignity of your Nature, and express your thankfulness to GOD for the benefits you enjoy by a due improvement of them. As I know very many of you do, who countenance that Piety which the men decry, and are the brightest Patterns of Religion that the Age affords; 'tis my grief that all the rest of our Sex do not imitate such illustrious Patterns,[1] and therefore I would have them encreas'd and render'd more conspicuous, that Vice being put out of countenance, (because Vertue is the only thing in fashion) may sneak out of the World, and its darkness be dispell'd by the confluence of so many shining Graces. The Men perhaps will cry out that I teach you false Doctrine, for because by their seductions some amongst us are become very mean and contemptible, they would fain persuade the rest to be as despicable and forlorn as they. We're indeed oblig'd to them for their management, in endeavouring to make us so, who use all the artifice they can to spoil, and deny us the means of improvement. So that instead of inquiring why all Women are not wise and good, we have reason to wonder that there are any so. Were the Men as much neglected, and as little care taken to cultivate and improve them, perhaps they wou'd be so far from surpassing those whom they now dispise, that they themselves wou'd sink into the greatest stupidity and brutality.[2] The preposterous returns that the most of them make, to all the care and pains that are bestow'd on them, renders this no uncharitable, nor improbable Conjecture. One wou'd therefore almost think, that the wise disposer of all things, foreseeing how unjustly Women are denied opportunities of improvement from *without*, has therefore by way of compensation endow'd them with greater propensions to Vertue and a natural goodness of Temper *within*, which if duly manag'd, would raise them to the most eminent pitch of heroick Vertue. Hither, Ladies, I desire you wou'd aspire, 'tis a noble and becoming Ambition, and to remove such Obstacles as lye in your way is the design of this Paper. We will therefore enquire what it is that stops your flight,

---

1 The 1695 and 1701 edns substitute "Examples" for "Patterns," an instruction suggested in the Errata list appended to the 1694 edn, 172.

2 The argument that society has allocated resources uneconomically in expending all its educational resources on one half of the human race is an argument that Judith Drake relentlessly pursues in her *Essay In Defence of the Female Sex* (1696), often taken to be Astell's work, and listed, for instance, in Locke's library under Astell's name. See John Harrison and Peter Laslet, *The Library of John Locke*, items #1104, #1105 and #1914.

that keeps you groveling here below, like *Domitian*[1] catching Flies when you should be busied in obtaining Empires?[2]

Altho' it has been said by Men of more Wit than Wisdom, and perhaps of more malice than either, that Women are naturally incapable of acting Prudently, or that they are necessarily determined to folly, I must by no means grant it; that Hypothesis would render my endeavours impertinent, for then it would be in vain to advise the one, or endeavour the Reformation[3] of the other. Besides, there are Examples in all Ages, which sufficiently confute the Ignorance and Malice of this Assertion.

---

1 Titus Flavius Domitianus, Roman Emperor AD 81-96, second son of Vespasian and Flavia Domitilla, twelfth of the Caesars and third of the Flavians. He made himself emperor on the death of his brother Titus, whom he is reported to have killed. Domitian, who promised peace and tranquillity, soon gave way to unnatural indulgences, commanding that he be addressed as God and Lord. He spent most of his day catching flies and killing them with bodkins, so that Vibius, upon being asked who was with the emperor, was able to reply, "Nobody, not even a fly." Suetonius records him in his *Lives*. (*Lemprière's Classical Dictionary of Proper Names mentioned in Ancient Authors*, 214.)

2 Astell has women and empire on the mind. By 1706 she has developed a brilliantly satirical disclaimer, denying any intention of encroaching upon the male domain in her famous Preface to *Reflections upon Marriage* (1706 edn, ii-iii, 1996 edn, ed. Springborg, 8; henceforth both editions will be cited):

> Far be it from her to stir up Sedition of any sort, none can abhor it more; and she heartily wishes that our Masters wou'd pay their Civil and Ecclesiastical Governors the same Submission, which they themselves exact from their Domestic Subjects. Nor can she imagine how she any way undermines the Masculine Empire, or blows the Trumpet of Rebellion to the Moiety of Mankind. Is it by exhorting Women, not to expect to have their own Will in any thing, but to be entirely Submissive, when once they have made choice of a Lord and Master, tho' he happen not to be so Wise, so Kind, or even so Just a Governor as was expected? She did not indeed advise them to think his Folly Wisdom, nor his Brutality that Love and Worship he promised in his Matrimonial Oath, for this required a Flight of Wit and Sense much above her poor Ability, and proper only to Masculine Understandings. However she did not in any manner prompt them to Resist, or to Abdicate the Perjur'd Spouse, tho, the Laws of GOD and the Land make special Provision for it, in a case wherein, as is to be fear'd, few Men can truly plead Not Guilty.

3 Astell anticipates her program for the reformation of manners.

The Incapacity, if there be any, is acquired not natural;[1] and none of their Follies are so necessary, but that they might avoid them if they pleas'd themselves. Some disadvantages indeed they labour under, and what these are we shall see by and by and endeavour to surmount; but Women need not take up with mean things, since (if they are not wanting to themselves) they are capable of the best. Neither God nor Nature have excluded them from being Ornaments to their Families[2] and useful in their Generation; there is therefore no reason they should be content to be Cyphers[3] in the World, useless at the best, and in a little time a burden and nuisance to all about them. And 'tis very great pity that they who are so apt to over-rate themselves in smaller matters, shou'd, where it most concerns them to know, and stand upon their Value, be so insensible of their own worth.

The Cause therefore of the defects we labour under, is, if not wholly, yet at least in the first place, to be ascribed to the mistakes

---

1 Astell seriously engages the question of the relation between gender and custom, arguing throughout that women's subordination is customary, not natural. There would appear to be an implicit contradiction between her Platonist belief in innate ideas and her subscription to nurture over nature as formative of character. It is a contradiction which she seeks to resolve by appeal to Malebranche's notion of "seeing all things in God," whereby the "innateness" of ideas is a consequence of divine design. When Astell later is persuaded, probably by Masham's critique, to give up the notion of the human mind as an efflux of the Divine, the contradiction, source of much confusion among her commentators, remains. What is clear, however, is that she does not subscribe to Lockean sensationalist psychology, which some have argued is the provenance of the nurture over nature argument for the power of custom and habit that she makes in *A Serious Proposal, Parts I* and *II*, and *Reflections upon Marriage*.

2 John Stuart Mill took seriously Astell's charge to women to be "Ornaments to their Families," a subject of disagreement between him and Harriet Taylor.

3 Variant of "cipher," from the Arabic term for zero, an arithmetical symbol or character of no value by itself, which increases the value of other figures according to its position; by transference, a person who fills a place, but is of no importance or worth, a nonentity, a "mere nothing" (*OED*).

of our Education; which like an Error in the first Concoction,[1] spreads its ill Influence through all our Lives.

The Soil is rich and would, if well cultivated, produce a noble Harvest, if then the Unskilful Managers not only permit, but incourage noxious Weeds, tho' we shall suffer by their Neglect, yet they ought not in justice to blame any but themselves, if they reap the Fruit of their own Folly.[2] Women are from their very Infancy debar'd those Advantages, with the want of which, they are afterwards reproached, and nursed up in those Vices which will hereafter be upbraided[3] to them. So partial are Men as to expect Brick where they afford no Straw; and so abundantly civil as to take care we shou'd make good that obliging Epithet of *Ignorant*, which out of an excess of good Manners, they are pleas'd to bestow on us!

One would be apt to think indeed, that Parents shou'd take all possible care of their Childrens Education, not only for *their* sakes, but even for their *own*. And tho' the Son convey the Name to Posterity, yet certainly a great Part of the Honour of their Families depends on their Daughters. 'Tis the kindness of Education that binds our duty fastest on us:[4] For the being instrumental to the bringing us into the World, is no matter of choice and therefore the less obliging: But to procure that we may live wisely and happily in it, and be capable of endless Joys hereafter, is a benefit we can never sufficiently acknowledge. To introduce poor Children into the World, and neglect to fence them against the temptations of it, and so leave them expos'd to temporal and eternal Miseries, is a wickedness, for which I want a Name; 'tis beneath Brutality; the Beasts are better natur'd for they take care of their off-spring, till they are capable of caring for themselves. And if Mothers had a due

---

1 Digestion of food. The old physiology recognized three phases: the *first concoction*, digestion in the stomach and intestines; the *second concoction*, the process whereby nutrients were turned into blood; and the *third concoction*, secretion (*OED*). Astell refers to the ingestion of bad food or poison.

2 The 2nd edn (1695, 22), substitutes for "their own Folly," "this their foolish Conduct," which the 1701 edn (16) repeats.

3 Be upbraided to them, brought forward, adduced, or alleged as a matter of censure or reproach against them (*OED*).

4 Bringing children into the world is more by accident than design, but education is a gift intentionally bestowed which obliges the recipient to gratitude.

regard to their Posterity, how *Great* soever they are, they wou'd not think themselves too *Good* to perform what Nature requires, nor thro' Pride and Delicacy remit the poor little one to the care of a Foster Parent. Or, if necessity inforce them to depute another to perform *their* Duty, they wou'd be as choice at least in the Manners and Inclinations, as they are in the complections of their Nurses, lest with their Milk they transfuse their Vices, and form in the Child such evil habits as will not easily be eradicated.[1]

Nature as bad as it is and as much as it is complain'd of, is so far improveable by the grace of GOD, upon our honest and hearty endeavours, that if we are not wanting to our selves, we may all in *some*, tho' not in an *equal* measure, be instruments of his Glory, Blessings to this World, and capable of eternal Blessedness in that to come. But if our Nature is spoil'd, instead of being improv'd at first; if from our Infancy we are nurs'd up in Ignorance and Vanity; are taught to be Proud and Petulent, Delicate and Fantastick,[2] Humorous and Inconstant, 'tis not strange that the ill effects of this Conduct appear in all the future Actions of our Lives. And seeing it is Ignorance, either habitual or actual,[3] which is the cause of all sin, how are they like to escape *this*, who are bred up in *that?* That therefore Women are unprofitable to most, and a plague and dishonour to some Men is not much to be regretted on account of the *Men*, because 'tis the product of their own folly, in denying them the benefits of an ingenuous[4]

---

1 It is not likely that Astell, who believed virtue to be acquired and not innate, would literally believe that children could imbibe the vices of wet-nurses. This appears to be a plea for nursing mothers. Astell's emphasis on an education for women that would produce serious mothers parallels Madame de Maintenon's proposals for Saint-Cyr, based on Fénelon's *De l'Education des filles* (1687, 1933 edn, 18, 100-01), and the admonitions of Richard Allestree in *The Ladies Calling*, Part 2, §2 and §3 "Of Wives" and "Of Widows" (1703 edn, 201 ff., 231 ff).

2 "Fantastick" (of persons, their actions and attributes): fanciful, impulsive, capricious, arbitrary (*OED*).

3 Astell distinguishes habitual ignorance from ignorance exhibited in deeds or discrete acts, active ignorance (*OED*).

4 Astell uses the term "ingenuous," more often than not satirically, in the obsolete seventeenth-century sense meaning "of high or excellent quality or character," i.e., a "Person of Quality," or "Befitting a free-born person, or one of honourable station; liberal, high-class" (*OED*); so for instance of White Kennett and John Locke in *An Impartial Enquiry* (1704 edn, 37, 43;1996 edn, ed. Springborg, 173, 180); and William Nicholls (1664-1712) in *Reflections upon Marriage* (1706 edn, ii, vi; 1996 edn, 8, 12).

and liberal Education, the most effectual means to direct them into, and to secure their progress in the ways of Vertue.

For that Ignorance is the cause of most Feminine Vices, may be instanc'd in that Pride and Vanity which is usually imputed to us, and which, I suppose, if throughly sifted, will appear to be some way or other, the rise and Original of all the rest. These, tho very bad Weeds, are the product of a good Soil; they are nothing else but Generosity degenerated and corrupted. A desire to advance and perfect its Being, is planted by GOD in all Rational Natures, to excite them hereby to every worthy and becoming Action;[1] for certainly next to the Grace of GOD, nothing does so powerfully restrain people from Evil and stir them up to Good, as a generous Temper. And therefore to be ambitious of perfections is no fault, tho to assume the Glory of our Excellencies to our selves, or to Glory in such as we really have not, are. And were Womens haughtiness express'd in disdaining to do a mean and evil thing; wou'd they pride themselves in somewhat truly perfective of a Rational nature, there were no hurt in it. But then they ought not to be denied the means of examining and judging what is so; they should not be impos'd on with tinsel ware. If by reason of a false Light, or undue Medium, they chuse amiss; theirs is the loss, but the Crime is the Deceivers. She who rightly understands wherein the perfection of her Nature consists, will lay out her Thoughts and Industry in the acquisition of such Perfections. But she who is kept ignorant of the matter, will take up with such Objects as first offer themselves, and bear any plausible resemblance to what she desires; a shew of advantage being sufficient to render them agreeable baits to her who wants Judgment and Skill to discern between reality and pretence. From whence it easily follows, that she who has nothing else to value her self upon, will be proud of her Beauty, or Money, and what that can purchase; and think her self mightily oblig'd to him, who tells her she has those Perfections which she naturally longs for. Her inbred self-esteem and desire of good, which are degenerat-

---

1 As Astell's correspondence with the Cambridge Platonist John Norris (1657-1711), *Letters Concerning the Love of God, between the Author of the Proposal to the Ladies and Mr. John Norris* (1695) demonstrates, Astell believes that the love of God is an active force, drawing the mind to its own perfection.

ed into Pride and mistaken Self-love,[1] will easily open her Ears to whatever goes about to nourish and delight them; and when a cunning designing Enemy from without, has drawn over to his Party these Traytors within, he has the Poor unhappy Person at his Mercy, who now very glibly swallows down his Poyson, because 'tis presented in a Golden Cup; and credulously hearkens to the most disadvantagious Proposals, because they come attended with a seeming esteem.[2] She whose Vanity makes her swallow praises by the whole sale, without examining whether she deserves them, or from what hand they come, will reckon it but gratitude to think well of him who values her so much; and think she must needs be merciful to the poor dispairing Lover whom her Charms have reduc'd to die at her feet. Love and Honour are what every one of us naturally esteem, they are excellent things in themselves and very worthy our regard; and by how much the readier we are to embrace what ever resembles them, by so much the more dangerous,[3] it is that these venerable Names should be wretchedly abus'd and affixt to their direct contraries, yet this is the Custom of the World: And how can she possibly detect the fallacy, who has no better Notion of either than what she derives from Plays and

---

1 Astell begins to speak the language of Pierre Nicole (1625-95) an influential member of the Jansenist Port Royal school, who, in his important *Essais de morale* (14 vols, 1671-79), distinguished between *amour-de-soi*, appropriate self-esteem, and *amour-propre*, pride, vanity or destructive self-love. It is a language she speaks throughout *A Serious Proposal, Parts I* and *II.* Nicole collaborated with Antoine Arnauld (1612-94) in publishing the work of the Port Royal school, with whose work Astell was clearly familiar. Arnauld's treatise *On True and False Ideas* (1683) was a refutation of Malebranche's *Search After Truth* (1678) and its thesis "that we see all things in God," a thesis which Astell addressed in *Letters Concerning the Love of God* (1695). Moreover, Locke, her chosen adversary, is reputed to have produced an early translation of Nicole's *Essais.*

2 Astell's own *Serious Proposal to the Ladies*, is thus juxtaposed to the fickle proposals (of marriage) with which their suitors woo them, and the work is in every sense a harbinger of Astell's *Reflections upon Marriage* (1700). The image of the Golden Cup and the language of war and treachery recall the classical suitors, such as Paris in pursuit of Helen, and all the Neoclassical conceits of courtship of the age.

3 Instruction in the Errata list appended to the 1694 edn, 172 to delete the comma.

Romances?[1] How can she be furnished with any solid Principles whose very Instructors are Froth and emptiness?[2] Whereas Women were they rightly Educated, had they obtain'd a well inform'd and discerning Mind, they would be proof against all those Batteries,[3] see through and scorn those little silly Artifices which are us'd to ensnare and deceive them. Such an one would value her self only on her Vertue, and consequently be most chary of what she esteems so much. She would know, that not what others say, but[4] what she her self does, is the true Commendation and the only thing that exalts her; the loudest Encomiums[5] being not half so satisfactory as the calm and secret Plaudit[6] of her own Mind; which moving on true Principles of Honour and Vertue, wou'd not fail on a review of it self to anticipate that delightful Eulogy she shall one day hear.

Whence is it but from ignorance, from a want of understanding to compare and judge of things, to chuse a right End, to proportion the Means to the End, and to rate ev'ry thing according to its proper value; that we quit the Substance for the Shadow, Reality for Appearance, and embrace those very things which, if we understood we shou'd hate and fly; but now are reconcil'd to, merely because they usurp the Name, tho' they have nothing of the Nature of those venerable Objects we desire and

---

1 Love and Honour were the values extolled in the plays and novels of William Davenant (1606- 68), Queen Henrietta Maria's poet and father of Charles Davenant (to whom Astell devotes the long prefatory essay of *Moderation truly Stated*, 1704), Beaumont and Fletcher and other Stuart and Restoration dramatists revived in her day. Astell disparages the sleight of hand by which they set traps, disguised as virtues, for females. Her disparagement of popular fiction parallels that of Fénelon, in *De l'Education des filles* (1687, 1933 edn, 23) and Richard Allestree's *The Ladies Calling*, Part 2, §3 (1705 edn, 257).

2 *The Ladies Library* ch. 13 on "Ignorance" (1714 edn, 438-534) reproduces Astell's text from this point to p. 58, with only minor changes.

3 Astell uses the language of assault. Short of the action of beating or battering, battery may be understood in the obsolete usage of a drum-beat, giving the signal for an assault (*OED*).

4 The Errata list appended to the 1694 edn, 172, instructs the substitution of "than."

5 A formal or high-flown expression of praise; a eulogy, panegyric (*OED*).

6 Round of applause, emphatic expression of approval (*OED*).

seek?[1] Were it not for this delusion, is it probable a Lady who passionately desires to be admir'd, shou'd ever consent to such Actions as render her base and contemptible? Wou'd she be so absurd as to think either to get love, or to keep it, by those methods which occasion loathing, and consequently end in hatred? Wou'd she reckon it a piece of her Grandeur, or hope to gain esteem by such excesses as really lessen her in the eyes of all considerate and judicious persons? Wou'd she be so silly as to look big, and think her self the better person, because she has more Mony to bestow profusely, or the good luck to have a more ingenious Taylor or Milliner than her Neighbour? Wou'd she who by the regard she pays to Wit,[2] seems to make some pretences to it, undervalue her Judgment so much as to admit the Scurrility[3] and profane noisy Nonsense of men, whose Fore-heads are better than their Brains, to pass under that Character? Wou'd she be so weak as to imagine that a few airy Fancies joyn'd with a great deal of Impudence and ill-nature (the right definition of modern Wit) can bespeak him a Man of sense,[4] who runs

---

1 Astell's emphasis on want of "understanding" as the cause of women's subordination may well be inspired by Locke's *Essay Concerning Human Understanding*. Her account of understanding as the capacity "to compare and judge of things, to chuse a right End, to proportion the Means to the End, and to rate ev'ry thing according to its proper value" is both Lockean and Aristotelian. But her addendum, that lack of understanding means "that we quit the Substance for the Shadow, Reality for Appearance," is pure Plato. This is an instance of Astell's not always happy syncretism of Cartesian rationalism (to which Locke himself was so indebted) and Aristotelian prudence.

2 Astell uses "Wit," often satirically, both to refer to the faculty for saying amusing or brilliant things, and to those persons known for such a capacity. Eighteenth-century cynics, sceptics, deists, and critics of Enthusiasm were commonly referred to as "Wits," as by Astell in *Bart'lemy Fair*. This meaning may be implied here.

3 Astell uses hyperbole; while she may refer to the "noisy Nonsense of men" as "scurrilous" to mean buffoon-like jocularity, it is unlikely that she attributes the further meanings: coarseness or indecency of language, especially in jesting and invective (*OED*).

4 "Man of sense" refers to the sensationalist psychology of Locke's *Essay Concerning Human Understanding*, which locates the origin of our ideas in sense experience. Astell makes explicit reference to a revised edn of Locke's *Essay*, vol. 2, ch. 33, "On the Association of Ideas," in *An Impartial Enquiry* (1704), 40/177, and throughout *The Christian Religion*; but it is clear that she is already familiar with the 1st edn, to judge by her long disquisitions on Understanding in *A Serious Proposal, Parts I* and *II*, especially *Part II*, ch. 3, which is an investigation of Locke's philosophy of mind.

counter to all the sense and reason that ever appear'd in the World? Than which nothing can be an Argument of greater shallowness, unless it be to regard and esteem him for it. Wou'd a Woman, if she truly understood her self, be affected either with the praises or calumnies of those worthless persons, whose Lives are a direct contradiction to Reason, a very sink of corruption, by whom one wou'd blush to be commended, lest they shou'd be mistaken for Partners[1] or Connivers at their Crimes?[2] Will she who has a jot of discernment think to satisfy her greedy desire of Pleasure,[3] with those promising nothings that have again and again deluded her? Or will she to obtain such Bubbles, run the risque of forfeiting Joys infinitely satisfying and eternal? In sum, did not ignorance impose on us, we would never lavish out the greatest part of our Time and Care, on the decoration of a Tenement, in which our Lease is so very short, and which for all our industry, may lose it's Beauty e'er that Lease be out, and in the mean while neglect a more glorious and durable Mansion![4] We wou'd never be so curious of the House, and so careless of the Inhabitant, whose beauty is capable of great improvement and will endure for ever without diminution or decay!

---

1 The 4th edn (1701), 26, reads "Partners in or Connivers at," but the 2nd edn (1695), 42-43, reads like the 1st.

2 The spiritedness of Astell's invective suggests a specific target and one wonders if Astell did not already know of Locke's relation to Damaris Masham, into whose household he entered in 1691, and where he lived until his death in 1704. John Edwards' exposure of Locke as "governor of the seraglio at Oates" was made in his *Brief Vindication of the Fundamental Articles of Christian Faith* of 1697 (see Cranston, *John Locke: A Biography*, 430-31; and S. O'Donnell, "Mr. Locke and the Ladies," 154). But Locke's influence on Lady Masham may well have been known in Cambridge Platonist circles earlier. It was almost certainly known to Astell by 1697, the year of *A Serious Proposal, Part II* (74/146), in which "every little warm Disputer and Pretender to Reason, whose Life is perhaps a continual contradiction to it," would seem to make reference to Locke's questionable domestic arrangements.

3 Astell parodies Epicurean pleasure and pain as the twin motivating principles of Locke's *Essay Concerning Human Understanding*.

4 Astell's use of edifice language is reminiscent of the New Testament, where John 14, 2 declares "my Father's house are many mansions." The grandness of her contrast between the body as a tenement, on which the soul has a short lease, and the mansions of heaven gives the metaphor great vividness and power.

Thus Ignorance and a narrow Education, lay the Foundation of Vice, and Imitation and Custom rear it up.[1] Custom, that merciless torrent that carries all before.[2] And which[3] indeed can be stem'd by none but such as have a great deal of Prudence and a rooted Vertue. For 'tis but Decorous that she who is not capable of giving better Rules, shou'd follow those she sees before her, lest[4] she only change the instance and retain the absurdity.[5] 'T wou'd puzzle a considerate Person to account for all that Sin and Folly that is in the World (which certainly has nothing in it self to recommend it,) did not Custom help to solve the difficulty.[6] For Vertue without question has on all accounts the preeminence[7] of Vice, 'tis abundantly more pleasant in the *Act*, as well as more advantageous in the *consequences*, as any one who will but rightly use her reason, in a serious reflection on her self and the nature of things, may easily perceive. 'Tis Custom therefore, that Tyrant Custom, which is the grand motive to all those irrational choices

---

1 Astell's wholesale denunciation of custom puts her squarely among the moderns in the battle of the books. Her sustained attack on customary authority in *A Serious Proposal, Parts I* and *II*, puts her in strange company, alongside the moderns as a supporter of science and reason. This does not prevent her, as it did not prevent any of the protagonists to the debate, from having favourites on the other side — so for instance her admiration for Mme Dacier. For a definitive treatment of the debate, see Levine, *Battle of the Books*.

2 The Errata list, appended to the 1694 edn, 172, suggests that "it" be inserted.

3 "that carries all before it, and which" in the 1695 (36) and 1701 (27) edns.

4 "least" in the 1695 (36), 1701 (27) edns.

5 Astell reproaches women for failing to be able to provide their own rational rules of conduct, their only innovation a variation of the instances of rules men set for them. This is a classic rationalist position, describing a classical theory of freedom as autonomy, as advanced later by J.-J. Rousseau, for instance: the capacity to elect a rule of conduct and follow it.

6 Here Astell seems to advance a Platonist argument that people would not knowingly commit a wrong, custom being the cause of the problem of evil. But, curiously, the arguments she advances to defend the proposition are utilitarian ones, in a resort to the language of interests, pleasure, and choices.

7 Surpassing or superior eminence, higher rank or distinction, priority of place, precedence or superiority (*OED*).

which we daily see made in the World, so very contrary to our *present* interest and pleasure, as well as to our Future. We think it an unpardonable mistake not to do as our neighbours do, and part with our Peace and Pleasure as well as our Innocence and Vertue, meerly in complyance with an unreasonable Fashion. And having inur'd ourselves to Folly, we know not how to quit it; we go on in Vice, not because we find satisfaction in it, but because we are unacquainted with the Joys of Vertue.

Add to this the hurry and noise of the World, which does generally so busy and pre-ingage us, that we have little time, and less inclination to stand still and reflect on our own Minds. Those impertinent Amusements which have seiz'd us, keep their hold so well and so constantly buz about our Ears, that we cannot attend to the Dictates of our Reason, nor to the soft whispers and winning persuasives[1] of the divine Spirit, by whose assistance were we dispos'd to make use of it, we might shake off these Follies, and regain our Freedom. But alas! to complete our misfortunes, by a continual application to Vanity and Folly, we quite spoil the contexture[2] and frame of our Minds, so loosen and dissipate, that nothing solid and substantial will stay in it.[3] By an habitual inadvertency we render our selves incapable of any serious and improving thought, till our minds themselves become as light and frothy as those things they are conversant about. To all which, if we further add the great industry that bad people use to corrupt the good, and that unaccountable backwardness that appears in too many good persons, to stand up for, and propagate the Piety they profess; (so strangely are things transposed, that Vertue puts on

---

1 Persuasions.

2 The action of or process of weaving together or intertwining, and the texture of a body so constituted; (by transference) the linking together of materials or elements to form a connected structure (natural or artificial); and the manner in which the parts of a thing are thus united. The *OED* notes that the term, common in the seventeenth century, is now rare, undoubtedly because notions of the mind/body relation have changed and because mechanism in general took over from more organic metaphors for the composition of a whole out of parts, a development to which Locke contributed and to which Astell was opposed.

3 The 1695 (39) and 1701 (29) edns follow the instruction in the Errata list appended to the 1694 edn, 172, and substitute "them." Note Astell's use of the infinitive or indicative forms, "loosen" and "dissipate," instead of the adjectival past participles, "loosened" and "dissipated."

the blushes,[1] which belong to Vice, and Vice insults with the authority of Vertue!) and we have a pretty fair account of the Causes of our non-improvement.

When a poor Young Lady is taught to value her self on nothing but her Cloaths,[2] and to think she's very fine when well accoutred.[3] When she hears say that 'tis Wisdom enough for her to know how to dress her self, that she may become amiable in his eyes; to whom it appertains to be knowing and learned; who can blame her if she lay out her Industry and Money on such Accomplishments, and sometimes extends it farther than her misinformer desires she should? When she sees the vain and the gay, making *Parade* in the World and attended with the Courtship and admiration of all about them,[4] no wonder that her tender Eyes are dazled with the Pageantry; and wanting Judgement to pass a due Estimate on them and their Admirers, longs to be such a fine and celebrated thing as they! What tho' she be sometimes told of another World, she has however a more lively perception of this, and may well think, that if her Instructors were in earnest when they tell her of *hereafter*, they would not be so busied and concerned about what happens *here*. She is, it may be, taught the Principles and Duties of Religion, but not Acquainted with the Reasons and Grounds of them; being told 'tis enough for her to believe, to examine why, and wherefore, belongs not to her.[5] And

---

1 The Errata list appended to the 1694 edn, 172, instructs that this comma be deleted.

2 Clothes.

3 Attired, dressed, equipped, arrayed; generally with the idea of being specially attired for some purpose (*OED*).

4 In the 1695 (41) and 1701 (39) edns, Astell substitutes for "of all about them," "of the gazing herd." Astell is no democrat, and in both her treatment of women and of citizens she shows scant regard for the mob. It follows, therefore, that she is also no defender of a right to free speech, freedom of the press or pulpit, as she makes clear in *A Fair Way with the Dissenters* (1704).

5 Astell's remarks anticipate her later scathing attack on Locke, for whom, she maintains (not quite fairly), the "Reasonableness of Christianity" does not extend to women. She generalizes from Locke's objection to Cambridge Platonism, that it was inaccessibile to those of "vulgar capacities," as if he meant by this religion in general. In the *Reasonableness of Christianity* (1695 edn, 279), he had declared condescendingly: "you may as soon hope to have all Day-Labourers and Tradesmen, the Spinsters and Dairy Maids perfect Mathematicians, as to have them perfect in *Ethicks* this way." Astell, who refers to this passage in two places in *The Christian*

therefore, though her Piety may be tall and spreading, yet because it wants foundation and Root, the first rude Temptation overthrows and blasts it, or perhaps the short liv'd Gourd decays and withers of its own accord.[1] But why should she be blamed for setting no great value on her Soul, whose noblest Faculty her Understanding is render'd useless to her? Or censur'd for relinquishing a course of Life, whose Prerogatives[2] she was never acquainted with, and tho' highly reasonable in it self, was put upon the embracing it with as little reason as she now forsakes it? For if her Religion it self be taken up as the Mode[3] of the Country, 'tis no strange thing that she lays it down again, in conformity to the Fashion. Whereas she whose Reason is suffer'd to display it self, to inquire into the grounds and Motives of Religion, to make a disquisition of its Graces, and search out its hidden Beauties; who is a Christian out of Choice, not in conformity to those about her;[4] and cleaves to Piety, because 'tis her Wisdom, her Interest, her Joy, not because she has been accustom'd to it; she who is not only eminently and unmoveably good, but able to give a Reason *why* she is so; is too firm and stable to be mov'd by the pitiful Allurements of sin, too wise and too well bottom'd[5] to be undermined and supplanted by the strongest Efforts of Temptation. Doubtless a truly Christian Life requires a clear Understanding as well as regular Affections, that both together may move the Will to a direct choice of Good and a stedfast adherence to it. For tho' the heart may

---

Religion (1705 edn, §307, 301; §400, 402-03), gave a pointed reply, declaring that her theology comprised only "plain Propositions and short Reasonings *about things familiar to our Minds, as* need not *amaze* any part of Mankind, no not the *Day Labourer and Tradesmen, the Spinsters and Dairy Maids*, who may very easily *comprehend* what a Woman cou'd write" (*The Christian Religion*, 1705, 402-03; see Perry, 1986, 92-93).

1 We are surprised as the nicely executed metaphor of the tree turns into a gourd, the large fleshy fruit of trailing or climbing plants, which when dried and hollowed out is used as a vessel (*OED*). Astell may have in mind Jonah, 4, 6-7, according to which the Lord prepared a gourd for Jonah, to his pleasure, but the next day contrived a storm, and it smote the gourd that it withered."

2 Probably the obsolete sense of pre-eminence, superiority (*OED*), rather than the language of rights or privilege (to which Astell has philosophical objections as the language of Whigs).

3 Fashion.

4 Phrase substituted in 1695 edn (43) and 1701 edn (32) "among whom she lives."

5 Well grounded (*OED*).

be honest, it is but by chance that the Will is right if the Understanding be ignorant and Cloudy And what's the reason that we sometimes see persons falling[1] off from their Piety, but because 'twas their Affections, not their Judgment, that inclin'd them to be Religious? Reason and Truth are firm and immutable, she who bottoms[2] on them is on sure ground: Humour and Inclination are sandy Foundations; and she who is sway'd by her Affections more than by her Judgment, owes the happiness of her Soul in a great measure to the temper of her Body; her Piety may perhaps blaze higher,[3] but will not last long. For the Affections are various and changeable, mov'd by every Object, and the last comer easily undoes whatever its Predecessor had done before it.[4] Such Persons are always in extreams, they are either violently good or quite cold and indifferent; a perpetual trouble to themselves and others, by indecent Raptures,[5] or unnecessary Scruples; there is no Beauty and order in their lives, all is rapid and unaccountable;[6] they are now very furious in such a course; but

---

1 In the 1696 edn, 44, and 1701 edn, 33, "unhappily falling off."

2 To set upon a foundation, based, found, ground upon (*OED*).

3 In the 1695 edn, 45, and 1701 edn, 33, "high."

4 No "it" in the 1695 edn, 45, 1701 edn, 33. Astell here takes a classic Platonist line in her account of the passions: that although a necessary appetitive and bodily motivational force, they blind reason and must be brought under its control. Her theory of the passions is developed at great length in chs ii and iv of *A Serious Proposal, Part II,* and summarized in the aphorism that "it is not the Head but the Heart that is the Seat of Atheism" (1697/2002, 31/130). Here she seems to follow the Port Royal theory of true and false desires, formulating the distinction in their terms as between "irregular" and "regular" forms of self-love.

5 By "indecent Raptures" Astell refers more to the ecstatic state of Enthusiasts or Neoplatonists than to the amorous transports that the term also conveyed in her day, although there may be word play. This indictment of Enthusiasm, or an emotion-based piety, seems to anticipate the accusations Damaris Masham was to make against Astell's proposal for a woman's retirement in *Discourse Concerning the Love of God* (1696,120); and to deny them. Referring to Astell's ecstatic faith demonstrated at length in *Letters Concerning the Love of God* (Astell, 1695, 261- 62), Masham accuses her of "as wild an Enthusiasm as any that has been yet seen; and which can End in nothing but Monasteries, and Hermitages; with all those sottish and Wicked Superstitions which have accompanied them where-ever they have been in use."

6 "Unaccountable" corrected as per Errata list, 172.

they cannot well tell why, and anon[1] as violent in the other extream. Having more *Heat* than *Light*, their Zeal out runs their knowledge, and instead of representing Piety as it is in it self, the most lovely and inviting thing imaginable, they expose it to the contempt and ridicule of the censorious World. Their Devotion becomes ricketed,[2] starv'd and contracted[3] in some of it's vital parts, and disproportioned and over-grown in less material instances; whilst one Duty is *over done*, to commute[4] for the neglect of another, and the mistaken person thinks the being often on her knees, attones for all the miscarriages of her Conversation: Not considering that 'tis in vain to petition for those Graces which we take no care to Practice, and a mockery to adore those Perfections we run counter to: and that the true end of all our Prayers and external Observances is to work our minds into a truly Christian temper, to obtain for us the Empire of Passions, and to reduce all irregular Inclinations, that so we may be as like GOD in Purity, Charity, and all his imitable excellencies, as is consistent with the imperfection of a Creature.[5]

And now having discovered the Disease and its cause, 'tis proper to apply a Remedy; single Medicines are too weak to cure such complicated Distempers, they require a full Dispensatory;[6] and what wou'd a good Woman refuse to do, could she hope by that to advantage the greatest part of the World, and improve her Sex in Knowledge and true Religion? I doubt not Ladies, but that the Age, as bad as it is, affords very many of you who will readily embrace whatever has a true tendency to the Glory of GOD and your mutual Edification, to revive the ancient Spirit of Piety in the World and to transmit it to succeeding Generations. I know there are many of you who so ardently love GOD, as to think no time too much to spend in his service, nor any thing too difficult to do for his sake; and bear such a hearty good-will to your Neighbours, as to grudge no Prayers or Pains to reclaim and improve them. I have therefore no more to do but to make the Proposal, to prove

---

1 Now again, now at this time, in contrast to at that time (*OED*).

2 Affected by rickets (*OED*).

3 Narrowed, shortened, shrunken (*OED*).

4 Compensate.

5 George Berkeley's extract from the first part of *A Serious Proposal* in *The Ladies Library* (1714 edn, vol. 1, 438-47), concludes here. A long extract comprising the important ch. 3 of *A Serious Proposal, Part II* (1697/2002, 68-194/144-97), follows (*The Ladies Library*, 1714 edn, vol. 1, 447- 524).

6 Place where medicines are made up, dispensary (obs. usage) (*OED*).

that it will answer these great and good Ends, and then 'twill be easy to obviate the Objections that Persons of more Wit than Vertue may happen to raise against it.

Now as to the Proposal it is to erect a *Monastery*, or if you will (to avoid giving offence to the scrupulous and injudicious, by names which tho' innocent in themselves, have been abus'd by superstitious Practices,) we will call it a *Religious Retirement*,[1] and such as shall have a double aspect, being not only a Retreat from the World for those who desire that advantage, but likewise, an institution and previous discipline, to fit us to do the greatest good in it; such an institution as this (if I do not mightily deceive my self,) would be the most probable method to amend the present and improve the future Age. For hère, those who are convinc'd of the emptiness of earthly Enjoyments, who are sick of the vanity of the world, and its impertinencies may find more substantial and satisfying entertainments, and need not be confin'd to what they justly loath. Those who are desirous to know and fortify their weak side, first do good to themselves, that hereafter they may be capable of doing more good to others; or for their greater security are willing to avoid *temptation*, may get out of that danger which a continual stay in view of the Enemy[2] and the familiarity and unwearied application of the Temptation may expose them to; and gain an opportunity to look into themselves, to be acquainted at home and no longer the greatest strangers to their own hearts. Such as are willing in a more peculiar and undisturb'd manner, to attend the great business they came into the world about, the service of GOD and improvement of their own Minds, may find a convenient and blissful recess from the noise and hurry of the World. A world so cumbersome, so infectious,[3] that altho' thro' the grace of GOD and their own strict watchfulness, they are kept from sinking down into its corruptions, 'twill however damp their flight to heav'n, hinder them from attaining any eminent pitch of Vertue.

---

1 Here Astell acidly anticipates her critics, including Bishop Gilbert Burnet, who was to counsel Queen Anne against supporting her proposal for a women's academy as smacking too much of an Anglican nunnery that would bring disrepute as being Popish (Ballard, *Memoirs of Several Ladies of Great Britain* [1752], 1985 edn, 383).

2 Although "the World, the Flesh and the Devil" are the real enemy, Astell's cadences rather suggest men.

3 Infectious in a pathological sense.

You are therefore Ladies, invited into a place, where you shall suffer no other confinement, but to be kept out of the road Of Sin: You shall not be depriv'd of your Grandeur, but only exchange the vain Pomps and Pageantry of the world, empty Titles and Forms of State, for the true and solid Greatness of being able to despise *them*.[1] You will only quit the Chat of insignificant people for an ingenious Conversation; the froth of flashy Wit for real Wisdom; idle tales for instructive discourses. The deceitful Flatteries of those who under pretence of loving and admiring you, really served their *own* base ends, for the seasonable Reproofs and wholsom Counsels of your hearty well-wishers and affectionate Friends, which will procure you those perfections your feigned lovers pretended you had, and kept you from obtaining. No uneasy task will be enjoyn'd[2] you, all your labour being only to prepare for the highest degrees of that Glory, the very lowest of which is more than at present you are able to conceive, and the prospect of it sufficient to out-weigh all the Pains of Religion, were there any in it, as really there is none.[3] All that is requir'd of you, is only to be as Happy as posssibly you can, and to make sure of a Felicity that will fill all the capacities of your Souls! A happiness, which when once you have tasted, you'l be fully convinc'd, you cou'd never do too much to obtain it; nor be too solicitous to adorn your Souls, with such tempers and dispositions, as will at present make you in some measure such holy and Heavenly Creatures, as you one day hope to be in a more perfect manner; without which Qualifications you can neither reasonably *expect*, nor are *capable* of enjoying the Happiness of the Life to come. Happy Retreat! which will be the introducing you into such a *Paradise* as your Mother *Eve* forfeited, where you shall feast on Pleasures, that do not like those of the World, disappoint your expectations, pall your Appetities, and by the disgust they give you, put you on the fruitless search after new Delights, which when obtain'd are as empty as the former; but such as will make you truly happy *now*, and prepare you to be *perfectly* so hereafter. Here are no Serpents to deceive you, whilst you entertain your selves in these delicious Gardens. No Provocations will be

---

1 Once again the emphasis on "them" suggests a personal object, men, a preparation for the following passionate attack on men as courtiers who subvert their subjects.

2 Imposed on, as of a task, penalty, duty or obligation (*OED*).

3 1701 edn (39) "are" none.

given in this Amicable Society, but to Love and to good Works, which will afford such an entertaining employment, that you'l have as little inclination as leisure to pursue those Follies which in the time of your ignorance pass'd with you under the name of love; altho' there is not in nature two more different things, than *true Love* and that *brutish Passion* which pretends to ape it. Here will be no Rivalling but for the of Love of GOD, no Ambition but to procure his Favour, to which nothing will more effectually recommend you, than a great and dear affection to each other. Envy, that Canker, will not here disturb your Breasts; for how can she repine[1] at anothers wel-fare, who reckons it the greatest part of her own? No Covetousness will gain admittance in this blest abode, but to amass huge Treasures of good Works, and to procure one of the brightest Crowns of Glory. You will not be solicitous to encrease your Fortunes, but enlarge[2] your Minds; esteeming no Grandeur like being conformable to the meek and humble JESUS. So that you only withdraw from the noise and trouble, the folly and temptation of the world, that you may more peaceably enjoy your selves, and all the innocent Pleasures it is able to afford you, and particularly that which is worth all the rest, a noble Vertuous and Disinteress'd[3] Friendship. And to compleat all, that *Acme* of delight which the devout Seraphic Soul[4] enjoys, when dead to the World, she devotes her self entirely to the Contemplation and Fruition of her Beloved; when having disengag'd her self from all those Lets[5] which hindered her from without, she moves in a direct and vigorous motion towards her true and only Good, whom now she embraces and acquiesces[6] in, with such an unspeakable pleasure, as is only intelligible to those who have tried and felt it, which we can no more describe to the dark and sensual part of Mankind, than we can the beauty of Colours and harmony of

---

1 Fret, murmur, or complain against (*OED*).

2 1696 edn, 55, and 1701 edn, 41, read "to enlarge," following the instruction in the 1694 Errata list.

3 Disinterested.

4 The saved soul is subsumed into the ranks of the angels, Seraphim, and Cherubim.

5 Hindrances, stoppages, obstructions, impediments (arch.) (*OED*).

6 To remain at rest (obs. usage) (*OED*).

Sounds to the Blind and Deaf.[1] In fine, the place to which you are invited is a Type[2] and Antepast[3] of Heav'n, where your Employment will be as there, to magnify GOD, to love one another, and to communicate that useful *knowledge*, which by the due improvement of your time in Study and Contemplation you will obtain; and which when obtain'd, will afford you a much sweeter and more durable delight, than all those pitiful diversions, those revellings and amusements, which now thro your ignorance of better, appear the only grateful[4] and relishing[5] Entertainments.

But because we were not made for our selves, nor can by any means so effectually glorify GOD, and do good to our own Souls, as by doing Offices of Charity and Beneficence to others; and to the intent,[6] that every Vertue, and the highest degrees of every Vertue may be exercis'd and promoted the most that may be; your Retreat shall be so manag'd as not to exclude the good Works of an *Active*, from the pleasure and serenity of a *contemplative* Life, but by a due mixture of both retain all the advantages and avoid the inconveniences that attend either. It shall not so cut you off from the world as to hinder you from bettering and improving it, but rather qualify you to do it the greatest Good, and be a Seminary to stock the Kingdom with pious and prudent Ladies; whose good Example it is to be hop'd, will so influence the rest of their Sex, that Women may no longer pass for those little useless and impertinent Animals, which the ill conduct of too many has caus'd them to be mistaken for.

We have hitherto consider'd our Retirement only in relation to Religion, which is indeed its *main,* I may say its *only* design; nor can this be thought too contracting[7] a word, since Religion is the adequate business of our lives, and largely consider'd, takes in all we

---

1 This passage is Neoplatonist in its invocation of celestial harmonies and the ecstatic transcendence of the sensual. It is reminiscent of the tone of the Astell-Norris correspondence, *Letters Concerning the Love of God*, which attracts hostile comment from the only child of Ralph Cudworth, Damaris Masham, now a Lockean, in her *Discourse Concerning the Love of God* (1696).

2 That by which something is symbolized or figured (theolog.) (*OED*).

3 Something taken before a meal to whet the appetite; a foretaste (*OED*).

4 Rewarding.

5 Satisfying.

6 Purpose, design, plan, project, endeavour (obs. usage) (*OED*).

7 Either in the sense of narrowing, confining, or binding, committing.

have to do; nothing being a fit employment for a rational Creature, which has not either a *direct* or *remote* tendency to this great and *only* end. But because, as we have all along observ'd, Religion never appears in it's true Beauty, but when it is accompanied with Wisdom and Discretion; and that without a good Understanding, we can scarce be *truly*, but never *eminently* Good; being liable to a thousand seductions and mistakes; for even the men themselves, if they have not a competent degree of Knowledge, they are carried about with every wind of Doctrine.[1] Therefore, one great end of this institution, shall be to expel that cloud of Ignorance, which Custom has involv'd us in, to furnish our minds with a stock of solid and useful Knowledge, that the Souls of Women may no longer be the only unadorn'd and neglected things. It is not intended that our Religious[2] shou'd waste their time, and trouble their heads about such unconcerning matters, as the vogue of the world has turn'd up for Learning, the impertinency of which has been excellently expos'd by an ingenious pen,[3] but busy them-

---

1 The concluding section of this sentence from "for even the men" is in parentheses in the 1695 edn, 61, and the 1701 edn, 45.

2 Here Astell refers to the members of her Academy as "Religious," the term designating members of a religious order, warranting perhaps the charges levelled against her by Masham and Bishop Burnet that this is a project for an Anglican nunnery. It is equally clear that essential elements of Astell's proposal conform to the Port Royal model, a famous Cistercian abbey singled out in 1223 by Pope Honorius III as a place of retreat for women who wished to withdraw from the world without taking the perpetual vows of a religious order.

3 *Mr. Nor. Conduct of Human Life* – Astell.

Marginal note to John Norris, *Reflections upon the Conduct of Human Life: with reference to the Study of Learning and Knowledge. In a Letter to the Excellent Lady, the Lady Masham*, (London, 1690, Wing N1267). Norris's homily on the appropriate education for women is based on a distinction between *contingent* and *necessary* truth as the basis for deciding what is necessary — and what superfluous — knowledge for a Christian, and not only for a Lady, summarized as follows (§34, 39):

> For as I have shewn, 'tis not *Contingent* but *Necessary* Truth, wherein the Perfection of the Understanding does consist. Whence it follows that True Learning ought to be placed in the Knowledge of *Necessary Truth*, in the Comprehension of those Arts and Sciences whose Foundations are not Arbitrary, but Stable and Immutable, and understanding the Eternal and Unchangeable Laws and Measures of *Reason* and *Consequence*.

selves in a serious enquiry after *necessary* and *perfective* truths, something which it *concerns* them to know, and which tends to their real interest and perfection, and what that is the excellent Author just now mention'd, will sufficiently inform them,[1] such a course of Study will neither be too troublesome nor out of the reach of a Female Virtuoso;[2] for it is not intended she shou'd spend her hours in learning *words* but *things*,[3] and therefore no more Languages than are necessary to acquaint her with useful Authors.[4] Nor need she trouble her self in turning over a great number of Books, but take care to understand and digest a few well chosen and good ones.[5] Let her but obtain right Ideas, and be truly acquainted with the nature of those Objects that present themselves to her mind, and then no matter whether or no she be able to tell what fanci-

---

1 The 1696 edn, 61, and 1701 edn, 45, begin a new sentence with "Such a course of Study...."

2 One with a special interest in the arts or sciences; a learned person, scientist, savant, or scholar (obs., *OED*). Note that this may be Astell's specific response to Thomas Wright's *The Female Virtuoso's: A Comedy*, published in 1693, which presented the learned lady as neglectful of her duty, lascivious, and "always a Pimp to her Pleasures" (Act 3, 26, cited in Mitzi Myers's "Domesticating Minerva," 177).

3 This is an argument about mistaking words for things that Astell cleverly turns against Locke, the linguistic philosopher, in *A Serious Proposal, Part II* (1697/2002,132/171): "Many times our Ideas are thought to be false when the fault is really in our language."

4 John Norris, in *Reflections upon the Conduct of Christian Life* (1690), §36, 42, includes "a variety of languages" in his catalogue of useless knowledge, which "gives a Man a Title to Learning without one Grain of Sense." Astell herself appears to be sufficiently in command of foreign languages to include a spattering of Italian proverbs in the 1st edn of *Reflections upon Marriage* (1700, 5, 44, 63), repeated in the 4th, but given only in English translation in the 3rd edn. Her argument that foreign languages functioned as a smoke-screen behind which men, privileged recipients of an education denied to most women, sheltered their commonplace knowledge, was made by other women writers of Astell's day. See for instance Bathsua Makin's *An Essay to Revive the Antient Education of Gentlewomen* (1673) and Judith Drake's *An Essay in Defence of the Female Sex* (1696, 35-38, see below 254-55).

5 Astell here anticipates the Cartesian argument concerning truth she develops, with respect to philosophers in general and Locke in particular, in *A Serious Proposal, Part II* (1697 edn, 122/167): "we are not oblig'd to tumble over many Authors, to hunt after a very celebrated Genius, but may have it for enquiring after in our own Breasts."

ful people have said about them: And throughly to understand Christianity as profess'd by the *Church of England*, will be sufficient to confirm her in the truth, tho' she have not a Catalogue of those particular errors which oppose it. Indeed a Learned Education of the Women will appear so unfashionable, that I began to startle at the singularity of the proposition, but was extremely pleas'd when I found a late ingenious Author (whose Book I met with since the writing of this),[1] agree with me in my Opinion. For speaking of the Repute that Learning was in about 150 years ago: *It was so very modish* (says he) *that the fair Sex seem'd to believe that* Greek *and* Latin *added to their Charms; and* Plato *and* Aristotle *untranslated, were frequent Ornaments of their Closets.*[2] *One wou'd think by the effects, that it was a proper way of Educating them, since there are no accounts in Histo-*

---

1 Mr *Wotton's Reflect. on Ant. and Mod. Learn.* p. 349, 350. – Astell.
The passage in italics, with roman type for emphasis, Astell quotes from William Wotton's, *Reflections upon Ancient and Modern Learning*, 1694, 349-50, with her customary accuracy, which, given the range of her sources, suggests that she is working in a library. Her view that foreign languages for women are an affectation, Astell claims to co-oincide with, but not derive from, the work of Wotton, which she must have come upon some time between the initial writing and publication of her *Serious Proposal*, because the disclaimer appears in the 1st edn (1694), 78, as well as subsequent edns. William Wotton (1666-1727) was a prodigy who at the age of five was said to read English, Latin, Greek, and Hebrew. But he took the side of the moderns in the famous debate occasioned by the essay entitled "Ancient and Modern Learning" by Sir William Temple (1628-99), which transported to England the debate begun in France between Bernard le Bouvier de Fontenelle (1657-1757) and Charles Perrault (1628-1703). Wotton's book stated the facts clearly, and as such provided a good summary of the discoveries in nature and physical science up to that time. That Astell should have quoted it favourably is in line with her belief that science, free from the clutter of ancient pedagogy, might be a field in which women would excel (see *The Christian Religion*, 1705 edn, 296). But in the "Battle of the Books," Astell's position was ambiguous, given that Wotton represented Cambridge and the Whigs, while Temple and his defender, Charles Boyle, represented Oxford and the Tories, among whom Astell's friends numbered.

2 Astell makes much play on the term "closet," in her day (1.a.) a room for privacy or retirement, (1.b.) a place of private devotion, (1.c.) a place of private study or secluded speculation; (2.a.) the private apartment of a monarch or potentate, (2.b.) a small room for storing utensils or provisions — a cupboard (*OED*, 2nd edn, (Oxford, 1989), vol. 3, 349).

ry of so many great Women in any one Age, as are to be found between the years 15 and 1600.

For since GOD has given Women as well as Men intelligent Souls, why should they be forbidden to improve them? Since he has not denied us the faculty of Thinking, why shou'd we not (at least in gratitude to him) employ our Thoughts on himself their noblest Object, and not unworthily bestow them on Trifles and Gaities and secular Affairs? Being the Soul was created for the contemplation of Truth as well as for the fruition of Good, is it not as cruel and unjust to preclude Women from the knowledge of the one, as well[1] as from the enjoyment of the other? Especially since the Will is blind, and cannot chuse but by the direction of the Understanding; or to speak more properly, since the Soul always *Wills* according as she *Understands*, so that if she *Understands* amiss, she *Wills* amiss.[2] And as Exercise enlarges and exalts any Faculty, so thro' want of using, it becomes crampt and lessened; if therefore we make little or no use of our Understandings, we shall shortly have none to use; and the more contracted,[3] and unemploy'd the deliberating and directive Power is, the more liable is the elective to[4] unworthy and mischievous options. What is it but the want of an ingenious Education that renders the generality of Feminine Conversations so insipid and foolish and their solitude so *insupportable*?[5] Learning is therefore necessary to render them more agreeable and useful in company, and to furnish them with becoming entertainments when alone, that so they may not be driven to those miserable shifts,[6] which too many make use of to put off their time, that precious Talent that never lies on the hands of a judicious Person. And since our Happiness in the next World, depends so far on those dispositions which we carry along with us out of this, that without a right habitude[7] and temper of mind we are not capable

---

1 The Errata list appended to the 1694 edn, 172, instructs that "as well" be omitted.

2 Astell here introduces the Stoic unitary theory of the will, that all cognition involves a degree of assent, which she develops at length in *A Serious Proposal, Part II,* chapters III and IV.

3 Narrowed, limited, confined.

4 Choice of.

5 Unbearable. Astell elides the subject of the final relative clause.

6 An expedient or ingenious device for effecting some purpose (*OED*).

7 Mental or moral constitution, disposition, or essential character (*OED*).

of Felicity; and seeing our Beatitude[1] consists in the contemplation of the divine Truth and Beauty, as well as in the fruition of his Goodness, can Ignorance be a fit preparative for Heaven? Is't likely that she whose Understanding has been busied about nothing but froth and trifles, shou'd be capable of delighting her self in noble and sublime Truths? Let such therefore as deny us the improvement of our Intellectuals,[2] either take up *his* Paradox, who said, *That Women have no Souls*;[3] which at this time a day, when they are allow'd to Brutes, wou'd be as unphilosophical as it is unmannerly; or else let them permit us to cultivate and improve them. There is a sort of Learning indeed which is worse than the greatest Ignorance: A Woman may study Plays and Romances all her days, and be a great deal more knowing but never a jot the wiser.[4] Such a knowledge as this serves only to instruct and put her forward in the practice of the greatest Follies; yet how can they justly blame her, who forbid, or at least, won't afford opportunity of better? A rational mind *will* be employ'd, it will never be satisfy'd in doing nothing; and if you neglect to furnish it with good materials, 'tis like to take up with such as come to hand.

We pretend not that Women shou'd teach in the Church, or usurp Authority where it is not allow'd them; permit us only to understand our *own* duty, and not be forc'd to take it upon trust from others; to be at least so far learned, as to be able to form in our minds a true Idea of Christianity, it being so very necessary to fence us against the danger of these *last* and *perilous* days,[5] in which

---

1 Eternal blessedness or happiness (*OED*).

2 Those things apprehensible to the intellect alone, non-material, spiritual (as opposed to what is perceived by the senses), ideal (*OED*).

3 Astell may be overstating the position of Nicholas Malebranche, who in *Recherche de la Vérité* (bk 2, pt 2, chap. 1) maintained that "the fibres in women's brains were too delicate and weak to plumb philosophical truths" ("n'a point assez de force et d'étendue pour en percer le fond"). Malebranche thus persuaded women to forget philosophy and concentrate on "deciding on fashion, choosing their words and discerning good tone and nice manners" ("à décider des modes, à juger de la langue, à discerner le bon air et les belles manières"). See *Oeuvres de Malebranche*, 1853 edn, 171-76, cited Perry, *Celebrated Mary Astell*, 78.

4 Astell has no time for drama or novels, at which Restoration women excelled, often Tories like herself, as in the case of Aphra Behn (1640-89).

5 Paul 2 Timothy, 3, 1 (Bible, Authorized Version, 1611, 1911 reprint).

Deceivers a part of whose Character is, to *lead captive silly Women*, need not *creep into Houses*[1] since they have Authority to proclaim their Errors on the *House top*.[2] And let us also acquire a true Practical Knowledge, such as will convince us of the absolute necessity of *Holy Living* as well as of *Right Believing*, and that no Heresy is more dangerous, than that of an ungodly and wicked Life. And since the *French Tongue* is understood by most Ladies, methinks they may much better improve it by the study of Philosophy (as I hear the *French Ladies* do) *Des Cartes*,[3]

---

1 Paul 2 Timothy, 3, 6: "For of this sort are they which creep into houses, and leade captive silly women laden with sinnes, led away with diuers lusts."

2 For preaching on housetops, see Matthew 10, 27; Luke 12, 3, none of which Astell quotes exactly, however. It may be that she is rather echoing the opening remarks on men's opinion of learned ladies of Bathsua Makin (b. 1612?) in *An Essay to Revive the Antient Education of Gentlewomen* (1673, sig. A2)

> To offer to the World the liberal Education of Women is to deface the Image of God in Man, it will make Women so high, and men so low, like Fire in the House-top, it will set the whole world in a Flame.

3 René Descartes (1596-1650), French philosopher whose main works, *Discours de la Methode* (1637) and *Principes de la Philosophie* (1644), Astell had read, it appears, and cites. From the age of ten he spent eight years at a Jesuit College, where his outstanding aptitude for mathematics became evident, and he remained a devout Catholic all his life. Serving in the Dutch army until 1619, Descartes then joined the army of Maximillian, Duke of Bavaria, for a further two years. After some European touring he settled in Holland for 20 years, and it was here he produced all his writings. Descartes is regarded as the father of modern philosophy, for his formulation of the relationship between mind and matter, and between mathematical ideas and reality. Despite the boldness and originality of his thinking, he was still a conformist, however, and his *Discourse on Method*, while acclaimed intellectually, incurred the displeasure of both Catholic and Calvinistic ecclesiastical authorities. To allay suspicions of heterodoxy he published two editions of *Meditations on the First Philosophy*, apparently as a genuine attempt to provide a *modus vivendi* for science and religion. (*European Authors, 1000-1900*). Locke and the Cambridge Platonists, were among the many profoundly influenced by his ideas, in particular by the *cogito* ("I think, therefore I am"), which epitomized Descartes' position on the capacity of humans to acquire true knowledge by introspection.

Malebranch[1] and others, than by reading idle *Novels* and *Romances*. 'Tis strange we shou'd be so forward to imitate their Fashions and Fopperies,[2] and have no regard to what is really imitable in them![3] And why shall it not be thought as genteel to understand *French Philosophy*, as to be accoutred in a *French Mode*? Let therefore the famous *Madam D'acier*[4] Etc. and our own incomparable *Orinda*, excite the Emulation of the English Ladies.

The Ladies, I'm sure, have no reason to dislike this Proposal, but I know not how the Men will resent it, to have their enclosure broke down, and Women invited to tast of that Tree of Knowledge they have so long unjustly *monopoliz'd*. But they must excuse me, if I be as partial to my own Sex as they are to theirs, and think Women as capable of Learning as Men are, and that it becomes them as well. For I cannot imagine wherein the hurt lyes, if instead of doing mischief to one another, by an uncharitable and vain Conversation, Women be enabled to inform and instruct those of their own Sex at least; the Holy Ghost having left it on record, that *Priscilla* as well as her Husband, catechiz'd the eloquent *Apollos* and the great Apostle found no fault with her.[5] It will therefore be very proper for our Ladies to spend part of their time in this Retirement, in adorning their minds with useful Knowledge.

---

1 Father Nicolas Malebranche (1638-1715), French philosopher of the Cartesian school and mathematician, published *De la Recherche de la Vérité* (1674), *Conversations Chrétiènnes* (1677), and *Traité de la Nature et de la Grace* (1680) — all of which were translated into English in the 1690s. He was much admired by John Norris, "the last of the Cambridge Platonists."

2 Foolishness, folly (*OED*).

3 Changed in the 1695 edn, 69, and 1701 edn, 51, to "really deserves our Imitation!"

4 "*Scudery*" added to the 1701 edn, 51. Madeleine de Scudéry (1607-1701), was a novelist who established her own salon (la société du Samedi) under the pseudonym of Sappho. Her immensely long novels were nevertheless highly popular and were translated into English. *Artamène ou le Grand Cyrus* (10 vols, 1648-53) included a discussion of female education and a self-portrait in vol. 10. *Ibrahim, ou l'illustre Bassa* (4 vols, 1641) and *Alhamide, ou l'esclave reine* (8 vols, 1661-63) were cast in an oriental mode but addressed current affairs. *Clélie* (10 vols, 1654-61) represented her contemporaries, Herminius, Paul Scarron and his wife in disguise. (*Encyclopaedia Britannica*, 11th edn, 1910-11, vol. 24, 487)

5 Acts 18, 26. Astell implies that Paul, who disdained women so often, had no comment on Priscilla's instructing the (Hellenized) Jew Apollos.

To enter into the detail of the particulars concerning the Government of the *Religious*, their Offices of Devotion,[1] Employments, Work, etc. is not now necessary. Suffice it at present to signify, that they will be more than ordinarily careful to redeem their time, spending no more of it on the Body than the necessities of Nature require, but by a judicious choice of their Employment, and a constant industry about it, so improve this invaluable Treasure, that it may neither be buried in Idleness, nor lavish'd out in unprofitable concerns. For a stated portion of it being daily paid to GOD in Prayers and Praises, the rest shall be employ'd in innocent, charitable, and useful Business; either in study (in learning themselves or instructing others; for it is design'd that part of their Employment be the Education of those of their own Sex)[2] or else in spiritual and corporal Works of Mercy,[3] relieving the Poor, healing the Sick, mingling Charity to the Soul with that they express to the Body, instructing the Ignorant, counselling the Doubtful, comforting the Afflicted, and correcting those that err and do amiss.

And as it will be the business of their lives, their meat and drink to *know* and *do* the Will of their Heavenly Father, so will they pay a strict conformity to all the Precepts of their holy Mother the *Church*, whose sacred Injunctions are too much neglected, even by those who pretend the greatest zeal for her. For, besides the daily performance of the Publick Offices after the Cathedral manner,[4] in the most affecting and elevating way, the celebration of the Holy Eucharist every Lords Day and Holyday, and a course of solid instructive Preaching and Catechizing; our *Religious*, considering that the holy JESUS punctually observ'd the innocent usages of the *Jewish* Church, and tho' in many instances the *reason* of the Command ceas'd as to him, yet he wou'd obey the *letter* to avoid giving

---

1 Astell refers to the daily roster of devotions prescribed for members of religious orders.

2 Parentheses retained in the 1695 edn, 72, but removed in the 1701 edn, 53.

3 "Medieval theology enumerated seven spiritual and seven corporal works of mercy" (*OED*), among them those that Astell goes on to enumerate.

4 Applied loosely to mean after the manner of a collegiate or abbey church (*OED*). Astell may mean the performance of the Sacred Office, or daily liturgy, according to High Church tradition.

offence and to set us an admirable pattern of Obedience;[1] therefore, tho' it may be thought such pious Souls have little occasion for the severities of fasting and mortification, yet they will consider it as a special part of their Duty to observe all the Fasts of the Church, *viz. Lent, Ember,*[2] and *Rogation-days,*[3] *Fridays* and *Vigils*; times so little heeded by the most, that one wou'd scarce believe them set apart for Religious Purposes, did we not find them in the antiquated Rubricks.[4] And as their Devotion will be regular, so shall it likewise be solid and substantial. They will not rest in the mere out-side of Duty, nor fancy the performance of their Fasts and Offices will procure them license to indulge a darling[5] Vice: But having long since laid the Ax to the root of sin, and destroy'd the whole body of it, they will look upon these holy times of recollection and extra-ordinary Devotion (without which Fasting signifies little) as excellent means to keep it down, and to pluck up every the least Fibre that may happen to remain in them. But we intend not by this to impose any intolerable burden on tender Constitutions, knowing that our Lord has taught us, that Mercy is to be prefer'd before Sacrifice: and that Bodily Exercise profiteth but a little, the chief business being to obtain a divine and God-like temper of Mind.

And as this institution will strictly enjoyn all pious and profitable Employments, so does it not only permit but recommend harmless and ingenious Diversions, Musick particularly, and such as may refresh the Body without enervating the Mind. They do a

---

1 Astell seems to be recommending the perpetuation of Medieval (i.e., Roman Catholic) liturgy in the modern age, on the model of Christ's incorporation of Jewish ritual in a Christian age. This provision may well have been targeted in her work as too "Romish" in the eyes of her detractors.

2 The English name of four periods of fasting and prayer, to be observed in the four seasons of the year, first prescribed by the Council of Placentia, AD 1095. Each of these fasts lasts three days, named Ember days, while the weeks in which they occur are named Ember weeks (*OED*).

3 The three days before Ascension Day, on which solemn supplications, including the litany of the saints, are prescribed by the litany of the Church of England (as of the Roman Catholic Church) (*OED*).

4 The instructions in prayerbooks and missals regarding religious rites, traditionally printed in red (hence the derivation of the name from red earth or red ochre) (*OED*).

5 Favourite (*OED*).

disservice to Religion who make it an enemy to innocent Nature, and injure the Almighty when they represent him as imposing burdens that are not to be born.[1] Neither GOD nor Wise men will like us the better for an affected severity and waspish sourness. Nature and Grace will never disagree, provided we mistake not the one, nor indulge the petulancy of the other; there being no Displacencies in Religion, but what we our selves have unhappily made. For true Piety is the most sweet and engaging thing imaginable, as it is most obliging to others, so most easie to our selves. 'Tis in truth the highest *Epicurism*[2] exalting our Pleasures by refining them; keeping our Appetites in that due regularity which not only Grace, but even Nature and Reason require, in the breach of which, tho' there may be a Transport,[3] there can be no true and substantial delight.

As to *Lodging, Habit* and *Diet*, they may be quickly resolv'd on by the Ladies who shall subscribe;[4] who I doubt not will make choice of what is most plain and decent, what Nature, not Luxury requires. And since neither Meat nor Cloaths commend us unto GOD, they'l content themselves with such things as are fit and convenient, without occasioning scruple to themselves or giving any trouble or offence to others. She who considers to how much better account that Money will turn which is bestow'd on the Poor, then that which is laid out in unnecessary Expences on her self, needs no Admonitions against superfluities. She who truly loves her self, will never waste that Money on a decaying Carkass, which if prudently disburs'd, wou'd procure her an eternal Mansion. She will never think her self so fine, as when the backs of the Poor do bless her; and never feast so luxuriously as when she treats an hungry person. No perfume will be thought so grateful as the Odour of Good Works; nor any Wash so Beautifying as her own tears. For her Heroick Soul is too great to ambition[5] any Empire but

---

1 Astell attacks Puritan prohibitions on music and innocent arts and amusements.

2 Astell may mean the word in both its technical sense (now rare), the philosophy of Epicureanism, and the general sense of pleasure-loving. Epicureanism had a new vogue in the seventeenth and eighteenth centuries, and the Earl of Shaftesbury, Locke's patron, was widely known as an Epicurean.

3 The state of being "carried out of oneself," rapture, ecstacy (*OED*).

4 Astell later (1694 edn, 157, see below 107) puts a figure of 500 pounds on the suggested "dowry" or entry fee for her female academy.

5 To move to ambition, to make desirous (obs.) (*OED*).

that of her own Breast, or to regard any other Conquest than the rescuing poor unhappy Souls[1] from the slavery of Sin and Satan, those only unsupportable Tyrants; and therefore what Decays[2] she observes in her Face will be very unconcerning[3] but she will with greatest speed and accuracy rectify the least Spot that may prejudice the beauty of her lovely Soul.

In a word, this happy Society will be but one Body, whose Soul is love, animating and informing it, and perpetually breathing forth it self in flames of holy desires after GOD, and acts of Benevolence to each other. Envy and Uncharitableness are the Vices only of little and narrow hearts, and therefore 'tis suppos'd, they will not enter here amongst persons whose Dispositions as well as their Births are to be Generous. Censure will refine into Friendly Admonition, all Scoffing and offensive Railleries will be abominated and banish'd hence; where not only the Words and Actions, but even the very Thoughts and Desires of the *Religious* tend to promote the most endearing Love and universal Good-will; for tho there may be particular Friendships, they must by no means prejudice the general Amity.[4] Thus these innocent and holy Souls shou'd run their Race, measuring their hours by their Devotions, and their days by the charitable Works they do. Thus wou'd they live the life of Heaven whilst on Earth, and receive an Earnest of its Joys in their hearts. And now, what remains for them to do at Night but to review the Actions of the Day? to examine what Passions have been stirring? How their Devotions were performed? in what temper their Hearts are? what good they have done? what progress made towards Heaven?[5] and with the plaudit of a satisfied Conscience sweetly to sleep in peace and safety, Angels pitching their Tents round about them, and he that neither slumbers or sleeps, rejoycing over them to do them good!

And to the end, that these great designs may be the better pursu'd, and effectually obtain'd, care shall be taken that our Religious be under the tuition of persons of irreproachable Lives, of a consummate Prudence, sincere Piety and unaffected Gravity. No

---

1 Occasionally arch. phraseology is a feature of Astell's initial *Serious Proposal*, that is not so evident in *Part II* or later works.

2 Ruined remains, ruins, debris (rarely in the singular, obs.) (*OED*).

3 Having no importance or relevance (*OED*).

4 The 1695 edn, 80, and 1701 edn, 59, conclude the sentence with "Good-will," omitting the final two clauses.

5 The 1695 edn, 81, and 1701 edn, 60, read "they've made."

Novices in Religion, but such as have spent the greatest part of their lives in the study and practice of Christianity; who have lived *much*, whatever the time of their abode in the world has been. Whose Understandings are clear and comprehensive, as well as their Passions at command and Affections regular, and their Knowledge able to govern their Zeal. Whose scrutiny into their own hearts has been so exact, they fully understand the weaknesses of human Nature,[1] are able to bear with its defects, and by the most prudent methods procure its Admendment. Plentifully furnish'd with instructions for the Ignorant and comfort for the disconsolate.[2] Who know how to quicken the slothful, to awaken the secure, and to dispel the doubts of the Scrupulous. Who are not ignorant when to use the Spur and when the Rein, but duly qualified to minister to all the spiritual wants of their Charge.[3] Watching over their Souls with tenderness and prudence; applying fitting Medicines with sweetness and affability. Sagacious is discovering the very approaches of a fault, wise in preventing, and charitable in bearing with all pityable Infirmities. The sweetness of whose Nature is commensurate to all the rest of their good Qualities, and all conspire together to make them lov'd and reverenc'd. Who have the perfect government of themselves, and therefore rule according to Reason, not Humour, consulting the good of the Society, not their own arbitrary sway. Yet know how to assert their Authority when there is just occasion for it, and will not prejudice their Charge, by an indiscreet remissness and loosning the Reins of discipline. Yet[4] what occasion will there be for rigour, when the design is to represent Vertue in all her Charms and native Loveliness, which must needs attract the eyes and enamour the hearts of all who behold her? To joyn the sweetness of Humanity to the strictness of Philosophy, that both together being improv'd and heighten'd by grace, may make up an accomplish'd *Christian*, who (if truly so)[5] is certainly the best-bred and best natur'd person in

---

1 The 1701 edn, 61, reads "humane Nature."

2 The 1701 edn, 61, runs this incomplete sentence into the next, separating them with a semicolon.

3 Again the 1701 edn, 61, runs this sentence into the next, separating them with a semicolon.

4 "Yet" replaced by "But" in the 1696 edn, 84, and the 1701 edn, 62, following the instruction in the Errata list appended to the 1694 edn, 172 (which lists it as line 13, instead of line 12).

5 Replaced in the 1701 edn, 62, with "for she who is truly so."

the world, adorn'd with a thousand Charms, most happy in her self and most agreeable and beneficial to all about her.[1] And that every one who comes under this holy Roof may be such an amiable, such a charming Creature, what faults they bring with them shall be corrected by sweetness not severity; by friendly Admonitions, not magisterial Reproofs; Piety shall not be roughly impos'd, but wisely insinuated by a perpetual Display of the Beauties of Religion in an exemplary Conversation, the continual and most powerful Sermon of an holy Life. And since Inclination can't be forc'd, (and nothing makes people more uneasy than the fettering themselves with unnecessary Bonds)[2] there shall be no Vows or irrevocable Obligations, not so much as the fear of Reproach to keep our Ladies here any longer than they desire. No: Ev'ry act of our Religious Votary shall be voluntary and free, and no other tye but the Pleasure, the Glory and Advantage of this blessed Retirement to confine her to it.

And now I suppose, you'll save me the labour of proving, that this Institution will very much serve the ends of Piety and Charity; it is methinks self-evident, and the very Proposal sufficient proof. But if it will not promote these great ends, I shall think my self mightily oblig'd to him who will shew me what will; for provided the good of my Neighbour be advanc'd, 'tis very indifferent to me, whether it be by my method or by anothers. Here will be no impertinent Visits, no foolish Amours, no idle Amusements to distract our Thoughts, and waste our precious time; a very little of which is spent in Dressing, that grand devourer, and its concomitants; and no more than necessity requires in sleep and eating; so that here's a vast Treasure gain'd, which for ought I know, may purchase an happy Eternity. But we need not rest in generals,[3] a cursory view of some particulars will sufficiently demonstrate the great usefulness of such a Retirement; which will appear by observing first,[4] a few of those inconveniences to which Ladies are expos'd by living in the World, and in the next place the positive advantages of a Retreat.

---

1 Replaced in the 1695 edn, 84, and 1701 edn, 63, with "She converses with."

2 Parentheses removed in the 1695 edn, 84, and 1701 edn, 63.

3 Generalities.

4 The Errata list appended to the 1694 edn, 172, instructs that the comma be deleted.

And first, as to the inconveniences of living in the World; no very small one is that strong *Idea* and warm perception it gives us of its Vanities; since these are ever at hand, constantly thronging about us, they must necessarily push aside all other Objects, and the Mind being prepossess'd and gratefully entertain'd with those pleasing Perceptions which external Objects occasion, takes up with them as its only Good, is not at leisure to tast those delights which arise from a Reflection on it self, nor to receive the *Ideas* which such a Reflection conveys, and consequently forms all its Notions by such *Ideas* only as it derives from sensation, being unacquainted with those more excellent ones which arise from its own operations and a serious reflection on them, and which are necessary to correct the mistakes, and supply the defects of the other.[1] From whence arises a very partial knowledge of things, nay, almost a perfect ignorance in things of the greatest moment. For tho' we are acquainted with the Sound of some certain words, *v.g.*[2] *God, Religion, Pleasure* and *Pain, Honour* and *Dishonour*, and the like; yet having no other *Ideas* but what are convey'd to us by those Trifles we converse with, we frame to our selves strange and awkard notions of them, conformable only to those *Ideas* sensation has furnish'd us with, which sometimes grow so strong and fixt, that 'tis scarce possible to introduce a new Scheme of Thoughts and so to disabuse us, especially whilst these Objects are thick in our way.[3]

Thus she who sees her self and others respected in proportion to that Pomp and Bustle they make in the world, will form her Idea of Honour accordingly. She who has relish'd no Pleasures but such as arise at the presence of outward Objects, will seek no high-

---

1 Here Astell uses the language of Locke on ideas and sensation, but with none of the theoretical rigour she displays in *A Serious Proposal, Part II*. Under the influence, no doubt, of the *Port Royal Logic*, which takes up the subject of self-reflection, Astell argues in *A Serious Proposal, Part II*, that sensation and reflection are alternative sources of *Ideas*. It is a premise of her developed theory that all perception involves a degree of assent and is more or less filtered by reflection. Platonist innate ideas are the basis of such a unitary theory of the mind, and grounds for her rejection of Locke's view of the mind as an empty vessel into which sensations are poured, and then combined to produce ideas.

2 Replaced by "*viz,*" in the 1695 edn, 89, and the 1701 edn, 66.

3 Astell develops her critique of language as a system of signs that may delude as well as inform, in *A Serious Proposal, Part II*, chapter 3, §4 (1697 edn, 132, see below 171).

er than her Senses for her Gratification. And thus we may account for that strange insensibility, that appears in some people when you speak to them of any serious Religious matter. They are then so dull you'll have much ado to make them understand the clearest Truth. Whereas if you rally the same persons or chat with them of some Mode or Foppery, they'll appear very quick, expert and ingenious. I have sometimes smil'd[1] to hear Women talk as gravely and concernedly about some trifling disappointment from their Milliner or Taylor, as if it had related to the weightiest concerns of their Soul,[2] nay, perhaps more seriously than others who wou'd pass for Good, do about their eternal Interest;[3] but turn the talk that way, and they grow as heavy and cold as they were warm and sensible before. And whence is this, but because their heads are full of the one, and quite destitute of such Ideas as might give them a competent notion of the other, and therefore to discourse of such matters, is as little to the purpose as to make Mathematical Demonstrations to one who knows not what an Angle or Triangle means.[4] (Hence by the way, will appear the great usefulness of

---

1 In the 1695 edn, 90, and 1701 edn, 67, the words "betwixt scorn and pity" are inserted according to the instruction in the Errata list appended to the 1694 edn, 172.

2 "Souls" in the 1695 edn, 90, and 1701 edn, 67.

3 Astell seems to be slighting Locke and the Whigs, by suggesting that their seriousness masks petty interest-seeking that may be compared with that of women being fitted for clothes and hats. In *An Impartial Enquiry*, 1704, the language of interests is singled out by her as the language of opportunism and political advantage, and in *The Serious Proposal, Part II* (1697, 74/148), she uses warmth as an example of sensationalist psychology to pillory Locke referred to in the class of "every little warm Disputer and Pretender to Reason, whose Life is perhaps a continual contradiction to it."

4 Locke in *An Essay Concerning Human Understanding*, bk 2, ch. 31, §3 (1694 edn), 208, used the example of the triangle as a complex abstract idea which was the product of computations of the mind, to refute the Platonists for whom such ideas are copies of divine archetypes. Astell's mention of the triangle here, the subject of a serious challenge to Locke later by Edward Stillingfleet, Bishop of Worcester, indicates she has already read *An Essay Concerning Human Understanding*, anathema to her views. Astell, in *A Serious Proposal, Part II* (1697 edn), ch. 3, §4, "A Natural Logic," 119/166, and *The Christian Religion* (1705, §259, §260, §264-§268, 250-51, 254-59) returns to the example of the triangle, having clearly read Locke's correspondence with Stillingfleet, citing *Mr* Lock's *Third Letter to the Bishop of Worcester*, 409, in the latter case (255-56).

judicious Catechizing,[1] which is necessary to form clear Idea's in the mind, without which it can receive but little benefit from the Discourses of the Pulpit, and perhaps the neglect of the former, is the reason that the great plenty of the latter has no better effect.)[2] By all which it appears, that if we wou'd not be impos'd on by false Representations and Impostures, if we wou'd obtain a due knowledge of the most important things, we must remove the little Toys and Vanities of the world from us, or our selves from them; enlarge our Ideas, seek out new Fields of knowledge, whereby to rectify our first mistakes.

From the same Original, *viz*. the constant flattery of external Objects, arises that querulousness and delicacy observable in most Persons of fortune, and which betrays them to many inconveniences.[3] For besides that it renders them altogether unfit to bear a change, which considering the great uncertainty and swift vicissitudes of worldly things, the Greatest and most established ought not to be unprepar'd for;[4] it likewise makes them perpetually uneasy, abates the delight of their enjoyments, for such persons will very rarely find all things to their mind, and then some little disorder which others wou'd take no notice of, like an aching Tooth or Toe, spoils the relish of their Joys. And tho' many great Ladies affect

---

1 Religious instruction.

2 The parentheses are removed, as well as the ungrammatical apostrophe in "Idea's," in the 1701 edn, 68. Astell continues her invective against Locke's (supposed) theological unorthodoxy.

3 Astell connects Locke's materialism and his interest-seeking as forms of opportunism, a theme on which she expands elsewhere. See *A Serious Proposal, Part II*, 115/164, 171-72/187-88.

4 Astell's warnings to political opportunists, particularly Whigs, that they are likely to be victims of their own machinations, are repeated in later works. See *An Impartial Enquiry* (1704, 40) where, after mentioning "Mr. *Lock's* Chapter *of the Association of Ideas*," Astell moves into free association herself, equating empiricism and opportunism and warning:

> till People will observe the excellent Precepts of our Holy Religion, and that in particular, of calling no Man Master upon Earth, of following no Popular Speaker and Leader of a Party, they will easily be persuaded to *think*, as every Cunning and Factious Man will have them.

In the same work she addresses evil ministers, intent on "appeas[ing] the Party ... obstruct[ing] the King's Business, and ... weaken[ing] his authority"; the cause of "perpetual Hurly-burly ... and ... Leap-frog Government" (Astell, *An Impartial Enquiry*, 1704, 7, 32; 1996 edn, 139, 169).

this temper, mistaking it for a piece of Grandeur, 'tis so far from that, that it gives evidence of a poor weak Mind; a very childish Humour, that must be cocker'd[1] and fed with Toys and Baubles to still its frowardness;[2] and is like the crazy stomach of a sick Person, which no body has reason to be fond of or desire.

This also disposes them to Inconstancy, (for she who is continually supply'd with variety knows not where to fix,)[3] a Vice which some Women seem to be proud of, and yet nothing in the world so reproachful and degrading, because nothing is a stronger evidence[4] of a weak and injudicious mind. For it supposes us either so ignorant as to make a wrong Choice at first, or else so silly as not to know and stick to it, when we have made a right one. It bespeaks an unthinking inconsiderate Mind, one that lives at Random without any design or end; who wanting judgment to discern when to fix, or to know when she's well, is ever fluctuating and uncertain, undoing to day what she had done yesterday, which is the worst Character that can be given of ones Understanding.

A constant Scene of Temptations and the infection of ill company, is another great danger which conversing in the world exposes to. 'Tis a dangerous thing to have all the opportunities of sinning in our power, and the danger is increas'd by the ill Precedents we daily see of those who take them. *Liberty* (as somebody says) *will corrupt an Angel*,[5] and tho' it is indeed more glorious to conquer than to fly, yet since our Vertue is so visibly weakned in other instances, we have no reason to presume on't in this. 'Tis become no easy matter to secure our Innocence in our necessary Civilities and daily Conversations; in which, if we have the good luck to avoid such as bring a necessity on us, either of seeming rude to them, or of being really so to GOD Almighty, whilst we tamely hear him, our best Friend and Benefactor affronted and swallow'd it,[6] at the same time, that we wou'd reckon't a very

---

1 Indulged or pampered (*OED*).

2 Perversity (*OED*).

3 Parentheses eliminated in the 1701 edn, 69-70.

4 In the 1695 edn, 94, and 1701 edn, 70, "evidence" is replaced with "indication." In all three edns "is" is understood before "so reproachful."

5 This saying cannot be traced. There are many biblical quotations warning of the dangers of liberty, but none sufficiently close in form of words to count.

6 The 1695 edn, 96, and the 1701 edn, 71, substitute "swallow," following the instruction in the Errata list appended to the 1694 edn, 172.

pitiful Spirit to hear an Acquaintance traduc'd[1] and hold our Tongue; yet if we avoid this Trial, our Charity is however in continual danger, Censoriousness being grown so modish, that we can scarce avoid being active or passive in it; so that she who has not her pert jest ready to pass upon others, shall as soon as her back is turn'd become a Jest her self for want of Wit.

In consequence of all this, we are insensibly betray'd to a great loss of time, a Treasure whose value we are too often quite ignorant of till it be lost past redemption. And yet, considering the shortness and uncertainty of Life, the great work we have to do, and what advantages accrew to us by a due management of our time, we cannot reconcile it with prudence to suffer the least minute to escape us. But besides our own lavish Expences (concerning which one may ask as *Solomon* does of Labour, *What Fruit have we of all that Sport and Pastime we have taken under the sun*?)[2] so unreasonble is the humour of the World, that those who wou'd reckon it a rudeness to make so bold with our Mony, never scruple to waite and rob us of this infinitely more precious Treasure.

In the last place, by reason of this loss of time and the continual hurry we are in, we can find no opportunities for thoughtfulness and recollection; we are so busied with what passes abroad, that we have no leisure to look at home, nor to rectify the disorders there. And such an unthinking mechanical way of living, when like Machins we are condemn'd every day to repent[3] the impertinencies of the day before; shortens our Views, contracts our Minds, exposes to a thousand practical Errors, and renders Improvement impossible, because it will not permit us to consider and recollect, which is the only means to attain it. So much for the inconveniences of living in the World; if we enquire concerning Retirement, we shall find it does not only remove all these, but brings considerable advantages of its own.

For first, it helps us to mate[4] Custom and delivers us from its Tyranny, which is the most considerable thing we have to do, it being nothing else but the habituating our selves to Folly that can reconcile us to it. But how hard is it to quit an old road? What

---

1 Defamed, maligned, censured (*OED*).

2 Astell's paraphrase of Ecclesiastes 1, 3; 2, 22; 3, 9.

3 Typographical error, corrected to "repeat" in 1695 edn, 98, and 1701 edn, 73.

4 Equal, rival, be a match for (*OED*).

courage as well as prudence does it require? How clear a Judgment to overlook the Prejudices of Education and Example and to discern what is best, and how strong a resolution, notwithstanding all the Scoffs and Noises of the world to adhere to it! For Custom has usurpt such an unaccountable Authority, that she who would endeavour to put a stop to its Arbitrary Sway and reduce it to Reason, is in a fair way to render her self the *Butt*[1] for all the Fops[2] in Town to shoot their impertinent Censures at. And tho a wise Woman will not value their Censure, yet she cares not to be the subject of their Discourse. The only way then is to retire from the World, as the *Israelites* did out of *Egypt* lest the Sacrifice we must make of its Follies, shou'd provoke its Spleen.[3]

This also puts us out of the road of temptation, and very much redeems our Time, cutting off those extravagancies on which so much of it was squandred away before.[4] And furnishing us constantly with good employment, secures us from being seduc'd into bad. Great are the Benefits of holy Conversation which will be here enjoy'd: As Vice is, so Vertue may be catching;[5] and to what heights of Piety will not she advance, who is plac'd where the sole Business is to be Good, where there is no pleasure but in Religion, no contention but to excel in what is truly commendable; where her Soul is not defil'd nor her Zeal provok'd, by the sight or relation of those Villanies the World abounds with?

And by that Learning which will be here afforded, and that leisure we have, to enquire after it, and to know and reflect on our own minds, we shall rescue our selves out of that woful incogitancy[6] we have slipt into, awaken our sleeping Powers and make use of that reason which GOD has given us. We shall then begin to wonder at our Folly, that amongst all the pleasures we formerly pursued, we never attended to that most noble and delicious one

---

1 Mark for archery practice (*OED*).

2 Foolish person, dandy, "pretender to wit" (obs.) (*OED*). Richard Allestree, in *The Ladies Calling*, part 2, §1 (1705 edn), 172, "Of Virgins," defined the Fop as "a bug-bear word, devis'd to fright all Seriousness and Sobriety out of the World."

3 As recounted in Exodus 13, 17ff.

4 In the 1695 edn, 100, and the 1701 edn, 75, this and the following sentence are run together, separated only by a comma.

5 Astell has "is" and "may" in italics for emphases in the 1695 edn, 101, and the 1701 edn, 75.

6 Thoughtlessness (*OED*).

which the chase of truth affords us;[1] and bless our selves at last, that our eyes are open'd to discern, how much more pleasantly we may be entertain'd by our own Thoughts, than by all the Diversions which the world affords us. By this means we are fitted to receive the influences of the holy Spirit and are put in a due frame for Devotion. No doubt but he[2] has often knock'd at the door of our hearts, when the croud and noise of our Vanities would not suffer us to regard or hear him, and could find no admittance when our house was so fill'd with other company. Here therefore is the fittest place for his Entertainment, when we are freed from outward disturbances, and entirely at leisure to attend so divine a Guest.[3] Our Devotions will be perform'd with due attention, those Objects that used to attract being now remov'd from us; simplicity of desire will beget simplicity of thought, and that will make our mind most intense and elevated, when we come to address our selves to the Throne of Grace. Being dead to the things of this world, we shall with greatest fervour petition for those of another; and living always in a lively and awful[4] sense of the divine Majesty, our hearts will ever be dispos'd to approach him in the most solemn, serious and reverent manner. 'Tis a very unseemly thing to jump from our Diversions to our Prayers; as if when we have been entertaining our selves and others with Vanity, we were instantly prepar'd to appear in the sacred presence of GOD. But a Religious Retirement and holy Conversation, will procure us a more serious Temper, a graver Spirit, and so both make us habitually fit to approach, and likewise stir us up to be more careful in our actual preparations when we do. For besides all other improvements of Knowledge, we shall hereby obtain truer Notions of GOD than we were capable of before, which is of very great consequence, since the want of right apprehensions concerning him, is the general cause of Mistakes in Religion, and in Practice;[5] for as GOD is the noblest Object of our Understanding, so nothing is more necessary or of

---

1 The 1695 edn, 102, and 1701 edn, 76, read "is to be found in the chase of truth," following the instruction in the Errata list appended to the 1694 edn, 172.

2 Capitalized to indicated God in the 1695 edn, 102, and 1701 edn, 76.

3 Phraseology changed in 1695 edn, 103, and 1701 edn, 76, to "for being freed from outward disturbances, we are entirely at leisure...."

4 I.e., full of awe.

5 The 1695 edn, 104-05 and 1701 edn, 78, read "of Errors in Speculation, and Indecorums in Practice."

such consequence to us as to busie our thoughts about him. And did we rightly consider his Nature, we shou'd neither dare to forget him, nor draw near to him with unclean hands and unholy hearts.

From this sacred Mountain where the world will be plac'd at our feet, at such a distance from us, that the steams of its corruptions shall not obscure our eye-sight; we shall have a right prospect of it, and clearly discern that all its Allurements, all those Gaities and Pageantries, which at present we admire so much are no better than insignificant Toys,[1] which have no value but what our perverse Opinion imposes on them. Things which contribute so very little to our real Good, that even at *present*, which is their only season, we may live much happier without than with them; and which are so far from being necessary to true[2] Felicity, that they shall vanish and be no more when that is consummate and perfect. Many are the Topics from whence we might declaim against the vanity of the world, but me-thinks Experience is so convincing that it supersedes all the rest, and wou'd certainly reclaim us from the immoderate love of earthly enjoyments, did we but seriously hearken to it. For tell me, Ladies, if your greatest Pleasures are not attended with a greater sting; when you think to grasp them, do they not either vanish into Froth,[3] or gall your fingers? To want, or to enjoy them, is equally tormenting; the one produces in you the Pain of Hunger the other of Loathing. For in reality, there is no good in them, nothing but the Shadow and Appearance; if there were, you cou'd not so easily loath your old Delights, and be so fond of variety, what is truly desirable never ending in disgust. They are not therefore Pleasures but Amusements which you now pursue, and which, through your ignorance of better Joys pretend to fill their place, toll[4] you on with fair pretences, and repay your Labour with defeated Hopes. Joys, not near so lasting as the slightest toy you wear,[5] the most capricious Humorist among you is

---

1 Echoes of Bathsua Makin's "Toyes and Trifles," *An Essay to Revive the Antient Education of Gentlewomen* (1673), sig. A2^{v}.

2 The 1695 edn, 106, and 1701 edn, 79, read "our Felicity."

3 "Air" in the 1695 edn, 107, and 1701 edn, 79, following the instruction in the Errata list appended to the 1694 edn, 172.

4 Pull, the sense having passed from "pull the bell-rope" (*OED*).

5 By toys you wear Astell probably means "trinkets," or it may be a specific usage, referring to "a close cap,or head-dress of linen or wool, with flaps coming down to the shoulders, formerly worn by women of the lower classes in Scotland" (*OED*).

more constant far than they. Come hither therefore and take a true view of 'em that you may no longer deceive your selves with that which profits not, but spurning away these empty nothings, secure a portion in such a Bliss as will not fail, as cannot disappoint you! A Felicity which depending on GOD only and your own Minds, is out of Fortunes reach, will place you above the Batteries of the world, above its Terrors and Allurements, and enable you at once to triumph over and despise it. And what can be more glorious than to have a mind unshaken by the blandishments of Prosperity, or the rough shocks of Adversity; that passes thro' both with the same indifferency[1] and integrity, is not to be tempted by either to a mean, unworthy and indecent Action?

Farther yet, besides that holy emulation which a continual view of the brightest and most exemplary Lives will excite in us; we shall have opportunity of contracting the purest and noblest Friendship; a Blessing, the purchase of which were richly worth all the World besides! For she who possesses a worthy Person, has certainly obtain'd the richest Treasure! A Blessing that Monarchs may envy, and she who enjoys is happier than she who fills a Throne! A Blessing, which next to the love of GOD is the choicest Jewel in our Caelestial Diadem, which, were it duly practic'd, wou'd both fit us for heav'n, and bring it down into our hearts whilst we tarry here. For Friendship is a Vertue which comprehends all the rest; none being fit for this, who is not adorn'd with every other Vertue. Probably one considerable cause of the degeneracy of the present Age, is the little true Friendship that is to be found in it; or perhaps you will rather say, that this is the effect of our corruption. The cause and the effect are indeed reciprocal; for were the World better, there wou'd be more Friendship, and were there more Friendship we shou'd have a better World. But because *Iniquity abounds*, therefore the *love of many* is not only *waxen*[2] *cold*, but quite benumb'd and perish'd. But if we have such narrow hearts, be so full of mistaken Self-love, so unreasonably fond of our selves, that we cannot spare a hearty Good-will to one or two choice Persons, how can it ever be thought, that we shou'd well acquit our selves of that Charity which is due to all Mankind? For Friendship is nothing else but Charity contracted;[3] it is (in the words of an admired

---

1 Indifference.

2 Grown. The source of this quotation is not known.

3 Astell probably means that friendship is charity writ small, the particular application of a general principle.

Author) a kind of revenging our selves on the narrowness of our Faculties, by exemplifying that extraordinary charity on one or two, which we are willing but not able to exercise towards all.[1] And therefore 'tis without doubt the best Instructor to teach us our duty to our Neighbour, and a most excellent Monitor[2] to excite us to make payment as far as our power will reach. It has a special force to dilate[3] our hearts, to deliver them from that vicious selfishness and the rest of those *sordid Passions* which express a narrow illiberal temper, and are of such pernicious consequence to Mankind. That institution therefore must needs be highly beneficial, which both disposes us to be friends our selves, and helps to find them. But by Friendship I do not mean any thing like those intimacies that are abroad in the world, which are often combinations in evil and at best but insignificant dearnesses; as little resembling true Friendship, as modern Practice does Primitive Christianity.[4] But I intend by it the greatest usefulness, the most refin'd and disinteress'd Benevolence, a love that thinks nothing within the bounds of Power and Duty, too much to do or suffer for its Beloved; And makes no distinction betwixt its Friend and its self, except that in Temporals[5] it prefers her interest. But tho' it be very desirable to obtain such a Treasure, such a Medicine of Life, (as the

---

1 These are the sentiments expressed by John Norris, who may well be the "admired Author," in the Astell-Norris correspondence, *Letters Concerning the Love of God* (published 1695, but begun in 1693).

2 One who admonishes or gives advice (*OED*).

3 Open.

4 Mention of the Primitive Church flags Arminians, Erastians, and all those who protested against the doctrine and ritual of the Laudean Church. The sheer number of political polemicists who undertook to examine Primitive Christianity in order to show the pagan deviations of the Catholic Church, to which Anglicanism of this type was deemed to have fallen heir, is very large. It included Hobbes, in his *Historia Ecclesiastica*, Locke's *Reasonableness of Christianity* and its imitators, works by James Owen (1654-1706), Astell's protagonist in *A Fair Way with the Dissenters* and William Whiston's five-volume *Primitive Christianity reviv'd* (1711-12). It is most surprising that Astell should appear to endorse the primitivism in vogue among many writers she otherwise considers to be her opponents. But in *An Impartial Enquiry* (1704, 30/163), she makes a similar remark, appealing to "Holy Scripture, and those best Expositors, as well as Practisers of Holy Writ, the Primitive Church."

5 Temporal matters, or matters concerned with life on earth.

wise man speaks)[1] yet the danger is great, least[2] being deceiv'd in our choice, we suck in Poyson where we expected Health. And considering how apt we are to disguise our selves, how hard it is to know our own hearts much less anothers, it is not advisable to be too hasty in contracting so important a Relation; before that be done, it were well if we could look into the very Soul of the beloved Person, to discover what resemblance it bears to our own, and in this Society we shall have the best opportunities of doing so. There are no Interests here to serve, no contrivances for another to be a stale to;[3] the Souls of all the Religious will be open and free, and those particular Friendships must be no prejudice to the general Amity.[4] But yet, as in Heav'n that region of perfect Love, the happy Souls (as some are of opinion) now and then step aside from more general Conversations, to entertain themselves with a peculiar Friend; so, in this little emblem[5] of this[6] blessed place, what shou'd hinder, but that two Persons of a sympathizing disposition, the *make* and *frame* of whose Souls bears an exact conformity to each other, and therefore one wou'd think were purposely design'd by Heaven to unite and mix; what shou'd hinder them from entring into an holy combination to watch over each other for Good, to advise, encourage and direct, and to observe the minutest fault in order to its amendment. The truest effect of love being to endeavour the bettering the beloved Person. And therefore nothing is more likely to improve us in Vertue, and advance us to the very highest pitch of Goodness than unfeigned Friendship, which is the most beneficial, as well as the most pleasant thing in the world.

But to hasten; such an Institution will much confirm us in Vertue and help us to persevere to the end, and by that substantial Piety and solid Knowledge we shall here acquire, fit us to propagate Religion when we return into the World. An habitual Practice of Piety for some years will so root and establish us in it, that

---

1 Parentheses removed in the 1701 edn, 84.

2 Lest.

3 To be uninterested in, or of diminished interest in (*OED*).

4 Friendship.

5 Fable or allegory (obs.), symbolic representation (*OED*). Astell understands "emblem" metonymically, as a part (the soul) representing the whole (the spiritual realm, heaven).

6 The Errata list appended to the 1694 edn, 172, instructs the substitution of "that" for "this."

Religion will become a second Nature, and we must do strange violences to our selves, if after that we dare venture to oppose it. For besides all the other Advantages that Vertue has over Vice, this will disarm it of *Custom*, the only thing that recommends it, bravely win its strongest Fort and turn its own Cannon against it self. How almost impossible wou'd it be for her to sin, whose Understanding being clearly illuminated with the knowledge of the Truth, is too wise to be impos'd on by those false *representations* that sin wou'd deceive it with; whose will has found out and united it self to its true *Centre*; and having been long habituated to move in a *right* line, has no temptation to decline to an *Oblique*.[1] Whose Affections have daily regaled[2] on those delicious Fruits of Paradice which Religion presents them with, and are therefore too sublime and refin'd to relish the muddy Pleasures of sensual Delights. It must certainly be a Miracle if such an one relinquish her Glory and Joy; she must be as bad as *Lucifer*[3] himself who after such Enjoyments can forsake her Heaven. 'Tis too unreasonable to imagine such an Apostacy, the supposition is monstrous, and therefore we may conclude will never, or very rarely happen. And then what a blessed World shou'd we have, shining with so many stars of Vertue![4] Who, not content to be happy themselves,[5] for that's a narrowness of mind too much beneath their God-like temper, would like the glorious Lights of Heav'n, or rather like him who made them, diffuse their benign Influences round about.[6] Having gain'd an entrance into Paradise themselves, they wou'd both shew the way, and invite all[7] others to partake of their felicity. In stead of that froth and impertinence, that Censure and Pragmaticalness,[8] with which Feminine Conversations so much

---

1 Slanting, crooked, deviant (*OED*).

2 Feasted on (obs.) (*OED*).

3 Literally, "Light Bearer," here the name of the Devil before his fall from the highest rank of archangel (*OED*).

4 This sentence is run into the next with a comma in the 1695 edn, 117, and the 1701 edn, 88.

5 In the 1695 edn, 117, and the 1701 edn, 88., "alone" is inserted here.

6 In the 1695 edn, 118, and the 1701 edn, 88., "where-ever they come" is substituted for "round about."

7 "All" omitted from the 1695 edn, 118, and the 1701 edn, 88.

8 "Officiousness, meddlesomeness, opinionativeness, dogmatism; practical or utilitarian quality" (*OED*).

abound, we should hear their tongues employ'd in making Proselytes[1] to heaven, in running down Vice, in establishing Vertue and proclaiming their Makers Glory. 'Twou'd be more genteel to give and take instructions about the ornaments of the Mind, than to enquire after the Mode;[2] and a Lecture on the Fashions wou'd become as disagreeable as at present any serious discourse is. Not the Follies of the Town, but the Beauties and the Love of JESUS wou'd be the most polite and delicious Entertainment.[3] 'Twould be thought as rude and barbarous to send our Visitors away uninstructed, as our foolishness at present reckons it to introduce a pertinent and useful Conversation. Ladies of Quality wou'd be able to distinguish themselves from their Inferiors, by the blessings they communicated, and the good they did. For this is their grand Prerogative, their *distinguishing Character*, that they are plac'd in a condition which makes that which is every ones chief business, to be their only employ. They have nothing to do but to glorify GOD, and to benefit their Neighbours, and she who does not thus improve her Talent, is more vile and despicable than the meanest Creature that attends her.

And if after so many Spiritual Advantages, it be convenient to mention Temporals,[4] here Heiresses and Persons of Fortune may be kept secure, from the rude attempts of designing Men; And she who has more Mony than Discretion, need not curse her Stars for being expos'd a prey to bold importunate[5] and rapacious Vultures. She will not here be inveigled and impos'd on, will neither be bought nor sold, nor be forc'd to marry for her own quiet, when she has no inclination to it, but what the being tir'd out with a restless importunity occasions. Or if she be dispos'd to marry, here she may remain in safety till a convenient Match be offer'd by her Friends, and be freed from the danger of a dishonourable one. Modesty requiring that a Woman should not love before Marriage, but only make choice of one whom she can love hereafter: She who has none but innocent affections, being easily able to fix them where Duty requires.

And though at first I propos'd to my self to speak nothing in particular of the employment of the Religious, yet to give a Spec-

---

1 Converts.

2 Fashion.

3 "Entertainments" in the 1695 edn, 119, and 1701 edn, 89.

4 Secular matters (*OED*).

5 "Persistent or pressing in solicitation" (*OED*).

imen how useful they will be to the World, I am now inclin'd to declare, that it is design'd a part of their business shall be to give the best Education to the Children of Persons of Quality,[1] who shall be attended and instructed in lesser Matters by meaner Persons deputed to that Office, but the forming of their minds shall be the particular care of those of their own Rank; who cannot have a more pleasant and useful employment than to exercise and encrease their own knowledge, by instilling it into these young ones, who are most like to profit under such Tutors. For how can their little Pupils forbear to credit them, since they do not decry the World (as others may be thought to do) because they cou'd not enjoy it; but when they had it in their power, were courted and caress'd[2] by it, for very good Reasons, and on mature deliberation, thought fit to relinquish and despise its offers for a better choice? Nor are mercenary people on other accounts capable of doing so much good to young Persons, because, having often but short views of things themselves, sordid and low Spirits, they are not like to form a generous temper in the minds of the Educated. Doubtless 'twas well consider'd of him, who wou'd not trust the breeding of his Son to a Slave, because nothing great or excellent could be expected from a person of that condition.

And when by the increase of their Revenue, the Religious are enabled to do such a work of Charity, the Education they design to bestow on the Daughters of Gentlemen who are fallen into decay, will be no inconsiderable advantage to the Nation. For hereby many Souls will be preserv'd from great Dishonours, and put in a comfortable way of subsisting, being either receiv'd into the House if they incline to it, or otherwise dispos'd of.[3] It being suppos'd that prudent Men will reckon the endowments they here acquire a sufficient *Dowry*; and that a discreet and vertuous Gentlewoman will make a better Wife than she whose mind is empty tho' her Purse be full.

---

1 Euphemism for persons of high birth or rank, nobility or gentry. Note that Astell's project, like that of Bathsua Makin, was aimed at rescuing the upper classes from their frivolous morals and mores and not at bettering the condition of the poor.

2 In the archaic sense of caress: "To treat with kindness of favour, pet, make much of" (*OED*). Allestree in *The Ladies Calling*, part 2, §3 (1705 edn), 232, speaks of "Frantick Embraces and Caresses of a Carcass," presumably in the same hyperbolic sense.

3 Managed (obs.) (*OED*).

But some will say, May not People be good without this confinement? may they not live at large in the World, and yet serve GOD as acceptably as here? 'Tis allow'd they may; truly wise and vertuous Souls will do it by the assistance of GOD's Grace in despite of all temptations; and I heartily wish that all Women were of this temper. But it is to be consider'd, that there are *tender* Vertues who need to be screened from the ill Airs of the World: many persons who had *begun* well might have gone to the Grave in peace and innocence, had it not been their misfortune to be violently tempted. For those who have honest Hearts have not always the strongest Heads; and sometimes the enticements of the World and the subtil insinuations of such as lye in wait to deceive, may make their Heads giddy, stagger[1] their Resolutions, and Overthrow all the fine hopes of a promising beginning. 'Tis fit therefore, such tender *Cyons*[2] shou'd be transplanted, that they may be supported by the prop of Vertuous Friendship, and confirm'd in Goodness by holy Examples, which alas! they will not often meet with in the world. And, such is the weakness of human Nature, that[3] bad People are not so apt to be better'd by the Society of the Good, as the Good are to be corrupted by theirs. Since therefore we daily pray against temptation, it cannot be amiss if we take all prudent care to avoid it, and not out of a vain presumption face the danger which GOD may justly permit to overcome us for a due correction of our Pride. It is not impossible for a man to live in an infected House or Town and escape with Life and Health; yet if he have a place in the Country to retire to, he will not make slight of that advantage; and surely the Health of our Souls is of greater consideration than the health of our Bodies. Besides, she has need of an establish'd Vertue and consummated[4] Prudence, who so well understands the great end she was sent into the world about,[5] and so faithfully pursues it, that not content to be wise and good her self alone, she endeavours to propagate Wisdom and Piety to all about her.[6] But neither this Prudence

---

1 Cause to waver or fall (obs.) (*OED*).

2 Obsolete form of "scion," twig, shoot, and by transference, heir, descendant (*OED*).

3 "That" omitted in the 1695 edn, 125, and the 1701 edn, 94.

4 Perfected (*OED*).

5 The 1695 edn, 125, and the 1701 edn, 95, substitute. "for which she came into the World."

6 The 1695 edn, 126, and the 1701 edn, 95, substitute, "for all within her Sphere," running the sentence into the next.

nor heroic Goodness are easily attainable amidst the noise and hurry of the world, we must therefore retire a while from its clamour and importunity,[1] if we generously design to do it good; and having calmly and sedately observ'd and rectify'd what is amiss in our selves, we shall be fitter to promote a Reformation in others. A devout Retirement will not only strengthen and confirm our Souls, that they be not infected by the worlds Corruptions, but likewise so purify and refine them, that they will become Antidotes to expel the Poyson in others, and spread a salutary Air on ev'ry Side.[2]

If any object against a Learned Education, that it will make Women vain and assuming, and instead of correcting encrease their Pride: I grant that a smattering in Learning may, for it has this effect on the Men, none so Dogmatical and so forward to shew their Parts as your little *Pretenders* to Science.[3] But I wou'd not have the Ladies content themselves with the *shew* my desire is, that they shou'd not rest till they obtain the *Substance*.[4] And then, she who is most knowing will be forward to own with the wise *Socrates*,[5] that she knows nothing: nothing that is matter of Pride

---

1 Demands.

2 Richard Allestree in *The Ladies Calling*, part 2, §3 (1705 edn), 125, had argued in favour of "Home-education" and against sending children abroad where "they may suck in all the Venom, and nothing of the Antidote."

3 Astell has no objections to science, which she discusses at great length in *A Serious Proposal, Part II* (78-79ff./150ff.), arguing, "Now tho there's a great difference between Opinion and Science, true Science being immutable but Opinion variable and uncertain." She had Locke clearly in her sights as among the "little *Pretenders* to Science" by then.

4 In fact, in *The Christian Religion* (1705 edn, 296), she claimed that science was a subject that women in retirement, as reflective by disposition, were especially suited:

> And since it is allow'd on all hands, that the Mens Business is without Doors, and theirs is an Active Life; Women who ought to be Retir'd, are for this reason design'd by Providence for Speculation: Providence, which allots every one an Employment, and never intended that any one shou'd give themselves up to Idleness and Unprofitable Amusements. And I make no question but great Improvements might be made in the Sciences, where not Women enviously excluded from this their proper Business.

5 Socrates (469-399 BC), Athenian philosopher and master of dialogic discourse, celebrated by Plato and Xenophon. In 399 BC Socrates was brought to trial in Athens before a popular court on the charge of introducing strange gods and corrupting youth, was condemned, and took hemlock rather than escape.

and Ostentation; nothing but what is attended with so much ignorance and imperfection, that it cannot reasonably elate and puff her up. The more she knows, she will be the less subject to talkativeness and its sister Vices, because she discerns, that the most difficult piece of Learning is to know when to use and when to hold ones Tongue, and never to speak but to the purpose.

But the men if they rightly understand their own interest, have no reason to oppose the ingenious[1] Education of the Women, since 'twou'd go a great way towards reclaiming the men; great is the influence we have over them in their Childhood, in which time, if a Mother be discreet and knowing as well as devout, she has many opportunities of giving such a *Form* and *Season*[2] to the tender Mind of the Child, as will shew its good effects thro' all the stages of his Life. But tho' you should not allow her capable of doing *good*, 'tis certain she may do *hurt*: If she do not *make* the Child, she has power to *marr* him, by suffering her fondness to get the better of discreet affection. But besides this, a good and prudent Wife wou'd wonderfully work on an ill man; he must be a Brute indeed, who cou'd hold out against all those innocent Arts, those gentle persuasives and obliging methods she wou'd use to reclaim him. Piety is often offensive when it is accompanied with indiscretion: but she who is as Wise as Good, possesses such Charms as can hardly fail of prevailing. Doubtless her Husband is a much happier Man, and more likely to abandon all his ill Courses, than he who has none to come home to, but an ignorant, froward[3] and fantastick[4] Creature. An ingenious Conversation will make his life comfortable, and he who can be so well entertain'd at home, needs not run into Temptations in search of Diversions abroad. The only danger is, that the Wife be more knowing than the Husband; but if she be 'tis his own fault, since he wants no opportunities of improvement; unless he be a natural *Blockhead*, and then such an one will need a wise Woman to govern him, whose prudence will conceal it from publick Observation, and at once both cover and supply his defects. Give me leave therefore to hope, that no Gentleman who has honourable designs, will henceforward decry Knowledge and Ingenuity in her he would pretend

---

1 "Intelligent, discerning, sensible" (obs.) (*OED*).

2 Flourishing (obs.) (*OED*).

3 Perverse, hard to please (*OED*).

4 Fanciful (*OED*).

to Honour: Or[1] if he does, it may serve for a Test to distinguish the feigned and unworthy from the real Lover.

Now, who that has a spark of Piety, will go about to oppose so Religious a design? What generous Spirit that has a due regard to the good of Mankind, will not be forward to advance and perfect it? Who will think 500 pounds too much to lay out for the purchase of so much Wisdom and Happiness? Certainly, we shou'd not think them too dearly paid for by a much greater Sum, did not our pitiful and sordid Spirits set a much higher value on Money than it deserves. But granting so much of that dear Idol is[2] given away, a person thus bred, will easily make it up by her Frugality and other Vertues: if she bring less, she will not waste so much as others do in superfluous and vain Expences. Nor can I think of any expedient so useful as this to Persons of Quality who are overstock'd with Children, for thus they may honourably dispose of them without impairing their Estates. Five or six hundred pounds may be easily spar'd with a Daughter, when so many thousand[3] would go deep; and yet as the world goes be a very inconsiderable Fortune for Ladies of their Birth; neither maintain them in that *Port*[4] which Custom makes almost necessary, nor procure them an equal Match, those of their own Rank (contrary to the generous custom of the *Germans*)[5] chusing rather to fill their Coffers than to preserve the purity of their Blood, and therefore think a weighty Bag the best Gentility, preferring a wealthy Upstart before the best Descended and best Qualified Lady; Their own Extravagancies perhaps having made it necessary, that they may keep up an empty shadow of Greatness, which is all that remains to shew what their Ancestors have been.

Does any think their Money lost to their Families when 'tis put in here? I will only ask what course they can take to save it, and at once to preserve their Money, their Honour and their Daughters too? Were they sure the Ladies wou'd die unmarried, I shou'd commend their Thrift; but Experience has too often shewn us the

---

1 "Or" omitted from the 1701 edn, 99.

2 The 1695 edn, 130, and the 1701 edn, 100, substitute "were."

3 The 1695 edn, 131, and the 1701 edn, 100, read "thousands." Astell means that such a charge would cause the guardians of girls to go deep into their pockets.

4 Style of living, social position, station (rare or obs.) (*OED*).

5 Apparently the Germans gave more attention to preserving the status and bloodlines of their families.

vanity of this expectation. For the poor Lady having past the prime of her Years in Gaity and Company, in running the Circle of all the Vanities of the Town, having spread all her Nets and us'd all her Arts for Conquest, and finding that the Bait fails where she wou'd have it take, and having all this while been so over-careful of her Body, that she had no time to improve her Mind, which therefore affords her no safe retreat now she meets with Disappointments abroad, and growing every day more and more sensible[1] that the respect which us'd to be paid her, decays as fast as her Beauty; quite terrified with the dreadful Name of *Old Maid*, which yet none but Fools will reproach her with, nor any wise Woman be afraid of; to avoid this terrible *Mormo*,[2] and the scoffs that are thrown on superanuated Virgins,[3] she flies to some dishonourable Match as her last, tho' much mistaken Refuge, to the disgrace of her Family and her own irreparable Ruin. And now let any Person of Honour tell me, if it were not richly worth some thousand Pounds, to prevent all this mischief, and the having an idle Fellow,[4] and perhaps a race of beggarly Children to hang on him, and to provide for?

Cou'd I think of any other Objection, I wou'd consider it; there's nothing indeed which witty Persons may not argue *for* and *against*, but they who duly weigh the Arguments on both sides, unless they be extreamly prejudiced, will easily discern the great usefulness of this Institution. The *Beaux*[5] perhaps, and topping Sparks of the Town[6] will ridicule and laugh at it. For Vertue her self as bright as she is, can't escape the lash of scurrilous Tongues; the comfort is, whilst they impotently endeavour to throw dirt on her, they are unable to soil her Beauty, and only[7] render themselves the more contemptible. They may therefore if they please, hug themselves in their own dear folly, and enjoy the diversion of their own insipid Jests. She has but little Wisdom and less Vertue, who is to be

---

1 Aware.

2 Hobgoblin, bugbear, from the Greek *mormo*, a hideous she-monster (obs.) (*OED*).

3 The epithet "superanuated Virgins," with which she was to become associated, and which was used against her, appears in Allestree's *The Ladies Calling*, part 2, §1, "Of Virgins" (1705 edn, 158).

4 The "Fellow" in this case is a woman.

5 Suitors.

6 Dandies.

7 In the 1695 edn, 134, and the 1701 edn, 103, read "defile and render themselves."

frighted from what she judges reasonable, by the scoffs and insignificant noises of ludicrous Wits and pert Buffoons. And no *wonder* that such as they, (who have nothing to shew for their pretences to Wit, but some scraps of Plays and blustring Non-sence; who fansie a well adjusted Peruke[1] is able to supply their want of Brains, and that to talk *much* is a sign of Ingenuity, tho't be never so little to the purpose,)[2] no wonder that they object against our Proposal; 'twou'd indeed spoil the Trade of the gay fluttering Fops, who wou'd be at a loss, had they no body as impertinent as themselves to talk with. The Criticism of their Dress wou'd be useless, and the labour of their *Valet de Chambre*[3] lost, unless they cou'd peaceably lay aside their Rivalling, and one Ass[4] be content to complement and admire another. For the Ladies wou'd have more discernment than to esteem a Man for such Follies as shou'd rather incline them to scorn and despise him. They wou'd never be so sottish[5] as to imagine, that he who regards nothing but his own brutish Appetite, shou'd have any real affection for them, nor ever expect Fidelity from one who is unfaithful to GOD and his own Soul. They wou'd not be so absurd as to suppose, that Man can esteem them who neglects his Maker; for what are all those fine Idolatries, by which he wou'd recommend himself to his pretended Goddess; but mockery and delusion from him who forgets and affronts the true Deity? They wou'd not value themselves on account of the Admiration of such incompetent Judges, nor consequently make use of those little trifling Arts that are necessary to recommend them to such Admirers; Neither wou'd they give them opportunity to profess themselves their Slaves so long till at last they become their Masters.

What now remains, but to reduce to Practice that which tends so very much to our advantage. Is Charity so dead in the world that none will contribute to the saving their own and their neighbours Souls? Shall we freely expend our Money to purchase Vanity, and often times both present and future Ruin, and find none for such an eminent good Work, which will make the Ages to come arise and call us Blessed? I wou'd fain persuade my self better things, and that I shall one day see this *Religious Retirement*

---

1 A wig (*OED*).

2 Parentheses removed in the 1701 edn, 103-04.

3 Valet, manservant (*OED*).

4 Fool.

5 Foolish, stupid, "of persons and their faculties" (obs.) (*OED*).

happily setled, and its great designs wisely and vigorously pursu'd; and methinks I have already a Vision of that lustre and glory our Ladies cast round about them![1] Let me therefore intreat the rest of our Sex, who tho' at liberty in the world, are the miserable Slaves of their own vile affections; let me intreat them to lay aside their Prejudices and whatever borders on Envy and Malice, and with impartial eyes to behold the Beauties of our *Religious*. The native innocency[2] and unaffectedness of whose Charms, and the unblameable Integrity of their Lives, are abundantly more taking[3] than all the curious Artifices and studied Arts the other can invent to recommend them, even bad men themselves being Judges, who often betray a secret Veneration for that vertue they wou'd seem to despise and endeavour to corrupt. As there is not any thing, no not the least shadow of a motive to recommend vice, but its fashionableness, and the being acustom'd to it; so there is nothing at all forbidding in Virtue but her uncouthness. Acquaint your selves with her a little, and you'll wonder how you cou'd be so foolish as to delight in any thing besides! For you'll find her Conversation most sweet and obliging; her Precepts most easy and beneficial; her very tasks Joys, and her Injunctions the highest Pleasures. She will not rob you of any innocent delight, not engage you to any thing beneath your Birth and Breeding: but will put a new and more grateful relish into all your Enjoyments, and make them more delicious with her Sweetness. She'll preserve and augment your Honour, by allying you to the King of Heaven; secure your Grandeur by fixing it on a firm bottom, such as the caprice of Fortune cannot shake or overthrow; she'll enlarge your Souls, raise them above the common level, and encourage that allowable Pride of Scorning to do a base unworthy action.[4] Make you truly amiable in the eyes of GOD and Man, preserve ever the Beauty of your Bodies as long as 'tis possible for such a brittle thing to last; and when it must of necessity decay, impress such a loveliness on your Minds, as will shine thro' and brighten your very Countenances; enriching you with such a stock of Charms, that Time which devours every other thing, shall never be able to decay. In

---

1 In the 1695 edn, 137, and the 1701 edn, 106, the words "far and near" are substituted for "round about them."

2 Innocence.

3 Engaging, affecting.

4 The 1701 edn, 108, runs this sentence into the next.

a word, 'tis Virtue only which can make you truly happy in the world as well as in the next.

There is a sort of Bravery and Greatness of Soul, which does more truly ennoble us than the highest Title, and it consists in living up to the dignity of our Natures, scorning to[1] do a degenerate and unbecoming thing; in passing differently[2] thro' Good and Evil Fortune, without being corrupted by the one or deprest by the other. For she that can do so, gives evidence that her Happiness depends not on so mutable a thing as this World; but, in a due subserviency to the Almighty, is bottom'd only on her own great Mind. This is the richest Ornament, and renders a Woman glorious in the lowest Fortune: So shining is real worth, that like a Diamond it loses not its lustre, tho' cast on a Dunghill. Whereas, she who is advanc'd to some eminent Station and wants this natural and solid Greatness, is no better than Fortunes *May-game*,[3] rendered more conspicuous that she may appear the more contemptible. Let those therefore who value themselves only on external accomplishments, consider how liable they are to decay, and how soon they may be depriv'd of them, and that supposing they shou'd continue, they are but sandy Foundations to build Esteem upon. What a disappointment will it be to a Ladies Admirer as well as to her self, that her Conversation shou'd lose and[4] endanger the Victory her eyes had gain'd! For when the Passion of a Lover is evaporated into[5] the Indifference of a Husband, and a frequent review has lessen'd the wonder which her Charms at first had rais'd, she'll retain no more than such a formal respect as decency and good breeding will require; and perhaps hardly that; but unless he be a very good Man (and indeed the world is not over full of 'em) her worthlessness has made a forfeit of his

---

1 In the 1695 edn, 139, and the 1701 edn, 108, the phrase "being so sensible of our own worth as to think our selves too great to" is substituted for "scorning to."

2 The 1695 edn, 139, and 1701 edn, 108, substitute "indifferently."

3 The festivities associated with May-day. May in an archaic sense meant a young virgin, "May and January" or "December," was an archaic idiomatic expression for the marriage of a young woman to an old man, and the May-game may well have been the maypole (*OED*), as a substitute for Fortune's wheel in Astell's metaphor.

4 The 1605 edn, 140, 1701 edn, 110, substitute "or."

5 The 1605 edn, 141, and the 1701 edn, 110, tone down the claim by substituting "Exchang'd for."

Affections, which are seldom fixt by any other thing than Veneration and Esteem. Whereas, a wise and good Woman is useful and valuable in all Ages and Conditions; she who chiefly attends the *one thing needful*, the *good part which shall not be taken from her*, lives a cheerful and pleasant life, innocent and sedate, calm and tranquile, and makes a glorious Exit; being translated from the most happy life on Earth, to unspeakable happiness in Heaven; a fresh and fragrant Name embalming her Dust, and extending its Perfume to succeeding Ages. Whilst the Fools, and the worst sort of them the wicked, *live* as well as *die* in Misery, go out in a snuff, leaving nothing but stench and putrefaction behind them.

To close all, if this *Proposal* which is but a rough draught and rude Essay, and which might be made much more beautiful by a better Pen, give occasion to wiser heads to improve and perfect it, I have my end. For imperfect as it is, it seems so desirable, that she who drew the Scheme is full of hopes, it will not want kind hands to perform and compleat it. But if it miss of that, it is but a few hours thrown away, and a little labour in vain, which yet will not be lost, if what is here offer'd may serve to express her hearty Good-will, and how much she desires your Improvement, who is

LADIES,

Your very humble Servant.

A Serious PROPOSAL to the LADIES

Part II

Wherein a Method is offer'd
for the Improvement
of their Minds

LONDON

Printed for *Richard Wilkin* at
the *King's Head* in St.*Paul's*
Church-yard, *1697*

THE

CONTENTS

Of the Second Part.

[THE DEDICATION][1]

To her Royal Highness
THE
Princess *ANN* of *Denmark*.

MADAM,

What was at first address'd to the Ladies in *General*, as seeming not considerable enough to appear in your Royal Highnesses Presence, not being ill reciv'd by them, and having got the Addition of a Second part, now presumes on a more *Particular* Application to Her who is the Principal of them, and whose Countenance and Example may reduce to Practice, what it can only Advise and Wish.

And when I consider you Madam as a Princess who is sensible that the Chief Prerogative of the Great is the Power they have of doing more Good than those in an Inferior Station can, I see no cause to fear that your Royal Highness will deny Encouragment to that which has no other Design than the Bettering of the World, especially the most neglected part of it as to all Real Improvment, the Ladies. It is by the Exercise of this Power that Princes become truly Godlike, they are never so Illustrious as when they shine as Lights in the World by an Eminent and Heroic Vertue. A Vertue as much above Commendation as it is above Detraction, which sits equally Silent and Compose'd when Opprest with Praises of Pursu'd with Calumnys, is neither hurt by these nor better'd by the other; for the Service of GOD, and the Resembling Him, being its

---

1 Princess Ann of Denmark (1665-1714), Queen of Great Britain from 1702 until her death, to whom *A Serious Proposal, Part II* is dedicated, was known to support women's causes and Astell hoped that she would provide financial support for her women's academy. For some time, it appears, she toyed with the idea, until dissuaded by Bishop Gilbert Burnet, because of the language in which Astell's proposal was couched: "a Monastery or if you will (to avoid giving offence...by names which tho' innocent in themselves have been abus'd by superstitious practices) we will call it a Religious Retirement." Burnet feared that the language of *A Serious Proposal* smacked too much of a Catholic nunnery, and would bring disrepute as being Popish (Ballard, 1985 edn, 383). The Dedication was printed in italics, as was the custom, but has been converted into Roman type.

only Aim, His Approbation[1] in a soft and inward Whisper, is more than the loud *Huzza's*[2] and Plaudits of ten thousand Worlds.

I shall not therefore offend your Royal Ear with the nauseous strain of Dedications; for what can one say, when by how much the more any Person deserves Panegyric, by so much the less they endure it? That your Royal Highness may be All that is truly Great and Good, and have a Confluence of Temporal, Sanctify'd and Crown'd with Spiritual and Eternal Blessings, is the unfeigned and constant desire of

MADAM,

Your Royal Highnesses

Most Humble and Most

Obedient Servant.

1 Approval.

2 Hurrah (*OED*).

THE
Introduction
Containing a farther
Perswasive
to the
LADIES
To endeavour the
Improvement of their Minds

Did the Author of the former Essay towards th' Improvement of the Ladies consult her own Reputation only, she wou'd not hazard it once more, by treating on so nice a Subject in a Curious and Censorious Age, but content herself with the favourable reception which the good natur'd part of the World were pleased to afford to her first Essay.[1] It is not unusual she knows for Writers to mind no more than their own Credit, to be pleas'd if they can make a handsom florish, get a Name amongst the Authors, come off with but a little Censure and some Commendations. Or if there are a few generous Souls who are got above the Hope or Fear of vulgar breath, who don't much regard that Applause which is dispenc'd more commonly by Fancy or Passion than by Judgment; they rest satisfied however in a good Intention, and comfort themselves that they've endeavour'd the Reformation of the Age, let those look to't who will not follow their Advices. But give her leave to profess, that as she is very indifferent what the Critics say, if the Ladies receive any Advantage by her attempts to serve them, so it will give her the greatest uneasiness if having prov'd that they are capable of the best things, she can't perswade to a pursuit of them. It were more to her satisfaction to find her Project condemn'd as foolish and impertinent, than to find it receiv'd with some Approbation, and yet no body endeavouring to put it in Practice. Since the former wou'd only reproach her own Understanding, but the latter is a shame to Mankind, as being a plain sign that 'tho they discern and commend what is Good, they have not the Vertue and Courage to Act accordingly.

And can you Ladies deny her so cheap a Reward for all the Good will she bears you, as the Pleasure of seeing you Wise and Happy? Can you envy her the Joy of assisting you at *Your*

---

1 Clearly the reception of the first part of *A Serious Proposal* was not entirely good natured. Pagination will be given for the 1694 edn and this edn.

Triumphs? for if ever she contend for Laurels it shall be only to lay them at the Ladies feet. Why won't you begin to think, and no longer dream away your Time in a wretched incogitancy?[1] Why does not a generous Emulation fire your hearts and inspire you with Noble and Becoming Resentments? The Men of Equity are so just as to confess the errors which the Proud and Inconsiderate had imbib'd to your prejudice, and that if you allow them the preference in Ingenuity, it is not because you *must* but because you *will*. Can you be in Love with servitude and folly? Can you dote on a mean, ignorant and ignoble Life? An Ingenious Woman is no Prodigy to be star'd on, for you have it in your power to inform the World, that you can every one of you be so, if you please your selves. It is not enough to wish and to would it, or t'afford a faint Encomium upon what you pretend is beyond your Power; Imitation is the heartiest Praise you can give, and is a Debt which Justice requires to be paid to every worthy Action. What Sentiments were fit to be rais'd in you to day ought to remain to morrow, and the best Commendation you can bestow on a Book is immediately to put it in Practice; otherwise you become self-condemn'd, your Judgment reproaches your Actions, and you *live* a contradiction to your selves. If you *approve*, Why don't you *follow*? And if you *Wish*, Why shou'd you not *Endeavour*? especially since that wou'd reduce your Wishes to Act, and make you of Well-wishers to Vertue and Good sense, become glorious Examples of them.

And pray what is't that hinders you? The singularity of the Matter? Are you afraid of being out of the ordinary way and therefore admir'd and gaz'd at? Admiration does not use to be uneasy to our Sex; a great many Vanities might be spar'd if we consulted only our own conveniency and not other peoples Eyes and Sentiments: And why shou'd that which usually recommends a trifling Dress, deter us from a real Ornament? Is't not as fine to be first in this as well as any other Fashion? Singularity is indeed to be avoided except in matters of importance, in such a case Why shou'd not we assert our Liberty, and not suffer every Trifler to impose a Yoke of Impertinent Customs on us? She who forsakes the Path to which Reason directs is much to blame, but she shall never do any thing Praiseworthy and excellent who is not got above unjust Censures, and too steady and well resolv'd to be sham'd from her Duty by the empty Laughter of such as have nothing but airy Noise and Con-

---

1 Want of thought or reflection (*OED*).

fidence to recommend them. Firmness and strength of Mind will carry us thro all these little persecutions, which may create us some uneasiness for a while, but will afterwards end in our Glory and Triumph.

Is it the difficulty of attaining the Bravery of the Mind, the Labour and Cost that keeps you from making a purchase of it? Certainly they who spare neither Money nor Pains t'obtain a gay outside and make a splendid appearance, who can get over so many difficulties, rack their brains, lay out their time and thoughts in contriving, stretch their Relations Purses in procuring, nay and rob the very Poor, to whom the Overplus of a full Estate, after the owners Necessaries and decent Conveniences according to her Quality are supplied, is certainly due, they who can surmount so many difficulties, cannot have the face to pretend any here. Labour is sweet when there's hope of success, and the thing labour'd after is Beautiful and Desireable: And if Wisdom be not so I know not what is; if it is not worth while to procure such a temper of mind as will make us happy in all Conditions, there's nothing worth our Thoughts and Care, 'tis best to fold our hands with *Solomon's* Sluggard and sleep away the remainder of a useless wretched Life.[1]

And that success will not be wanting to our Endeavours if we heartily use them, was design'd to be evinc'd in the former Essay, and I hope I have not lost my Point, but that the Theory is sufficiently establish'd; and were there but a General Attempt, the Practice wou'd be so visible that I suppose there wou'd remain no more place to dispute it. But this is your Province Ladies: For tho I desire your improvement never so passionately, tho I shou'd have prov'd it feasible with the clearest Demonstration, and most proper for you to set about; yet if you *will* believe it impossible, and upon that or any other prejudice forbear t'attempt it, I'me like to go without my Wishes; my Arguments what ever they may be in themselves, are weak and impertinent to you, because you make them useless and defeat them of the End they aim at. But I hope better things of you; I dare say you understand your own interest too well to neglect it so grossly and have a greater share of sense, whatever some Men affirm, than to be content to be kept any longer under their Tyranny in Igorance and Folly, since it is in your Power to regain your Freedom, if you please but t'endeavour it. I'me unwill-

---

1 Probably a reference to Solomon's exhortations against idleness in Proverbs, 6,9: "How long wilt thou sleepe, O sluggard?"

ing to believe there are any among you who are obstinately bent against what is praise-worthy in themselves, and Envy or Detract from it in others; who won't allow any of their Sex a capacity to write Sense, because they want it, or exert their Spleen where they ought to shew their Kindness or Generous Emulation; who sicken at their Neighbours Vertues, or think anothers Praises a lessening of their Character; or meanly satisfie ill-nature by a dull Malicious Jest at what deserves to be approv'd and imitated. No Ladies, Your Souls are certainly of a better Make and Nobler temper, your Industry is never exerted to pull down others but to rise above them, the only Resentment that arises at your Neighbours Commendations is a harmless blush for your own Idleness in letting them so far outstrip you, and a generous Resolution to repair your former neglects by future diligence; One need not fear offending you by commending an other Lady in your Presence, or that it shou'd be thought an affront or defect in good breeding to give them their lawful Eulogies: You have too just a Sentiment of your own Merit to envy or detract from others, for no Body's addicted to these little Vices but they who are diffident of their own worth; You know very well 'tis infinitely better to *be* good than to *seem* so,[1] and that true Vertue has Beauty enough in her self t'attract our hearts and engage us in her service, tho she were neglected and despis'd by all the World. 'Tis this therefore you endeavour after, 'tis the approbation of GOD and your own Consciences you mainly esteem, which you find most ascertain'd by an humble Charity, and that you never merit Praise so much, because you never make so great a progress in what is truly praise-worthy, as when your own defects are often in your eyes t'excite you to watch against and amend them, and other peoples Vertues continually represented before you in their brightest lustre, to the end you may aspire to equal or surpass them.

I suppose then that you're fill'd with a laudable Ambition to brighten and enlarge your Souls, that the Beauty of your Bodies is but a secondary care, your Dress grows unconcerning, and your Glass is ne're consulted but in such little intervals of time as hang loose between those hours that are destin'd to nobler Employments, you now begin to throw off your old Prejudices and smile on 'em as antiquated Garbs; false Reasoning won't down with you, and glittering Non-sense tho address'd to your selves in the specious appearance of Respect and Kindness, has lost its *haut*

---

1 Astell appeals to the Socratic dictum, "Be what you wish to appear."

goust;[1] Wisdom is thought as better recommendation than Wit, and Piety than a *Bon-mien*;[2] you esteem a Man only as he is an admirer of Vertue, and not barely for that he is yours; Books are now become the finest Ornaments of your Closets and Contemplation the most agreeable Entertainment of your leisure hours; your Friendships are not cemented by Intrigues nor spent in vain Diversions, but in the search of Knowledge, and acquisition of Vertuous Habits, a mutual Love to which was the Origin of 'em; nor are any Friends so acceptable as those who tell you faithfully of your faults and take the properest method to amend 'em. How much better are you entertain'd now your Conversations are pertinent and ingenious, and that Wisdom never fails to make one in your Visits? Solitude is no more insupportable; you've conquered that silly dread of being afraid to be alone, since Innocence is the safest Guard, and no Company can be so desirable as GOD's and his holy Angels conversing with an upright mind; your Devotion is a Rational service, not the repetition of a Set of good words at a certain season; you read and you delight in it, because it informs your Judgments, and furnishes Materials for your thoughts to work on; and you love your Religion and make it your Choice because you understand it; the only Conquest you now design and lay out your care to obtain is over Vice and Prophaness; you study to engage men in the love of true Piety and Goodness, and no farther to be Lovers of your selves than as you are the most amiable and illustrious examples of 'em; you find your Wit has lost nothing of its salt and agreeableness by being employ'd about its proper business, the exposing Folly; your Raillery[3] is not a whit less pleasant for being more Charitable, and you can render Vice as ridiculous as you please, without exposing those unhappy Persons who're guilty of it; your Humour abates not of its innocent gaity now that it is more upon the Guard, for you know very well that true Joy is a sedate and solid thing, a tranquility of mind, not a boisterous and empty flash: Instead of Creditors your doors are fill'd with indigent Petitioners who don't so often go without your Bounty as the other us'd to do without their just demands; nor are you unjust to some under colour of being Charitable to others, and when you

---

1 A seventeenth-century form of *bon gout*, "high flavour" (*OED*).

2 "*Mien*," the English poetic form of French "*mine*," expression, aspect of countenance, look, appearance (*OED*), so "good appearance."

3 Mockery.

give Liberally, give no more than what is lawfully your own. You disdain the base ungenerous Practice of pretending Kindness where you really mean none; and of making a poor Country Lady less instructed in the formalities of the Town than your selves, pay sufficiently for your seeming Civility and kind Entertainment by becoming the Subject of your mirth and diversion as soon as she is gone; but one may now pretty securely relie on your Sincerity, for when this lower sort of Treachery is abhorr'd, there can certainly be no place for that more abominable one of betraying and seducing unwary Innocence. I do not question Ladies but that this is the Practice of the greatest number of you, and would be of all the rest were it not for some little discouragments they meet with, which really are not so great as their own modesty and diffidence of themselves represent 'em. They think they've been bred up in Idleness and Impertinence, and study will be irksome to them, who have never employ'd their mind to any good purpose, and now when they wou'd they want the method of doing it; they know not how to look into their Souls, or if they do, they find so many disorders to be rectified, so many wants to be supplied, that frighted with the difficulty of the work they lay aside the thoughts of undertaking it. They have been barbarously us'd, their Education and greatest Concerns neglected, and Guardians were busied in managing their Fortunes and regulating their Mien; who so their Purse was full and their outside plausible[1] matter'd not much the poverty and narrowness of their minds, have taught them perhaps to repeat their Catechism and a few good Sentences, to read a Chapter and *say* their Prayers, tho perhaps with as little Understanding as a Parrot, and fancied that this was Charm enough to secure them against the temptations of the present world and to waft them to a better; and so thro want of use and by misapplying their Thoughts to trifles and impertinences, they've perhaps almost lost those excellent Capacities which probably were afforded them by nature for the highest things. For such as these I've a world to Kindness and Compassion, I regret their misfortune as much as they can themselves, and suppose they're willing to repair it and very desirous to inform themselves were't not for the shame of confessing their ignorance. But let me intreat them to consider that there's no Ignorance so shameful, no Folly so absurd as that which

---

1 Deserving of applause or approval (obs.) (*OED*). Astell invariably uses the word in this sense.

refuses Instruction, be it upon what account it may. All good Persons will pity not upbraid[1] their former unhappiness, as not being their own but other Peoples fault; whereas they themselves are responsible if they continue it, since that's an Evidence that they are silly and despicable, not because they *cou'd* not, but because they *wou'd* not be better Informed. But where is the shame of being taught? for who is there that does not need it? Alas, Human Knowledge is at best defective, and always progressive, so that she who knows the most has only this advantage, that she has made a little more speed than her Neighbours. And what's the Natural Inference from hence? Not to give out, but to double our diligence; perhaps we may out-strip 'em, as the Penitent often does him who needs no Repentance. The worst that can be is the perishing in a glorious attempt, and tho we shou'd happen to prove successless, 'tis yet worth our while to've had such a noble design. But there's no fear of ill success if we are not wanting to our selves, an honest and laborious mind may perform all things. Indeed an affected Ignorance, a humorous delicacy and niceness which will not speculate a notion for fear of spoiling a look, nor think a serious thought lest she shou'd damp the gaity of her humour; she who is so top full of her outward excellencies, so careful that every look, every motion, every thing about her shou'd appear in Form, as she employs her Thoughts to a very pitiful use, so is she almost past hopes of recovery, at least so long as she continues this humour, and does not grow a little less concern'd for her Body that she may attend her Mind. Our directions are thrown away upon such a temper, 'tis to no purpose to harp to an Ass, or to chant forth our Charms in the Ears of a deaf Adder;[2] but I hope there are none so utterly lost in folly and impertinence: If there are, we can only afford them our Pity for our Advice will do no good.

As for those who are desirous to improve and only want to be assisted and put into the best method of doing it, somewhat was attempted in order to do them that service in the former Essay, in which they may please to remember that having so mov'd

---

1 Allege as a ground for censure (rare); reproach (*OED*).

2 Possibly a reference to Psalm 58: 4-5, which exclaims of the wicked that "Their poyson is like the poyson of a serpent; they are like the deaf adder that stoppeth her eare: which will not hearken to the voice of charmers, charming never so wisely" (Bible, Authorized Version, 1611).

that groundless prejudice against an ingenious Education of the Women, which is founded upon supposition of the impossibility or uselessness of it, and having assign'd the reasons why they are so little improv'd, since they are so capable of improvement, and since tis so necessary that others as well as themselves shou'd endeavour it; which reasons are chiefly Ill-nurture, Custom, loss of time, the want of Retirement, or of knowing how to use it, so that by the disuse of our Faculties we seem to have lost them if we ever had any are sunk into an Animal life wholly taken up with sensible objects; either have no Ideas of the most necessary things or very *false* ones; and run into all those mischiefs which are the natural Consequences of such mismanagements; we then proceeded to propose a Remedy for these Evils, which we affirm'd cou'd hardly be rectified but by erecting a Seminary where Ladies might be duly Educated, and we hope our Proposition was such that all impartial Readers are convinc'd it wou'd answer the Design, that is, tend very much to the real advantage and improvement of the Ladies. In order to which it was in general propos'd to acquaint them with Judicious Authors, give them opportunity of Retirement and Recollection and put them in a way of Ingenious Conversation, whereby they might enlarge their prospect, rectify their false Ideas, form in their Minds adequate conceptions of the End and Dignity of their Natures, not only have the Name and common Principles of Religion floating in their Heads and sometimes running out at their Mouths, but understand the design and meaning of it, and have a just apprehension, a lively sentiment of its Beauties and Excellencies; know wherein the Nature of a true Christian consists; and not only feel Passions, but be able to direct and regulate their Motions; have a true Notion of the Nothingness of Material things and of the reality and substantialness of immaterial, and consequently contemn this present World as it deserves, fixing all their Hopes upon and exerting all their Endeavours to obtain the Glories of the next. But because this was only propos'd in general, and the particular method of effecting it left to the Discretion of those who shou'd Govern and Manage the Seminary, without which we are still of Opinion that the Interest of the Ladies can't be duly serv'd [yet][1] in the mean time till that can be erected and that nothing in our power may be wanting to do them service, we shall attempt to lay down in this second part some more minute Directions, and such as we hope if attended to may be of use to them.

1 "Yet" should be deleted according to Errata list (1697 edn, 298).

The Second part of the Proposal to the Ladies

CHAP. I

Of the Mutual Relation between Ignorance and Vice, and Knowledge and Purity.

What are Ignorance and Vice but Diseases of the Mind contracted in its two principal Faculties the Understanding and Will? And such too as like many Bodily distempers do mutually foment each other. Ignorance disposes to Vice, and Wickedness reciprocally keeps us Ignorant, so that we cannot be free from the one unless we cure the other; the former part of this Proposition has been already shewn,[1] and the latter may easily be made apparent; for as every Plant does Naturally draw such juices towards it as serve for its Nutrition, as every Creature has an aptness to take such courses as tend to its preservation; so Vice that spawn of the Devil, that *Ignis fatuus*[2] which can't subsist but in the dark night of Ignorance, casts forth Vapours and Mists to darken the Soul and eclipse the clear light of Knowledge from her View. And tho a Wicked Man may pretend to Wit, tho he have never so much Acumen and Facetiousness of Humour, yet his Impiety proclaims his Folly; he may have a lively Fancy, an Intriguing Cunning and Contrivance, and so may an Ape or a Fox, who probably if they had but Speech, tho destitute of Reason, wou'd outdo him in his own way; but he wants the Ingenuity of a Man, he's a Fool to all Rational Intents and Purposes. She then who desires a clear Head must have a pure Heart; and she who has the first in any Measure will never allow herself to be deficient in the other. But you will say what degrees of Purity are requisite in order to Knowledge, and how much must we Know to the end we may heartily endeavour to Purify?

---

1 Part I. page 22, *Etc.* – Astell.
Astell's marginal note to *A Serious Proposal, Part I* (1694 edn).

2 Will-o'-the-wisp. See *Oxford Dictionary of Foreign Phrases and Classical Quotations*, 54.

Now in Order to satisfie this demand I consider, That there are certain Notices which we may call the Rudiments of Knowledge, which none who are Rational are without however they came by them. It may happen indeed that a habit of Vice or a long disuse has so obscur'd them that they seem to be extinguish'd but it does only *seem* so, for were they really extinguish'd the person wou'd be no longer Rational, and no better than the Shade and Picture of a Man. Because as Irrational Creatures act only by the Will of him who made them, and according to the Power of that Mechanisme by which they are form'd, so every one who pretends to Reason, who is a Voluntary Agent and therefore Worthy of Praise or Blame, Reward or Punishment, must *Chuse* his Actions and determine his Will to that Choice by some Reasonings or Principles either true or false, and in proportion to this Principles and the Consequences he deduces from them he is to be accounted, if they are Right and Conclusive a Wise Man, if Evil, Rash and Injudicious a Fool. If then it be the property of Rational Creatures, and Essential to their very Natures to Chuse their Actions, and to determine their Wills to that Choice by such Principles and Reasonings as their Understandings are furnish'd with, they who are desirous to be rank'd in that Order of Beings must conduct their Lives by these Measures, begin with their Intellectuals, inform themselves what are the plain and first Principles of Action and Act accordingly.[1]

---

1 This passage of Astell's is a paraphrase of the opening statement of Antoine Arnauld (1612-94), in *Logic, or the Art of Thinking*, and probably of the English translation of 1693 (1-2), which sets out the purpose of Arnauld's educational project:

> There is nothing more worthy of Esteem, than soundess of Judgment, and an exact measure of Wit to discern between truth and falsehood. All the other Faculties of the Mind are of singular use, but exactness of Reason is universally profitable upon all occasions, and in all the employments of Life. For it is not only in the Sciences that it is a difficult thing to discern Truth or Error, but also in all those Affairs and Actions both of the Body and Mind, which are the Subjects of Human Discourse. There is in every one a signal difference, while some are true and some are false; and therefore it belongs to Reason to make the choice. Who chuse aright, are they who are indu'd with an equal poise of Wit; such as make a wrong choice, are they whose Judgments are deprav'd; wherein consists the chiefest and most important Difference between the Faculties of the Understanding.
>
> And therefore it ought to be the most principal Study of a Man to form and shape his Judgment, and to render it the most exact that possible [*sic*] may be; the main aim to which his utmost diligence ought to tend.

By which it appears that there are some degrees of Knowledge necessary before there can be *any* Human Acts, for till we are capable of Chusing our own Actions and directing them by some Principle, tho we Move and Speak and so many such like things, we live not the Life of a Rational Creature but only of an Animal. If it be farther demanded what these Principles are? Not to dispute the Number of 'em here, no body I suppose will deny us one, which is, *That we ought as much as we can to endeavour the Perfecting of our Beings, and that we be as happy as possibly we may*. For this we see is Natural to every Creature of what sort soever, which endeavours to be in as good Condition as its Nature and Circumstances will permit. And now we have got a Principle which one would think were sufficient for the Conduct of our Actions thro the whole Course of our Lives; and so indeed it were, Cou'd we as easily discern, wherein our Happiness consists as 'tis natural to wish and desire it. But herein lies our great mistake and misfortune; for altho we all pursue the same end, yet the means we take to obtain it are Indefinite: There needs no other Proof of this than the looking abroad into the World, which will convince us of the Truth and raise our Wonder at the absurdity, that Creatures of the same Make shou'd take not only so many different, but every contrary Ways to accomplish the same End! We all agree that its fit to be as Happy as we can, and we need no Instructor to teach us this Knowledge, 'tis born with us, and is inseparable from our Being, but we very much need to be Inform'd what is the true Way to Happiness. When the Will comes to ask the Understanding this Question, What must I do to fill up my Vacuities, to accomplish my Nature? Our Reason is at first too weak, and afterwards too often too much sophisticated to return a proper Answer, tho it be the most important concern of our Lives, for according as the Understanding replies to it so is the Moral Conduct of the Will, pure and right if the first be well Inform'd irregular and vitious if the other be weak and deluded. Indeed our power of Willing exerts it self much

---

Antoine Arnauld was born in Paris, the twentieth child of Antoine Arnauld, a lawyer who was distinguished for his powerful and successful defense of the University of Paris against the Jesuits in 1594. His family formed the nucleus of the sect of Jansenists of whom the young Antoine became a leader and literary defender. His treatise *On True and False Ideas* (1683) was a refutation of Malebranche's *Search After Truth* (1678) and its thesis "that we see all things in God." (See Moyer, *Who Was Who in Church History*.)

sooner than that Rational Faculty which is to Govern it, and therefore t'will either be left to its own range, or to the Reason of another to direct it; whence it comes that we generally take that Course in our search after Happiness, which Education, Example or Custom puts us in, and, tho not always, yet most commonly, we tast of our first seasoning; which shou'd teach us to take all the care we can that it be Good, and likewise that how Good soever it appear, we be not too much Wedded to and biass'd by it. Well then, the first light of our Understanding must be borrow'd, we must take it on trust till we're furnish'd with a Stock of our own, which we cannot long be without if we do but employ what was lent us in the purifying of our Will, for as this grows more regular the other will enlarge, if it clear up, that will brighten and shine forth with diffusive Rays.

Indeed if we search to the bottom I believe we shall find, that the Corruption of the Heart contributes *more* to the Cloudiness of the Head, than the Clearness of our Light does to the regularity of our Affections, and 'tis oftner seen that our vitious Inclinations keep us Ignorant, than that our Knowledge makes us Good. For it must be confess'd that Purity is not *always* the product of Knowledge; tho the Understanding be appointed by the Author of Nature to direct and Govern the Will, yet many times it's headstrong and Rebellious Subject rushes on precipitately, [not only] without[, but against] its directions.[1] When a Truth comes thwart our Passions, when it dares contradict our mistaken Pleasures and supposed Interests, let the Light shine never so clear we shut our Eyes against it, will not be convinced not because there's any want of Evidence, but because we're *unwilling* to Obey. This is the Rise of all that Infidelity that appears in the World; it is not the Head but the Heart that is the Seat of Atheism. No Man without a brow of Brass, and an Impudence as strong as his Arguments are weak, cou'd demur to the convincing Proofs of Christianity, had not he contracted such diseases in his Passions as make him believe 'tis his Interest to oppose *those* that he may gratify *these*. Yet this is no Objection against what we have been proving, it rather confirms what was said concerning the mutual Relation between the Understanding and the Will, and shews how necessary it is to take care of both, if we wou'd improve and advance either.

---

1 Material in square brackets indicated as requiring to be deleted in the Errata list, 298.

Where we must begin.[1] The result of all then, and what gives a satisfactory Answer to the Question where we must begin is this; that some Clearness of Head, some lower degrees of Knowledge, so much at least as will put us on endeavouring after more, is necessary to th'obtaining Purity of Heart. For tho some Persons whom we vulgarly call Ignorant may be honest and Vertuous, yet they are not so in these particulars in which they are Ignorant, but their Integrity in Practising what they know, tho it be but little, causes us to overlook that wherein they Ignorantly transgress. But then any eminent degree of Knowledge, especially of Mortal and Divine Knowledge, which is most excellent because most necessary and useful, can never be obtain'd without considerable degrees of Purity: And afterwards when we have procur'd a competent measure of both, they mutually assist each other; the more Pure we are the clearer will our Knowledge be, and the more we Know, the more we shall Purify. Accordingly therefore we shall first apply our selves to the Understanding, endeavouring to inform and put it right, and in the next place address to the Will, when we have touch'd upon a few Preliminaries and endeavour'd to remove some Obstructions that are prejudicial to both.

CHAP. II

Containing some Preliminaries. As 1. The removing of Sloth and stupid Indifferency. II. Prejudices arising. (1.) From Authority, Education and Custom. (2.) From Irregular Self-Love, and Pride. How to cure our Prejudices. Some Remarks upon Change of Opinions, Novelty and the Authority of the Church. III. To arm our selves with Courage and Patient Perseverance against (1.) The Censures of ill People, and (2.) our own Indocility. IV. To propose a Right End.

§I. The first thing I shall advise against is Sloth, and what may be joyn'd with it a stupid Indifference to any thing that is excellent; shall I call it Contentedness with our Condition how low and imperfect soever it be? I will not abuse the Word so much, 'tis rather an ungenerous inglorious Laziness, we doze on in a Circle with our Neighbours, and so we get but Company and Idleness enough, we consider not for what we were made, and what the Condition of our present State requires. And we think our selves

---

1 This instruction is given as a marginal note in Astell's text.

good humble Creatures for this, who busy not our Heads with what's out of our Sphere and was never design'd for us, but acquiesce honestly and contentedly in such Employments as the generality of Women have in all Ages been engaged in; for why shou'd we think so well of our selves as to fancy we can be wiser and better than those who have gone before? They went to Heav'n no doubt, and we hope that by treading in their steps we likewise in due time may come there. And why should we give our selves any farther trouble? The lowest degree of Bliss in that happy place is more than we deserve, and truly we have too much Humility and Modesty to be Ambitious of a higher.

Thus we hide our faults under the borrowed name of Vertue; an old device taught us by the Enemy of our Souls, and by which he has often deceiv'd us. But 'tis all mistake and nonsense to hope to get to Heaven if we stint our Endeavours and care for no more but just to get there. For what's at the bottom of this pretended humble temper? No real love to GOD and longing to enjoy him, no appetite for Heaven, but since we must go thither or to Hell when we quit this dear beloved World, a taking up with that as the more tolerable place. Had we indeed any true Idea of the Life to come, did we but fix our Eyes and Thoughts in the Contemplation of that unconceivable Blessedness, 'twould be impossible not to desire it with the warmest vigor, not to be Ambitious of all we are able to attain. For pray wherein do the Joys of Heaven conflict, but in the Fruition of GOD the Only and All satisfying Good? and how can we Enjoy Him but by Loving him? And is it not the property of that Passion to think it can never Enjoy enough but still to thirst for more? How then can we Love GOD if we do not Long and Labour for the *fullest* Enjoyment of him? And if we do not Love Him how are we like to Enjoy Him in *any* the *least* Degree? He needs neither our Services nor our Company, he loses nothing of His Happiness, tho we will not fit our selves to receive those Communications of it He is desirous t'impart to us; and therefore we've no reason to think He will force His Bliss upon us, render those Faculties He has given us needless, and make us Happy how unfit soever, we are for Beatitude. What did we come into the World for? To Eat and to Drink and to pursue the little Impertinences of this Life? Surely no, our Wise Creator has Nobler Ends whatever we have; He sent us hither to pass our Probation, to Prepare our selves and be Candidates for Eternal Happiness in a better. And how shall this be done but by Labour and Industry? A Labour indeed, but such as carried its Reward with it, besides what it is entituled to hereafter.

The Truth is, that the Condition of our Present State is such, that we can't do *any* thing, much less what's Great and Excellent without some Pain and Weariness of the Flesh; even our very Pleasures are accompanied with Pain, nor wou'd they relish without it, this is the Sauce that recommends them. And why then shall we be averse to the taking a little Pains in that Case only in which 'twill be worth our while? A Title, an Estate, or Place, can neither be got nor kept without some difficulty and trouble; an Amour, any even a paltry Dress can't be manag'd without some Thought and Concern, and are our Minds the only thing that do not need, or not deserve them? Has our Bountiful Lord set no limits to our Happiness but the Capacity of our Nature, and shall we set less, and not strive to extend our Capacities to their utmost reach? Has the obliging Son of GOD thought no difficulties too mighty, no Pain too great to undergo for the Love of us, and shall we be so disingenuous[1] and ungrateful as to think a few hours Solitude, a little Meditation and Watchfulness too much to return to his Love? No certainly, we cannot have such narrow groveling hearts; no we are all on Fire, and only want to know wherein to employ our Activity, and how to manage it to the best advantage, which if we wou'd do we must in the next place,

§II. Disengage our selves from all our former Prejudices, from our Opinion of Names, Authorities, Customs and the like, not give credit to any thing any longer because we have once believ'd it, but because it carries clear and uncontested Evidence along with it. I shou'd think there needed no more to persuade us to this, than a consideration of the mischiefs these Prejudices do us. These are the grand hindrance in our search after Truth; these dispose us for the reception of Error, and when we have imbib'd confirm us in it; Contract our Souls and shorten our views, hinder the free range of our Thoughts and confine them only to that particular track which these have taken, and in a word, erect a Tyranny over our free born Souls, whilst they suffer nothing to pass for True that has not been stampt at their

1 Insincere, morally fraudulent (*OED*).

own Mint.[1] But this is not all their mischief, they are really the root of Scepticism; for when we have taken up an Opinion of weak Grounds and stifly adher'd to it, coming afterwards by some chance or other to be convinced of its falseness, the same disposition which induc'd us to receive the Premises without Reason, now inclines us to draw as false a Conclusion from them; and because we seem'd once well assur'd of what now appears to have no thing in't to make us so, therefore we fancy there's nothing certain that all our Notions are but Probabilities, which stand or fall according to the Ingenuity of their Managers, and so from an unreasonable Obstinancy we pass on to as unreasonable a Levity; so smooth is the transition from believing too easily and too much, to the belief of just nothing at all.

But pray, where's the force of this Argument, "This is true because such a Person or such a Number of Men have said it. Or, which commonly weighs more, because I my self, the dear Idol of my own Heart have sometimes embrac'd and perhaps very zealously maintain'd it?"[2] Were we to Poll for Truth,[3] or were our own particular Opinions th' Infallible Standard of it, there were reason to subscribe to the Sentiments[4] of the *Many*, or to be tenacious of our *Own*. But since Truth tho she is bright and ready to reveal her self to all sincere Inquirers, is not often found by the generality of those who pretend to seek after her, Interest, Applause, or some other little sordid Passion, being real-

---

1 This argument, that the very men who press for Liberty exempt themselves from its constraints on the exercise of their power (at home), is an important anticipation of the argument mounted against the social contract theory of "Great *L—k* in his *Two Discourses of Government*" by Charles Leslie in 1703 and by Astell in her famous 1706 Preface to *Reflections upon Marriage*. Debate over the reception of Locke's anonymously published *Two Treatises of Government* (1690) has never given Astell her due. Not only is her critique more trenchant than that of Leslie's, published in the Supplement (4-7) to his *The New Association, Part II* (London, 1703), but it is earlier by two counts, having been introduced in the body of the text of *Reflections upon Marriage* (London, 1700, 29, 32, 38-41, 92-95), as well. (See 1706/1996 edns, 27/46, 31/48, 36-41/51-54, 87-92/76-80.)

2 This is clearly a rhetorical question of Astell's own devising.

3 "To plunder by or as by excessive taxation; to pillage, rob, fleece, strip, to despoil; to practise extortion, commit depredations" (obs.) (*OED*).

4 Astell plays on the now obsolete meaning, personal experience, one's own feeling, sensation (*OED*), to refer specifically to Lockean sensationalist psychology.

ly the Mistress they court, whilst she (like Religion in another Case) is made use of for a Stale[1] to carry on the Design the better; since we're commonly too much under the power of Inordinate Affections to have our Understandings always clear and our Judgments certain, are too rash, too precipitate not to need the assistance of a calmer thought, a more serious review; Reason wills that we shou'd think again, and not form our Conclusions or fix our foot till we can honestly say, that we have with our Prejudice or Prepossession view'd the matter in Debate on all sides, seen it in every light, have no bias to encline us either way, but are only determined by Truth it self, shining brightly in our eyes, and not permitting us to resist the force and Evidence it carries. This I'me sure is what Rational Creatures ought to do, what's then the Reason that they do't not?

Laziness and Idleness in the first place; Thinking is a pain to those who have disus'd it, they will not be at the trouble of carrying on a thought, of pursuing a Meditation till it leads them into the confines of Truth, much less till it puts 'em in possession of her. 'Tis an easier way to follow on in a beaten road, than to launch out into the main Ocean, tho it be in order to the making of new Discoveries; they therefore who would be thought knowing without taking too much pains to be so, suppose 'tis enough to go on in their Fore-fathers steps, to say as they say, and hope they shall get as much Reputation by it as those who have gone before.

Again Self-love,[2] an excellent Principle when true, but the

---

1 Probably used by Astell in the legal sense of a claim or demand that has been allowed to lie dormant for an unreasonable length of time. But undoubtedly she plays on the meaning, when used of a bachelor or spinster, as past the prime, or fitting season for marriage (*OED*).

2 Astell uses the term made famous by Pierre Nicole (1625-95) in a theory of the passions which distinquished between healthy self-love, *amour-de-soi*, and a form of self-love that was destructive, *amour propre*, based on pride and vanity. Astell, who makes much of the distinction in this work, follows Nicole, like Arnauld a Jansenist and member of the Port Royal school, of which his aunt, Marie de Agnes Suireau, had been for a short time Abbess. Although only a cleric in minor orders, Nicole, like Arnauld, with whom he worked in close cooperation, worked as a general editor and advocate for the school, assisting in the publication of Pascal's *Provincial Letters* (1656), which he translated into Latin pseudonymously in 1658. Nicole's most famous work, in which the theory of true and false passions appears, the 14-volume *Essais de morale*, was published from 1671 on. The first four volumes were translated into English in the 1680's by a "Person of Quality," generally believed to have been John Locke. (See *Encyclopaedia Britannica*, 11th edn, vol. 19, 663.)

worst and most mischievous when mistaken, disposes us to be retentive of our Prejudices and Errors, especially when it is joyn'd as most commonly it is with Pride and Conceitedness. The Condition of our present State (as was said before) in which we feel the force of our Passions e're we discern the strength of our Reason, necessitates us to take up with such Principles and Reasonings to direct and determine these Passions as we happen to meet with, tho probably they are far from being just ones, and are such as Education or Accident not right Reason disposes us to; and being inur'd[1] and habituated to these, we at last take them for our own, for parts of our dear beloved selves, and are as unwilling to be divorced from them as we wou'd be to part with a Hand or an Eye or any the most useful Member. Whoever talks contrary to these receiv'd Notions seems to banter us, to persuade us out of our very Senses, and does that which our Pride cannot bear, he supposes we've been all along deceiv'd and must begin anew: We therefore instead of depositing[2] our old Errors, fish about for Arguments to defend 'em, and do not raise Hypotheses on the Discoveries we have made of Truth, but search for Probabilities to maintain our Hypotheses. And what's the result of all this? Having set out in a wrong way we're resolved to persist in it, we stumble in the dark and quarrel with those who wou'd lead us out of it?

But is there no Remedy for this disorder, since we hope that All are not irrecoverably lost, tho too many are so invellop'd in Prejudice that there's little probability of disengaging them? Why really the best that I can think of at present is, to Resolve to be Industrious, and to think no Pains too much to purchase Truth; to consider that our Forefathers were Men of like Passions with us, and are therefore not to be Credited on the score of Authority but of Reason; to remember likewise our own Infirmity, the shortness of our Views, and the bias, which our Passions and secular Interests give us; generously to disengage our selves from the deceptions of sense, from all sinister and little Designs, and honestly to search after Truth for no other End but the Glory of GOD, by the accomplishing of our Own and our Neighbours Minds, and when we have humbly implor'd as now we may very well hope for the Divine Assistance, that the Father of Lights will shine upon us, and that He who is *the Way, the Truth and the Life* will lead us in to all

---

1 Accustomed, habituated (*OED*).

2 Laying them up for safe-keeping (*OED*).

Truth; why then we shou'd do well to take notice, That it is of no great consequence to us what our old Opinions are any farther than as we persist in 'em; that there's not necessity that they shou'd be true, but 'tis highly necessary we shou'd fix on what is so; therefore these also must be made to pass the Scrutiny and be cashier'd if they stand not the Test of a Severe Examination and sound Reason.[1]

'Tis a great mistake to fancy it a reproach to change our Sentiments, the infamy lies on their side who wilfully and unreasonably adhere to 'em. Not but that it is mean and shameful to be ever on the tip-toe, and indeed to change in any Case where pure and disinterest'd Reason does not oblige us to it. To be once willing to alter our sentiments if there be just occasion for 't, wou'd for ever after secure us from Changing, to which the Precipitate and Obstinate are most liable; whereas such as suspend their Judgments till after a Sufficient Examination and Weighing of all things they see cause to fix them, do seldom Change, because they can hardly meet with any Reason to do so; and indeed whatever may be the Character of a Wit, Stay'dness[2] and Deliberation is that of a Wise Person.

But as there is an extream on one hand in being too resolutely bent on our Old Opinions, so is there on the other in inordinately thirsting after Novelty. An Opinion is neither better nor worse for being Old or New, the Truth of it is the only thing considerable; tho properly speaking all Truth is Antient, as being from Eternity in the Divine Ideas, 'tis only New in respect of our Discoveries. If we go about to assign a Reason for this insatiable desire of Novelty, I know not how to find a better than our Credulity and easy assent to things inevident. Truth being the proper Object of the Understanding it does naturally search after it, and tho this search will never wholly cease, because our Understandings are

---

1 Locke in the *Essay Concerning Human Understanding*, bk 4, ch. 10, §7, argued that those who appeal to an innate idea of God and "out of an over-fondness of that darling invention, cashier, or at least endeavour to invalidate all other arguments," choose "an ill way ... of silencing atheists" and a poor way to establish the truth, "for it is evident, some men have none, and some a worse than none." Edward Stillingfleet, Bishop of Worcester (1635-99), fastened on the claim, as reported by Locke in the his first *Letter to the Bishop of Worcester*, dated Jan 7, 1696/7 (see John Locke, *Works*, 1823 edn, vol. 3, 52).

2 Steadfastness (archaic).

more capacious than our Discoveries, and the view of one Truth is but a Preparative[1] to look farther; yet had we clear and certain Evidence for our Conclusions, tho that wou'd not end our Inquiries, it wou'd however satisfy us, so far at least as they have gone. Whereas on the contrary your hunters after Novelty are commonly never satisfied, they pull down today what they had built up yesterday, and Why? But because they concluded too soon? and their Novel Hypothesis is founded on Fancy or Passion, or any thing rather than Right Reason.

But when I speak of the little deference that is to be given to Names, Authorities, and receiv'd Opinions, I extend it no farther than to matters purely Philosophical to mere Humane Truths, and do not design any Prejudice to the Authority of the Church which is of different consideration. For those it be necessary even in this Case, to deposite[2] whatever may look like a Prejudice, arising from that particular way of Worship, whereby that Communication in which we've been Educated is distinguish'd from all other Christians, yet as to the Substantials of Faith and Practice, tho every one be allow'd to Examine, for they will bear the Test, yet it is not fit that he shou'd draw Conclusions, contrary to what has been already determin'd by the Catholick Church,[3] or even by that particular Church of which he is a Member, unless where it does plainly and evidently contradict that sense of Holy Scripture which has been receiv'd by the Church Universal. Nor is this a giving up our selves to Authority barely as such, 'tis only a modest deference to Truth, Philosophical Truths are not open to every Inquirer, an elevated Genious and great application of Mind is requir'd to find them out, nor are they of that importance but that Men may give Scope to their Thoughts, and very often think, tho indeed unreasonably, that they're oblig'd in point of Honour to defend their own Hypotheses. But the Articles of our Faith and the great Principles of Christian Morality are of another Nature, GOD *wou'd*

1 Serving as a preparation, introduction; applied to a pre-dinner drink (obsolete) (*OED*). Note that this is the language of Allestree, who speaks of the "needful preparative to Sacred commerce," etc. (*The Ladies Calling*, part 1, §5, 1705 edn, 116).

2 To put to rest (*OED*).

3 Universal Church. Astell subscribed to Church of England doctrine that the Reformation had not disturbed institutional continuity between the medieval Roman Catholic Church and its successor, the national Anglican church.

have all Men to be sav'd and to come the Knowledge of these Truths,[1] tho he did not design 'em all for Philosophers, and therefore they carry a Proof and Evidence suited to the very Vulgar, which he who runs may read, which every one ought to acquiesce in, tho according to their leisure and capacity 'tis fit they inquire why. And being a matter of the highest concern such as our Eternal Happiness or Misery depends on, it may reasonable be suppos'd (tho to the shame of our Folly we sometimes find the contrary) that Men won't play fast and loose in a Business of so vast importance, but that all Christians have as they are oblig'd seriously and fully consider'd it, and especially those who are more peculiarly set apart by the Divine Appointment for the study of Sacred Truths. So that to acquiesce in the Authority of the Church, so far as it is here pleaded for is no more than this, The calling in to our assistance the Judgment and Advice of those whom GOD hath set over us, and consequently whom he assists in a more especial manner to discharge that Function to which he has call'd them; and, in such disputable points as we're not able to determine for our selves, a quiet submission to the Voice of our Guides, whom Modesty will incline us to think have greater Abilities and Assistances, as well as more Time and Opportunity to find out the Truth than we.

As Prejudice fetters the Understanding so does Custom manacle the Will, which scarce knows how to divert from a Track which the generality around it take, and to which it has it self been habituated. It wou'd be too large a digression, to examin thoroughly a Subject so fit to be consider'd being it is the root of very much Evil, the last refuge of Vice where it fortifies it self when driven from all other retreats We shall therefore forbear to enquire from what mistakes it draws its force, what Considerations are proper to disarm it of its power, and what else might be of use to deliver us from its Slavery, and only remark; That tho great deference is to be paid to the Ways and Usages of the Wise and Good, yet considering that these are the least number of Mankind, 'tis the Croud who will make the Mode,[2] and consequently it will be as absurd as they are: Therefore Custom cannot Authorise a Practice if Reason Condemns it, the following a Multitude is no excuse for the doing

---

1 This is the text of much of the Christian literature of instruction and devotion which Astell cites, especially the works by Allestree, *The Ladies Calling* and *The Gentleman's Calling*.

2 Fashion.

of Evil. None but the Weak and Inconsiderable[1] swim down with the Torrent, brave Spirits delight to stem the Tide, they know no Conquest so Glorious, because none so difficult, as that which is obtain'd over foolish and ill-grounded Maxims and sinful Customs; What wou'd they not do to restore Mankind to their Lawful Liberty, and to pull down this worst of Tyrannies, because it enslaves the very Souls of Men?

§III. But a Generous Resolution and Courageous Industry are not only necessary to enable us to throw off Sloth and to Conquer the Prejudices of Education, Authority and Custom, the same Resolution and Courage which help'd us to this Victory, must secure and continue to us the Fruits of it. We shall have need of Patience and constant Perseverance thro the whole course of our Lives if we mean to prosecute the noble Design we have begun; we must not think the Business is over when we have smooth'd the entrance; there will still be Difficulties, tho no insuperable ones, but such as will wear off by degrees, the greatest uneasiness being in the first effort. And tho our Progress shou'd not happen to be answerable to our Desires, there's no reason to be discouraged, we shou'd rather be animated by such noble Desires to greater Industry. Where's the Glory of an easy Victory? 'Tis Labour and Cost that inhances the value of every thing. And to the end we may not be discourag'd, 'tis fit that we arm our selves against all Accidents by considerating them before hand. We have the Malice and Industry of many Cunning and Powerful Adversaries, as well as our own indocility to contend with. The grand Enemy of Mankind is very unwilling that they shou'd arrive at that State of Innocence and Perfection from which he fell, and of all the Artifices he makes use of to hinder it, scarce any's more effectual than the mischief he excites us to do one another. What are they employ'd in but his Service who will neither do any thing that's excellent themselves, nor if they could hinder, suffer it to be done by others? Who employ all their little Wit and Pains in Scoffing at such who they say in derision wou'd be wiser than their Neighbours? We must be content to suffer a scornful steer,[2] a parcel of hard Names and a little ridiculing, if we're Resolv'd to do such things as do not deserve 'em. Dogs will bark at the Moon, and perhaps for no other reason but because she

---

1 Insignificant.

2 Piece of advice (*OED*).

is out of their reach, elevated above them. But the Author of our Nature to whom all the Inconveniences we are liable to in this Earthly Pilgrimage are fully known, has endow'd us with Principles sufficient to carry us safely thro them all, if we will but observe and make use of 'em. One of these is *Generosity*, which (so long as we keep it from degenerating into Pride) is of admirable advantage to us in this matter. It was not fit that Creatures capable of and made for Society, shou'd be wholly Independent, or Indifferent to each others Esteem and Commendation; nor was it convenient considering how seldom these are justly distributed, that they shou'd too much regard and depend on them. It was requisite therefore that a desire of our Neighbours Good Opinion shou'd be implanted in our Natures to the end we might be excited to do such things as deserve it, and yet withall a Generous neglect of it, if they unjustly withheld it where it was due. There's so little reason that we shou'd be discourag'd from what is truly excellent and becoming on account of being Scoft and Laugh'd at for it, that on the contrary this is a new accession to our Glory, we never shine so Illustriously as when we break thro these little Clouds and Oppositions which impotently attempted to obscure our Rays. To be Reproach'd for Welldoing is a higher Encomium, than the loftiest Praises when we do not deserve them: So that let the World think as it list,[1] whilst we are in the pursuit of true Wisdom, our Reputation is secur'd, our Crown is furbishing[2] and tho it do not shine out in this Envious and Ill-natur'd World, it will however, which is infinitely more desirable appear in all its Lustre and Splendor in a better.

And as we disregard the Censures of ill People, so are we patiently to bear with our own backwardness and indocility. There goes a good deal of Time and Pains, of Thought and Watchfulness to the rooting out of ill-habits, to the fortifying our Minds against foolish Customs, and to the making that easie and pleasant which us'd to be irksom to us. But we ought not to be dishearten'd, since 'tis necessary to be done, and we cannot reasonably say 'tis Impossible, till we've attempted and fail'd in't. But then let's attempt it in the most prudent Method, use the properest Means, allow sufficient Time for their Operation and to make the essay: Let's not set about it by fits, or in one or two good Moods, nor expect it will

---

1 Likes.

2 Being polished up, burnished, brightened (archaic) (*OED*).

be done on a sudden, but by degrees and in a proper season, making it our main Design and Business, and then I dare confidently affirm the success will answer the Pains we have spent about it.

§IV. But one thing more, and then I shall go on as well as I can, to lay down what seems to be the best Method for Improvement. Whoever wou'd Act to purpose must propose some End to them selves, and keep it still in their Eye thro' out their whole progress. Life without this is a disproportionate unseemly thing, a confused huddle of broken, contradictory Actions, such as afford us nothing but the being asham'd of 'em. But do we need to be taught our End? One wou'd rather think there were no occasion to mention it, did not Experience daily convince us how many there are who neglect it. What End can Creatures have but their Creators Glory? And did they truly understand their own Happiness 'tis certain they wou'd have no other, since this is the only way of procuring their own Felicity. But it is not enough to have barely an implicit and languid desire of it, 'twere much better to hold it ever in view, and that all our Actions had in their proportion a warm and immediate tendency thither. This wou'd stamp the impression of Holiness upon the most indifferent Action, and without this what is Materially and to all outward appearance very good, is really and truly no better than a specious folly. We are not made for our selves, nor was it ever design'd we shou'd be ador'd and idoliz'd by one another. Our Faculties were given us for Use not Ostentation, not to make a noise in the World, but to be serviceable in it, to declare the Wisdom, Power and Goodness, of that All-Perfect Being from whom we derive *All* our Excellencies, and in whose Service, they ought *Wholly* to be employ'd. Did our Knowlege serve no other purpose than the exalting us in our own Opinion, or in that of our Fellow Creatures, the furnishing us with Materials for a quaint Discourse, an agreeable Conversation, 'twere scarce worth while to be at the trouble of attaining it. But when it enlarges the Capacity of our Minds, gives us nobler ideas of the Majesty, the Grandeur and Glorious Attributes of our adorable Creator, Regulates our Wills and makes us more capable of Imitating and Enjoying him, 'tis then a truly sublime thing, a worthy Object of our Industry: And she who does not make this the End of her Study, spends her Time and Pains to no purpose or to an ill one.

We have no better way of finding out the true End of any thing, than by observing to what Use it is most adapted. Now the Art of

Well-Living, the Study of the Divine Will and Law, that so we may be Conformable to it in all things, is what we're peculiarly fitted for and destin'd to, what ever has not such a Tendency, either Directly or at least Remotely, is besides the purpose. Rational Studies therefore next to GOD's Word bid fairest for our Choice, because they best answer the Design above mention'd. Truths merely Speculative and which have no influence upon Practice, which neither contribute to the good of Soul or Body, are but idle Amusements, an impertinent and criminal wast of Time. To be able to speak many Languages, go give an Historical Account of all Ages Opinions and Authors, to make a florid Harangue, or defend right or wrong the Argument I've undertaken, may give me higher thoughts of my Self but not of GOD,[1] this is the *Knowlege that pufeth up*, in the Words of the Apostle, and seldom leads us to that *Charity which Edifieth.*[2]

And as the Understanding so the Will must be duly directed to its End and Object. Morality is so consonant to the Nature of Man, so adapted to his Happiness, that had not his Understanding been darkn'd by the Fall, and his whole Frame disorder'd and weakned, he wou'd Naturally have practis'd it. And according as he recovers himself, and casts off those Clouds which Eclipse his Reason, so proportionably are his Actions more agreeable to Moral Precepts, and tho we suppose him ignorant of any higher end, he will however do such things as they enjoyn him, to th'intent he may be easy, obtain a good Reputation, and enjoy himself and this World the better. Now were we sure that Reason wou'd always maintain its ground against Passion and Appetite, such an one might be allow'd to be a good Neighbour, a Just Ruler, a plausible Friend or the like, and wou'd well enough discharge the Relative Duties of Society, and do nothing misbecoming the dignity of Human Nature. But considering how weak our Reason is, how unable to maintain its Authority and oppose the incursions of

---

1 Astell waxes eloquent on a theme already introduced in *A Serious Proposal, Part I* (1694 edn, 76-77, see above 78):

> Such a course of Study will neither be too troublesome nor out of the reach of a Female Virtuoso; for it is not intended she shou'd spend her hours in learning *words* but *things*, and therefore no more Languages than are necessary to acquaint her with useful Authors. Nor need she trouble her self in turning over a great number of Books, but take care to understand and digest a few well-chosen and good ones.

2 1 Corinthians, 8: 1.

sense, without the assistance of an inward and Spiritual Sensation[1] to strengthen it, 'tis highly necessary that we use due endeavours to procure a lively relish of our true Good, a Sentiment that will not only Ballance, but if attended to and improv'd, very much outweigh the Pleasures of our Animal Nature. Now this is no otherwise to be obtain'd than by directing the Will in an elicit Act to GOD as its only Good, so that the sole End of all its movements may be to draw near, to acquiesce in and be united to him. For as all Natural Motions are easie and pleasant, so this being the only Natural Motion of the Will must needs be unspeakably delightful to it. Besides that peculiar delectation,[2] which this Fountain of Joy bestows as a Donative,[3] on all who thus sincerely address themselves to him. So that it is not enough to be Morally Good because 'tis most Reputable and Easie, and most for our Pleasure and Interest in the present World, as this will never secure our Duty, so is it too low an End for a Creature capable of Immortality to propose, nothing less than an intire devoting of our selves to the End for which we were made, the Service and Enjoyment of the most amiable and only Good, can keep us Constantly and Uniformly in our Duty, or is a Design that's worthy of us.

CHAP. III

Concerning the Improvement of the Understanding. I. Of the Capacity of the Humane Mind in General. II. Of Particular Capacities. III. The most common Infirmities incident to the Understanding and their Cure. IV. A Natural Logic, And V. Rhetoric propos'd. VI. The Application and Use of our Knowlege.

The perfection of the Understanding consisting in the Clearness and Largness of its view, it improves proportionably as its Ideas become Clearer and more Extensive.[4] But this is not so to be

---

1 Astell's use of "spiritual sensation" suggests that she might endorse the corresponding notion of "spiritual" or "mental substance," under contest in the debate between Malebranche and Arnauld, which in *The Christian Religion* she later rejected.

2 Action of delighting, delight, pleasure (*OED*).

3 Donation, especially of a benefice (*OED*).

4 George Berkeley's extract from *A Serious Proposal, Part II*, in *The Ladies Library* (1714 edn, vol. 1, 447-524) commencing here, comprises almost all of her important ch. 3, with exclusions noted below.

understood as if all sorts of Notices contributed to our Improvement, there are some things which make us no wiser when we know 'em, others which 'tis best to be ignorant of. But that Understanding seems to me the most exalted, which has the Clearest and most Extensive view of such Truths as are suitable to its Capacity, and Necessary or Convenient to be Known in this Present State.[1] For being that we are but Creatures, our Understanding in its greatest Perfection has only a limited excellency. It has indeed a vast extent, and it were not amiss if we tarried a little in the Contemplation of its Powers and Capacities, provided that the Prospect did not make us giddy, that we remember from whom we have receiv'd them, and ballance those lofty Thoughts which a view of our Intellectuals may occasion, with the depressing ones which the

---

1 Astell's *Letters Concerning the Love of God, between the Author of the Proposal to the Ladies and Mr. John Norris* deals with Malebranche's principle, which explains human cognition in terms of receptivity to divine ideas. Astell endorsed the notion, although not without criticism of Norris's conclusions. In *A Serious Proposal, Part I,* she still appears to endorse it. But in *Part II* of 1697 she is less sure, turning instead to Antoine Arnauld of the Port Royal School, a friend-turned-critic of Malebranche. Without doubt her change of heart reflects the devastating attack by Damaris Masham in *Discourse Concerning the Love of God* (1696). It is important to note, however, that the passage under review owes a good deal to the arguments of John Norris's *Reflections upon the Conduct of Human Life* (1690), already cited by Astell as a source in *A Serious Proposal, Part I* (1694 edn, 76, see above, 78). Astell nobly overlooks the fact that Norris's *Reflections* was dedicated to Lady Masham, replete with addresses to "Her Ladyship," whose invective Astell had enjoyed in the interim. She appears to have in mind Norris's argument at §15 (1690 edn, 17-18). Or did she? There are rather specific sounding references to malignant *Reflections* throughout *A Serious Proposal, Part II.* However, in answer to the question "what is it that is perfective of the Understanding," Norris says:

> To the Question then I answer, that the Perfection of the Understanding, as that of the will, is either *Formal* or *Objective.* The *Formal Perfection* of the understanding, as that of the will, is no other than its Exercise or Operation, which is *Thinking* and *Perception*, as that of the other is *Willing* and *Chusing.* According to the vulgar Maxim, that *the Perfection of every thing is its Operation*, which must be understood only the *Formal Perfection.* The *Objective Perfection* of the understanding is *Truth*, as that of the will is *Good.* The Result of these two Perfections joyn'd together is what in the understanding we call *Knowledge*, and what in the will we call *Vertue.*

irregularity of our Morals will suggest, and that we learn from this inspection, how indecorous[1] it is to busy this bright side of us in mean things, seeing it is capable of such noble ones.

Human Nature is indeed a wonderful Composure admirable in its outward structure, but much more excellent in the Beauties of its Inward, and she who considers in whose Image her Soul was Created, and whose Blood was shed to Redeem it, cannot prize it too much, nor forget to pay it her utmost regard. There's nothing in this Material World to be compar'd to 't, all the gay things we dote on, and for which we many times expose our Souls to ruin, are of no consideration in respect of it. They are not the good of the Soul, it's happiness depends not on 'em, but they often deceive and withdraw it from its true Good. It was made for the Contemplation and Enjoyment of its GOD, and all Souls are capable of this tho in a different degree and by measures somewhat different, as we hope will appear from that which follows.

§I. Truth in general is the Object of the Understanding, but all Truths are not equally Evident, because of the Limitation of the Humane Mind, which tho' it can gradually take in many Truths, yet cannot any more than our sight attend to many things at once: And likewise, because GOD has not thought fit to communicate such Ideas to us, as are necessary to the disquisition[2] of some particular Truths. For knowing nothing without us but by the Idea we have of it, and Judging only according to the Relation we find between two or more Ideas when we cannot discover the Truth we search after by Intuition or the immediate comparison of two Ideas, 'tis necessary that we shou'd have a third by which to compare them. But if this middle Idea be wanting, though we have sufficient Evidence of those two, which we wou'd compare, because we have a Clear and Distinct Conception of them, yet we are Ignorant of those Truths which wou'd arise from their Comparison, because we want a third by which to compare them.[3]

---

1 Inappropriate.

2 Exposition.

3 Clear and distinct ideas are a major topic raised by Stillingfleet in terms of "Descartes' general rule of certainty" and in the possibility or impossibility of clear ideas of God, in response to Locke's *Essay Concerning Human Understanding*, bk 4, ch. 4, §10; bk 4, ch. 10, etc. Locke responds in his First Letter to Stillingfleet (Locke, *Works*, 1823 edn, vol. 3).

To give an instance of this in a point of great consequence, and of late very much controverted[1] tho to little purpose, because we take a wrong method, and wou'd make that the Object of Science which is properly the Object of Faith, the Doctrin of the Trinity.[2] Revelation which is but an exaltation and improvement of Reason has told us That the Father is GOD, the Son is GOD, and the Holy Ghost is GOD, and our Idea of the Godhead of any one of these Persons, is as clear as our Idea of any of the other. Both Reason and Revelation assure us that GOD is One Simple Essence, Undivided, and Infinite in all Perfection, this is the Natural Idea which we have of GOD. How then can the Father be GOD, the Son GOD, and the Holy Ghost GOD, when yet there is but One GOD? That these two Propositions are true we are certain, both because GOD who cannot lie has Reveal'd 'em, and because we have as clear an Idea of 'em as it is possible a Finite Mind, shou'd have of an Infinite Nature. But we cannot find out how this should be, by the bare Comparison of these two Ideas without the help of a third by which to compare them. This GOD has not thought fit

---

1 Debated.

2 Stillingfleet entered into an important controversy with Locke over the doctrine of the Trinity in 1696-97, which went to the heart of Locke's epistemology in *An Essay Concerning Human Understanding* (1690). Astell's clear familiarity with this debate gives some indication of the speed with which she was able to digest and respond to philosophical controversy. Locke's *Letter to the Bishop of Worcester* takes up Stillingfleet's objections to Locke on the Trinity as being Unitarian, or asserting God as being one substance and one person. In *An Essay Concerning Human Understanding* (bk 2, ch. 23, §2, 1690 edn, 157-58), which Stillingfleet parodies, Locke had argued that because the Trinity is not accessible to sensation or reflection:

> it is "only an uncertain supposition of we know not what." And therefore it is paralleled, more than once, with the Indian philosopher's "He-knew-not-what"; which supported the tortoise, that supported the elephant, that supported the earth: so substance was found only to support accidents. And that when we talk of substances, we talk like children; who, being asked a question about somewhat which they knew not, readily give this satisfactiory answer, that it is something.

Locke in his *Letter to the Bishop of Worcester* of 1696/97 (1823 edn, 5) stood by his claim, clearly Unitarian and undoubtedly blasphemous to Astell even in the very way it is expressed, comparing the pantheistic god of the Brahmin to the Christian God.

to impart to us, the Prospect it wou'd have given us wou'd have been too dazling, too bright for Mortality to bear, and we ought to acquiesce in the Divine Will. So then, we are well assur'd that these two Propositions are true. *There is but one GOD; And, There are three Persons in the Godhead:* but we know not the *Manner* how these things are. Nor can our acquiescence be thought Unreasonable, nor the Doctrin, we subscribe to be run down as absurd and contradictory by every little warm Disputer and Pretender to Reason, whose Life is perhaps a continual contradiction to it, and he knows little of it besides the Name. For we ought not to think it strange that GOD has folded up his own Nature, not in Darkness, but in an adorable and inaccessible Light, since his Wisdom sees it fit to keep us ignorant of our own. We know and feel the Union between our Soul and Body, but who amongst us sees so clearly, as to find out with Certitude and Exactness, the secret ties which unite two such different Substances,[1] or how they are able to act upon each other? We are conscious of our own Liberty, who ever denies it denies that he is capable of Reward and Punishments, degrades his Nature and makes himself but a more curious piece of Mechanism;[2] and none but Atheists will call in question on the Providence of GOD, or deny that he Governs *All*, even the most Free of all his Creatures.[3] But who can reconcile me these? Or adjust the limits between GOD's Prescience[4] and Mans Free-will? Our Understandings are sufficiently illuminated to lead us to the Fountain of Life and Light, we do or may know enough to fill our Souls with the noblest Conceptions, the humblest Adoration, and the intirest Love of the Author of our Being, and what can we desire farther? If we make so ill a Use of that Knowledge which we have, as to be so far puffed up with it, as to turn it against him

---

1 Discussed by Locke in his first Letter to Stillingfleet, 1823 edn, 8 and 51, with reference to his *Essay Concerning Human Understanding*, bk 4, ch. 4, §18; and again 52-55, Locke referring to his *Essay*, bk 4, ch. 10, §7.

2 Astell intuited the trajectory Lockean sensational psychology took with the "man-machine" theorists, Abbé Étienne de Condillac (1715-80), Claude Adrien Helvétius (1715-71) and Baron Paul Heinrich Dietrich d'Holbach (1723-89), who made of it a mechanistic theory of environmental conditioning.

3 Referring to Locke's assertion about atheists in the *Essay Concerning Human Understanding*, bk 4, ch. 10, §7 (reported by him in the first Letter to Stillingfleet), 1823 edn, 52.

4 God's foreknowledge of actions that lie in the future.

who gave it, how dangerous would it be for us to have more Knowledge, in a State in which we have so little Humility! But if vain Man will pretend to Wisdom, let him first learn to know the length of his own line.

Tho the Human Intellect has a large extent, yet being limited as we have already said, this Limitation is the Cause of those different Modes of Thinking, which for distinction sake we call Faith, Science and Opinion. For in this present and imperfect State in which we know not any thing by Intuition, or [immediate][1] View, except a few first Principles which we call Self-evident, the most of our Knowlege is acquir'd by Reasoning and Deduction: And these three Modes of Understanding, Faith, Science and Opinion are no otherwise distinguish'd, than by the different degrees of Clearness and Evidence in the Premises from whence the Conclusion is drawn.

Knowlege in a proper and restricted Sense and as appropriated to Science, signifies that clear Perception which is follow'd by a firm assent to Conclusions rightly drawn from Premises of which we have clear and distinct Ideas. Which Premises or Principles must be so clear and Evident, that supposing us reasonable Creatures, and free from Prejudices and Passions, (which for the time they predominate as good as deprive us of our Reason) we cannot withhold our assent from them without manifest violence to our Reason.

But if the Nature of the thing be such as that it admits of no undoubted[2] Premises to argue from, or at least we don't at present know of any, or that the Conclusion does not so necessarily follow as to give a perfect satisfaction to the Mind and to free it from all hesitation, that which we think of it is then call'd Opinion.

Again, If the Medium[3] we make use of to prove the Proposition be Authority, the Conclusion which we draw from it is said to be Believ'd; This is what we call Faith, and when the Authority is GOD's a Divine Faith.

Moral Certainty is a Species of Knowlege whose Proofs are of a compounded Nature, in part resembling those which belong to Science, and partly those of Faith. We do not make the whole

1 "immediate" to be deleted according to Errata list, 298.

2 Certain.

3 Middle term.

Process our selves, but depend on another for the *immediate* Proof, but we our selves deduce the *Mediate* from Circumstances and Principles as Certain and almost as Evident as those of Science, and which lead us to the immediate Proofs and make it unreasonable to doubt of 'em. Indeed we not seldom deceive our selves in this matter, by inclining alternately to both extremes. Some times we reject Truths which are Morally Certain as Conjectural and Probable only, because they have not a Physical and Mathematical Certainty, which they are incapable of. At another time we embrace the slightest Conjectures and any thing that looks with Probability, as moral Certainties and real Verities, if Fancy, Passion or Interest recommend them; so ready are we to be determin'd by these rather than by solid Reason.

In this enumeration of the several ways of Knowing. I have not reckon'd the Senses, in regard that we're more properly said to be *Conscious* of than to *Know* such things as we perceive by Sensation.[1] And also because that Light which we suppose to be let into our Ideas by our Senses is indeed very dim and fallacious, and not to be relied on till it has past the Test of Reason; neither do I think there's any Mode of Knowlege which mayn't be reduc'd to those already mentioned.

Now tho there's a great difference between Opinion and Science, true Science being immutable but Opinion variable and uncertain, yet there is not such a difference between Faith and Science as is usually suppos'd. The difference consists not in the Certainty but in the way of Proof; the Objects of Faith are as Rationally and as Firmly Prov'd as the Objects of Science, tho by another way. As Science Demonstrates things that are *Seen*, so Faith is the Evidence of such as are *Not Seen*. And he who rejects the Evidence of Faith in such things as belong to its Cognizance,[2] is as unreasonable as he who denies Propositions in Geometry that are prov'd with Mathematical exactness.

There's nothing true which is not in itself demonstrable, or which we should not pronounce to be true had we a Clear and Intuitive View of it. But as was said above we see very few things by Intuition, neither are we furnish'd with Mediums to make the

---

1 This is an important objection to Locke's notion of ideas as a mental reflex produced by sensations. The distinction between consciousness, or unreflected knowledge, and self-consciousness, raised by the Cartesian *cogito*, was only beginning to be investigated.

2 Understanding.

Process our selves in Demonstrating all Truths, and therefore there are some Truths which we must either be totally ignorant of or else receive them on the Testimony of another Person, to whose Understanding they are clear and manifest tho not to ours. And if this Person be one who can neither be Deceiv'd nor Deceive, we're as certain of those Conclusions which we prove by his Authority, as we're of those we demonstrate by our own Reason; nay more Certain, by how much his Reason is more Comprehensive and Infallible than our own.

Science is the following the Process our Selves upon Clear and Evident Principles; Faith is a Dependance on the Credit of another, in such matters as are out of our View. And when we have very good Reason to submit to the Testimony of the Person we Believe, Faith as is Firm, and those Truths it discovers to us as truly Intelligible, and as strongly Prov'd in their kind as Science.

In a word, as every Sense so every Capacity of the Understanding has its proper Object. The Objects of Science are things within our View, of which we may have Clear and Distinct Ideas, and nothing shou'd be determin'd here without Clearness and Evidence. To be able to repeat any Persons *Dogma* without forming a Distinct Idea of it our selves, is not to Know but to remember; and to have a Confuse Indeterminate Idea is to Conjecture not to Understand.

The Objects of Faith are as Certain and as truly Intelligible in themselves as those of Science, as has been said already, only we become persuaded of the Truth of them by another Method, we do not *See* them so clearly and distinctly as to be unable to disbelieve them. Faith has a mixture of the Will that it may be rewardable, for who will thank us for giving our Assent where it was impossible to withold it? Faith then may be said to be a sort of Knowlege capable of Reward, and Men are Infidels not for want of Conviction, but thro an *unwillingness* to Believe.

But as it is a fault to Believe in matters of Science, where we may expect Demonstration and Evidence, so it is a reproach to our Understanding and a proof of our Disingenuity,[1] to require that sort of Process peculiar to Science, for the Confirmation of such Truths as are not the proper Objects of it. It is as ridiculous as to reject Musick, because we cannot Tast or Smell it, or to deny there is such a thing as Beauty because we do not hear it. He who wou'd

---

1 Lack of frankness, insincerity (*OED*).

See with his Ears and Hear with his Eyes may indeed set up in *Bedlam*[1] for a Man of an extraordinary reach, a Sagacious Person who won't be impos'd on, one who must have more Authentick proofs than his dull Fore-fathers were content with. But Men of dry Reason and a moderate Genius, I suppose will think Nature has done very well in allotting to each Sense its proper employment, and such as these will as readily acknowlege that it is as Honourable for the Soul to Believe what is truly the Object of Faith, as it is for her to Know what is really the Object of her Knowlege. And were we not strangely perverse we shou'd not scruple Divine Authority when we daily submit to Human. Who-ever has not seen *Paris* has nothing but Human Authority to assure him there is such a place, and yet he wou'd be laugh'd at as ridiculous who shou'd call it in question, tho he may as well in this as in another Case pretend that his Informers have designs to serve, intend to impose on him and mock his Credulity. Nay how many of us daily make that a matter of Faith which indeed belongs to Science, by adhering blindly to the Dictates of some famous Philosopher in Physical Truths, the Principles of which we have as much right to examine, and to make deductions from 'em as he had?

To sum up all: We may know enough for all the purposes of Life, enough to busie this active Faculty of Thinking, to employ and entertain the spare Intervals of Time and to keep us from Rust and Idleness, but we must not pretend to fathom all Depths with our short Line, we shou'd be Wise unto Sobriety, and reckon that we know very little if we go about to make our *Own* Reason the Standard of all Truth.[2] It is very certain that nothing is True but what is conformable to Reason, that is to the Divine Reason of which ours is but a short faint Ray, and it is as certain that there are many Truths which Human Reason can-not Comprehend. Therefore to be thoroughly sensible of the Capacity of the Mind, to discern precisely its Bounds and Limits and to direct our Studies and Inquires accordingly, to Know what is to be Known, and to Believe what is to be Believ'd is the property of a Wise person. To be content with too little Knowlege, or to aspire to over-much is equally a fault, to make that use of our Understandings which

---

1 The Hospital of St. Mary of Bethlehem, founded in 1247 and rebuilt in 1676, used as an asylum for the mentally deranged, lent its name to madness or lunacy in general (*OED*).

2 Astell's implicit criticism of Locke.

GOD has Fitted and Design'd them for is the Medium which we ought to take. For the difference between a plow-man and a Doctor does not seem to me to consist in this, That the Business of the one is to search after Knowlege, and that the other has nothing to do with it.[1] No, whoever has a Rational Soul ought surely to employ it about some Truth or other, to procure for it right Ideas, that its Judgments may be true tho its Knowlege be not very extensive. But herein lies the difference, that tho Truth is the Object of every Individual Understanding, yet all are not equally enlarg'd nor able to comprehend so much; and they whose Capacities and Circumstances of Living do not fit 'em for it, lie not under that obligation of extending their view which Persons of a larger reach and greater leisure do. There is indeed often times a mistake in this matter, People who are not fit will be puzling their heads to little purpose, and those who are prove Slothful and decline the trouble; and thus it will be if we do not thoroughly understand our selves, but suffer Pride or Ease to make the estimate.

§II. It is therefore very fit that after we have consider'd the Capacity of the Understanding in general, we shou'd descend to the view of our own particular, observing the bent and turn of our own Minds, which way our Genius lies and to what it is most inclin'd. I see no reason why there may not be as great a variety in Minds as there is in Faces, that the Soul as well as the [Body][2] may not have something in it to distinguish it, not only from all other Intelligent Natures but even from those of its own kind. There are different proportions in faces which recommend them to some Eyes sooner than to others, and tho *All* Truth is amiable to a Reasonable Mind, and proper to employ it, yet why may there not be some particular Truths, more agreeable to each individual Understanding than others are? Variety gives Beauty to the Material World and why not to the Intellectual? We can discern the different Abilities which the Wise Author of all things has endow'd us with, the different Circumstances in which he has plac'd us in ref-

---

1 Locke, in *The Reasonableness of Christianity* (1695 edn, 279), had argued from the impossibility of making "the Day-Labourers and Tradesmen, the Spinsters and Dairy Maids ... perfect Mathematicians," an equal impossibility of perfecting them "in Ethicks" in the Neoplatonist mode. Astell turns the argument against him here.

2 Errata list, 298, indicates Body should be deleted but it is hard to see how it can be and preserve the sense.

erence to this World and the Concerns of an Animal Life, that so we may be mutually useful, and that since each single Person is too limited and confin'd to attend to many, much less to all things, we may receive from each other a reciprocal advantage, and why may we not think he has done the like in respect of Truth? that since it is too much for one, our united Strength shou'd be employ'd in the search of her. Especially since the Divine Being who contains in himself all Reality and Truth is Infinite in Perfection, and therefore shou'd be Infinitely Ador'd and Lov'd; and If Creatures are by their being so uncapable of rendering to their Incomprehensible Creator, an Adoration and Love that's worthy of him, it is but decorous that they shou'd however do as much as they can. All that variety of sublime Truths of Beautiful and Wondrous Objects which surround us, are nothing else but a various display of his unbounded Excellencies, and why shou'd any of 'em pass unobserv'd? Why shou'd not every individual Understanding be in a more especial manner fitted for and employ'd in the disquisition of some particular Truth and Beauty? 'Tis true after all our researchers we can no more sufficiently Know GOD than we can worthily Love him, and are as much unable to find out all his Works as we are his Nature, yet this shou'd only prompt us to exert *All* our Powers and to do our best, since even *that* were too little cou'd we possibly do more. We can never offer to him so much Praise as he deserves, and therefore it is but fit that he shou'd have *All* that Mankind can possibly render him. He is indeed immutable in his own Nature, but those discoveries we daily make of his Operations will always afford us somewhat New and Surprizing, for this All glorious Sun the Author of Life and Light is as inexhaustible a Source of Truth as he is of Joy and Happiness.

If then we are convinced that there's some peculiar Task allotted us, our next business will be to enquire what it is. To know our own Strength and neither to over nor underrate our selves is one of the most material[1] points of Wisdom and which indeed we are most commonly ignorant of, else we shou'd not reach at all, how unable soever we are to attain it, nor make so many successless attempts and be forc'd to come off with that pitiful Apology, *I was mistaken, I did not think it*. But we can scarce duly estimate our Understandings till we have regulated our Wills, reform'd Self-love

1 Germane, material to the issue.

and a train of immortified[1] Passions, which it is not our Business to speak of here, we shall have occasion to do't hereafter. Let it suffice that we remark a frequent Error which these engage us in, that is, an aptness to lessen the Human Mind, to detract from its Grandeur and abridg its Powers when we consider it in General, and as great a forwardness when we look on our selves to extend our Abilities beyond their bounds. Are we conscious of a Defect? the shallowness of Human Reason at large must bear the blame, we Harrangue very excellently on the Ignorance and Vanity of Mankind, and it were well if we rested there, and wou'd forbear to murmur even at our Creator himself for allowing us so scanty a Portion. But if Reason has shon out, dispelling those Clouds which Eclips'd the bright face of Truth, we arrogate all to our selves. *My* Discovery, *My* Hypothesis, the Strength and Clearness of *My* Reasonings, rather than the Truth are what we wou'd expose to view;[2] 'tis that we Idolize our selves and wou'd have every one Admire and Celebrate. And yet all this is no more perhaps than another has done before us, or at least might have done with our Opportunities and Advantages. The reverse of this procedure wou'd become us better, and it were more Glorious as well as more Just to ascribe the Excellencies of the Mind to Human Nature in the Lump[3] and to take the Weaknesses to our selves. By this we shou'd both avoid Sloth, (the best use we can make of our Ignorance and Infirmity being first to be humbled for, and then sedulously to endeavour their Amendment) and likewise secure our Industry from the Mixtures of Pride and Envy. By looking on our own Acquisitions as a general Treasure, in which the Whole have a Right, we shou'd pretend to no more than a share; and considering our selves as Parts of the same Whole, we should expect to find our own account in th' improvement of every part of it, which wou'd restrain us from being puft up with the Contemplation of our Own, and from repining at our Neighbours Excellencies. For let Reason shine forth where it may, as we can't engross,[4]

---

1 Unmortified passions, those for which no guilt or shame has been expressed.

2 A comment on the hubris of philosophers who claim authorial privilege in deciding the truth for others while claiming Reason to be transparent.

3 As a whole.

4 Buy up wholesale, gain or keep exclusive possession of, monopolize (obsolete) (*OED*).

so neither can we be excluded from sharing in the Benefit, unless we wilfully exclude our selves; every one being the better for True Worth and Good Sense, except the little Soul'd Enviers of 'em.

To help us to the Knowledge of our own Capacities, the Informations of our Friends, nay even of our Enemies may be useful. The former if Wise and True will direct us to the same Course to which our Genius Points, and the latter will industriously endeavour to divert us from it, and we can't be too careful that these don't disguise themselves under the specious appearance of the former, to do us an ill-turn the more effectually. For it is not seldom seen that such as pretend great Concern for us, will press us on to such Studies or Ways of Living as inwardly they know we are unfit for, thereby to gratify their Secret Envy, by diverting us from that to which our Genius disposes, and in which therefore they have reason to suppose we wou'd be Excellent. But tho we may make use of the Opinions of both, yet if we will be Sincere and Ingenuous we cannot have a more faithfull Director than our own heart. He who gave us these Dispositions will excite us to the Use and Improvement of 'em; and unless we drive him from us by our Impurity, or thro negligence and want of Attention let slip his secret Whispers, this Master within us will lay most in our view such Lessons as he wou'd have us take. Our care then must be to open our Eyes to that Beam of Light which does in a more especial manner break in upon us, to fix them steadily, and to examine accurately those notices which are most vividly represented to us, and to lay out our Thoughts and Time in the Cultivation of 'em. It may be our Humor won't be gratified, nor our Interest served by such a Method. Other Business or Amusements put on a finer Garb, and come attended with more Charms and Grandeur, these recommend us to the World make us Belov'd and Illustrious in it: Whilst the followers of Truth are despis'd and look'd askew on, as fantastick Speculatists,[1] unsociable Thinkers, who pretend to see farther than their Neighbours, to rectifie what Custom has establish'd, and are so Unmannerly as to Think and Talk out of the Common way. He who speaks Truth makes a Satyr[2] on the greatest part of Mankind, and they are not over apt to forgive him, he contradicts the vogue of the Times, is so hardy as to lay open Mens

---

1 One who speculates, theorist; very common from 1750 (*OED*).

2 Seventeenth-century spelling of satire.

darling Errors, to draw a lively Picture of their most secret Corruptions, a Representation which they cannot bear. Their Gall is touch'd proportionably as their Wounds are more deeply search'd into, altho it be only in order to a Cure. They therefore who Love Truth shall be Hated by the Most, who tho they openly pretend to Honour, yet secretly Malign her, because she reproaches them. And as a plausible Life is not often a very Religious one, which made the best Judge pronounce a Wo on those whom all Men shall speak well of so neither is the most Just and Illuminated Understanding the most admir'd and trusted to, but a plausible Speaker, as well as a plausible Liver,[1] commonly bears away the Bell.[2] If then we consult our Passions and Vanity we shall go near to determine amiss, and make that use of our Intellectuals which Fancy or Interest pushes us on to, not which Nature has fitted us for. Hence it is that those who might have done very well in some Studies and Employments, make but bungling work when they apply themselves to others. We go on apace when the Wind and Tide are on our side, but it costs us much Labour, and we make little speed, when we Row against both.

And as a due Consideration of our Particular Capacity wou'd put us right in our own Studies, so wou'd it keep us from clashing with our Neighbours, whom we many times Contend with not so much out of Love to Truth, as thro a humor of Contradiction, or because we think this the best way to shew our Parts, and by this tryal of Skill to exalt our selves above them. But is there no better way to discover our Penetration, and to try our Strength, than by a Malicious and Litigious Opposition?[3] The field of Truth is large, and after all the Discoveries that have been made by those who have gone before, there will still be untroden Paths, which they who have the Courage and Skill may beat out[4] and beautify. If then instead of Jostling and Disputing with our Fellow Travellers, of bending all the force of our Wit to Contradict and Oppose those advances which they make, we wou'd well understand, duly Employ and kindly Communicate our Peculiar Talent, how much more Service might we do our Lord, how much more useful

---

1 One whose life is worthy of applause, praiseworthy.

2 *The Ladies Library* extract (1714 edn, vol 1, 467) substitutes for "commonly bears away the Bell" a paraphrase, "commonly has the Applause of the World."

3 Astell characterizes the forensic methods of debate.

4 Tread out.

might we be to one another? What vast Discoveries wou'd be made in the wide Ocean of Truth? How many Moral Irregularities wou'd be observ'd and rectify'd? We shou'd be restrain'd from aspiring to things above our reach, move regularly in our own Sphere, not abuse those good Parts which were given us for Common Benefit, to the Destruction of our selves and others, be in a fair way to discern the Defects of our Mind and to proceed to the Cure of 'em.

§III. We have already exprest our thoughts concerning the Capacity and Perfection of the Understanding, and what has been said if duly consider'd is sufficient to bring every particular Person acquainted with their own defects.[1] But because they who need Amendment most, are commonly least dispos'd to make such reflections as are necessary to procure it, we will spend a few Pages in considering for them, and in observing the most usual defects of the Thinking Faculty.

If we are of their Opinion who say that the Understanding is only Passive, and that Judgment belongs to the Will, I see not any Defect the former can have, besides Narrowness and a disability to extend it self to many things, which is indeed incident to all Creatures, the brightest Intelligence in the highest Order of Angels is thus defective, as well as the meanest Mortal, tho in a less degree. Nor ought it to be complain'd of, since 'tis Natural and Necessary, we may as well desire to be Gods as desire to Know all things. Some sort of Ignorance therefore, or Non perception we cannot

---

1 Astell in *A Serious Proposal, Part I* (1694 edn, 76/78 above) had discussed "*necessary* and *perfective* truths" with reference to the arguments of John Norris's *Reflections upon the Conduct of Human Life* (1690). What follows owes a good deal to Norris's argument at §15 of the same work (1690 edn, 17-18) where, in answer to the question "what is it that is perfective of the Understanding," he asserted:

> To the Question then I answer, that the Perfection of the Understanding, as that of the will, is either *Formal* or *Objective*. The *Formal Perfection* of the understanding, as that of the will, is no other than its Exercise or Operation, which is *Thinking* and *Perception*, as that of the other is *Willing* and *Chusing*. According to the vulgar Maxim, that *the Perfection of every thing is its Operation*, which must be understood only the *Formal Perfection*. The *Objective Perfection* of the understanding is *Truth*, as that of the will is *Good*. The Result of these two Perfections joyn'd together is what in the understanding we call *Knowledge*, and what in the will we call *Vertue*.

help; a Finite Mind, suppose it as large as you please, can never extend it self to Infinite Truths. But no doubt it is in our Power to remedy a great deal more than we do, and probably a larger Range is allowed us than the most Active and Enlightned Understanding has hitherto reach'd. Ignorance then can't be avoided but Error may, we cannot Judge of things of which we have no Idea, but we can suspend our Judgment about those of which we have, till clearness and evidence oblige us to pass it. Indeed in strictness of Speech the Will and not the Understanding is blameable when we Think amiss, since the latter opposes not the Ends for which GOD made it, but readily extends it self as far as it can, receiving such Impressions as are made on it; 'tis the former that directs it to such Objects, that fills up its Capacity with such Ideas as are foreign to its Business and of no use to it, or which does not at least oppose the incursions of Material things, and deface[1] as much as it is able those impressions which Sensible Objects leave in the Imagination. But since it is not material to the present Design, whether Judgment belongs to the Understanding or Will, we shall not nicely distinguish how each of 'em is employ'd in acquiring Knowledge, but treat of 'em both together in this Chapter, allotted to the Service of the Studious, who when they are put in the way may by their own Meditations and Experience, rectifie the mistakes and supply the Omissions we happen to be guilty of.

They who apply themselves to the Contemplation of Truth, will perhaps at first find a Contraction or Emptiness of Thought, and that their Mind offers nothing on the Subject they wou'd consider, is not ready at unfolding, nor in representing correspondent[2] Ideas to be compar'd with it, is as it were asleep or in a Dream, and tho' not empty of all Thought, yet Thinks nothing clearly or to the purpose. The Primary Cause of this is that Limitation which all Created Minds are Subject to, which Limitation appears more visible in some than in others, either because some Minds are endow'd by their Creator with a larger Capacity than the rest, or if you are not inclin'd to think so, then by reason of the Indisposition of the Bodily Organs, which cramps and contracts the Operations of the Mind. And that Person whose Capacity of receiving Ideas is very little, whose Ideas are disorder'd, and not capable of being so dispos'd as that they may be compar'd in order to the

---

1 Blot out, obliterate, efface (*OED*).

2 Corresponding.

forming of a Judgment, is a Fool or little better. If we find this to be our Case, and that after frequent tryals there appears no hopes of Amendment, 'tis best to desist, we shall but lose our Labour, we may do some Good in an Active Life and Employments that depend on the Body, but we're altogether unfit for Contemplation and the Exercises of the Mind. Yet e'er we give out let's see if it be thus with us in all Cases: Can we Think and Argue Rationally about a Dress, an Intreague, an Estate? Why then not upon better Subjects? The way of Considering and Meditating justly is the same on all Occasions. 'Tis true, there will fewest Ideas arise when we wou'd Meditate on such Subjects as we've been least conversant about; but this is a fault which it is in our power to remedy, first by Reading or Discoursing, and then by frequent and serious Meditation, of which hereafter.

As those we have been speaking of are hindred[1] in their search after Truth, thro a want of Ideas out of which to deduce it, so there are another sort who are not happy in their Enquiries, on account of the multitude and Impetuosity of theirs. Volatileness of Thought, very pernicious to true Science, is a fault which People of warm Imaginations and Active Spirits are apt to fall into. Such a Temper is readily dispos'd to receive Errors and very well qualified to propagate them, especially if a volubility of Speech be join'd to it. These thro an immoderate nimbleness of Thinking skip from one Idea to another, without observing due Order and Connexion, they content themselves with a superficial view, a random glance, and depending on the vigor of their Imagination, are took with Appearances, never tarrying to penetrate the Subject, or to find out Truth if she float not upon the Surface. A multitude of Ideas not relating to the matter they design to think of rush in upon them, and their easie Mind entertains all comers how impertinent soever; instead of examining the Question in debate they are got into the Clouds, numbring the Cities in the Moon and building Airy Castles there. Nor is it easie to cure this Defect, since it deceives others as well as those who have it with a shew of very great Ingenuity. The vivacity of such Persons makes their Conversation plausible, and taking with those who consider not much, tho not with the Judicious; it procures for them the Character of Wit, but hinders them from being Wise. For truth is not often found by such as won't take Time to examine her Counterfeits, to distinguish

---

1 Hindered.

between Evidence and Probability, Realities and Appearances, but who thro a conceit of their own sharp-sightedness think they can pierce to the bottom with the first glance.

To cure this Distemper perfectly perhaps it will be necessary to apply to the body as well as to the Mind: The Animal Spirits must be lessen'd, or rendred more Calm and Manageable; at least they must not be unnaturally and violently mov'd by such a Diet, or such Passions, Designs and Divertisments[1] as are likely to put 'em in a ferment. Contemplation requires a Governable body, a sedate and steady Mind, and the Body and the Mind do so reciprocally influence each other, that we can scarce keep the one in tune if the other be out of it. We can neither Observe the Errors of our Intellect, nor the Irregularity of our Morals whilst we are darkned by Fumes, agitated with unruly Passions, or carried away with eager Desires after Sensible things and vanities. We must therefore withdraw our Minds from the World, from adhering to the Senses, from the Love of Material Beings, of Pomps and Gaieties; for 'tis these that usually Steal away the Heart, that seduce the Mind to such unaccountable Wandrings, and so fill up its Capacity that they leave no room for Truth, so distract its Attention that it cannot enquire after her. For tho' the Body does partly occasion this fault, yet the Will no doubt may in good measure Remedy it, by using its Authority to fix the Understanding on such Objects as it wou'd have Contemplated; it has a Rein which will certainly curb this wandring, if it can but be persuaded to make use of it. Indeed Attention and deep Meditation is not so agreeable to our Animal Nature, does not flatter our Pride so well as this agreeable *Reverie*, which gives us a pretence to Knowledge without taking much Pains to acquire it, and does not choak us with the humbling thoughts of our own Ignorance, with which we must make such ado e're it can be enlightened. Yet without Attention and strict Examination we are liable to false Judgments on every occasion, to Vanity and Arrogance, to Impertinent Prating of things we don't understand, are kept from making a Progress, because we fancy our selves to be at the top already, and can never attain to true Wisdom. If then we wou'd hereafter think to purpose, we must suffer our selves to be convinced how oft we have already thought to none, suspect our Quickness, and not give our desultory Imagination leave to ramble.

---

1 Diversions.

And in order to the restraining it we may consider, what a loss of Time and Study such irregular and useless Thoughts occasion, what a Reproach they are to our Reason, how they cheat us with a *shew* of Knowledge, which so long as we are under the power of this giddy Temper will inevitably escape us And if to this we add a serious perusal of such Books as are not loosly writ, but require an Attent and Awakened Mind to apprehend, and to take in the whole force of 'em, obliging our selves to Understand them throughly,[1] so as to be able to give a just account of them to our Selves, or rather to some other Person intelligent enough to take it and to correct our mistakes, it is to be hop'd we shall obtain a due poise of Mind, and be able to direct our Thoughts [to][2] the thorow[3] discussion of such Subjects as we wou'd Examine. Such Books I mean as are fuller of Matter than words, which diffuse a light through every part of their Subject, do not Skim, but penetrate it to the bottom, yet so as to leave somewhat to be wrought out by the Reader's own Meditation; such as are writ with Order and Connexion, the Strength of whose Arguments can't be sufficiently felt unless we remember and compare the whole System. 'Tis impossible to prescribe absolutely, and every one may easily find what Authors are most apt to stay[4] their Attention, and shou'd apply to them. But whenever they Meditate, be it on what Object it may, let 'em fix their Minds stedily on it, not removing till it be throughly Examin'd, at least not until they have seen all that's necessary to their present purpose.

Doing so we shall prevent Rashness and Precipitation[5] in our Judgments, which is occasion'd by that Volatileness we have been speaking of, together with an over-weaning opinion of our Selves. All the irregularities of our Will proceed from those false Judgments we make, thro want of Consideration, or a partial Examination when we do consider. For did we Consider with any manner of Attention, we cou'd not be so absurd as to call Evil, Good, and Chuse it as such, or prefer a less Good before a greater, a poor Momentary Trifle, before the Purity and Perfection of our Mind, before an Eternal and Immutable Crown of Glory! But we seek no farther than the first Appearances of Truth and Good here we Stop,

1 Sic, i.e., thoroughly.
2 Errata list, 298, requires insertion of "to."
3 I.e., thorough.
4 To hold.
5 Undue haste (*OED*).

allowing neither Time nor Thought to search to the bottom, and to pull off those Disguises which impose on us. This Precipitation is that which gives birth to all our Errors, which are nothing else but a hasty and injudicious Sentence, a mistaking one thing for another, supposing an Agreement or Disparity amongst Ideas and their Relations where in reality there is none, occasion'd by an imperfect and cursory view of 'em. And tho' there are other things which may be said to lead us into Error, yet they do it only as they seduce us into Rash and Precipitate Judgments. We love Grandeur and every thing that feeds our good Opinion of our Selves, and therefore wou'd Judge off hand, supposing it a disparagement[1] to our Understandings to be long in Examining, so that we greedily embrace whatever seems to carry Evidence enough for a speedy Determination, how slight and superficial soever it be. Whereas did we calmly and deliberately Examine our Evidence, and how far those Motives we are acted by ought to Influence, we shou'd not be liable to this Seduction. For hereby the Impetuosity of a warm Imagination wou'd be cool'd, and the extravagancies of a Disorderly one Regulated; we shou'd not be Deceiv'd by the Report of our Senses; the Prejudices of Education; our own Private Interest, and readiness to receive the Opinions whether True or False of those we Love because we think they will serve us in that Interest; our inordinate thirst after a great Reputation, or the Power and Riches, the Grandeurs and Pleasures of this World, these wou'd no longer dissipate our Thoughts and distract our Attention, for then we shou'd be sensible how little Concern is due to them. We shou'd neither mistake in the End and Object by not employing our Understandings at All about such things as they were chiefly made for, or not Enough, or by busying them with such as are out of their reach, or beneath their Application; nor shou'd we be out in the Method of our Meditation, going a wrong or a round about way. For the GOD of Truth is ready to lead us into all Truth, if we Honestly and Attentively apply our selves to him.

In sum, whatever false Principle we embrace, whatever wrong Conclusion we draw from true ones, is a disparagement to our Thinking Power, a Weakness of Judgment proceeding from a Confuse and Imperfect view of things, as that does from want of attention, and a hasty and partial Examination. It were endless to reckon up all the false Maxims and Reasonings we fall into, nor is it

---

1 Discredit.

possible to give a List of them, for there are innumerable Errors opposite to one single Truth. The General Causes have been already mention'd, the particulars are as many as those several Compositions which arise from the various mixtures of the Passions, Interests, Education, Conversation and Reading, etc. of particular persons. And the best way that I can think of to Improve the Understanding, and to guard it against all Errors proceed they from what Cause they may, is to regulate the Will, whose Offense it is to determine the Understanding to such and such Ideas, and to stay it[1] in the Consideration of them so long as is necessary to the Discovery of Truth; for if the Will be right the Understanding can't be guilty of any Culpable Error. Not to Judge of any thing which we don't Apprehend, to suspend our Assent till we see just cause to give it, and to determine nothing till the Strength and Clearness of the Evidence oblige us to it. To withdraw our selves as much as may be from Corporeal things,[2] that pure Reason may be heard the better; to make that use of our senses for which they are design'd and fitted, the preservation of the Body, but not to depend on their Testimony in our Enquiries after Truth. Particularly to divest our selves of mistaken Self-love, little Ends and mean Designs, and to keep our inclinations and Passions under Government. Not to engage our selves so far in any Party or Opinion as to make it in a manner necessary that that shou'd be Right, lest from wishing it were, we come at last to persuade our selves it is so. But to be passionately in Love with Truth, as being throughly sensible of her Excellency and Beauty. To embrace her how opposite soever she may sometimes be to our Humours and Designs, to bring these over to her, and never attempt to make her truckle to them. To be so far from disliking a Truth because it touches us home, and lances our tenderest and dearest Corruption,[3] as on the contrary to prize it the more, by how much the more plainly it shews us our Errors and Miscarriages. For indeed it concerns us most to know such Truths as these, it is not material to us what other Peoples Opinions are, any farther than as the Knowlege of their Sentiments may correct Our Mistakes. And the higher our Station is in the World, so much the greater need have we to be curious in this particular.

---

1 To control, restrain (obsolete) (*OED*).

2 Material things.

3 Astell suggests the image of lancing a boil.

The mean and inconsiderable often stumble on Truth when they seek not after her, but she is commonly kept out of the way, and industriously conceal'd from the Great and mighty; either out of Design or Envy, for whoever wou'd make a Property of another must by all means conceal the Truth from him; and they who Envy their Neighbours Preeminence in other things, are willing themselves to excel in exactness of Judgment, which they think and very truly, to be the greatest Excellency. And to help forward this deception, the Great instead of being Industrious in finding out the Truth, are generally very impatient when they meet with her. She does not treat them so tenderly and fawningly, with so much Ceremony and Complaisance as their Flatterers do. There's in her that which us'd to be the Character of our Nation, an honest Plainness and Sincerity, Openness and blunt Familiarity: She cannot mould her self into all Shapes to be rendred agreeable, but standing on her Native Worth is regardless of Out-side and Varnish. But to return from this Digression.[1]

Above all things we must be throughly convinced of our entire Dependance on GOD, for what we *Know* as well as for what we Are, and be warmly affected with the Sense of it, which will both Excite us to Practise, and Enable us to Perform the rest. Tho' we are Naturally Dark and Ignorant, Yet in *his Light we may* hope to *see Light*, if with the Son of *Syrac*[2] we Petition for *Wisdom that sits by his Throne* to *labour with me*, and Sigh with *David* after his *Light and Truth*. For then he who is *The Light that Lightneth every one who comes in to the World*, the Immutable Truth, and Uncreated Wisdom of His Father, will *Teach us in the way of Wisdom and lead us in right Paths*,[3] he will instruct us infinitely better by the right use of our own Faculties than the brightest Human reason can. For in him are all the Treasures of Wisdom and Knowlege which he Liberally dis-

---

1 Astell's digression — an attack on politicians, in particular the whigs, Shaftesbury, Locke, etc. — is familiar from her later writings. The digression is included in *The Ladies Library* extract, but the following paragraph is not.

2 "The Wisdome of Jesus the sonne of Sirach, or Ecclesiasticus" is the name of one of the books of the Apochrypha. Richard Allestree, who may be Astell's source, refers his reader in *The Ladies Calling*, part 1, §1 (1705 edn), 527, to Eccesiasticus, 23, for the Son of *Syrach* on the wantonness of women.

3 Astell echoes the formulaic language of Psalms 23: 3 and 35: 4. Proverbs 4: 11 and 8: 20, etc.

pences to all who Humbly, Honestly and Heartily ask 'em of him. To close this Head: Whatever the Notion That we see all things in GOD, may be as to the Truth of it, 'tis certainly very commendable for its Piety, in that it most effectually humbles the most dangerous sort of Pride, the being Proud of our Knowlege, and yet does not slacken our Endeavours after Knowlege but rather Excites them.[1]

§IV. As to the *Method* of Thinking, if be proper for me to say any thing of that, after those better Pens which have treated of it already, it falls in with the Subject I'me now come to, which is, that *Natural Logic* I wou'd propose. I call it natural because I shall not send you further than your Own Minds to learn it, you may if you please take in the assistance of some well chosen book, but a good Natural Reason after all, is the best Director, without this you will scarce Argue well, tho you had the Choicest Books and Tutors to Instruct you, but with it you may, tho' you happen to be destitute of the other. For as a very Judicious Writer on this Subject (to whose Ingenious Remarks and Rules[2] I am much obliged) well observes, "These Operations [of the Mind][3] proceed meerly from Nature, and that sometimes more perfectly from those who are altogether ignorant of Logic, than from others who have learn'd it."

That which we propose in all our Meditations and Reasonings is, either to deduce some Truth we are in search of, from such Principles as we're already acquainted with; or else, to dispose our Thoughts and Reasonings in such a manner, as to be able to Convince others of those Truths which we our selves are Convinc'd of. Other Designs indeed Men may have, such as the Maintenance of their Own Opinions, Actions and Parties without regard to the Truth and Justice of 'em of the Seduction of their unwary Neigh-

---

1 Astell appears to accept Masham's critique in *Discourse Concerning the Love of God* (1696) of the Malebranchean principle of "Seeing all things in God," to which Astell had subscribed in her *Letters Concerning the Love of God* (1695). But in *The Christian Religion* (1705) she reindorses Malebranche's principle.

2 *Art of Thinking* – Astell.

Astell's Marginal note is to Antoine Arnauld's *Logic, or the Art of Thinking*. The quotation is from the introduction to Part I, ch. 1, and almost certainly from the English edn of 1693, 38, which Astell reproduces almost exactly. She elsewhere indicates her indebtedness to Arnauld for the rules of logic which she sets out.

3 These are Astell's square brackets.

bours,[1] but these are Mean and Base ones, beneath a Man, much more a Christian, who is or Ought to be endow'd with greater Integrity and Ingenuity.

Now Reasoning being nothing else but a Comparison of Ideas, and a deducing of Conclusions from Clear and Evident Principles, it is in the first place requisite that our Ideas be Clear and Just, and our Principles True, else all our Discourse will be Nonsense and Absurdity, Falshood and Error. And that our Idea may be Right, we have no more to do but to look attentively into our own Minds, having as was said above, laid aside all Prejudices and whatever may give a false tincture[2] to our Light, there we shall find a Clear and Lively Representation of what we seek for, unsophisticated with the Dross[3] of false Definitions and untelligible Expressions. But we must not imagine that a transient view will serve the turn, or that our Eye will be Enlightened if it be not fix'd.[4] For tho' Truth be exceeding bright, yet since our Prejudices and Passions have darkned our Eye-sight, it requires no little Pains and Application of Mind to find her out, the neglect of which Application is the Reason that we have so little Truth, and that the little we have is almost lost in that Rubbish of Error which is mingled with it. And since Truth is so near at hand, since we are not oblig'd to tumble over many Authors, to hunt after a very celebrated Genius, but may have it for enquiring after in our own Breasts,[5] are we not inexcusable if we don't obtain it? Are we not unworthy of Compassion if we suffer our Understandings to be over-run with Error? Indeed it seems to me most Reasonable and most agreeable to the Wisdom and Equity of the Divine Operations, that every one shou'd have a Teacher in their own Bosoms, who will if they seriously apply themselves to him, immediately Enlighten them so far as that is necesary, and direct them to such Means as are sufficient for their Instruction both in Humane and Divine Truths; for as to the lat-

---

1 Astell appears to be impugning Locke as the seducer of Masham.

2 Colouring matter, dye, pigment (obsolete), tint, hue, colour (rare) (*OED*).

3 Extraneous matter thrown off in melting metals (as in the frequent Biblical comparison between dross and gold); scum (*OED*).

4 Astell parodies the language of Locke's exclusively optical perspective, which pretends the transparency of reason, but omits the functions of deliberation and the will.

5 Astell's restatement of Descartes' "cogito" and its implications: that individuals understand ultimate truths by self-reflection.

ter, Reason if it be Right and Solid, will not pretend to be our sole Instructor, but will send us to Divine Revelation when it may be had.

GOD does nothing in vain, he gives no Power of Faculty which he has not allotted to some proportionate use, if therefore he has given to Mankind a Rational Mind, every individual Understanding ought to be employ'd in somewhat worthy of it. The Meanest Person shou'd Think as *Justly*, tho' not as *Capaciously*, as the greatest Philosopher. And if the Understanding be made for the Contemplation of Truth, and I know not what else it can be made for, either there are many Understandings who are never able to attain what they were design'd and fitted for, which is contrary to the Supposition that GOD made nothing in Vain, or else the very meanest must be put in a way of attaining it: Now how can this be if all that which goes to the composition of a Knowing Man in th' account of the World, be necessary to make one so? All have not leisure to Learn Languages and pore on Books, nor Opportunity to Converse with the Learned; but all may *Think*, may use their own Faculties rightly, and consult the Master who is within them.[1]

By Ideas we sometimes understand in general all that which is the immediate Object of the Mind, whatever it Perceives; and in this large Sense it may take in all Thought, all that we are any ways capable of Discerning: So when we say we have no Idea of a thing, 'tis as much as to say we know nothing of the matter. Again, it is more strictly taken for that which represents to the Mind some Object distinct from it, whether Clearly or Confusedly; when this is its import, our Knowledge is said to be as Clear as our Ideas are. For that Idea which represents a thing so Clearly, that by an Attent and Simple View we may discern its Properties and Modifications, at least so far as they can be Known, is never false; all our Certainty and Evidence depends on it, if we Know not Truly what is thus represented to our Minds we know nothing. Thus the Idea of Equality between 2 and 2 is so evident that it is impossible to doubt of it, no Arguments could convince us of the Contrary, nor

---

1 Astell turns the Cartesian *cogito*, the "I think, therefore I am," which democratizes the proofs of existence, against Locke, presumably the Genius in question, rehearsing an argument she has made earlier, that if Locke is right we cannot believe him (as the product of environmental conditioning he cannot make truth claims), and if Descartes is right Locke is superfluous.

be able to persuade us that the same may be found between 2 and 3.[1]

And as such an Idea as this is never False, so neither can any Idea be said to be so, if by False we mean that which has no Existence; our Idea certainly Exists, tho' there be not any thing in Nature Correspondent to it. For tho' there be no such thing as a Golden Mountain, yet when I think of one, 'tis certain I have an Idea of it.[2]

But our Ideas are then said to be False, or rather Wrong, when they have no Conformity to the Real Nature of the Thing whose Name they bear.[3] So that properly speaking it is not the Idea but the Judgment that is False; we err in supposing that our Idea is answerable to something without us when it is not. In simple Perceptions we are not often deceiv'd but we frequently mistake in Compounding them, by Uniting several things which have no Agreement, and Separating others which are Essentially United. Indeed it may happen that our Perceptions are faulty sometimes, thro the Indisposition of the Organs or Faculties thus a Man who has the *Jaundice* sees everything ting'd with Yellow, yet even here the Error is not in the Simple Idea but in the Compos'd one, for we do not mistake when we say the Object appears Yellow to our Sight, tho' we do, when we affirm that it does, or ought to do so to others. So again, when the Mind does not sufficiently Attend to her Ideas nor Examine them on all sides, 'tis very likely she will Think amiss, but this also is a false Judgment, that which is amiss in the Perception being rather the Inadequateness than the Falshood. Thus in many Cases we enquire no farther than whether an Action be not Directly Forbidden, and if we do not find it Absolutely Unlawful, we think that sufficient to Authorize the Practise of it, not considering it as we ought to do, Cloathed with the Circumstances of Scandal, Temptation, etc. which place it in the same Classes with things unlawful, at least make it so to us.

Rational Creatures shou'd endeavour to have right Ideas of every thing that comes under their Cognizance, but yet our Ideas

---

1 See Locke's first letter to Stillingfleet (1823 edn, 52-53).

2 The source of the golden mountain example is unknown. Locke in the *Essay*, bk 3, ch. 6, §50 (1690 edn, 264) gives a nominalist account of "Gold," whose various usages, he insists, connote no underlying substance or essence.

3 Astell subscribes to the classical theory of truth which accords human cognition the capacity to know things as they really are. It is this confidence which Locke's scepticism seemed to undermine.

of Morality, our thoughts about Religion are those which we shou'd with greatest speed and diligence rectifie, because they are of most importance, the Life to come, as well as all the Occurences of This, depending on them. We shou'd search for Truth in our most abstracted Speculations, but it concerns us nearly to follow her close in what relates to the Conduct of our Lives. For the main thing we are to drive at in all our Studies, and that which is the greatest Improvement of our Understandings is the Art of Prudence, the being all of a Piece, managing all our Words and Actions as it becomes Wise Persons and Good Christians.

Yet in this we are commonly most faulty; for besides the deceits of our Passions, our Ideas of Particular Vertues and Vices, Goods and Evils, being an assemblage of divers simple Perceptions, and including several Judgments are therefore liable to mistake, and much more so considering how we commonly come by them. We hear the Word that Stands for such a Thing, suppose Honor and then instead of enquiring what it is at the Fountain-head the Oracles of GOD, and our own, or the Impartial Reason of the Wisest and the Best, Custom and the Observations we make on the Practice of such as Pretend to it forms our Idea, which is seldom a Right one, the Opinions and Practices of the World being very fallacious and many times quite opposite to the Dictates of Reason wou'd we but give ear to them. For what a strange distorted Idea of Honor must they needs have, who can think it Honourable to break a Vow that ought to be Kept, and Dishonourable to get loose from an Engagement that ought to be broken? Who cannot endure to be tax'd with a Lye, and yet never think fit to keep their Word? What do they think of Greatness who support their Pomp at the Expence of the Groans and Tears of many Injur'd Families? What is their Idea of Heaven, who profess to Believe such a thing, and yet never endeavour to Qualifie themselves for the Enjoyment of it? Have they any Idea at all of these things when they speak of 'em? Or, if they have, is it not a very false one?[1]

---

1 Here Astell anticipates her challenge to Locke and the Whigs in *Reflections upon Marriage* (1700, 29, 32, 38-41, 92-95; 1706/1996, 27/46, 31/48, 36-41/51-54, 87-92/76-80), to apply in the private sphere the democracy they advocate in the public. "How much soever Arbitrary Power may be dislik'd on a Throne, not *Milton* himself wou'd cry up Liberty to poor *Female Slaves*, or plead for the Lawfulness of Resisting a Private Tyranny," Astell dismally concluded (27/46-47). Charles

Now that we may avoid mistake the better, and because we usually join Words to our Ideas even when we only Meditate, we shou'd free them from all Equivocation, not make use of any Word, which has not a Distinct Idea annex'd to it, and where Custom has join'd many Ideas to one Word, carefully separate and distinguish them. For if our Words are Equivocal, how can we by Pronouncing such and such, excite the same Idea in another that is in our own Mind, which is the End of Speech, and consequently how can we be Understood? And if sometimes we annex one Idea to a Word, and sometimes another, we may for ever wrangle with those who perhaps wou'd be found to agree with us if we Understood each other, but can neither Convince them, nor clear up the Matter to our own Mind. For instance: Shou'd I dispute Whether Evil were to be Chosen? Without defining what I mean by Evil, which is a Word customarily apply'd to things of different Natures, and shou'd conclude in the Affirmative, meaning at the same time the Evil of Pain, or any Corporal Loss or Punishment, I were not mistaken, tho' another Person who annexes no other Idea but that of Sin to the word Evil, might Justly contradict me and say that I was. Or if in the Process of my Discourse, I shou'd without giving notice of it, substitute the Idea of Sin instead of that of Pain, when I mention Evil, I shou'd argue falsly. For it is a Maxim that we may Chuse a less Evil to avoid a greater, if both of them be Corporal Evils, or if one of them be so, and we chuse it to avoid a Sin, between which and the Evil of Pain there is no Comparison: But if the two Evils proposed to our Choice be both of them Sinful, that Principle will not hold, we must Chuse neither, whatever comes on't, Sin being Eligible no manner of way.

Thus many times our Ideas are thought to be false when the fault is really in our Language, we make use of Words without joyning any, or only loose and indeterminate Ideas to them, Prating like Parrots who can Modify Sounds, and Pronounce Syllables, and sometimes martial them as a Man wou'd, tho without the use of Reason or understanding any thing by them. So that after a long Discourse and many fine Words, our Hearer may justly ask us what

---

Leslie in his "Supplement," March 25, 1703 (6-7), "With a short Account of the *Original of Government* Compared with the *Schemes* of the *Republicans* and *Whigs*," appended to *The New Association, Part II*, laid down the same challenge in what is believed to be the first published critique of Locke's *Two Treatises* — erroneously, as I maintain (Springborg, 1995).

we have been saying? And what it is we wou'd be at? And so a great part, of the Good Breeding of the World, many Elegant Complements pass for nothing, they have no meaning, or if they have, 'tis quite contrary to what the Words in other Cases signifie.

From the Comparison of two or more Ideas clearly Conceived arises a Judgment, which we may lay down for a Principle, and as we have occasion Argue from. Always observing that those Judgments which we take for Axioms or Principles, be such as carry the highest Evidence and Conviction, such as every one who will but in the least Attend may Clearly see, and be fully convinced of, and which need not another Idea for their Demonstration. Thus from the Agreement which we plainly perceive between the Ideas of GOD and of Goodness singly consider'd, we discern that they may be joyn'd together so as to form this Proposition, *That GOD is Good*: And from the evident disparity that is between GOD and Injustice, we learn to affirm this other, *That he is not Unjust.* And so long as we Judge of Nothing but what we see Clearly, we can't be mistaken in our Judgments, we may indeed in those Reasonings and Deductions we draw from them, if we are Ignorant of the Laws of Argumentation, or Negligent in the Observation of them.

The First and Principal thing therefore to be observed in all the Operations of the Mind is, That we determine nothing about those things of which we have not a Clear Idea, and as Distinct as the Nature of the Subject will permit, for we cannot properly be said to Know any thing which does not Clearly and Evidently appear to us. Whatever we see Distinctly we likewise see Clearly, Distinction always including Clearness, tho this does not necessarily include that, there being many Objects Clear to the view of the Mind, which yet can't be said to be Distinct.

That (to use the words of a Celebrated Author)[1] may be said to be "Clear which is Present and Manifest to an attentive Mind;" so as we say we see Objects Clearly, when being present to our Eyes they sufficiently Act on 'em, and our Eyes are dispos'd to regard 'em. And that Distinct, which is so Clear, Particular, and Different from all other things, that it contains not any thing in it self which appears not manifestly to him who considers it as he ought. Thus

---

1 *Les Princip. del la Philosof. de M. Des Cartes* Pt. I. §45 – Astell.

Astell's marginal note, section note added as per Errata list, 298. Note that the material in parentheses, i.e., the attribution to Descartes, is omitted from the extract reproduced in *The Ladies Library* (1714 edn), vol 1, 490.

we may have a Clear, but not a Distinct and Perfect Idea of GOD and of our own Souls; their Existence and some of their Properties and Attributes may be Certainly and Indubitably Known, but we can't Know the Nature of our Souls Distinctly, for Reasons too long to be mentioned here, and less that of GOD, because he is Infinite. Now where our Knowlege is Distinct, we may boldly deny of a subject, all that which after a careful Examination we find not in it: But where our Knowlege is only Clear, and not Distinct, tho' we may safely Affirm what we see, yet we can't without a hardy Presumption Deny of it what we see not. And were it not very common to find People both Talking and Writing of things of which they have no Notion, no Clear Idea; nay and determining Dogmatically concerning the entire Nature of those of which they cannot possibly have an Adequate and Distinct one, it might seem Impertinent to desire them to speak no farther than they Apprehend. They will tell you Peremptorily[1] of Contradictions and Absurdities in such matters as they themselves must allow they cannot Comprehend, tho others as Sharp sighted as themselves can see no such thing as they complain of.

As Judgments are form'd by the Comparing of Ideas, so Reasoning or Discourse arises from the Comparison or Combination of several Judgments. Nature teaches us when we can't find out what Relation one Idea bears to another by a Simple view or bare Comparison, to seek for a Common Measure or third Idea, which Relating to the other two, we may by Comparing it with each of 'em, discern wherein they agree or differ. Our Invention discovers it self in proposing readily apt Ideas for this Middle Term, our Judgment in making Choice of such as are Clearest and most to our purpose, and the excellency of our Reasoning consists in our Skill and Dexterity in Applying them.

Invention indeed is the hardest part, when Proofs are found it is not very difficult to manage them. And to know precisely wherein their Nature consists, may help us somewhat in our enquiries after 'em. An Intermediate Idea then which can make out an Agreement between other ideas, must be Equivalent to, and yet Distinct from those we compare by it. Where Ideas agree it will not be hard to find such an Equivalent, and if after diligent search we cannot meet with any, 'tis a pretty sure Sign that they do not agree. It is not necessary indeed that our Middle Idea be Equivalent in all

1 Decisively, conclusively, in a manner to preclude debate (*OED*).

respects, 'tis enough if it be in such as make the Comparison: And when it is so to one of the Compar'd Ideas but not to the other, that's a Proof that they do not agree amongst themselves.

All the Commerce and Intercourse[1] of the World is manag'd by Equivalents, conversation as well as Traffick.[2] Why do we Trust our Friends but because their Truth and Honesty appears to us Equivalent to the Confidence we repose in 'em? Why do we perform Good Offices to others, but because there's a proportion between them and the Merit of the Person, or our own Circumstances? And as the way to know the Worth of things is to Compare them one with another, so in like manner we come to the Knowlege of the Truth of 'em by an Equal Ballancing.[3] But you will say, Tho I may learn the value of a *Spanish* Coin by Weighing, or Comparing it with some other Money whose Standard I know, and so discern what proportion it bears to those Goods I wou'd exchange;[4] yet what Scales shall I find to weigh Ideas? What Hand so even as to poize them Justly? Or if that might be done, yet where shall I meet with an Equivalent Idea when I have occasion to use one?[5]

In answer to this Demand I consider, that as Light is always visible to us if we have an Organ to receive it, if we turn our Eyes towards it, and that nothing interpose between it and us; so is Truth, we are surrounded with it, and GOD has given us Faculties to receive it. If it be ask'd, Why then do we so seldom find it? The

---

1 Trade.

2 A marvellously Lockean statement of the principle of general equivalence. But in fact the phraseology is directed at Masham, who in *Discourse Concerning the Love of God* (1696 edn, 121) had convicted Astell's project of denying human sociability, making "it impossible to live in the daily Commerce and Conversation of the World, and love God as we ought to do."

3 The remainder of this, and the following two paragraphs, are omitted from *The Ladies Library* extract (1714 edn), vol. 1, 492.

4 Astell demonstrates knowledge of the value of money as an expression of exchange-value, taken by Locke after the manner of the Church Fathers, from Aristotle in the *Politics*, bk 1, ch. 3, 1257a–1257b.

5 Astell challenges extension of the notion of general equivalence in economics to the realm of ideas as an instance of the fallacy of misplaced concreteness. Scales to weigh coin, and money as the expression of exchange value, are items to hand, but not so for an "Equivalent Idea." It is of course ironic that Astell should be charging Locke with over-concretizing ideas, but she draws attention to Locke's arbitrariness in retaining a role for ideas at all in a mechanistic materialist system.

Reason is, because instead of making right use of our Faculties we employ them in keeping it out; we either shut our Eyes, or if we vouchsafe to open them, we are sure to view it thro such unsuitable Mediums as fail not to misrepresent it to us. As for those few Noble Spirits, who open the Windows of their Souls to let in Truth, and take the Films of Interest, Passion and Prejudice from before their Eyes, they will certainly be Enlighten'd, and cannot miss of obtaining as much Truth as they are capable of Receiving. For, to go on with the Comparison, as we can See no farther than our own Horizon, tho the Light shine never so bright around us; and as we cannot discern every Object even within that Compass Clearly, nor Any Distinctly but what we particularly apply our selves to; So neither are our Capacities large enough to take in *All* Truth, as has been often said, nor are we capable of attaining *Any*, without Attention and diligent Examination. But if we carefully Consider those Ideas we already have and Attend to those Truths we are acquainted with, we cannot want Mediums to discover more, if our Enquiries be after that which is within our Reach. He who is the Fountain of Truth is also a GOD of Order, and has so regularly connex'd one Truth with another, that the discovery of one is a step towards a further Progress; so that if we diligently Examine those Truths which, we Know, they will clear the way to what we search after: For it seldom happens but that the Question it self directs us to some Idea that will serve for the Explanation or Proof of it.

There is no Object, no Accident of Life but affords us matter of Instruction. GOD has so dispos'd all the Works of his Hands, all the Actings of his Providence, that every one of 'em ministers to our Improvement, if we will but Observe and Apply them. Indeed this Living *Ex Tempore* which most of us are guilty of, our making no Reflections, our Gay and Volatile Humour which transports us in an Instant from one thing to another, e're we have with the Industrious Bee suck'd[1] those Sweets it wou'd afford us, frequently renders his gracious Bounty ineffectual. For as the Diligent-hand maketh Rich, whil'st the Slothful and Prodigal come to nothing, so the Use of our Powers improves and Encreases them, and the most Observing and Considerate is the Wisest Person: For she lays up in her Mind as in a Store-house, ready to produce on all

---

1 Astell appears to echo the song from Shakespeare's *Tempest* (V, i, 88 ff.), "Where the bee sucks, there suck I."

Occasions, a Clear and Simple Idea of every Object that has at any time presented itself. And perhaps the difference between one Womans Reason and anothers may consist only in this, that the one has amass'd a greater number of such Ideas than the other, and dispos'd them more Orderly in her Understanding, so that they are at hand, ready to be apply'd to those Complex Ideas whose Agreement or Disagreement cannot be found out but by the means of some of 'em.

But because Examples are more familiar than Precepts, as condescending to shew us the very manner of Practising them, I shall endeavour to make the matter in Hand as plain as I can by subjoining Instances to the following Rules, which Rules as I have not taken wholly on Trust from others, so neither do I pretend to be the Inventer of 'em.[1]

We have heard already that a Medium is necessary when we can't discern the Relation that is between two or more Ideas by Intuition or a simple View. Could this alone procure us what we seek after, the addition of other Ideas wou'd be needless, since to make a shew of Wit by tedious Arguings and unnecessary Flourishes, does only Perplex and Incumber the Matter, Intuition being the Simplest, and on that account the best way of Knowing.

Rule I. And therefore we shou'd in the first place, *Acquaint our selves throughly with the State of the Question, have a Distinct Notion of our Subject whatever it be, and of the Terms we make use of, knowing precisely what it is we drive at:* that so we may in the second.

Rule II. *Cut off all needless Ideas and whatever has not a necessary Connexion to the matter under Consideration*, which serve only to fill up the Capacity of the Mind, and to Divide and Distract the Attention. From the neglect of this comes those causless Digressions, tedious Parentheses and Impertinent Remarques which we meet with in some Authors. For, as when our Sight is diffus'd and

---

1 Astell takes her rules of logic from Arnauld, who acknowledged having taken them from "a small *Manuscript* of the deceas'd *Monsieur Paschal*, entitled, *The Soul of Geometry*," i.e., the work of that title by Blaise Pascal (1623-62). (See Arnauld's *Logic, or the Art of Thinking*, 1693 edn, 12.) But the rules set out by Arnauld in the Introduction to Part I of his work (40) and in Part 4, ch. 4 (413 ff.) are five in number, to which Astell adds a sixth, and her formulations do not correspond to the phraseology of the 1693 translation.

extended to many Objects at once we see none of them Distinctly; so when the Mind grasps at every Idea that presents it self, or rambles after such as relate not to its present Business, it loses its hold and retains a very feeble Apprehension of that which it shou'd Attend. Some have added another Rule (*viz*). *That we Reason only on those things of which we have Clear Ideas*; but I take it to be a Consequence of the first, and therefore do not make it a distinct one: For we can by no means Understand our Subject, or be well acquainted with the State of the Question, unless we have a Clear Idea of all its Terms.

Rule III. Our Business being stated, the next Rule is *To conduct our Thoughts by Order, beginning with the most Simple and Easie Objects, and ascending as by Degrees to the Knowledge of the more Compos'd.* I need not tell you, that Order makes everything, Easie, Strong and Beautiful, and that the Superstructure is neither like to Last or Please unless the Foundation be duly laid, for this is obvious to the most Superficial Reader. Nor are they likely to solve the Difficult, who have neglected or slightly pass'd over the Easie Questions. Our Knowledge is gradual, and by passing Regularly thro Plain things, we arrive in due time at the more Abstruse.

Rule IV. In this Method we are to practise the Fourth Rule which is, *Not to leave any part of our Subject unexamin'd*, it being as necessary to Consider All that can let in Light, as to shut out what's Foreign to it. We may stop short of Truth as well as over run it; and tho we look never so attentively on our proper Object, if we view but half of it, we may be as much mistaken, as if we extended our Sight beyond it. Some Objects agree very well when observ'd on one side, which upon turning the other shew a great disparity. Thus the Right Angle of a Triangle may be like to one part of a Square, but compare the Whole, and you'l find 'em very different Figures.[1] And a Moral Action may in some Circumstance be not

---

1 To Locke's further extended discussion of the triangle, an example of abstract ideas as products of the mind rather than Platonic archetypes, Stillingfleet, like Astell, raised serious objections. Antoine Arnauld, whose *Art of Thinking* Astell goes on to treat, opens ch. 5 of that work, "Of the Universality, Particularity and Singularity of Ideas," with a discussion of any given triangle as "a Figure containing three Lines and as many Angles; which *Idea* so inform'd may serve for the apprehension of all other Triangles" (London, 1693 edn, 65).

only Fit but Necessary, which in others, where Time, Place, and the like have made an alteration, wou'd be most Improper; so that if we venture to Act on the former Judgment, we may easily do amiss, if we wou'd Act as we ought, we must view its New Face, and see with what Aspect that looks on us.

To this Rule belongs that of *Dividing the Subject of our Meditations into as many Parts, as we can, and as shall be requisite to Understand it perfectly*. This is indeed most necessary in difficult Questions, which will scarce be unravell'd but in this manner by Pieces: Ever taking care to make Exact Reviews, and to Sum up our Evidence justly e're we pass Sentence and fix our Judgment.

Rule V. To which purpose we must *Always keep our Subject Directly in our Eye, and Closely pursue it thro all, our Progress*; there being no better Sign of a good Understanding than Thinking Closely and Pertinently,[1] and Reasoning dependently, so as to make the former part of our Discourse a support to the Latter, and *This* an Illustration of *That*, carrying Light and Evidence in ev'ry step we take. The neglect of this Rule is the Cause why our Discoveries of Truth are seldom Exact, that so much is often said to so little purpose; and many Intelligent and Industrious Readers when they have Read over a Book are very little wiser than when they began it. And that the two last Rules may be the better observ'd, 'twill be fit very often to look over our Process so far as we have gone, that so by rendring our Subject Familiar, we may the sooner arrive to an Exact Knowlege of it.

Rule VI. All which being done we are in a fair way towards keeping the last Rule, which is, *To judge no further than we Perceive, and not to take any thing for Truth, which we do not evidently Know to be so*. Indeed in some Cases we are forc'd to content our selves with Probability, but 'twere well if we did so only where 'tis plainly Necessary. That is, when the Subject of our Meditation is such as we cannot possibly have a Certain Knowledge of, because we are not furnish'd with Proofs which have a Constant and Immutable Connexion with the ideas we apply them to, or because we can't perceive it, which is our Case in such Exigencies as oblige us to Act presently, on a cursory view of the Arguments propos'd to us, when

1 To the point.

we want time to trace them to the bottom, and to make use of such means as wou'd discover Truth.

I cannot think we are often driven to such straits in any considerable Affair, tho I believe that very many Subjects may be propos'd to us, concerning which we cannot readily pass our Judgment, either because we never consider'd them before, or because we are wanting in some Means that lead to the Knowlege of 'em. In which Case Reason wills that we suspend our Judgment till we can be better Inform'd; nor wou'd it have us remit our Search after Certainty, even in those very Cases in which we may sometimes be forc'd to Act only on Probable Grounds. For Reason can't rest satisfy'd with Probabilities where Evidence is possible, our Passions and Interest may, but *That* does not incline us to leave off Enquiring lest we happen to meet somewhat contrary to our Desires. No, Reason requires us to continue our Enquiries with all the Industry we can, till they've put us in Possession of Truth, and when we have found, enjoyns us to follow her how opposite so ever she may cause our Latter Actions to be to our Former. But by this we may learn (and so we may by every thing that such weak and fallible Creatures as we are perform) to think Candidly of those whose Opinions and Actions differ from our own. Because we do not know the necessity of their Affairs, nor in what ill Circumstances they are plac'd in respect of Truth.

And now to Apply what has been said; The State of the Question being Distinctly known, and certain Ideas fixt to the Terms we make use of, we shall find sometimes that the Difference which was suppos'd to be between the Things themselves, is only in words, in the divers ways we make use of to express the same Idea.

For if upon looking into our selves we discern, that these different Terms have but one and the same Idea, when we have corrected our Expressions the Controversie is at an End, and we need enquire no further. Thus, If we are ask'd *Whether GOD is Infinitely Perfect*?[1] There needs no Intermediate Ideal to compare the Idea of

1 Locke in his reply to the Bishop of Worcester, Edward Stillingfleet, revisited this question, which he had raised in the *Essay Concerning Human Understanding*, at great length. Astell follows Stillingfleet in maintaining that the conditions Locke sets for invalidating the idea of God are impossible, because we can have no standard of comparison for him, precisely Locke's argument, in fact.

GOD with that of Infinite Perfection, since we may discern them on the very first view to be one and the same Idea differently express'd, which to go about to explain or prove were only to cumber with needless words, and to make what is Clear, Obscure. For we Injure a Cause instead of Defending it, by attempting an Explanation or Proof of things so Clear, that as they do not need, so perhaps they are not Capable of any.

But if it be made a Question *Whether there is a GOD, or a Being Infinitely Perfect?*[1] We are then to Examin the Agreement between our Idea of GOD and that of Existence.[2] Now this may be discern'd by Intuition, for upon a View of our Ideas we find that Existence is a Perfection, and the Foundation of all other Perfections, since that which has no Being cannot be suppos'd to have any Perfection. And tho the Idea of Existence is not Adequate to that of Perfection, yet the Idea of Perfection Includes that of Existence, and if *That* Idea were divided into parts, one part of it wou'd exactly agree with *This*. So that if we will allow that *Any* Being is Infinite in All Perfections, we cannot deny that Being Exists; Existence it self being one Perfection, and such an one as all the rest are built upon.

If unreasonable Men will farther demand, *Why is it necessary that All Perfection shou'd be Centred in One Being, is't not enough that it be parcel'd out amongst many? And tho it be true that that Being who has all Perfection must needs Exist, yet where's the Necessity of an All-Perfect Being?*[3] We must then look about for Proofs and Intermediate Ideas, and the Objection it self will furnish us with one. For those *Many* whose Particular Ideas it wou'd have joyn'd together to make a Compound one of All Perfection, are no other than Creatures, as will appear if we consider our Idea of Particular Being and of

---

1 Discussed by Locke in reply to Stillingfleet (*Letter to the Bishop of Worcester,* in John Locke, *Works*, 1823 edn, vol. 3, 8 and 51), with reference to his *Essay Concerning Human Understanding*, bk 4, ch. 4, §18; from pages 52-55 of the same Letter, Locke refers to his *Essay*, bk 4, ch. 10, §7.

2 See Locke's reply to Stillingfleet (8-9) on substance and existence, addressing the question in the terms of the Scholastics — "'Ens' or res per se subsistens et substans accidentibus?'" — to which he answers that simple qualities presuppose a substratum or substance.

3 Discussed by Locke in reply to Stillingfleet, 8; again on 46, citing the *Essay Concerning Human Understanding*, bk 4, ch. 10, §1; and on 51, with reference to his *Essay*, bk 4, ch. 4, §18.

Creature, which are so far from having any thing to distinguish 'em, that in all Points they resemble each other. Now this Idea naturally suggests to us that of Creation, or a Power of giving Being to that which before the exerting of that Power had none, which Idea if we use it as a Medium, will serve to discover to us the necessity of an All-Perfect Being.

For in the first place, what ever has any Perfection or Excellency (for that's all we mean by Perfection here) must either have it of it self, or derive it from some other Being. Now Creatures cannot have their Perfections from themselves because they have not their Being, for to suppose that they Made themselves is an Absurdity too ridiculous to be seriously refuted, 'tis to suppose them to Be and not to Be at the same time, and that when they were Nothing, they were able to do the greatest Matter. Nor can they derive either Being or Perfection from any other Creature. For tho some Particular Beings may seem to be the Cause of the Perfections of others, as the Watch-maker may be said to be the Cause of the Regular Motions of the Watch,[1] yet trace it a little farther, and you'l find this very Cause shall need another, and so without End, till you come to the Foundation-head, to that All-Perfect Being, who is the last resort of our Thoughts, and in whom they Naturally and Necessarily rest and terminate. If to this it be Objected that we as good as affirm that this All-Perfect Being is his own Maker, by saying he is Self-Existent, and so we fall into the same Absurdity which we imputed to that Opinion which supposes that Creatures were their own Maker. The reply is easie, That we do not say he Made him self, we only affirm that his Nature is such, that tho we can't sufficiently Explain because we can't comprehend it, yet thus much we can discern, that if he did not Exist of himself no other Being could ever have Existed. So that either All must be swallow'd up in an Infinite Nothing, if Nothing can properly have that Epithet, and we must suppose, that neither we our selves, nor any of those Creatures about us ever had, or ever can have a Being, which is too ridiculous to imagine, or else we must needs have recourse to a Self-Existing Being, who is the Maker and Lord of all things. And since Self-Existence must of necessity be plac'd somewhere, is it not much more Natural and Reasonable to place it in Infinite Perfection, than amongst poor, frail Creatures, whose Origin we may trace, and whose End we see daily hastning?

---

1 This famous analogy points to Descartes.

To Sum up all: Since there are Innumerable Beings in the World, which have each of them their several Excellencies or Perfections; Since these can no more derive their Perfections than their Being from themselves or from any other Creature; Since a Self-Existing Being is the result of our Thoughts; the First and only True Cause, without whom it is impossible that any thing should ever have Existed; since Creatures with their Being receive all that depends on it from him their Maker; Since none can give what he has not,[1] and therefore he who Communicates an innumerable variety of Perfections to his Creatures, even all that they enjoy, must needs contain in himself all those Beauties and Perfections he is pleas'd to Communicate to Inferior Beings; nothing can be more Plain and Evident than that there is a GOD, and that the Existence of an All-Perfect Being is Absolutely necessary.

Perhaps these Arguments are not in Form, I do not oblige my Self to follow servilely the Rules of Art, nor know I what better Judges will think of 'em, but they seem to me to be Clear, Rational and Concluding, which is all I aim at. And I hope the Reader will receive from hence more light into the way of Arguing, than she cou'd have gain'd had I spent as many Pages in prescribing Rules and giving trifling Examples, which when they are known, merit only to be forgot again. But if some are better pleas'd with the usual way of Syllogism,[2] and think an Argument cannot be rightly managed without one, for their Satisfaction we will add another Instance.

---

1 Astell's phraseology is curiously close in form of words to the principle on which Locke's argument against slavery is based in the *Two Treatises of Government* (1988 edn, Bk 2, §23, 284): "No body can give more power than he has himself; and he that cannot take away his own life cannot give another power over it." Astell is already citing Locke's *Two Treatises* in *The Christian Religion* of 1705, and I believe that there is clear evidence she had read the work by 1700 (see Springborg, "Mary Astell, Critic of Locke"), but could she have read it by 1697? The first systematic comment on Locke's political treatises is usually credited to Charles Leslie, in his "Supplement," dated March 25, 1703, to *The New Association, Part II* (6-7).

2 The syllogism is a standard form of argument in Aristotelian logic comprising two premises which contain a common or middle term, from which the third term or conclusion is derived by deduction. Astell's discussion of the technical rules governing the syllogism follows Arnauld's *The Art of Thinking: Port Royal Logic*, part 3, chs 2-10 (1693 edn, 215-382).

Suppose the Question were put *Whether a Rich Man is Happy*? By a Rich Man understanding one who possesses the Wealth and Good things of this World, and by Happy the Enjoyment of the Proper Good of Man. We compare the two Terms Riches and Happiness together, to discern if they be so much one and the same, that what is affirm'd of the one may be said of the other; but we find they are not. For if Riches and Happiness were terms Convertible, then all who are Happy must be Rich, and all who are Rich must be Happy, to affirm the last of which is to beg the Question, and the contrary appears by the following Argument, which makes use of *Satisfaction with ones own Condition* for the middle Idea or Common Measure.

He who is Happy is satisfied with his Condition and free from Anxious Cares and Solicitude (for these proceeding from the want of Good, he who enjoys his proper Good cannot be subject to them.) But Riches do not free us from Anxieties and Solicitude, they many times encrease them, Therefore to be Rich and to be Happy are not one and the same thing.

Again, If there are some who are Happy and yet not Rich, then Riches and Happiness are two distinct things. But a Good Poor Man is Happy (in the Enjoyment of GOD who is better to him than Thousands of Gold and Silver,) therefore Riches and Happiness are to be distinguish'd.

We may further consider, that if the Enjoyment of Riches can make a Man Happy according to our Notion of Happiness, they must be his Proper Good. Now if we compare the Idea of Riches with that which we have of Man, we shall find in the former nothing but what's Material, External and Adventitious, but our Idea of the latter represents to us somewhat that Thinks, and so is of an Immaterial and more noble Nature, a Nature altogether different from the former, and much more excellent and Superior to it; and by Consequence the less Noble cannot be the Good of the more, nor a Body or an Extended Substance, the Proper Good of the Mind, a Spiritual or Thinking Substance, So that upon the whole matter we find, that we cannot affirm a Man is Happy because he is Rich, neither can we deny it; Riches consider'd absolutely in 'emselves, neither make a Man Happy nor hinder him from being so. They Contribute to his Happiness or they Obstruct it according to the Use he makes of 'em.

As for the Common Rules of Disputation they do more frequently Intangle than Clear a Question, nor is it worth while to know any more of them than may help to guard us from the

Sophistry of those who use them, and assist us in the managing an Argument fairly, so long as it is Tenable, and till we are driven from it by the meer dint of Truth. To be able to hold an Argument Right or Wrong may pass with some perhaps for the Character of a Good Disputant, which yet I think it is not, but must by no means be allow'd to be that of a Rational Person, it belongs to such to detect as soon as may be the Fallacies of an ill one, and to establish Truth with the Clearest Evidence. For indeed Truth not Victory is what we shou'd contend for in all Disputes, it being more Glorious to be Overcome by her than to Triumph under the Banners of Error. And therefore we pervert our Reason when we make it the Instrument of an Endless Contention, by seeking after Quirks and Subtilties, abusing Equivocal Terms and by practising the rest of those little Arts every Sophister is full of, which are of no service in the discovery of Truth, all they can do is to Ward off an Opponents blow, to make a Noise and raise a Dust, that so we may escape in the Hurry, our foil being undiscover'd.

It were endless to reckon up all the Fallacies we put on our selves and endeavour to obtrude on others. On our selves in the first place, for however we may be pleas'd in the Contemplation of our own Craft or to use those softer Names we are apt to give it, our Acuteness and Ingenuity; who ever attempts to impose on others is first impos'd on himself, he is cheated by some of those grand Deceivers, the World, the Flesh, and the Devil, and made to believe that Vain-glory, Secular Interest, Ambition or perhaps Sensuality or Revenge, or any the like contemptible Appetites are preferable to Integrity and Truth.

Neither is it necessary to reduce the most usual Sophisms to general Heads since that's already very well perform'd in a Book to which I'de rather refer you, than be at the trouble of Transcribing,[1] having nothing to add but this, that if I be not mistaken, all the false Arguing enumerated there, and what other you may happen to meet with may be discover'd and avoided by the Rules already

---

1 *Art of Thinking*, Pt.3, Ch. 19, 20 – Astell.

Astell's preceding arguments about the possibility of certitude restate the case against the Pyrrhonic sceptics in Arnauld's *Logic, or the Art of Thinking*, (1693 English edn), 309-82, referenced in this marginal note. Chs 19 and 20 of the *Port Royal Logic* are entitled "Of the several sorts of vicious Arguments call'd Sophisms," and "Of bad reasoning in civil Conversation and common Discourse."

given, and do indeed proceed, so far as they relate to the Understanding, from the Non-observation of some of 'em.

But it is to little purpose to guard our selves against the Sophisms of the Head, if we lie open to those of the Heart. One irregular Passion will put a greater Obstacle between us and Truth, then the bright Understanding and clearest Reasoning can easily remove. This every one of us is apt to discern in others but we're blind to it in our selves. We can readily say that it is Pride or Obstinacy, Interest or Passion or in a word Self-love that keeps our Neighbour from Conviction, but all this while imagine our own Hearts are very clear of 'em, tho' more Impartial Judges are of another Mind.

I wish there were no Reason to think that there are some who attempt to maintain an Opinion which they know to be false, or at least which they have cause to suspect, and therefore industriously avoid what wou'd manifest their Error.[1] Tis hop'd however that the greatest part of the Disputers of the World are not of this number, and that the reason why they offer their Neighbours Sophistical Arguments, is because they are not aware of it themselves. That what makes them so Positive is their firm persuasion that they are acted only by a Zeal for GOD, an honest Constancy and Stanch Integrity, tho at the very same time quite different Motives move them under these Appearances.

And indeed he must be an extraordinary good Man, a Wonder scarce produc'd in an Age, who has no Irregular Passion stirring; Who receives no Manner of Tincture[2] from Pride and Vitious Self-Love, to which all are so prone, and which hide themselves under so many disguises; Who is got above the World it's Terrors and Allurements, has laid up his Treasure in Heaven, and is fully Contented with his Present Circumstances, let them be what they will, having made them the boundaries of his Desires; who knows how

---

1 Astell's claim, in apparent contradiction with her earlier affirmation of the Platonist position that one cannot knowingly do wrong, is resolvable in terms of corruption of the will. When the will is corrupted even cognition is skewed, and it is by failing to discipline the will that individuals "industriously avoid what wou'd manifest their error."

2 In the sense favoured by the Cambridge Platonists (especially Henry More), but now obsolete: "a supposed spiritual principle or immaterial substance whose character or quality may be infused into material things, which are then said to be tinctured; the quintessence, spirit, or soul of a thing" (*OED*).

to live on a Little very happily and therefore receives no Bias from his own Conveniency, nor is weigh'd down by the dead Weight of his Appetites and Interests; which ought to be the Temper of every Person who wou'd find out Truth, and who desires to make a high Judgment in all things.

We all pretend to this it's true, and think our selves Injur'd if it be not believ'd that we are Disinteress'd[1] and free from Passion; that no Humour or Private End, nothing but an honest Zeal for Truth gives warmth to our Discourses; and yet it often happens that e're we Conclude them, we give just occasion to have it thought, that how large soever our Knowlege in other things may be, we are not well acquainted with our own Hearts. All which consider'd, how confidently soever we're perswaded of our own Integrity, tho we think we have penetrated to the very bottom of our Hearts, it wou'd not be amiss to suspect our selves sometimes, and to fear a Bias, even at the very instant we take care to avoid one.

For Truth being but One, and the Rational Faculties not differing in Kind but in Degree, tho there may be different Measures of Understanding, there could not be such Contradictions in Mens Opinions as we find there are, even in those who examin as well as in those who do not, were they acted only by the Love of Truth, and did not Self-Love perswade them that they shall find their own particular account by such an Opposition. I wou'd not be so understood as if I thought that in all Controversies one side must needs be Criminal, if not be Wilfully Opposing Truth, yet at least by an indulgence of such un-mortifi'd Passions as estrange them from her. No, without doubt great allowances are to be made on the score of Education, Capacity, [the][2] Leisure, and Opportunity of Information we have had. But this we may venture to say, that had we but a Modest Opinion of our selves, believing it as possible for us as for those who contradict us to be mistaken, did we behave[3] our selves answerable to such a belief; were we seriously convinc'd that nothing is so much our Interest as a readiness to admit of Truth, from what ever Hand it comes, greatest part of our Disputes wou'd have a better Issue than we generally find. At least if we cou'd not be so happy as to Convince one another, our Contests wou'd be manag'd with more Temper and Moderation, wou'd

---

1 Disinterested.

2 Insertion as per Errata list, 298.

3 Hold or conduct ourselves.

not conclude in such a breach of Charity, or at best in such a Coldness for each other, as they usually do.

If we consider wisely we shall find it to be our Present Interest as well as our Future, to do that in Reality which all of us Pretend to, that is, to Search after and to Follow Truth. And to do it with all that Candor and Ingenuity which becomes a true Philosopher as well as a good Christian, making use of no Arguments but what we really believe, and giving them up contentedly when we meet with stronger. Our *Present Interest*, which is that which weighs most with the generality, and to which we make all other considerations give place; For what is it we Contend for? They who have such little Souls as to bait at any thing beneath the highest End,[1] make Reputation their Aim, and with it that Authority and Wealth which usually attends it. But now Reputation cannot be acquir'd, at least not a lasting one, by Fallacious Reasonings; we may perhaps for a while get a Name by them amongst unwary Persons, but the World grows too quick-sighted to be long impos'd on. If a Love of Truth do not, yet Envy and Emulation will set other heads a Work to discover our Ignorance or Fraud, they are upon the same Design, and will not suffer us to go away with the Prize undeservedly, And besides, with how ill an Aspect must he needs appear who does not Reason fairly, and by consequence, how unlike is he to gain on those who hear him? There are but three Causes to which false Arguments can be refer'd, Ignorance, Rashness, or Design, and the being suspected for any one of these hinders us very much in acquiring that Reputation, Authority or Preferment we desire.[2] I must confess were we sure the Fallacy wou'd not be detected, and that we shou'd not lie under Suspicion of it, we might gain our point; for provided the Paint do not rub off, good Colouring may serve a present turn as well as a true Complection: But there is little reason to hope for this, because of what was just now mention'd, and for other Reasons that might be added.

Now what can be more provoking than the Idea we have of a Designing Person? of one who thinks his own Intellectuals so strong and ours so weak, that he can make us swallow any thing,

---

1 Astell's aside to her critics.

2 Here again Astell appears to be answering her critics, pointing in the direction of Locke, whom she elsewhere convicts of expedient arguments, a party man from Shaftesbury's stable.

and lead us where he pleases? such an one seems to have an Intention to reduce us to the vilest Slavery,[1] the Captivation of our Understandings, which we justly reckon to be the highest Insolence. And since every one puts in for a share of Sense, and thinks he has no reason to complain of the distribution of it, whoever supposes that another has an over-weaning Opinion of his own, must needs think that he undervalues his Neighbours Understanding, and will certainly repay him in his own Coin, and deny him those advantages he seems to arrogate.[2]

The most we can say for our selves when the weakness of our Arguments comes to be discover'd, is that we were mistaken thro Rashness or Ignorance, which tho more pardonable than the former, are no recommending Qualities. If we argue falsly and know not that we do so, we shall be more pittied than when we do, but either way disappointed. And if we have added Rash Censures of those who are not of our Mind, Pride or Positiveness[3] to our Errors as we cannot so handsomely Retreat so neither will so fair a Quarter be allow'd as those who Argue with Meekness, Modesty and Charity may well expect. So that when we have cast up our Account and estimated the Present Advantages that false Arguings bring us, I fear what we have got by a Pretence to Truth, won't be found to countervail the loss we shall sustain by the Discovery that it was no more. Which may induce us (if other Considerations will not) to be wary in receiving any Proposition our selves, and restrain us from being forward to impose our Sentiments on others.

After all, 'tis a melancholy reflection that a great part of Mankind stand in need of Arguments drawn from so low a Motive as Worldly Interest, to persuade them to that to which they have much greater inducements. It is strange that we shou'd need any other considerations besides the bare performance of our Duty, and

---

1 Astell introduces the rhetoric of slavery, for which *Reflections upon Marriage* (1700) and the 1706 Preface are so famous.

2 Astell's argument against Locke as an opportunist takes a new twist. Locke, assistant to the Earl of Shaftesbury in the 1670's and 1680's, during the period of his commercial involvement in the slave-owning American colonies, had argued strongly against slavery in the second of the *Two Treatises of Government* (Bk 2, §149, Laslett edn, 1988, 367). But Astell convicts him of impugning the capacity of human understanding in the *Essay* in order to enslave people to his opinions.

3 Subjective certainty, confidence, assurance (*OED*).

those unspeakable advantages laid up for all such as do it sincerely, hereafter. When we have the Approbation of GOD and the infinite Rewards he has propos'd to those who study to recommend themselves to him, for our Encouragement, how low are we sunk if the Applause of Men and the little Trifles which they can bestow weigh any thing with us! I am therefore almost asham'd of proposing so mean a consideration, but the degeneracy of the Age requir'd it, and they who perhaps at first follow Truth as the Jews did once, for the Loaves only,[1] may at last be attracted by its own Native Beauties.

§V. As Nature teaches us Logic, so does it instruct us in Rhetoric much better than Rules of Art, which if they are good ones are nothing else but those Judicious Observations which Men of Sense have drawn from Nature, and which all who reflect on the Operations of their own Minds will find out 'em selves. The common Precepts of Rhetoric may teach us how to reduce Ingenious ways of speaking to a certain Rule, but they do not teach us how to Invent them, this is Natures work and she does it best; there is as much difference between Natural and Artificial Eloquence as there is between Paint and True Beauty. So that as a good Author well observes,[2] all that's useful in this Art, "is the avoiding certain evil ways of Writing and Speaking, and above all an Artificial and Rhetorical Stile Compos'd of false Thoughts, Hyperboles and forc'd Figures which is the greatest fault in Rhetoric."

I shall not therefore recommend under the name of Rhetoric an Art of speaking floridly on all Subjects, and of dressing up Error and Impertinence in a quaint and taking garb; any more than I did that Wrangling which goes by the name of Logic, and which teaches to dispute *for* and *against* all Propositions indefinitely whether they are True or False. It is an abuse both of Reason and Address to press 'em into the Service of a Trifle or an Untruth; and

---

1 Astell's phraseology suggests an Old Testament parable, probably I Samuel, 10, 3-4; 17, 17; 21, 3; 25, 18 or II Samuel, 16, 1. But she could have the New Testament parable of the loaves and fishes in mind from Matthew, 14, 17 to 15, 36; Mark 6, 38 to 8, 19; Luke, 9, 13 to 11, 5; or John, 6, 9-26.

2 *L'art de Penser*, p. 22 – Astell.

Astell quotes in fact from the introductory Second Discourse of the English edn of the *Port Royal Logic* (1693, edn, 24-25), already cited by her as a marginal note (1697 edn, 164).

a mistake to think that any Argument can be rightly made, or any Discourse truly Eloquent that does not illustrate and inforce Truth. For the design of Rhetoric is to remove those Prejudices that lie in the way of Truth, to Reduce the Passions to the Government of Reasons; to place our Subject in a Right Light, and excite our Hearers to a due consideration of it. And I know not what exactness of Method, pure and proper Language, Figures,[1] insinuating ways of Address and the like signify, any farther than as they contribute to the Service of Truth by rendring our Discourse Intelligible, Agreeable and Convincing. They are indeed very serviceable to it when they are duly managed, for Good Sense loses much of its efficacy by being ill express'd, and an ill stile is nothing else but the neglect of some of these, or over doing others of 'em.

Obscurity, one of the greatest faults in Writing, does commonly proceed from a want of Meditation, for when we pretend to teach others what we do not understand our selves, no wonder that we do it at a sorry rate. Tis true, Obscurity is sometimes design'd, to conceal an erroneous opinion which an Author dares not openly own, or which if it be discover'd he has a mind to evade. And sometimes even an honest and good Writer who studies to avoid may insensibly fall into it, by reason that his Ideas being become familiar to himself by frequent Meditation, a long train of 'em are readily excited in his mind, by a word or two which he's us'd to annex to them; but it is not so with his Readers who are perhaps strangers to his Meditations, and yet ought to have the very same Idea rais'd in theirs that was in the Authors mind, or else they cannot understand him. If therefore we desire to be intelligible to every body, our Expressions must be more plain and explicit than they needed to be if we writ only for our selves, or for those to whom frequent Discourse has made our Ideas familiar.

Not that it is necessary to express at length all the Process our Mind goes thro in resolving a Question, this wou'd spin out our Discourse to an unprofitable tediousness, the Operations of the Mind being much more speedy than those of the Tongue or Pen.

1 *The Art of Speaking*, by Bernard Lamy (1640-1715), followed the programme of the *Port Royal Logic* on rhetoric, devoting part 4 to "Figures," defined by him as "Rhetorical Figments, invented for ornaments of discourse" (1676 edn, 99).

But we shou'd fold up our Thoughts so closely and neatly, expressing them in such significant tho few words, as that the Readers Mind may easily open and enlarge them. And if this can be done with facility we are Perspicuous[1] as well as Strong, if with difficulty or not at all, we're then perplext and Obscure Writers.

Scarce any thing conduces more to Clearness, the great Beauty of writing, than Exactness of Method; nor perhaps to Persuasion, for by putting every thing in its proper place with due Order and Connexion, the Readers Mind is gently led where the Writer wou'd have it. Such a Stile is Easy without Softness; Copious as that signifies the omission of nothing necessary, yet not Wordy and Tedious; nor stuft with Nauseous Repetitions, which they who do not Think before they Write and dispose their Matter duly, can scarce avoid. The Method of Thinking has been already shewn, and the same is to be observ'd in Writing, which if it be what it ought, is nothing else but the communicating to others the result of our frequent and deep Meditations, in such a manner as we judge most effectual to convince them of those Truths which we believe. Always remembring that the most natural Order is ever best that we must first prepare their minds by removing those Prejudices and Passions which are in our way, and then propose our Reasons with all the Clearness and Force, with all the Tenderness and Good-Nature we can.

And since the Clearness and Connexion as well as the Emphasis and Beauty of a Discourse depends in the great measure on a right use of the Particles, whoever wou'd Write well ought to inform themselves nicely in their Proprieties. a[n][2] *And*, a *The*, a *But*, a *For*, Etc. do very much perplex the Sense when they are misplac'd, and make the Reader take it many times quite otherwise than the Writer meant it. But this is not a place to say all that this Subject deserves; they who wou'd have much in a little, may consult an Ingenious Author who has touch'd upon't,[3] and from thence take hints to observe how these little words are applied in

---

1 Clearly understood, lucid (*OED*).

2 an, as per Errata list, 298.

3 *Locke* of Hum. Und. B. 3, Ch. 7 – Astell.

Astell's marginal note to Locke's *Essay Concerning Human Understanding*, bk 3, ch. 7, "Of Particles" (1690 edn, 265-66), in which he discusses the uses of the definite and indefinite articles, conjunctions, etc. This is a topic discussed at length in Lamy's *Art of Speaking*, Part I, chs 1 and 2.

good Authors, and how themselves may best use them to express the several Postures of their own Minds.

In a word, I know not a more compendious way to good Speaking and Writing, than to chuse out the the most excellent in either as a Model on which to form our selves. Or rather to imitate the Perfections of all, and avoid their mistakes; for few are so perfect as to be without fault, and few so bad as to have nothing good in them. A true Judgment distinguishes, and neither rejects the Good for the sake of the Bad, nor admits the Bad because of the Good that is mingled with it. No sort of Style but has its excellency and is liable to defect: If care be not taken the Sublime which subdues us with Nobleness of Thought and Grandeur of Expression, will fly out of sight and by being Empty and Bombast become contemptible. The Plain and Simple will grow Dull and Object; the Severe dry and Rugged, the Florid vain and impertinent. The Strong instead of rousing the Mind will distract and intangle it by being Obscure; even the Easy and Perspicuous if it be too diffuse, or over delicate tires us instead of pleasing. Good Sense is the principal thing without which all our polishing is of little Worth, and yet if Ornament be wholly neglected very few will regard us. Studied and artificial periods[1] are not natural enough to please, they shew too much solicitude about what does not deserve it, and a loose and careless Style declares too much contempt of the Public. Neither Reason nor Wit entertain us if they are driven beyond a certain pitch, and Pleasure it self is offensive if it be not judiciously dispenc'd.

Every Author almost has some beauty or blemish remarkable in his Style from whence it takes its name; and every Reader has a peculiar tast of Books as well as Meats. One wou'd have the Subject exhausted, another is not pleas'd if somewhat be not left to enlarge on in his own Meditations. This affects a Grave that a Florid Style; One is for Easiness, a second for Plainness, a third for Strength, and a fourth for Politeness. And perhaps the great secret of Writing is the mixing all these in so just a proportion that every one may tast what he likes without being disgusted by its contrary. And may find at once that by the Solidity of the Reason, the purity and propriety of Expression, and insinuating agreeableness of Address, his Understanding is Enlightned, his Affections subdued and his Will duly regulated.

---

1 Concluding sentences, perorations (archaic).

This is indeed the true End of Writing, and it wou'd not be hard for every one to judge how well they had answer'd it, wou'd they but lay aside Self-Love,[1] so much of it at least, as makes them partial to their own Productions. Did we consider our own with the same Severity, or but Indifferency that we do anothers Writing, we might pass a due Censure on it, might discern what Thought was Crude or ill exprest, what Reasoning weak, what passages superfluous, where we were flat and dull, where extravagant and vain, and by Criticizing on our selves does greater kindness to the World than we can in making our Remarques on others. Nor shou'd we be at a loss, if we were Impartial, in finding out Methods to Inform, Persuade and Please; for Human Nature is for the most part much alike in all, and that which has a good effect on us, will generally speaking have the same on others. So that to guess what success we are like to have, we need only suppose our selves in the place of those we Address to, and consider how such a Discourse wou'd operate on us, if we had their Infirmities and Thoughts about us.

And if we do so I believe we shall find, there's nothing more improper than Pride and Positiveness, nor any thing more prevalent than an innocent compliance with their weakness: Such as pretends not to dictate to their Ignorance, but only to explain and illustrate what they did or might have known before if they had consider'd it, and supposes that their Minds being employ'd about some other things was the reason why they did not discern it as well as we. For Human Nature is not willing to own its Ignorance; Truth is so very attractive, there's such a natural agreement between our Minds and it, that we care not to be thought so dull as not to be able to find out by our selves such obvious matters. We shou'd therefore be careful that nothing pass from us which upbraids our Neighbours Ignorance, but study to remove't without appearing to take notice of it, and permit 'em to fancy if they please, that we believe them as Wise and Good as we endeavour to make them. By this we gain their Affections which is the hardest part of our Work, excite their Industry and infuse a new Life into all Generous Tempers, who conclude there's great hopes they may with a little pains attain what others think they Know already, and

---

1 Astell compares the negative form of self-love, *amour propre* with the positive form, *amour-de-soi,* as discussed in the multi-volume *Moral Essays* of Pierre Nicole (see *A Serious Proposal, Part I* (1694 edn, 35), p. 63 n.1 above.

are asham'd to fall short of the good Opinion we have entertain'd of 'em.

And since many wou'd yield to the Clear Light of Truth were't not for the shame of being overcome, we shou'd Convince but not Triumph, and rather Conceal our Conquest than Publish it. We doubly oblige our Neighbours when we reduce them into the Right Way, and keep it from being taken notice of that they were once in the Wrong, which is certainly a much greater satisfaction than that blaze of Glory which is quickly out, that noise of Applause which will soon be over. For the gaining of our Neighbour, at least the having honestly endeavour'd it, and the leading our own Vanity in Triumph are Real Goods and such as we shall always have the Comfort of. It is to be wish'd that such Propositions as are not attended with the Clearest Evidence were deliver'd only by way of Enquiry, since even the brightest Truth when Dogmatically dictated is apt to offend our Readers, and make them imagine their Liberty's impos'd on, so far is Positiveness from bringing any body over to our Sentiments. And besides, we're all of us liable to mistake, and few have Humility enough to confess themselves Deceiv'd in what they have confidently asserted, but think they're obliged in Honour to maintain an Opinion they've once been Zealous for, how desirous soever they may be to get rid on't, cou'd they do it handsomely. Now a Modest way of delivering our Sentiments assists us in this, and leaves us at liberty to take either side of the Question as Reason and Riper Considerations shall determine.

In short, as Thinking conformably to the Nature of Things is True Knowledge, so th' expressing our Thoughts in such a way, as more readily, and with the greatest Clearness and Life, excites in others the very same Idea that was in us, is the best Eloquence. For if our Idea be conformable to the Nature of the thing it represents, and in Relations duly stated, this is the most effectual way both to Inform and Perswade, since Truth being always amiable, cannot fail or attracting when she's plac'd in a Right Light, and those to whom we offer her, are made Able and Willing to discern her Beauties. If therefore we thoroughly understand our Subject and are Zealously affected with it, we shall neither want suitable word to explain, nor perswasive Methods to recommend it.

And since Piety and Vertue should in spite of the mistaken Customs of the Age be the principal Theme of a Christians Conversation; that which those who bear that Sacred Name ought always to regard some way or other, even when it might be unseasonable to speak of it directly, the way to be good Orators is to be good Christians, the Practice of Religion will both instruct us in the Theory, and most powerfully inforce what we say of it. Did we truly relish the Delights of GOD'S Service, we cou'd neither refrain from talking of the Pleasure, nor be so ill-natur'd as not to strive to Communicate it; and were we duly warm'd with a Zeal for his Glory and concern for our Neighbours Soul, no Figures of Rhetoric, no Art of Perswasion wou'd be wanting to us. We shou'd diligently watch for Opportunities, and carefully improve them, accommodating our Discourse to the Understanding and Genius of all we cou'd hope to do good to.

Besides, by being True Christians we have Really that Love for others which all who desire to perswade must pretend to; we've that *Probity* and *Prudence*, that *Civility* and *Modesty* which the Masters of this Art say a good Orator must be endow'd with; and have pluck'd up those Vicious Inclinations from whence the most distastful faults of Writing proceed. For why do we chuse to be Obscure but because we intend to Deceive, or wou'd be thought to see much farther than our Neighbours? One sort of Vanity prompts us to be Rugged and Severe, and so possess'd with the imagin'd Worth and Solidity of our Discourse, that we think it beneath us to Polish it: Another disposes us to Elaborate and Affected ways of Writing, to Pompous and improper Ornaments; and why are we tediously Copious but that we fancy every Thought of ours is extraordinary? Contradiction is indeed for our advantage as tending to make us wiser, yet our Pride makes us impatient under it, because it seems to Lessen that Esteem and Deference we desire shou'd be paid us. Whence come those sharp Reflections, those imagin'd strains of Wit, not to be endur'd amongst Christians, and which serve not to Convince but to Provoke, whence come they but from Ill-nature or Revenge, from a Contempt of others and a desire to set forth our own Wit? Did we write less for our selves we should sooner gain our Readers, who are many times disgusted at a well writ Discourse if it carries a tange of Ostentation: And were our Temper as Christian as it ought to be, our Zeal wou'd be spent on the most Weighty things, not on little differences of Opinions.

I have made no distinction in what has been said between Speaking and Writing, because tho they are talents which do not always meet, yet there is no material difference between 'em. They Write best perhaps who do't with the gentile and easy air of Conversation; and they Talk best who mingle Solidity of Thought with th' agreableness of a ready Wit. As for *Pronunciation*, tho it takes more with some *Auditors* many times than Good Sense, there needs little be said of it here, since Women have no business with the Pulpit, the Bar or *St. Stephens Chapel*:[1] And Nature does for the most part furnish 'em with such a Musical Tone, Perswasive Air and winning Address as renders their Discourse sufficiently agreeable in Private Conversation. And as to spelling which they're said to be defective in, if they don't believe as they're usually told, that its fit for 'em to be so, and that to write exactly is too Pedantic, they may soon correct that fault, by Pronouncing their words aright and Spelling 'em accordingly. I know this Rule won't always hold because of an Imperfection in our Language which has been oft complain'd of but is not yet amended; But in this case a little Observation or recourse to Books will assist us; and if at any time we happen to mistake by Spelling as we Pronounce, the fault will be very Venial,[2] and Custom rather to blame than we.

I've said nothing of *Grammar* tho we can't Write properly if we transgress its Rules, supposing that Custom and the reading of English Books are sufficent to teach us the Grammar of our own Tongue, If we do but in any measure attend to them. And tho Women are generally accus'd of Writing false English, if I may speak my own Experience, their Mistakes are not so common as is pretended, nor are they the only Persons guilty. What they most commonly fail in is the Particles and Connexion, and that generally thro a Briskness of temper which make them forget, or Hast which will not suffer 'em to read over again what went before. And indeed, those who Speak true Grammar unless they're very Careless cannot write false, since they need only peruse what they've

---

1 St. Stephen's Chapel, built by King Stephen, became the meeting place for the House of Commons from 1547, once it had moved venues from the chapter house of Westminster Abbey (*Encyclopaedia Britannica*, vol, 28, 551). Astell later uses St. Stephen's Chapel to refer metonymically to the Houses of Parliament in *A Fair Way with the Dissenters* (1704/1996, 21/196). Her remarks here may echo the famous epithet of Fénelon in *De l'Education des filles* (1687, 1933 edn, 18), that women "ought neither to govern the state, nor make war, nor enter into the sacred ministry."

2 Worthy of forgiveness, pardonable (*OED*).

Writ, and consider whether they wou'd express 'emselves thus in Conversation.[1]

But for this and for Figures Etc. and indeed for all that relates to this Subject, I must refer you to an Ingenious Treatise[2] which handles it fully, and to which I'me oblig'd in great measure for what little skill I have. Observing only, that whatever it is we Treat of, our Stile shou'd be such as may keep our Readers Attent, and induce them to go to the End. Now Attention is usually fixt by Admiration, which is excited by somewhat uncommon either in the Thought or way of Expression. We fall asleep over an Author who tells us in an ordinary manner no more than we knew before: He who wou'd Take[3] must be Sublime in his Sense, and must cloath it after a Noble way. His Thoughts must not be superficial, such as every one may fall into at the first glance, but the very Spirits and Essence of Thinking, the sum of many hours Meditation folded up in one handsome and comprehensive Period, whose Language is Intelligible and Easy that the Readers may not lose the pleasure of the Kernel, by the pain they find in cracking the Shell. The most difficult Subject must be made easy by his way of handling it; tho his Matter may deserve a Meditation, yet his Expressions must be so Clear that he needs not be read twice to be Understood; *these* are to be Natural and Familiar, condiscending to the meanest Capacity, whilst his Thoughts are Great enough to entertain the highest. He Discourses always on a Useful Subject in a manner agreeable to it, and Pleases that he may Instruct; Nothing seems Studied in his whole Composition, yet every thing is Extraordinary, a Beautiful Harmony shining thro all its parts. No Sentence is Doubtful, no word Equivocal, his Arguments are Clear and his Images Lively; all the Ideas he excites in your Mind, as nearly resemble the thing they represent as Words can make them. Whilst th' exactness of his Method, and Force of his Reason Enlighten and Convince the Mind; the Vivacity of his Imagination and insinuating Address, gain the Affections and Conquer the Will. By the weight and closeness of the former you wou'd take him for

---

1 *The Ladies Library* ch. 13 on "Ignorance" (1714 edn, 438-534), reproduced from Astell's text with only minor changes, concludes at this point.

2 *Art of speaking* – Astell.

Astell's marginal note is to Lamy's *The Art of Speaking* (1696), a theory of rhetoric derived, as Lamy's title states, from the *Port Royal Logic*.

3 Be effective.

an Angel, and the tender and affable sweetness of the last bespeaks him a Friend. He considers that as mere Florish and Rhetorick are good for nothing, so neither will bare Reason dull and heavily express'd perform any great matter, at least not on those who need it most, whose Palates being deprav'd their Medicines must be administred in a pleasing Vehicle. Since Mankind are averse to their Real Happiness, he does not only tell 'em their Duty but Interesses them in it; and thinking it not enough to run 'em down with the strength of Reason, he draws 'em over to a Voluntary Submission by th' attractives of his Eloquence. For he has a peculiar Turn and Air which animates every Period, so that the very same Truth which was dry and Unaffecting in a vulgar Authors words, Charms and Subdues you when cloath'd in his. He shews no more warmth than may convince his Readers that he's heartily persuaded of the Truths he offers them; and if it is necessary at any time to make use of Figures to give a more Lively Representation than plain Expressions cou'd, to describe his own Passions and excite the same in others upon a just occasion, in a word to awaken a Stupid and Clear the Mind of A Prejudic'd Reader, his Figures are duly chosen and discreetly us'd. For he knows that scarce any thing speaks a greater want of Judgment than the shewing concern where there needs none, or is a worse fault in Oratory than the polishing a Wrong or a Trifling Thought, the neatness of whose dress may strike with Admiration perhaps at first sight, but upon a review it will certainly appear Contemptible. And therefore as he does not abound in Superfluous Ornaments, so neither does he reject anything that can promote his End, which is not his own Reputation but the Glory of his GOD and his Neighbours Edification. He considers the narrowness of the Humane Mind, and says all that is necessary but no more; Understands it so well as to know what will move and Please, and has so much command of himself as to give over when he has done enough. Yet he can exhaust the most fruitful Subject without making the Reader weary; for when he enlarges it is in Things not Words, and he mingles Variety without Confusion. All the diverse excellencies of different Stiles meet in his to make up a perfect one, Strength and Ease, Solidity and Liveliness, the Sublime and the Plain. He's neither so Lofty as to fly out of Sight, nor so humble as to become Creeping and Contemptible. His Strength does not make him Rugged and Perplext nor his Smoothness Weak and Nice; tho every thing is Neat, there's not a grain of Affectation; he is gratefull to the Ear, but far remov'd from jingling Cadence. Brief when there is occasion without Dryness or

Obscurity, and Florid enough to entertain th' Imagination without Distracting the Mind. There's not an Antiquated or Barbarous Word to be found in him, all is Decent, Just and Natural; no peculiar or Affected Phrases, whether Courtly or Clownish, Grave or Burlesque. For Plain and Significant Language is ever best, we have a mistaken Idea of Learning if we think to pretend to't by sending our Reader every minute to the Dictionary. Words out of the common way are only allowable when they express our Sense with greater Force than Ordinary ones cou'd, or when they are so significant as to ease us of Circumlocutions, a hard word which I cou'd not avoid without using half a dozen words.

After all, it may not be amiss to take notice that Ornaments are common to Falshood and Truth, but Clearness and strength of Reasoning are not. They who wou'd propagate Error usually disguise it in Equivocal Terms and Obscure Phrases; they strive to engage our Passions, rather than to Convince our Reason, and carry us away in the torrent of a warm Imagination. They endeavour to refute, or if they can't do that, to Ridicule the contrary opinion, and think this Sufficient to establish their own. Being much better skill'd in pulling down former Systems than in building new ones, for it requires no great skill to Object, and there are many Truths which we're very Certain of, and yet not able to answer every Impertinent Enquiry concerning 'em. Their greatest Art is in confounding things, in giving a probable Air to what they write, in pretending to Demonstration where the nature of the Truth does not require't, and in evading it where it does. An Immoral or Heretical Discourse therefore may be *Cunningly* but not *well* writ, for we can never plead for Error and Vice with true Eloquence. We may trick 'em up in a handsom Garb, adorn 'em with quaint Expressions, and give them such a plausible turn as may enable them to do very much Mischief; but this is only a fulsom Carcass, the substance and Life are not there if Vertue and Truth are wanting.

§VI. For it is to little purpose to Think well and speak well, unless we *Live well*, this is our Great Affair and truest Excellency, the other are no further to be regarded than as they may assist us in this. She who does not draw this Inference from her Studies has Thought in vain, her notions are Erroneous and Mistaken. And all her Eloquence is but an empty noise, who employs it in any other design than in gaining Proselytes to Heaven. I am therefore far from designing to put Women on a vain pursuit after unnecessary and useless Learning, nor wou'd by any means persuade them to endeavour after Knowledge cou'd I be convinc'd that it is improper for 'em. Because I know every well that tho a thing be never so excellent in it self, it has but an ill grace if it be not suitable to the Person and Condition it is apply'd to. Fine Cloaths and Equipage do not become a Beggar, and a Mechanic who must work for daily bread for his Family, wou'd be wickedly Employ'd shou'd he suffer 'em to starve whilest he's solving Mathematical Problems. If therefore Women have another Duty incumbent on 'em, and such as is inconsistent with what we here advise, we do ill to take them from it: But to affirm this is to beg the Question, and is what I will never grant till it be better prov'd than as yet it appears to be. For if the Grand Business that Women as well as Men have to do in this World be to prepare for the next, ought not all their Care and Industry to Centre here? and since the matter is of Infinite Consequence is it equitable to deny 'em the use of any help? If therefore Knowledge were but any ways Instrumental, tho at the remotest distance, to the Salvation of our Souls, it were fit to apply our selves to it; and how much more when it is so necessary, that without it we can't do any thing that's Excellent, or Practise Vertue in the most Perfect manner. For unless we Understand our Duty and the Principles of Religion, we don't perform a Rational Service, it is but by Chance that we are Good or so much as Christians. We are their Property into whose hands we fall, and are led by those who with greatest Confidence impose their Opinions on us; Are as moveable as the different Circumstances that befall us; or if we happen to be Constant in our first way, it is not Reason but Obstinacy that makes us so. A great deal of Good will be omitted, and very much Evil, or Imperfection at least, stick to us, if we are not throughly acquainted with the Law of God and the secret springs and windings of our Hearts, which is scarce to be obtain'd without much Meditation and the helps that study affords.

And as when a rash young Traveller is about to run into dangerous places beset with Theives and full of Precipices,[1] if you have

1 This complex passage alludes to the parable of the Good Samaritan (Luke 10, 33) and possibly to the famous examples of the "high-way man" employed by Hobbes in *Leviathan* (ch. 14, 1991 edn, 98) and Locke in the second *Treatise of Government* (1988 edn, §119, 347-48; §176, 385; §182, 390; §186, 393; §202, 401; §207, 403-04). If Astell already knows the provenance of Locke's *Two Treatises of Government*, which she clearly

any hearty concern for his safety, you'l not think it enough barely to shew him his way, or even to tell him of the Danger, especially if the entrance seems fair and inviting and treacherous Companious are upon the watch to decoy him into it: But you'l expose it in all its frightful Circumstances, endeavour to quicken his vigilance and excite his Passions, and all little enough for his Security. So it cannot be thought sufficient that Women shou'd but just know whats Commanded and what Forbid, without being inform'd of the Reasons why, since this is not like to secure them in their Duty. For we find a Natural Liberty within us which checks at an Injunction that has nothing but Authority to back it; And tho Religion is indeed supported by the Strongest Reasons, and inforc'd by the most powerful Motives, yet if we are not acquainted with 'em, tis all one to us as if it were not. But having spoke of this in the first part we shall not farther enlarge on it here.

Perhaps it will be objected that we've said *the great Truths of Religion carry a force and Evidence suited to the very Vulgar, and that GOD has not design'd All for Philosophers.*[1] And therefore if the way to the most necessary Knowlege be so very plain, and all Capacities are not fitted for higher attainments, what needs this ado about th' Improvement of our minds? the only thing necessary is to be good Christians, and we may be that without being Philosophers. Suppose we may: This will Justify such as want Time and Capacity, but can never excuse the Sloth and Stupidity of those who have both.

For unless we have very strange Notions of the Divine Wisdom we must needs allow that every one a placed in such a Station as they are fitted for. And if the necessity of the world requires that some Person shou'd Labour for others, it likewise requires that

---

shows in her *Reflections upon Marriage* of 1700, then this strengthens my case for her importance as the first systematic critic of that work (see Springborg, "Astell, Critic of Locke"). To the 3rd edn of *Reflections upon Marriage* in 1706, Astell had added a cautionary homily on the pitfalls of marriage, invoking the image of the highway-man to characterize the rogue government of husbands: "And if mere Power gives a Right to Rule, there can be no such thing as Usurpation; but a Highway-Man so long as he has strength to force, has also a Right to require our Obedience" (*Reflections upon Marriage*, 1706 edn, x/16).

1 The thesis of much of the devotional literature to which Astell refers, especially the works by Allestree cited above.

others shou'd Think for them. Our Powers and Faculties were not given us for nothing, and the only advantage one Woman has above another, is the being allotted to the more noble employment. Nobody is plac'd without their own fault, in such unhappy Circumstances as to be incapable of Salvation, but some are plac'd in such happy ones as to be capable of attaining much greater degrees of Happiness than others if they do not neglect them: And shou'd these last do no more than the very utmost that is expected from the former, I know not how they wou'd acquit themselves, or what account they cou'd give of their great Advantages. And therefore tho no body shall be condemn'd because they *Cou'd* not, yet we have reason to fear if our Case be such as that we *Might* but *Wou'd* not receive Instruction. She then who makes this Objection must not take it amiss if we Judge of her in other Cases according to what the Pleads in this: She must never set up for a Wit, or a censurer of her Neighbours, must not pretend to be a fine Lady or any thing extraordinary: but be content to herd amongst the Drudges of the World who eat Their Bread in the Sweat of their Brows, if she says she wants Leisure; or in a less acceptable rank amongst the Fools and Idiots, or but one degree above them, if she says she wants Capacity for this Employment. It is one thing to be content with Ignorance, or rather with a less degree of Knowledge, on account of the Station that GOD has plac'd us in, and Another to Chuse and Delight in't thro a Stupid Carelesness, a fear of Trouble, or an Inordinate pursuit of the Cares and Pleasures of this Mortal Life. This last only shews our Disesteem of our Souls, our Contempt of GOD and the Talents he has given us, and exposes us to all the dreadful consequences of such a neglect; to Punishments to which not only those who misemploy their Lord's Talent, but even they who don't employ it at all, are Obnoxious.

And indeed as unnecessary as it is thought for Women to have Knowledge, she who is truly good finds very great use of it, not only in the Conduct of her own Soul but in the management of her Family, in the Conversation of her Neighbours and in all the Concerns of Life. Education of Children is a most necessary Employment, perhaps the chief of those who have any; But it is as Difficult as it is Excellent when well perform'd; and I question not but that the mistakes which are made in it, are a principal Cause of that Folly and Vice, which is so much complain'd of and so little mended. Now this, at least the foundation of it, on which in a great measure the success of all depends, shou'd be laid by the Mother, for Fathers find other Business, they will not be confin'd to such a laborious work, they have not such opportunities of observing a Childs Temper, nor are the greatest part of 'em like to do much good, since Precepts contradicted by Example seldom prove effectual. Neither are Strangers so proper for it, because hardly any thing besides Paternal Affection can sufficiently quicken the Care of performing, and sweeten the labour of such a task. But Tenderness alone will never discharge it well, she who wou'd do it to purpose must throughly understand Human nature, know how to manage different Tempers Prudently, be Mistress of her own, and able to bear with all the little humours and follies of Youth, neither Severity nor Lenity are to be always us'd, it wou'd ruin some to be treated in that manner which is fit for others. An Mildness makes some ungovernable and as there is a stupor in many from which nothing but Terrors can rouse them, so sharp Reproofs and Solemn Lectures serve to no purpose but to harden others, in faults from which they might be won by an agreeable Address and tender application. GOD Himself waits to be gracious and administers his Medicines in the most proper season, and Parents shou'd imitate him in this, for the want of observing it, and of accomodating their Methods to the several Dispositions they have to deal with, is perhaps the reason that many Pious Persons lose the fruit of their Pains and Care.

Nor will Knowledge lie dead upon their hands who have no Children to Instruct; the whole World is a single Lady's Family, her opportunities of doing good are not lessen'd but encreas'd by her being unconfin'd. Particular Obligations do not contract her Mind, but her Beneficence moves in the largest Sphere. And perhaps the Glory of Reforming this Prophane and Profligate Age is reserv'd for you Ladies, and that the natural and unprejudic'd Sentiments of your Minds being handsomly express'd, may carry a more strong conviction than the Elaborate Arguments of the Learned. Such as fence themselves against the Cannon they bring down, may lie open to an Ambuscade[1] from you. And whilst the strong arguings of the Schools like the Wind in the Fable,[2] seems but to harden these Sturdy Sinners, your Persuasions like the Suns mild and powerful rays, may oblige them to cast off that Cloak of

---

1 Ambush (obsolete except as a formal military term) (*OED*).

2 Possibly the book of Job which, extremely old and elemental, is full of wind, see esp., Job 8: 2, where the words "of thy mouth be like a strong wind."

Maliciousness in which they are so much intangled. And surely it is worth your while to fit your selves for this: Tis a Godlike thing to relieve even the Temporal wants of our Fellow Creatures, to keep a *Body* from perishing, but it, is much more Divine, to *Save a Soul from Death*! A Soul which in his estimate who best knows the value of it is worth more than all the World. They who are thus *wise shall shine as the brightness of the Firmament, and they who turn many to Righteousness as the Stars for ever*;[1] which is a Glory we may honestly Contend for, a Beauty we may lawfully Covet; O that we had but Ambition enough to aspire after it! O that we had but so much at least as we see daily thrown away on a poor transitory Earthly Diadem, which sets uneasy on his head who wears it, and which a longer arm may wrest from his Brows! But alas it was in our fore-fathers days that the Kingdom of Heav'n was took by violence; they thought nothing, and we think every thing too much to Do or Suffer to obtain it! Nor but that it is still as bright and glorious, as truly attractive, but we are dull and stupid we shut our eyes and won't behold its Charms. Were we but duly sensible of this we shou'd think no Posterity so desireable as the Offspring of our Minds, nor any state so great as the carrying a large Train of Followers with us to the Court of Heaven! So much Knowledge therefore as is necessary to engage and keep us firm in our Christian Course, to fit us to help others in theirs, to stir us up to pursue, and direct us in our endeavours after one of the brightest Crowns of Glory, does very well become us and more than this I do not contend for, being far from desiring that any one shou'd neglect her Necessary Affairs to amuse her self with nice Speculations. No, She who has a Family is discharging part of her Christian Calling whilst She's taking care for it's Support and Government, and wou'd be very much out, if she lock'd her self in her Study, when her Domesticks had need of her direction. But there are few of those to whom I write, who have not a good deal of time to spare, if you reckon whats thrown away on fantastic Impertinencies, and tis this I wou'd have better employ'd: Were not a Morning more advantageously spent at a Book than at a Looking Glass, and an Evening in Meditation than in Gaming? were not Pertinent and Ingenious Discourse more becoming in a visit, than Idle twattle and uncharitable

---

1 Daniel 12: 3.

Remarks? than a Nauseous repetition of a set of fine words which no body believes or cares for? And is not the fitting our selves to do Real Services to our Neighbours, a better expression of our Civility than the formal performance of a thousand ridiculous Ceremonies, which every one condemns and yet none has the Courage to break thro?

CHAP. IV.

Concerning the Regulation of the Will and the Government of the Passions.

As the Capacity which we find in our selves of Receiving and Comparing Ideas is what we call the Understanding, so the Power of Preferring any Thought or Motion, of Directing them to This or That thing rather than to another is what we mean by the Will: Whose Regularity consists in a constant Tendency towards such things as ought to be Prefer'd, or in a word, in Conformity to the Will of GOD. That GOD'S Will is the Rule of ours is methinks so plain that it needs no proof; for why do we Prefer a thing but because we Judge it Best? and why do we Chuse it but because it Seems Good for us? Now GOD being Infintely Wise all his Judgments must be Infallible, and being Infintely Good he can will nothing but what is best, nor prescribe any thing that is not for our Advantage. This is I dare say what every one Thinks, if they think at all about the matter, and is the Rule they wou'd Act by, did they given themselves leave upon all occasions duly to Consider and Weigh what is propos'd to them.

But as there are some Ideas which our Understandings receive so early that they seem to be born with us, which are never totally absent from our minds, and are in a manner the source of all the rest; so there are certain Motions of Inclinations inseparable from the Will, which push us on to the use of that Power, and determine it to the Choice of such things as are most agreeable to them. Nor shou'd we do amiss in following these Inclinations did they keep that Impression which the Author of Nature gave them, which is towards Good in general, or towards himself, for he only is our True Good, and these are the Wings of the Soul which shou'd carry it on vigorously towards him.

Whether there is not in us an Inclination to do what is *Fit*, that is to think and Act agreeably to a Rational Nature, without considering our own particular advantage I shall not here dispute. For whether this be so or no, tis certain that in our present Circumstances, we cannot separate *Fit* and *Good* in Reality, tho we may have distinct Ideas of them. What is really proper for Rational Creatures to do, tending necessarily to their Happiness, and nothing being able to make them truly Happy but that which is fit to be done. Besides, so pure an Inclination being wholly abstracted from Self-Love and Prejudice is not subject to any Irregularity, and so needs not be spoken of here; and perhaps so few are acquainted with it, that it will hardly be known what we mean by it.

An Inclination therefore after Happiness is that to which we shall at present reduce all the rest; which Happiness we pursue by removing as far as we can from that which is uneasie to us, and by uniting our selves as much as we are able to some Good which we suppose we want. The former of these being indeed a pursuit of Good, tho not so directly as the latter. Good then is the Object of the Will, and hitherto one wou'd think there were no probability of our straying from the Will of GOD, and that there were so little need of advising us to Will as GOD Wills that it is impossible we shou'd Will otherwise; because whenever we oppose our Wills to his, we change in a manner the very Constitution of our Nature and fly from that Happiness which we wou'd pursue.

But the misfortune is as has been once observ'd already, that we Will e're we are capable of examining the Reasons of our Choice, or of viewing our Ideas so exactly as we must if we wou'd Judge aright. And the frequent repetition of such unreasonable Choices makes them Customary to us, and consequently gives a new and wrong bias to our Inclinations, which upon all occasions dispose the Will to the Choice of such things as we suppose, tho by mistake, to contribute to our Happiness. Add to this, that the Passions which are certain Commotions in the Bloud and Animal Spirits accompanying these Inclinations, design'd in the Order of Nature for the good of the Body, as the Inclinations were intended for the Good of the Soul, do so unite us to sensible things, and represent 'em with such advantage, that Spiritual Good which seems at a greater distance relishes very little, and abstracted Truths do not find us so Impartial as to examin them throughly, and to give them their due Weight, when they're ballanc'd against such things as may be Seen and Felt; these being commonly preferr'd, not for their intrinsic worth, but for their outward Shew and the Bulk they carry.

That we always endeavour to be Happy is sufficiently evident, and that we too frequently fly from GOD who only can make us so, Experience sadly Demonstrates. Which cou'd not be did we not grossly mistake our Happiness, as we certainly do whenever we Will any thing in opposition to the Will of GOD, whatever Appearance of Good it may happen to carry. 'Tis true the Will does always pursue Good, or somewhat represented to it as such, but it is not always, or rather very seldom, determin'd to the Choice of what is in it self the greatest Good. And though I suppose we always Chuse that which in that Juncture in which it is propos'd seems fittest for our present turn, yet it is often such as we wou'd not prefer, did we impartially examin and observe the Consequences. But we will not do that, chusing rather to Act by the Wrong Judgments we have formerly made, and to follow blindly the Propensities they have given us, than to suspend our Inclinations as we both May and Ought, and restrain them from determining our Will, till we have fairly and fully examin'd and ballanc'd, according to the best of our Knowledge, the several degrees of Good and Evil present and future that are in the Objects set before us. The neglect of which is at once both our Fault and Misery; Our Fault in that we precipitate our Choice, refusing to Consider sufficiently to rectifie our Mistakes. And our Misery because we shall certainly be Disappointed sooner or later, and be convinc'd that what was so Hastily and Unreasonably Chosen, ought not even then to have been prefer'd, how Pleasant soever it appear'd, seeing it neither Was nor Cou'd be Good for us.

It seems indeed the greatest wonder in the World how any Man in his Senses can prefer the Short Pleasures of Sin, which are attended even in this Life with Pain and Shame, and a thousand Inconveniencies, to the Present Delights of Vertue, and the Prospect of a Felicity Infinite and Eternal, if he does at all compare them. An Eternity of Joys must needs be preferable to Fifty or Threescore Years of Sinful Pleasures, weigh them in what Scales you please, and supposing these much greater than ever any Sinner found 'em, especially since they are attended with Eternal Pains, and no perverse Inclination can make us think otherwise if it will allow us to consider. But it will not allow Consideration, or if it does a little permit it, it deceives us however with Fallacious Salvoes. It fixes our Thoughts on a Present Uneasiness which it says must be remov'd, and our Desires gratify'd at any rate, without suffering us to weigh the ill Consequences of doing so. And perhaps the Wrong bias which we receive from our Evil Inclinations does not consist in the persuading us that a Present Sinful Pleasure or Profit, is the Greatest Good, or that it ought to be Prefer'd before the Favour of GOD and Eternal Beatitude, which whenever we Think of we must needs acknowledge to be infinitely greater, but in keeping us from a full Conviction that th' one can't be Chosen without Renouncing th' other, and in making us unwilling to examine throughly, lest we shou'd want the pretence of Ignorance or Passion to excuse what our Conferences can't but Reproach us with as an unworthy Choice, whenever we permit our selves to Reflect.

So that the great aggravation of Sin seems to consist in this, That the commission of it is a pretending to be Wiser or Stronger than GOD, an attempt to out wit him by Fineness, or else by plain Force to wrest his Felicity from him whether he Will or no. For seeing we always Will happiness, and yet wou'd be Happy after another manner than GOD Wills we shall, we express a Desire, and an Endeavour so far as we're able to Oppose and Alter his Will and Order, by reconciling the gratification of a present unreasonable Appetite with the Enjoyment of Happiness, tho he has declar'd they can't be reconciled, and made it in the ordinary course of things impossible they shou'd.

The Will of GOD then is the Rule of ours, and if it be ask'd how we shall come to the Knowledg of it? the Answer is ready, that the Eternal Word and Wisdom of GOD declares his Fathers Will unto us, by *Reason* which is that Natural and Ordinary Revelation by which he speaks to every one; and by that which is call'd *Revelation* in a stricter Sense, which is nothing else but a more perfect and infallible way of Reasoning, whereby we are Clearly and Fully instructed in so much of GOD's Will as is fit for us to know. We must therefore Improve our Reason as much as our Circumstances in the World permit, and to supply its deficiency Seriously, Devoutly and Diligently study the Holy Scriptures "than which" (to use the words of a most excellent Person)[1] "a Christian needs under-

1 Mr. *Boyle* Style of Scripture – Astell.

Marginal note (1697 edn), p. 226/208. Astell refers to Robert Boyle's *Some Considerations Touching the Style of the Holy Scriptures* (1661), an early work based on his knowledge of the original biblical languages (in addition to Latin, Aramaic, Syriac, French, and Italian) and his concern for a proper English translation. Boyle argues for a freer translation which will result in a proper communication of the sense of the Hebrew and Greek

stand no other Book to know the duty of his Faith and Life, tho indeed to understand it well, 'tis ordinarily requisite that a pretty number of other Books be understood."

In the former Chapter[1] we have laid down a Method of using our Reason so as to discover Truth, by observing of which 'tis hop'd we may escape from considerable Errors, and consequently from great Offences. And tho I can't say we shall never be Mistaken nor chuse amiss, yet our Infirmities will be very pitiable, such as our Just and Merciful Lord God will never impute to us, tho we our selves ought to be humbled for and always endeavouring to rectifie 'em.

After all, the best way to be further Instructed in the Knowledg of our Duty is to Practise so much of it as we Know already. By keeping GOD's Commandments, we get such a sound and strong Constitution of Soul, as leads us naturally to our True Good. For as a healthy person whose Tast is not vitiated, is directed by that, without examining the Philosophy of Bodys to such things as are fit for the nourishment of his own: So a Divine Sensation gives us a lively relish of what's Good, and a perfect aversion to the contrary. It endues the Soul not only with a Sagacity of Understanding to discern readily what is best, but likewise with such a Regularity of Will, as makes it even Hate and Abhor all evil ways.

A most desirable Temper no doubt, the very top of Human Felicity, but how shall we obtain it? We find our selves under the

---

texts. This in turn will encourage people to study the Bible for themselves. Boyle, a prominent member of the Royal Society, advanced the inductive reasoning of Bacon to focus on a philosophy which he called "new, corpuscularian, atomical, Cartesian or Mechanical" that was built on two foundations: "reason and experience." He is best known for the discovery, arrived at through detailed experimentation, that the volume of a gas is inversely proportional to its pressure, known as Boyle's law. Boyle was among the group of seventeenth century "Virtuosi," a term used by Astell to describe men of leisure who used their free time to engage in an esoteric examination of nature. But in *The Christian Virtuoso* (1690-91) Boyle redefined the term to describe a person who is interested in the investigation of natural science. The Christian Virtuoso is one who is "dispos'd to make use of the knowledge of the Creatures to confirm his belief, and encrease his Veneration, of the Creator."

1 See P. 114, Etc. – Astell.

power of quite contrary Inclinations and Relishes, and how to get rid of 'em we know not. This is indeed a very wretched condition, the only thing that deserves our Sorrow, yet the Case is not so desperate, but that by the help of an Almighty Physician we may be Cured, if in good earnest we set about it. And because the not discerning our true Happiness and the being accustom'd to pursue a false one is the cause of our Disorder, somewhat must be done by way of Mediation and somewhat by way of Exercise.

Now I know not any Subjects more proper for our Meditation on this and all occasions, than our own Nature, the Nature of Material Beings, and the Nature of GOD; because it is thro the mistake of some of these that our Inclinations take a wrong bias, and consequently that we transgress against GOD, our Neighbour and our selves. For did we consider what we Are, that Humane Nature consists in the Union of a Rational Soul with a Mortal Body, that the Body very often Clogs the Mind in its noblest Operations, especially when indulg'd. That we stand not singly on our own Bottom, but are united in some measure to all who bear a Human Form, especially to the Community amongst whom we live, and yet more particularly to those several Relations we may have in it. Did we go on to consider what are the proper Duties and Enjoyments of such a nature as ours, that is, what performances do naturally result from those Capacities we find our selves endow'd with, which may therefore be reasonably expected from us, and what sort of Pleasures we are made to relish. Again, were we so far at least Philosophers, as to be able to pass a due estimate on material Beings, did we know 'em so well as not to prize them above their real value. Did we in the last place contemplate the Author of our Being, *from* whom we Derive and *to* whom we owe our *All*; and insted of prying saucily into his Essence, (an insufferable presumption in Creatures who are ignorant of their own) or pretending to know more of him than he has thought fit to communicate in his Word, and in that Ideal of Infinite Perfection which he has giv'n us, Frequently, Seriously and Humbly Meditate on what he has been pleas'd to unveil. Did we but employ so much of our Time and Thoughts on these things as we do on our Sins and Vanities, we shou'd not be long in discerning the good effects.

For I question not but that we shou'd be convinc'd that the Body is the Instrument of the Mind and no more, that it is of a much Inferior Nature, and therefore ought to be kept in such a Case as to be ready on all occasions to serve the Mind. That the true and proper Pleasure of Human Nature consists in the exercise of that Dominion which the Soul has over the Body, in governing every Passion and Motion according to Right Reason, by which we most truly pursue the real good of both, it being a mistake as well of our Duty as our Happiness to consider either part of us singly, so as to neglect what is due to the other. For if we disregard the Body wholly, we pretend to live like Angels whilst we are but Mortals; and if we prefer or equal it to the Mind we degenerate into Brutes. The former indeed is not frequent, it is only to be found amongst a few Scrupulous Persons, who sometimes impose such rigors on the Body, as GOD never requires at their hands, because they are inconsistent with a Human Frame. The latter is the common and dangerous fault, for the most of us accustom our selves to tast no other Pleasures than what are convey'd to us by the Organs of Sense, we pamper our Bodies till they grow resty[1] and ungovernable, and instead of doing Service to the Mind, get Dominion over it.

Thus we learn what is truly to Love our selves: for tho Self-Love as it is usually understood has a very ill Character and is the Root of Evil, yet rightly apply'd it is Natural and Necessary, the great inducement to all manner of Vertue. They cannot be said to Love their Body who wou'd not willingly suffer a little pain in a Finger to preserve an Arm, much more to save their Life; nor do they in reality love themselves, who wou'd not readily suffer any uneasiness in their Body, which may conduce to the good of their Mind; and who do not prefer the least probability of bettering their condition in the next Life, to all the Conveniencies of this, nay even to Life it self.

Again, when we consider that we are but several Parts of one great Whole, and are by Nature so connected to each other, that whenever one part suffers the rest must suffer with it, either by Compassion or else by being punish'd for the want of it, we shall never be so absurd as to fancy we can do our selves a Service by any thing Injurious to our Neighbours.

And finding both that we're endow'd with many excellent Faculties, which are capable of great Improvement, such as bespeak in us somewhat too Divine, to have it once imagin'd that it was made for nothing else but to move a portion of Matter 70 or 80 Years;[2]

---

1 Restive.

2 Astell's sarcasm is directed at the materialism of Hobbes and Locke.

to Act only on the Stage of an Unjust and Ill-natur'd World, where Folly and Wickedness usually go away with the Reward that is due to Wisdom and Vertue: And yet that for all these Excellencies, somewhat is still wanting to complete our Happiness, we do not find intire Felicity in our selves, but we are conscious of many wants which must be supply'd elsewhere. We therefore look about to see where we may meet with this Supply, and Material Beings with which we're compass'd do first present themselves. These are the Objects of our Senses, it is at their presence that the Body tasts all its Pleasures, no wonder therefore if it endeavour to persuade us that our Good is here, tho a little Consideration, if not our frequent disappointments when we seek no further, were sufficient one wou'd think to convince us that it is not. For when we come to weigh 'em in an impartial Consideration we discern, that as they are GOD's Work they have a Perfection suitable to their several Natures, and are as perfect as is consistent with the several Ranks and Stations they are plac'd in , so that consider'd Positively they are not to be Contemn'd, since they set forth the Wisdom, Power and Goodness of their Maker. But if we compare them with the Human Soul they appear of little value, and of none at all in comparison of Him who made them; and since their Nature is beneath, and their Worth much less than ours, we cannot find our Happiness in 'em. They contribute 'tis true to the Preservation and Ease of the Body, they help to make it fit for the Service of the Mind; But since a very few of 'em will do this, the rest are but a load and trouble, so far from being useful, that they indeed hurt us, unless they're made to minister to Charity and Contemplation.

Let then these little things be drawn aside, these Clouds that hide the most adorable Face of GOD from us, these Mud-walls that enclose our Earthly Tabernacle and will not suffer us to be pierc'd with the Beams of his Glory, and wounded, not to Death but Life, with the Arrows of his Love and Beauty. In him we find that infinite Good which alone can satisfie us, and which is not to be found elsewhere. Somewhat in which we lose our selves with Wonder, Love and Pleasure! Somewhat too ineffable to be nam'd, too Charming, too Delightful not to be eternally desir'd! And were we not sunk into Sense, and buried alive in a crowd of Material Beings, it might seem impossible to think of any thing but Him. For whether we consider the Infinite Perfection of his Nature, or the Interest we have in, and our intire dependance on him. Whether we consider him as Maker and Governor of all things, as filling all places, intimately acquainted with all Events, as Righteous in all his ways, and holy in all his works Whether we contemplate his Almighty Power; or what seems more suitable to our Faculties and Condition, the Spotless Purity of his Nature, which guided by Infallable Wisdom always Chuses what is Best. And more particularly his Infinite Goodness, his Beneficence to the Children of Men; that he is not only Good in himself, but that he is also *Our* Good, the only Amiable Being, who is altogether Lovely and worthy of All our Love, the Object of our Hope, the Sum of our Desire, the Crown of our Joy without whom we shall for ever Languish and Grieve; Enjoying whom we have nothing to Fear, nor any thing to Hate but what wou'd deprive us of that Enjoyment. If we consider how much he has done to render us capable of this Happiness even when we fled from it; what affronts he has put up, with what Patience he bears our Follies and solicits our Return, in a Word, all the Wonders of his Love in Christ Jesus! We cannot sure do less than fix our Thoughts for ever on Him, and devote our selves Intirely to Him! All our Passions will be Charm'd, and every Inclination attracted! We shall no more dispute his Will, nor seek exemption from it, but with all Sincerity of Heart, and ardent Desire cry out, *Lord what wilt thou have me to do? Not my Will Lord, but thine be done*![1] The business of our Lives will be to improve our Minds and to stretch our Faculties to their utmost extent, that so we may have the fullest enjoyment our Nature will admit, of this ever satisfying and yet ever desirable, because an Infinite, and our True, Good.

As to what is to be done by way of Exercise, not to enter too far into the Philosophy of the Passions, suffice it briefly to observe: That by the Oeconomy of Nature such and such Motions in the Body are annext in such a manner to certain Thoughts in the Soul, that unless some outward force restrain, she can produce them when she pleases barely by willing them, and reciprocally several Impressions on the Body are communicated to, and affect the Soul, all this being perform'd by the means of the Animal Spirits. The Active Powers of the Soul, her Will and Inclinations are at her own dispose, her Passive are not, she can't avoid feeling Pain or other sensible Impressions so long as she's united to a Body, and that Body is dispos'd to convey these Impressions. And when

---

1 The words of Christ to his Father on the Mount of Olives (Luke, 22, 42) echoed in The Lord's Prayer, Matthew, 6, 10.

outward Objects occasion such Commotions in the Bloud and Animal Spirits, as are attended with those Perceptions in the Soul which we call the Passions, she can't be insensible of or avoid 'em, being no more able to prevent these first Impressions than she is to stop the Circulation of the Bloud, or to hinder Digestion.[1] All she can do is to Continue the Passion as it was begun, or to Divert it to another Object, to Heighthen or to let it Sink by degrees, or some way or other to Modifie and Direct it. The due performance of which is what we call *Vertue*, which consists in governing Animal Impressions, in directing our Passions to such Objects, and keeping 'em in such a pitch, as right Reasons requires.

By which it appears that it is not a fault to have Passions, since they are natural and unavoidable, and useful too; for as the Inclinations are the Wings of the Soul, so these give Life and Vigor to the Inclinations, by disposing the Body to act according to the Determination of the Mind. But the fault lies here, we suffer 'em too often to get the Mastry of the Mind, to hurry it on to what Objects they please and to fix it there, so that it is not able to consider any Idea but what they present. Whereas the Soul can if she please and if she makes use of her Authority in time, divert the Course of the Spirits, and direct 'em to a new Object, by Limiting or Extending her Ideas, and by laying aside those the Passions excited, and entertaining new ones. Nay, if we do but forbear to revolve such Considerations as are apt to continue the Commotion of the Spirits, it will cease of it self. This is what we *can* and *ought* to do, and if we do not perform it, we act rather like the Slaves of Sense than Creatures endued with Reason; but if we do, we can hardly receive any Injury from the Passions.

---

1 Astell's theory of the passions owes much to Cambridge Platonists like Simon Patrick (1626- 1707), Bishop of Ely (Simon Patrick, *Works*, ed. Taylor, vol. 9, 425-26), for whom inflamed animal passions represented the physiology of the soul whose natural motion was towards God. She articulated this physiology early in the *Letters Concerning the Love of God* (Astell, Letter IX, St. Philip and St. James, 1694, 209-10):

> 'tis our Misfortune that we live an animal before we live a rational Life; the good we enjoy is mostly transmitted to us through Bodily Mediums, and contracts such a Tincture of the Conveyance through which it passes, that forgetting the true Cause and Source of all our good, we take up with those occasional goods that are more visible, and present to our animal Nature.

The way therefore to Govern 'em is to be always in a Temper fit for this, Recollect and Compos'd, holding our Minds in as even a poise as ever we can between Mirth and Melancholy, one of which Stupifies the Soul and the other Dissolves it; and both of 'em weaken and dispose it for Passion. Nothing but what feeds the ill humour will make Impression whilst it is under the power of *this*, nor any useful thing stay in it, but it lies open to all manner of evil, when it is violently agitated by *that*. Too much of either rendring us unfit to Converse with our selves or others; such a mixture of both as makes us Serious without Sourness, and Chearful without Levity, being the happy Temper. It is by surprize that the Passions injure us, they violently attack our Reason when she is not prepar'd to receive them, so that the Will is determin'd all of a sudden by Confuse Perceptions and Sensations. Nor is it easie to repulse them when once they have gain'd ground, because they often bribe our Guard, and get the Mastry of us by those very Considerations which shou'd have been aim'd against 'em. But Recollection, a sedate and sober frame of Mind, prevents this Mischief, it keeps our Reason always on her Guard and ready to exert her self; it fits us to Judge truly of all occurrences, and to draw advantage from whatever happens. This is the true Art of Prudence, for that which properly speaks us Wise, is the accommodating all the Accidents of Life to the great End of Living. And since the Passiveness of our Nature makes us liable to many Sufferings which we cou'd wish to avoid, Wisdom consists in the using those Powers, which GOD has given us the free disposal of, in such a manner, as to make those very things which befal us against our Will, an occasion of Good to us.

For if we do not live like Machines,[1] but like Reasonable Creatures, that is if we Observe, Examine and Apply whatever comes under our Cognizance, every Turn in our own and our Neighbours Life will be Useful to us. It is not to be deny'd that we're generally Critical Observators on our Neighbours, but I'm afraid it is with an Ill not a Good Design. We do't to feed our Pride by an ungenerous insulting over their Infirmities, or thinking to Excuse and Justifie our own Faults by theirs. But we seldom set a mark on the Precipices from whence they fell that we

1 Astell appears to anticipate the man-machine theories of Condillac Helvétius and d'Holbach, developments from Hobbesian mechanism, and Lockean sensationalist psychology.

may avoid 'em, or note their False Steps, that ours may be more Exact.

And indeed as things are usually manag'd, since Modesty, Breeding, or Sheepish Cowardise, restrains even those who are capable of bettering Conversation, from Edifying Discourses, the only use we can make of that Time which the World borrows of us and Necessary Civility exacts, is to lay in Matter of Observation. I do not mean that we shou'd make Ill-natur'd Remarks, or Uncharitable Reflections on Particular Persons, but only that we take notice of the several workings of Human Nature, the little turns and distinctions of Various Tempers; there being somewhat peculiar almost in every one, which cannot be learn'd but by Conversation and the Reflections it Occasions. For as to the main, we learn it by looking into our own Hearts, one Person being but the Counterpart of another, so that they who thorowly Know themselves have a right Idea of Mankind in general, and by making reasonable allowances for Circumstances, may pretty well guess at Particulars.

But even the Knowledge of our selves is not to be had without the Temper here recommended. For since the Passions do mostly depend on the Constitution of the Body, Age, Education and way of Living; so that the same Object does not only Affect several Persons differently, but variously moves the very same Person at several Seasons; and there was once a time perhaps, when that which puts us now in a ferment had no power to move us: We must therefore to the general consideration of Human Nature already spoken of, add a more minute inquiry into our own; Observing our Particular Passions, that especially to which we're most inclin'd by Nature, on which all the rest in manner depend; and all the Peculiarities that are to be found in our own Temper. Very great things many times depending on a trivial Humour; nor is it so often Reason, as our particular way of using it that determines our Thoughts and Actions. Now nothing less than a continual Watch and Application can procure us a sufficient Acquaintance with our selves, we cannot well discern what Objects most sensibly touch us; which is our weakest side; by what means it is Expos'd or Strengthened; how we may Restrain or rightly Employ a Passion we cou'd not Prevent; and consequently grow strong by our very Infirmities, whilst we make them an occasion of Exercising and Encreasing our Vertue; unless we're always in a watchful Frame, unless we make Remarks even whilst the Passion is working and Constantly attend the least beatings of our own Heart. Our own Heart which is indeed one of the best Books we can Study, especially in respect of Morality, and one principal Reason why we're no better Proficients in useful Knowledg, is because we don't duly consult it.

Again, we shou'd endeavour to render Spiritual and Future things as Present and Familiar as may be, and to withdraw as much as we can from sensible Impressions, especially from such as attack us violently. She whose Mind is busied about the former will find 'em of Weight and Moment sufficient to employ all her Passions, whilst the other will be scarce taken notice of; or be look'd on with Indifferency,[1] because they appear to deserve very little Admiration, Joy, or Sorrow, and are not of value enough to discompose[2] the Mind. And tho we have not Ambition to aspire to St. *Paul's* Perfection, who was *Crucified to the World and the World to him*,[3] a greater Character than that of *Universal Monarch*;[4] tho we think it impossible to be wholly Insensible to it whilst we live in it: Yet sure we can't deny that it is Possible, and very much our Duty, to be more indifferent to the Objects of Sense than the most of us are. For we certainly do amiss if we fix our Eyes and Thoughts so constantly on 'em, as that at last we take them for the most considerable things, and imagine that our Happiness is here; or, tho we can't be so gross as to *believe* this, yet if we *act* as if we did; It wou'd become us much better to argue, that the Possession of these Worldly Advantages which Mankind so much contend for, is Good if it can procure us Eternal Felicity; and that the Want of 'em is an Evil, if it exclude us from the Kingdom of Heav'n.

By which we learn how necessary it is to Retire and Meditate frequently; and how much it becomes us to keep out of the way of Theatrical Shows and inordinate Merriments, and not so much as to enter into a Parley[5] with those Pomps and Vanities we renounc'd in our Baptism. For tho some extraordinary Tempers may make use of these to stir up the Powers of their Soul, and to give them a greater aversion to Vanity, as some Poysons are said to be Antidotes against others, yet for the most part they have an ill Effect: Because they deprive the Soul of real Joy and divine Seren-

---

1 Indifference.

2 Destroy the composure of, agitate (*OED*).

3 Paul, Galatians 6, 14.

4 Universal Monarch does not appear in the Bible, nor anything close to it; Astell may be comparing St. Paul with the Roman Emperor.

5 Conversation, debate (*OED*).

ity, by making too strong an Impression on the Senses, whereby the Animal Spirits are very much Mov'd and Exhausted, and being spent on trifles the Mind is left Dull, Unactive, and Melancholy too, especially if it Reflect on its Action as it ought; so natural and necessary is it, that Vain Mirth shou'd conclude in Heaviness.

Again, the Passions consider'd as Bodily Impressions only, excite us any times to the Gratification of the Animal in prejudice of the Rational Nature. For tho Mankind had Originally no Appetites but what might Innocently be satisfied; yet since our Degeneracy, and that we have lost the true Relish of Good and Evil, they often give us false alarms, stirring us up to Pursue or Avoid what indeed we Ought not, if we consult our Good in the Main, and not the pleasing of a Part, nay the Worst part of us. But if we consider 'em as attending our Inclinations, they can do no hurt, let 'em be as Brisk and Active as they can, provided they fix on their Proper Objects. Now what these are is to be found by the Nature of the Passions, by which we are led to the Use of 'em, since every thing ought to be employ'd about that which it is fitted for. But this being already accounted for by *Des Cartes*[1] and *Dr. More*, in his excellent *Account of Vertue*,[2] I cannot pretend to add any thing to what they have so well Discours'd. Only as a further confirmation of what has been already said we may observe; That Admiration gives Rise to all the Passions; for unless we were Affected with the Newness of an Object, or some other remarkable Circumstance, so as to be attentively engag'd in the Contemplation of it, we shou'd not be any wise mov'd, but it wou'd pass by unregarded. And therefore 'tis very necessary not to be struck with *little* things, or to busie our Minds about 'em, but to fix all our Attention on, and to keep all our Admiration for things of the greatest moment, such as are those which relate to another World.

---

1 *Les Passions de l'Ame.* – Astell.

Descartes' *Passions of the Soul*, published in Latin, by Elzevir of Amsterdam in 1650, was published in English in the same year.

2 Henry More (1614-87), theologian, dedicated works to Ralph Cudworth and corresponded with John Norris of Bemerton. A Cambridge Platonist, he gradually moved away from Cartesianism, which he had earlier admired. His works were said to be so popular in the Restoration that they "ruled all the Booksellers in London." *An Account of Virtue: or Dr Henry More's abridgment of morals*, a popularization of his beliefs, was published posthumously in 1690.

We may further observe, that there is a leading Passion almost in every one, to which the Temper of their Body inclines, and on which the rest do in a manner wholly depend, especially if it be confirm'd by Education and Custom, so that if we duly manage *this*, we have the Command of all. Some are more subject to *Fear*, some to *Hope*, to *Joy*, *Sorrow* or the like, than others; but *Love* seems to be the predominant Passion in every one, and that which makes one of the former more remarkable than another, is only because it has been oftner mixt with Love. And indeed, since this is at the bottom of all the Passions, one wou'd think they're nothing else but different Modifications of it, occasion'd by some Circumstance in the Subject or Object of this Passion. Thus *Desire* is a Love to Good consider'd as Future, *Hope* the Passion that disposes us to believe we may, and *Fear* that we shall not obtain it. *Joy* is a pleasant Commotion of the Soul in the Fruition of the Good we Love; and *Sorrow* a disagreeable one occasion'd by the want of it, or presence of its contrary. The like may be said of the rest, for even *Hatred* tho it appear directly opposite to Love, may be refer'd to it, the very same motion that carrys the Soul towards Good, carrying her also from those things which wou'd deprive her of it, which on that account are call'd Evils, and why do we Hate any thing, but because it does some way or other hinder our Enjoyment of what we Love?

If therefore our Love be Right, the rest of our Passions will of course be so; and our Love which is *a motion of the Soul to joyn it self to that which appears to be grateful to it*,[1] will then be right when our Notions of Good and Evil are; That is, when we do not take up with Imaginary or Particular, but pass on to the Sovereign Good, to GOD who is the only proper and adequate Object of our Love, as Sin is of our Hatred, all things, else being no other wise to be Pursued or Avoided, than in proportion to the Relation they bear to these, So that if we Love GOD with *All* our Soul, as He certainly Deserves, and as we certainly Must if we wou'd be Happy; we shall be so taken up with the Contemplation and *Admiration* of his Beauties, have so boundless an *Esteem*, such an awful *Veneration* for, and so great a *Contempt* of all things in Comparison of Him; that our *Desires* will be carried out after nothing but GOD and such things as may further our Union with Him. His Favour, and the Light of His Countenance will be the Object of our

1 The language is that of More, but the quotation has not been traced.

Hopes, nor shall we much *Fear* any thing but His Displeasure. No *Grief* will pierce our Heart but for our many Offences against, and our Imperfect *Enjoyment of Him. We shall perfectly Hate all evil ways*, be *Jealous* of Sin at the remotest distance, and *suspect* every thing that has the least appearance of a Temptation. We shall be extremely Watchful over all our Actions, and never Resolve upon any till we're fully assur'd it is conformable to his Will and Pleasure. Whither will not our *Emulation* rife, what Difficulties won't our *Courage* surmount, when th' Enjoyment of a GOD is what we aspire to! The defects of our Services, and our failings is our Duty towards Him, will be the only occasion of *Shame*; for Reproach from Men when suffer'd for His sake will be counted a high Encomium, and his Approbation our only *Glory*. If ever we are *Angry* it will be when His Laws are Contemn'd and Right Reason violated; a just *Indignation* will arise when the Worthless are Prefer'd, and Merit is left unregarded. His Favourites will be ours, we shall dispense our *Good will* to every one proportionably as they are dear to Him; and shall think our *Gratitude* can never enough express it self, to that Bountiful Being from who we receiv'd our All. And Oh! with what *Joy* and *Satisfaction of Mind* shall we proceed in every step of this! how pure and exalted is that Pleasure, how highly entertaining, which results from the right use of our Faculties, and Fruition of the Sovereign Good! Happiness is the natural Effect as well as the Reward of an Ardent Love to GOD, and what necessarily flows from it, Universal Piety. That Holy Soul is always serene, and full of unutterable Bliss, whose Reason Directs, and whose Passions readily Obey, whilst both are Guided by his Will and Spirit who is Infallible. She tasts a Pleasure which the World can neither give nor take away, nor can Worldly Minds so much as Imagine it: She is satisfied with the Past, Enjoys the Present, and has no Solicitude for, but a Joyful Expectation of what's approaching, for which the Dawnings of a Blisful Endless Day, break forth already in that Happy Mind, whose Temper and Constitution is Heavenly; it has a Foretaste, and thereby a well-grounded Assurance, of never-ceasing Joys to Come!

So far (by the way) is Religion from being an Enemy either to Nature or Pleasure, that it perfects the one, and raises the other to the greatest height. It teaches us the true Use of the Creatures, keeps us from expecting more in them than we can ever find, and leads us to the Enjoyment of the Creator who only can satisfie us. For I wou'd fain know of any experienced Person, whether any of the Delights of this World did ever answer Expectation when

Enjoy'd, and whether the Joys of Religion do not exceed it? We come to the first with mighty hopes and are always Disappointed, to the last we approach with Fear and Trembling, supposing it will rob us of all the Satisfactions of Life, we shrink at the Pain and Difficulty, and thats the only thing in which after a little Trial we find our selves much mistaken. Good Christians being indeed the truest *Epicures*,[1] because they have the most tastful and highest Enjoyment of the greatest Good.

For GOD is too Kind and Bountiful to deny us any Pleasure befitting our Nature; he does not require us to relinquish Pleasure, but only to exchange the Gross and Insipid for the Pure and Relishing, the Pleasures of a Brute for those of a Man. He wou'd not have us enslav'd to any Appetite, or so taken up with any Created Good whatever, as not to be able to maintain the Empire of our Reason and Freedom of our Will and to quit it when we see occasion. And this is all that the Rules of Self-Denial and Mortification tend to so far as they are Rational, they mean no more than the procuring us a Power and Disposition to do that which we come now in the last place to recommend, which is To sanctifie our very Infirmities, to make even the disorderly Commotions of our Spirits an occasion of producing Holy Passions. It were better indeed if they were rais'd upon a right Principle; that the Passions did not move the Mind, but the Mind the Passions; and that the Motives to Religion were not Sensitive but Rational. However in the Infancy of our Vertue, it may not be amiss to make some use of our Vices, and what we advise if it serve no other end, 'twill help at least to break Ill-Habits and that's a con-

---

1 In *Letters Concerning the Love of God* (Letter VII, 1695 edn, 128) Astell condemned: "the sottishness of those dull *Epicureans*, who make it their Business to hunt after Pleasures as vain and unsatisfactory as their admirers are Childish and Unwise." Anthony Ashley Cooper, First Earl of Shaftesbury, was known as an Epicurean, and Locke was known to be his admirer. Astell repeats the charge in *Moderation Truly Stated* (1704, 106-07):

> To see a bloated luxurious Epicure whose business is to gather Wealth rapaciously, that he may spend it on his Vices, indulging himself in all the Softness and Debaucheries of Licentious Age. Who thinks there is no Felicity but in Riches, and no Honour but in making a Figure, as they call it, in having a great Equipage and Bustle about him! To see these set up for Patriots who have nothing of the Temper of the Truly Noble Patriots to pretend to!

siderable benefit. Agreeable to which did an excellent Author[1] bespeak the Ladies sometime ago: *Let her that is Amorous, place her Love upon him who is the Chiefest among ten thousand; she that is Angry turn her edg against her Sins; she that is haughty disdain the Devils Drudgery; she that is Fearful dread him who can destroy, both Body and Soul in Hell; and she that is sad reserve her Tears for her Penitential Offices.* Which, with the rest of that Authors Ingenuous[2] and Kind Advice, I heartily wish were not only to be seen in their Closets, but transcrib'd in their Hearts and Legible in their Lives and Actions.

Now in order to this, if our guard has been surpriz'd, and some sensible Impression has strongly broke in upon us, so that we find our selves all in a ferment, let us manage the Opportunity discreetly, change the Object and hallow the Passion. Which is no very difficult thing, for when a Passion is boyling it will spend it self on any Object that we please to fix it on. And the Proper Objects of our Passions, being most considerable in 'em selves, and naturally most apt to move us if we'll but give them fair play, that is allow 'em a place in our Thoughts, they'll work out the other, and make our Passions what they shou'd be: We have a plain Instance of this in Afflictions, in which our *Grief* is at first excited by some outward Cause, and when that has softned us, the Spirit of GOD who is never wanting unless we Neglect or Quench him, improves this Worldly into a *Godly Sorrow* that worketh Repentance not to be Repented of.

Besides, as there is a Pleasure in the Passions as well as in all the genuine Operations of Nature, so there's a Pain accompanying 'em when misplac'd, which disposes the Mind to a readiness to rectifie

---

1 *Ladies Calling.* – Astell.

Richard Allestree (1619-81), a Divine from Christ Church College, Oxford, who suffered for the Royalist cause, published *The Ladies Calling* pseudonymously in 1673. Running to 8 editions before 1700, the work argued that while women "in respect of their intellects ... are below men," their souls are the equal of men's, enjoining women to obedience to superiors, lest their insubordination be "the spring and original of infinite confusions, a grand incendiary which sets Kingdoms, Churches, Families in combustion." (Allestree, *The Ladies Calling*, part 1, §2 (1705 edn), 43. (See *DNB* and Bridget Hill, *The First English Feminist*, 22). I have not been able to locate the passage cited here in the 1705 edn of *The Ladies Calling*, to which Astell owes a great debt, as elsewhere noted.

2 *Ingenious*, according to Errata list, 298.

them, that so it may enjoy the Pleasure without mixture of Pain. If therefore we assist it with a little Meditation, it will readily come over; and tho we may find it difficult absolutely to quash[1] a Passion that is once begun, yet it is no hard matter to transfer it, so that it may pour forth it self in all its pleasing transports, without fear of danger, or mixture of uneasiness.

But a Caution will not be amiss, which is, that we don't mistake the Fits of Passion for a Spirit of Piety and Devotion. They are good beginnings 'tis true, but if we're only wafted up to Heaven in our Closet and shew forth nothing or very little of it in our Lives and Conversations, we may cheat our selves with the conceit of being Holy, but neither GOD nor Man will be so impos'd on.[2] She who mourns for her Sins, tho never so bitterly, and yet returns to them at the next occasion, gives a very good Evidence of her Weakness, but none of her Repentance. She who pretends to never so great transports of Love to GOD, and yet is wedded to the world, can part with nothing for his sake, nor be content and easie when He only is her Portion, gives Him good words, and makes Him many fine Complements and that's the whole of the matter. She who makes shew of great Awe and Reverence towards the Divine Majesty at Church and has no regard to Him in the World his larger Temple, as good as declares that she thinks his Presence confin'd to a place, or that she hopes to commute[3] a Days neglect for an Hours Observance, and expresses her Contempt of GOD much more than her Veneration. How can she profess to Hope in Him who is Anxious and Solicitous about the least Event? Or say that her Desires are fix't on GOD who has a great many Vanities and Sensual Aptites[4] to be Satisfied?

Nor are we less out of the way when we tincture[5] our Religion with our Passions, and fashion an Idea of it according to our own

---

1 Suppress, crush, utterly subdue (now rare) (*OED*).

2 Richard Allestree, in *The Ladies Library*, part 1, §5, "Of Piety" (1705 edn, 126), advised that "private Devotion, tho' of excellent effect, cannot commute for the omission of publick," using closet metaphor: "if God please to visit them in their Closets, they are even, by their own Laws of Civility, oblig'd to return his visits, and attend him in his House."

3 Exchange.

4 This may be a typographical error, because the word is broken at the end of the line thus: Ap-tites.

5 To impart a tincture or hue to; to imbue or impregnate with a quality; tinge, taint (*OED*).

Complection[1] not the tenor of the Gospel. Hence comes that great diversity we meet with both in Practice and Theory, for as there is somewhat Peculiar almost in every ones Temper, so is there in their Religion. Is our Disposition Sad and Cloudy, are we apt to take Offence, Suspicious and hard to be pleas'd? we imagine GOD so, Religion is not our Joy but our Task and Burden, we become extremely scrupulous and uneasie to our selves and others. And if Resolution and Daring be joyn'd with our Melancholy, and Temptations fall pat in our way, we discard such a troublesome Religion and set up for Atheism and Infidelity. On the other hand, if we're Fearful and Timerous our Superstition has no bounds, we pay less regard to those Laws our Maker has prescrib'd, than we do to those Chimera's our own Fancy has invented to reconcile Him. A mistake which the Brisk and Jovial are sensible of, but not of the contrary extreme they run into; they discern that GOD's ways are ways of Pleasantness, and all his Paths are Peace, that Good Christians live the Happiest Lives, 'tis their Duty to Rejoyce evermore and all the good things of the World are at their service. All which is very true, but then it is as true, that their Pleasures are not Sensual but Rational and Spiritual, which is not a lessening, but an Addition to their Character; that we are to Use the World so as not to abuse either our selves or it, to testify on all occasions our Moderation and Contempt of it, to be ready to quit it, nay even to part with Life it self when ever they come in competition with our Duty. In a word, if our Anger against our own Sins provokes us to be Peevish with others, tho not so good as they shou'd be, it goes too far. If our Zeal finds fault with all who do not come up to our Heights, or who don't express their Devotion in our way, it is not according to Knowlege, that is, it is not Discreet and Christian. If our great Love to GOD takes us up so much, that we think we may be morose and ill-natur'd to our Neighbour, we express it in a very disagreeable way: And I dare say it wou'd be more acceptable to Him, if instead of spending it all in Rapture and Devotion, a part of it were employ'd in Imitating his Beneficence to our Fellow-Creatures.

---

1 Complexion. In medieval physiology and natural philosophy, the combination of supposed qualities, *cold* or *hot*, and *moist* or *dry* (i.e., the four humours), in a certain proportion, determining the nature of a body, plant, etc. (*OED*).

To wind up all; The Sum of our Duty and of all Morality, is to have a Temper of Mind so absolutely Conform'd to the Divine Will, or which is the same in other words, such an Habitual and Intire Love to GOD, as will on all occasions excite us to the Exercise of such Acts, as are the necessary consequents of such a Habit. This frame and Constitution of Soul is what we must all our Life time Labour after, it is to be begun, and some Proficiency made in it whilst we stay on Earth, and then we may joyfully wait for its consummation in Heaven, the reason why we cannot be perfectly Happy whilst we tarry here, being only because we can have this Temper but Imperfectly. The want of which is the Hell of the Damn'd, the degree of their misery bearing a proportion to their opposition to the Divine Will. For Happiness is not *without* us, it must be found in our own Bosoms, and nothing but a Union with GOD can fix it there; nor can we ever be United to Him any other wise than by being like Him, by an Intire Conformity to his Will.

Now she who has obtain'd this blessed Temper, whose Will is Right, and who has no Passion but for GOD's Service, is pleas'd that his Wisdom shou'd Chuse her Work, and only prepares to dispatch it with the greatest Diligence and Chearfulness. She keeps All his Precepts, and does not pick and Chuse such as are for her turn, and most agreeable to her own Humor; but as she does every thing for His Sake, so is she easy and pleas'd under all his Dispensations; is truly indifferent to Applause, and fully content with GOD's Approbation. Indeed the Conquest of our Vanity is one of our last Triumphs, and a Satisfaction in all GOD's Choices for us, from a full Conviction that they are most for our advantage, the best Test of a Regular Will and Affections. For these are heights to which we can't arrive till we have travers'd over all the Paths of Vertue, and when once our Passions are reduc'd to this, I know not in what they can oppose us.

Not but that we're strictly oblig'd to *Provide for honest things in the Sight of Men* as well as of GOD, to do nothing but what is of GOD, to do nothing but what is of *Good Report*; *to Abstain* from all Appearance of Evil; not to *give Occasion* of Slander to those who desire and *Seek* it; but to *Let our Light so shine before Men, that they may see our Good-works and Glorify our Father who is in Heaven.*[1] But

1 Astell could be quoting from the Bible, in what is a familiar form of words, or from *The Ladies Calling*.

when we have done this, and have taken all possible care to approve our selves to GOD and Man, can we be at Ease if we fail in the latter? Are we more desirous of a Good than a Great Reputation? and wou'd we not to get a Name amongst our Fellow Servants, do any thing that may in the least Offend, or be less acceptable to our Common Master? Can we bear the being Censur'd as Singular and Laugh'd at for Fools, rather than comply with the evil Customs of the Age? and are we much more Covetous of the Substance *Vertue*, than of the Shadow *Fame*? If it be so we're pretty sure that all is Right, and that GOD's will is the Rule, and his Glory the End of all our Actions. It goes to a good Womans heart to receive that Commendation which the good-nature or Civility of another bestows on her, when she knows she does not Merit it, and to find whilst she's applauded abroad, a thousand Follies, Mistakes and Weaknesses in her own Mind. All the use that she makes of her Credit and Esteem in the World, is to excite her to Deserve it, tho at present perhaps she does not, and *Really* to come up to that Character which all are Ambitious to have.

Again, what is said of Submission and a perfect acquiescence in the Divine Will, is not to be so understood as if it were a fault to change our Circumstances when we're fairly and honestly call'd to't, or that we might not seek by honourable ways to enlarge them if they fit too strait. But it is design'd to correct that Complaining humour, which makes us always dissatisfied with the Present, and longing after a Change; which, how Religious soever we wou'd appear, is a very sure sign that our Passions are not mortified nor our Will reduced to a due Regularity: As hers is without doubt who can be pleas'd when even her most innocent Desires are denied, when she is disappointed in what she thinks her Best Designs. For such an one has nothing in her Temper that Sensible Impressions can so strongly fasten on, as to discompose her Mind; and what can she meet with to seduce her to Unlawful, who desires not to be her own Chuser in Lawful and Indifferent things?

The Laws of GOD have a Natural and Inward Goodness, which wou'd recommend them to a Rational Mind tho they were not injoyn'd, and therefore no wonder that Temper inclines one, Conveniency another, and Reputation a third to the Practise of some of them. But a Will duly regulated passes over these and is acted by a higher Motive, she who is Religious upon a Right Principle regards the Will of GOD only, for that and that alone is able to carry her Uniformly and Constantly thro all her Duty.

Thus Acts of Beneficence, Liberality and Charity, are full of Lustre, they procure for their Possessor a lofty Character, and therefore whether we Value them or no, we're willing however to *seem* to be fond of 'em. We fancy what mighty things we wou'd do were we in such or such a Persons Circumstances, and long to be Rich and Great that we may Relieve the Needy and Rescue the Oppressed. But we are not so forward in aspiring after Poverty, tho nothing shews a Braver Mind than the bearing it Nobly and Contentedly; we care not to be the Oppressed Person, that we might exercise Meekness and Forgiveness, Patience and Submission. Not but that the Vertues of Adversity are as lovely in themselves, and as Acceptable to GOD as those of Prosperity, or rather more so, because they express a greater Love to GOD, are more opposite to Vicious Self-Love, and do more eminently declare the Veneration we have for the Divine Wisdom and Goodness, which we can Adore and Delight in, which we can Justify and Applaud even in the most uneasy Circumstances. But they don't make so great a Figure in the World, they don't feed our Vanity so much, nor are so agreeable to Flesh and Bloud, and that's the reason why we care not for them.

Tis true we profess that we desire Riches and Honour, a great Reputation and Theater in the World, on no other account but to do GOD Service. But if we are real in this, why don't we perform so much as we might in our present Station? Alas! we Cheat our selves, as well as endeavour to impose on others; and under Pretence of seeking GOD'S Glory, in Reality Pursue nothing but our own. For had we indeed that Esteem for GOD and Intire Conformity to his Will, which is at once both the Duty and Perfection of all Rational Beings, we shou'd not complain of his Exercise of that Power, which a Prince or even an Ordinary Master has a Right to; which is, to set his Servants about such work as he thinks them fittest for. If we allow that GOD Governs the Universe, can we so much as imagine that it is not Govern'd with the Greatest Justice and Equity, Order and Proportion? Is not every one of us plac'd in such Circumstances as Infinite Wisdom discerns to be most suitable, so that nothing is wanting but a careful observation whither they lead us, and how we may best improve them? What reason then to complain of the Management of the world? and indeed except in the Morals of Mankind which are visibly and grossly deprav'd, I see not why we shou'd so much as wish for any alteration. The Wicked Prosper sometimes and what then? shall we grudge them their Portion *here*, since that's their All, and alas a very sorry one!

Besides, this world is not a soil for perfect Happiness to Grow in, Good and Evil are blended together, every Condition has its Sweet and Bitter, we may be Made by Adversity and ruin'd by Prosperity according as we manage them. Riches and Power put opportunities of doing Good into our hands, if we have a Will to Use them, but at the same time they furnish us with Instruments of doing Evil. They afford us at once the Conveniencies of Life and fuel for irregular Appetites. They make us known to others, but many times hinder us from being acquainted with our selves. They set us in view, so that if our Example be Bright it becomes the more Illustrious; but we must also remember that our Faults are as conspicuous as our Vertues, and that Peoples eyes are most intent on *those*, and most inquisitive to find 'em, so that even our innocent Liberties are many times misconstrued.

By Obscurity, and a Narrow Fortune, we're depriv'd of somewhat Necessary or Commodious to our Present Living, but are quickned to a more diligent concern for a Life to Come; we don't find our Good things *here*, and common Prudence will teach us to take care that we may enjoy them *hereafter*. If we do not Possess much, we have not much to Lose, nor such great Accounts to make; have little Business and less Authority with others, but hereby the more Command of our own Time and Thoughts. Our Vertue is plac'd in an ill-light, and our Wisdom rejected with a *What Impertinents are these, who pragmatically attempt to Instruct their Betters*?[1] but we have fewer Temptations to shock the one, and greater Advantages, as things are commonly manag'd to improve both. We're expos'd to the Contempt and Outrage of the World, but that makes us less in love with it, and more ready to welcome Death, whene're it brings the kind Releasing Summons.

It may be thought a considerable omission that no directions have bin given, any further than the management of our *Own* Inclinations and Passions; tho't be very advantageous to know how to deal with other Peoples, both in regard of Education, and of the Influence that they have on ours. But I have this to say, that Education is a beaten Subject, and has been accounted for by better Pens than mine: And that in this as in all other things, we are

---

1 Source not traced, but could be *The Ladies Calling*.

to treat our Neighbours as we do our selves, shew 'em the unsuitableness of those Objects which Irregular Affections pursue, and persuade them to a willing use of such methods as we take to Cure our own. It requires I confess, no little Skill to do this to purpose, and to convince them that we're really their Friends, whilst we strive to divorce them from such Objects as they're endear'd and fastned to by a thousand tyes: And this is so nice a matter, so laborious a task, that the more I consider it the more unable I find my self to give fit Directions for the performance of it. They who wou'd do that, must have a more exact Knowlege of Human Nature, a greater Experience of the World, and of those differences which arise from Constitution, Age, Education, receiv'd Opinions, outward Fortune, Custom and Conversation, than I can pretend to. And perhaps there is no need of Directions since few will attempt to practise them; for if a Passion that is young and tender gives us work enough, as the difficulty of Education plainly shews it does, they had need be very Kind, very Good, and very Wise, who set about the Cure of an Old and inveterate one. Nor can they who have so much Divinity in their Mind as to design such a noble work, be thought to stand in need of any advice how to perform it.

However, I'le venture to say in general, that we must never oppose Commotion with Commotion, nor be in Passion our selves if we wou'd reform anothers, else we lose many good Opportunities and seem to seek the gratification of our own humor rather than our Neighbours good. No discouragements shou'd shock us, no ungrateful returns shou'd sower our Temper, but we must expect and be prepar'd to bear many repulses and wild disorders, and patiently sustain that greatest uneasiness to a Christian Mind, the bitter appearance that our Hopes are lost, and that all the Labour of our Love is ineffectual! We must abound both in Good-Nature and Discretion, and not seldom make use of quite contrary means to bring about the End we aim at. Removing all Fuel from the Passion sometimes; and sometimes Indulging it as far as Innocently we may; and if nothing else will do, give it line enough, that so it may destroy it self in its own Excesses.

But ah! will any one drive us to such a desperate Remedy as often Kills, and cannot Cure without a very great Care, and a more than Ordinary assistance of GOD's Grace, which they have little reason to hope for, who abandon themselves to Temptations, and push things to such Extremities! Will nothing less than Temporal Ruin which unreasonable Passions naturally end in, serve to prevent Eternal? and it were well if even that wou'd do, for they usually involve in both. If therefore such as are in Passion are capable of hearing any thing but what sooths 'em in their own way, I wou'd beg of 'em for GOD's sake and their own, to grant but this one very easy and equitable Request, which is Calmly to Hear and to Consider what may be said against their darling Passion. For if it be Right it will stand the test of all that can be urg'd against it; if it be not, is it Good for them to retain and cherish it any longer?

And if they refuse to listen to the *Kind*, tho according to them, unreasonable and mistaken advice that is given, and seek no further than for Arguments to Justifie themselves, do they not by so great a Partiality secretly confess that they are in the Wrong, and wou'd not have it discover'd that they are so, because they're resolv'd with or without Reason to continue their irregular Passion?

And the cause of this strange Resolution seems to be this, That a Passion of any sort having got the hank of one, it becomes so Natural, so Agreeable, that the going about to wean them from it, looks like an attempt to deprive them of all their Joy; and they're hardly persuaded to part with what's a *Present* Delight, let its Consequences be what they may, and tho the quitting of it be in order to th' enjoyment of that much Sweeter, as well as Nobler Pleasure, which arises from the due use of Reason; and with which those Wise and Holy Souls are entertain'd, who prefer the relishes of a Rational before those of an Animal Life.

But they ought not to think us their Enemies, when we endeavour their Cure, tho we happen to Lance and Scarifie them. They who are Sick of Passion are like People in a Lethargy, insensible of their Danger; nay they're fond of their Disease, and set themselves against our Medicines; tho the greater unwillingness they show to be Disturb'd, so much the more need of Rousing 'em out of their pleasing slumber. The more secure they think themselves, the more wretched is their Condition, for that's a sign that the Passion has got an intire Possession of their Soul, and has fortified all its Avenues against Reason and Wholesome Advice. And 'tis worth being remarqued, that our Inclinations how Innocent and Harmless soever they appear, are always to be suspected if the Passions that accompany them are violent. For Violence does not Answer but Destroy the Use of Passion, it hinders th' Operations of the Soul, insted of disposing the Body to follow her Directions Vigorously.

And as to the Influence that another Persons Passion may have on us, enough has bin said to warn us, not to dally with the Flame when our Neighbours house is on Fire, lest we be consum'd in it; and carefully to avoid doing any thing which may excite, or encrease their Passions. But when we discern that the Plague is begun, let's remove with all possible speed out of the infected Air. Great Passions arise from very small beginnings, and that which appear'd Innocent at first if allow'd on that account, does often become our Ruin, or gives us at least the greatest trouble in overcoming it.

The CONCLUSION

Thus you have Ladies, the best Method I can at present think of for your Improvement, how well it answers my Design the World must judge. If you are so favourable as to think it comes up to't in any measure, what remains but to put it in Practise, tho in the way in which you live, 'tis not probably that all of you either Will or Can, for reasons mention'd in the first Part,[1] and particularly because of the great waste of your Time, without Redeeming of which there's nothing to be done. It is not my intention that you shou'd seclude your selves from the World, I know it is necessary that a great number of you shou'd live in it; but it is Unreasonable and Barbarous to drive you into't, e're you are capable of doing Good in it, or a least of keeping Evil from your selves. Nor am I so fond of my Proposal, as not to lay it aside very willingly, did I think you cou'd be sufficiently serv'd without it. But since such Seminaries are thought proper for the Men, since they enjoy the fruits of those Noble Ladies Bounty who were the foundresses of several of their Colleges,[2] why shou'd we not think that such ways

---

1 P. 72, *Etc.* – Astell.

2 Astell refers to the Port Royal School. Established south-west of Paris in 1204 by Mahaut de Garlande, wife of Mathieu de Montmorenci-Marli. Its modern history commences in 1598 with the appointment of Angélique Arnauld, sister of the famous Jansenist, to the post of coadjutor to the Abbess. Angélique Arnauld herself made the contact with Jean Duvergier, Abbot of Sain Cyran, and chief apostle of Jansenism, a movement with which her family and her convent became inextricably associated. In 1648 the abbey set up a school for the sons of Jansenist parents, but doctrinal skirmishing with the papacy consumed the next two decades, leading to its eventual destruction. (See the *Encyclopaedia Britannica*, 11th edn, vol 12, 130.)

of Education wou'd be as advantageous to the Ladies? or why shou'd we despair of finding some among them who will be as kind to their own Sex as their Ancestors have been to the other? Some Objections against this design have already been consider'd, and those which I have since met with are either too trifling to deserve a serious Answer, or too illnatur'd not to require a severer than I care to give them.[1] They must either be very Ignorant or very Malicious who pretend that we wou'd imitate Foreign Monastries, or object against us the Inconveniencies that they are subject to; a little attention to what they read might have convinc'd them that our Institutions is rather *Academical* than *Monastic.* So that it is altogether beside the purpose, to say 'tis too Recluse, or prejudicial to an Active Life; 'tis as far from that as a Ladys Practising at home is from being a hindrance to her dancing at court. For an Active Life consists not barely in *Being in the World*, but in *doing much Good in it*: And therefore it is fit we Retire a little, to furnish our Understandings with useful Principles, to set our Inclinations right, and to manage our Passions, and when this is well done, but not till then, we may safely venture out.

As for those who think so Contemptibly of such a considerable part of GOD's Creation, as to suppose that we were made for nothing else but to Admire and do them Service, and to make provision for the low concerns of an Animal Life, we pity their mistake, and can calmly bear their Scoffs, for they do not express so much Contempt of us as they do of our Maker; and therefore the reproach of such incompetent Judges is not an Injury but an Honour to us.

The Ladies I hope pass a truer estimate on themselves, and need not be told that they were made for nobler purposes. For tho I wou'd by no means encourage Pride, yet I wou'd not have them take a mean and groveling Spirit for true Humility. A being content with Ignorance is really but a Pretence, for the frame of our nature is such that it is impossible we shou'd be so; even those very Pretenders value themselves for some Knowlege or other, tho it be a trifling or mistaken one. She who makes the most Grimace at a Woman of Sense, who employs all her little skill in endeavouring to render Learning and Ingenuity ridiculous, is yet very desirous to

1 Astell clearly refers to Masham's demeaning characterization of her as an acolyte of Norris, who fails to see the quietism to which her proposal would lead (Masham, *Discourse*, 1696, 120).

be thought Knowing in a Dress, in the Management of an Intreague, in Coquetry or good Houswifry.[1] If then either the Nobleness or Necessity of our Nature unavoidably excites us to a desire of Advancing, shall it be thought a fault to do it by pursuing the best things? and since we *will* value our selves on somewhat or other, why shou'd it not be on the most substantial ground? The Humblest Person that lives has some Self-Esteem, nor is it either Fit or Possible that any one should be without it. Because we always Neglect what we Despise, we take no care of its Preservation and Improvement, and were we throughly possess'd with a Contempt of our selves, we shou'd abandon all Care both of our Temporal and Eternal Concerns, and burst with Envy at our Neighbours. The only difference therefore between the Humble and the Proud is this, that whereas the former does not prize her self on some Imaginary Excellency, or for any thing that is not truly Valuable; does not ascribe to her self what is her Makers due, nor Esteem her self on any other account but because she is GOD's Workmanship, endow'd by him with many excellent Qualities, and made capable of Knowing and Enjoying the Sovereign and Only Good; so that her Self-Esteem does not terminate in her *Self* but in GOD, and she values her self only for GOD's sake. The Proud on the contrary is mistaken both in her Estimate of Good, and in thinking it is her Own; She values her self on things that have no real Excellency, or which at least add none to her, and forgets from whose Liberality she receives them: She does not employ them in the Donors Service, all her care is to Raise her self, and she little considers that the most excellent things are distributed to others in an equal, perhaps in a greater measure than to herself, they have opportunities of advancing as well as she, and so long as she's puft up by this Tumor of Mind, they do really excel her.

The Men therefore may still enjoy their Prerogatives for us, we mean not to intrench on[2] any of their Lawful Privileges, our only

---

1 This could be directed at Lady Masham, who in the Locke correspondence reveals herself desirous to be thought the good household manager. Astell once again resorts to Plato's response to Thrasymachus in the *Republic*: the housewifely claim to the superiority of *techne* or practical wisdom (like Thrasymachus' claim to know that the ruling class rules in its own interest) against the truths of philosophy and book learning is a knowledge claim which presupposes philosophical truth.

2 To encroach or trespass upon, to infringe rights or laws (now rare) (*OED*).

Contention shall be that they may not out-do us in promoting his Glory who is Lord both of them and us; And by all that appears the generality will not oppose us in this matter, we shall not provoke them by striving to be better Christians. They may busy their Heads with Affairs of State, and spend their Time and Strength in recommending themselves to an uncertain Master, or a more giddy Multitude, our only endeavour shall be to be absolute Monarchs in our own Bosoms. They shall still if they please dispute about Religion, let 'em only give us leave to Understand and Practise it. And whilst they have unrival'd the Glory of speaking as *many* Languages as *Babel*[1] afforded, we only desire to express our selves Pertinently and Judiciously in *One*. We will not vie with them in thumbing over Authors, nor pretend to be walking Libraries, provided they'll but allow us a competent Knowlege of the Books of GOD, Nature I mean and the Holy Scriptures: And whilst they accomplish themselves with the Knowlege of the World; and experiment all the Pleasures and Follies of it, we'll aspire no further than to be intimately acquainted with our own Hearts. And sure the Complaisant and Good natur'd Sex will not deny us this; nor can they who are so well assur'd of their own Merit entertain the least Suspicion that we shall overtop them. It is upon some other account therefore that they object against our Proposal, but what that is I shall not pretend to guess, since they do not think fit to speak out and declare it.

Some indeed are pleas'd to say, that tho this appears in Speculation to be a very Happy and Useful way of Living, it will be quite another thing when reduc'd to Practice. Variety of Humours will occasion Resentments and Factions, and perhaps other inconveniencies not yet forseen; nor can we expect that every Person there will be of such an agreeable, obliging and teachable Temper, as neither to Give nor Take Offence. And supposing the first Company were as tractable and as happily cemented by the mutual love of Vertue, and prudent Management, as we cou'd desire, yet how can we be secure of their Successors, or that this as well as other good Institutions shall not degenerate?

I agree so far with this Objection as to grant that our Proposal is not such a piece of Perfection that nothing can be said

1 Babel (Babylon), ruled by Nimrod in Genesis, 10, 10; so named "because the LORD did there confound the language of all the earth," Genesis, 11, 9.

against it, but is there any thing in this World that is so? Or do Men use to quit their Employments and Houses, their Wives and Children, Relations and Friends, upon every little pet, or because they very often find trouble or disagreeableness? do they not rather if they are good Christians, bear with Infirmities and endeavour to mend them? He then who wou'd Object to purpose must shew that the Good it may do is not equivalent to the Evil which may attend it; that the Ladies will suffer greater Inconveniencies with, than without it, and that it will not in the *Main* be best. Otherwise we shall take liberty to believe that it is Humor, Covetousness or any thing rather than Reason which restrains him from Approving and Promoting it. There is a certain Pride in the Mind of Man, which flatters him that he can See farther and Judge better than his Neighbour, and he loves to feed it by scrupling and objecting against what another proposes, who perhaps has not over-look'd those fine discoveries in which he hugs himself, but having view'd them on all sides has discern'd and despis'd their insignificancy. I wou'd only ask our Objectors whether they think the World so good as that it needs none, or so bad as that it is not capable of Amendment? If neither of these, let them tell me whether Complaining and Wishing will ever do the business, or who is the greatest Benefactor to Mankind, he who finds fault with every Project set on foot to better and improve them, because it is not exactly after the Pattern in the Mount,[1] that is indeed according to his own tooth and relish; it is not beyond exception, but has a touch of Humane Weakness and Ignorance mingled with it? Or he who vigorously and sincerely with a pure heart and a diligent hand, sets about doing what he Can, tho not so much as he Wou'd, were his abilities greater? We're all apt enough to cry out against the Age, but to what purpose are our Exclamations unless we go about to Reform it? Not faintly and coldly as if we were unconcern'd for the success, and only wou'd do somewhat to still the reproaches of our Consciences and to exalt us in our own Imaginations, with the Pompous Idea of Zeal and Public Spiritedness; but *with all our Might*, with an Unwearied Industry and Vigor, I'me asham'd to say like that which the Instruments of Satan express in making Proselytes to Wickedness and Prophaneness; but rather with such as becomes the Servants of Christ, which bears some

1 Sermon on the Mount, Matthew, 5-7, Luke, 6, 20.

sort of proportion to the Greatness of our Master, the Importance of the Work and the Excellency of the Reward.

We do not expect that all who come into this Society will be perfect, but we will endeavour to make them and our selves so as much as may be. Nor shall any be admitted who either have not, or are not desirous to have, that Divine yet humble, that Great and Generous, yet Meek and Condescending Spirit, that unfeigned Love to GOD and all mankind which was in Christ Jesus. We set no other Rules than those of the Gospel, Christianity being the highest Improvement of a Rational Nature, and every one's oblig-'d to keep its Institutions whether they Live in such a Society or out of it.

And as for that degeneracy which it may fall into, 'tis too general an objection to have any weight, and may as well be urg'd against Universities, all sorts of Government, and indeed against every thing, as against this. *May be's* and *if's* are endless, and he who undertakes to provide against all Future Contingencies, either believes no GOD or fancies himself to be one. A Prudent Man will look as far as he can, and provide to the utmost of his Knowlege and Power, but when that's done, he knows he's but a Man and therefore can't possibly Forsee and Remedy all things.

Let's then do what we *Can*, and leave the rest to our Great Benefactor and Governor, but let us set about our own part, not only when the way is open and easy, who shall give us thanks for that? but in spite of all Difficulties and Discouragement, since we have so Glorious a Leader, so indefatigable in his Labours, so boundless in his Love, such an Omnipotent Assister who neither wants Power nor Will to help us. The Peevishness and Obstinacy of such as Quarrel with our Labour of Love and let themselves against all we can do to serve them, will only add to our Laurels and enlarge our Triumphs, when our Constancy in doing Good has at last o'ercome those Perverse Opposers of it.

THE END

Appendix A: Judith Drake, An Essay in Defence of the Female Sex *(1696)*

[Judith Drake *Essay in Defence of the Female Sex* (Wing, A4058), London: 1696]

AN ESSAY In Defence of the *FEMALE SEX* In which are inserted the CHARACTERS OF *A Pedant,*[1] *A Vertuoso,*[2] *A Squire, A Poetaster,*[3] *A Beau,*[4] *A City-Critick,*[5] etc. In a Letter to a Lady. Written by a Lady. LONDON. Printed for *A. Roper* and *E. Wilkinson* at the *Black Boy*, and *R. Clavel* at the *Peacock*, in *Fleetstreet*, 1696.

Since each is fond of his own ugly Face;
Why shou'd you when we hold it break the Glass?
Prol. to Sir *F.* Flutter.[6]

AN ESSAY In Defence of the Female Sex, *etc.*[7]

---

1 For Drake's depiction of the character of the pedant see below (250-51).

2 A learned person, savant, scholar (obs.). (*OED*). Drake characterizes the virtuoso (96-110) as: "one who has sold an Estate in Land to purchase one in *Scallop, Conch, Muscle, Cockle Shells, Periwinkles, Sea Shrubs, Weeds, Mosses, Sponges, Coralls, Corallines, Sea Fans, Pebbles, Marchasites* and *Flint stones*; and has abandoned the Acquaintance and Society of Men for that of *Insects, Worms, Grubs, Maggots, Flies, Moths, Locusts, Beetles, Spiders, Grasshoppers, Snails, Lizards* and *Tortoises*" (96).

3 A rimester, a writer of poor or trashy verse. (*OED*) Drake characterizes the poetaster (79-82): "the most voluminous Fool is the Fop Poet, who is one that has always more Wit in his Pockets than anywhere else...." (79).

4 A man who gives special or excessive attention to appearance, a fop, a dandy. (*OED*) As Drake describes him (68-75), "one that has more Learning in his Heels than his Head, which is better cover'd than fill'd" (68).

5 Journalist or satirist. Drake begins her characterization (119-24): "A *Critick* of this sort is one that for want of *Wit* sets up for *Judgment*; yet has so much Ambition to be thought a *Wit* that he lets his *Spleen* prevail against *Nature* and turns *Poet*" (119).

6 Sir Fopling Flutter is a character in Etherege's *The Man of Mode* (1676), and the quotation is the last two lines of the Prologue to that play.

7 Dedicatory preface and commendary verses by James Drake omitted. Errata incorporated.

The Conversation we had 'tother day, makes me, Dear *Madam*,[1] but more sensible, of the unreasonableness of your desire; which obliges me to inform you further upon a Subject, wherein I have more need of your instruction. The strength of Judgment, sprightly Fancy,[2] and admirable Address, you shew'd upon that Occasion, speak you so perfect a Mistress of that Argument (as I doubt not but you are of any that you please to engage in) that whoever, would speak or write well on it, ought first to be your Schollar. Yet to let you see how absolutely you may command me, I had rather be your *Eccho*,[3] than be silent when You bid me speak, and beg your excuse rather for my Failures, than want of Complacence. I know You will not accuse me for Plagiary[4] if I return You nothing, but what I have glean'd from You, when You consider, that I pretend not to make a Present, but to pay the Interest only of a Debt. Nor can You tax me with Vanity, since no Importunity[5] of a Person less lov'd, or valu'd by me than your self could have extorted thus much from me. This Consideration leaves me no room to doubt but that you will with your usual Candour pardon those Defects, and correct those Errors, which proceed only from an over forward Zeal to oblige You, though to my own Disadvantage.

The defence of our Sex against so many and so great Wits as have so strongly attack'd it, may justly seem a Task too difficult for a Woman to attempt. Not that I can, or ought to yield, that we are by Nature less enabled for such an Enterpize,[6] than Men are; which I hope at least to shew plausible Reasons for, before I have done: But because through the Usurpation of Men, and the Tyranny of Custom (here in *England* especially) there are at most but few, who are by Education, and acquir'd Wit, or Letters sufficiently quallified for such an Undertaking. For my own part I shall readily own, that as few as there are, there may be and are abundance,

---

1 The work is dedicated to Princess, later Queen, Anne (1665-1714), wife of Prince George of Denmark.

2 Imagination.

3 The personification of Echo may be a literary allusion to Ovid's *Metamorphoses*, or the famous opening lines of Virgil's *Eclogues*, 1.4-5, ed. Guy Lee (Harmondsworth: Penguin, 1984), 31: "you, Tityrus, cool in shade,/ Are teaching woods to echo *Lovely Amaryllis*."

4 Plagiarism.

5 Solicitation.

6 Enterprise — typographical error.

who in their daily Conversations approve[1] themselves much more able, and sufficient Assertors of our Cause, than my self; and I am sorry that either their Business, their other Diversions, or too great Indulgence of their Ease, hinder them from doing publick Justice to their Sex. The Men by Interest or Inclination are so generally engag'd against us, that it is not to be expected, that any one Man of Wit shoud arise so generous as to engage in our Quarrel, and be the Champion of our Sex against the Injuries and Oppressions of his own. Those Romantick days are over, and there is not so much as a *Don Quixot*[2] *of the Quill left to succour the distressed Damsels. 'Tis true, a Feint*[3] *of something of this Nature was made three or four Years since by one; but how much soever his Eugenia may be oblig'd to him,*[4] *I am of Opinion the rest of her Sex are but little beholding to him. For as you rightly observ'd, Madam,* he has taken more care to give an Edge to his Satyr,[5] than force to his Apology; he has play'd a sham Prize, and receives more thrusts than he makes; and like a false Renegade fights under our Colours only for a fairer Opportunity of betraying us. But what could be expected else from a Beau? An Animal that can no more commend in earnest a Womans Wit, than a Man's Person, and that compliments ours, only to shew his own good Breeding and Parts.[6] He levels his Scandal at the whole Sex, and thinks us sufficiently fortified, if out of the Story of Two Thousand Years he has been able to pick up a few Examples of Women illustrious for their Wit, Learning or Vertue, and Men infamous for the contrary; though I think the most inveterate of our Enemies would have spar'd him that labour, by granting that all Ages have produc'd Persons famous or infamous of both Sexes; or they must throw up all pretence to Modesty, or Reason.

---

1 Prove.

2 Don Quixote, the hero of the romance (1605-15) by Cervantes, satirizing chivalric beliefs and conduct.

3 Sham.

4 William Walsh (1663-1708), critic and poet, author of *Pastorals* and other amorous verses, as well as *A Dialogue Concerning Women, being a Defence of the Sex. Written to Eugenia* (1691).

5 Satire.

6 Abilities, capacities, talents (archaic).

I have neither Learning, nor Inclination to make a Precedent, or indeed any use of Mr. W's. labour'd Common Place Book;[1] and shall leave Pedants and School-Boys to rake and tumble the Rubbish of Antiquity, and muster all the *Heroes* and *Heroins* they can find to furnish matter for some wretched Harangue, or stuff a miserable Declamation with instead of Sense or Argument.

[*Some advantages to be allow'd to the disparity of Education.*][2] I shall not enter into any dispute, whether Men, or Women be generally more ingenious,[3] or learned; that Point must be given up to the advantages Men have over us by their Education, Freedom of Converse,[4] and variety of Business and Company. But when any Comparison is made between 'em, great allowances must be made for the disparity of those Circumstances. Neither shall I contest about the preheminence[5] of our Virtues; I know there are too many Vicious, and I hope there are a great many Virtuous of both Sexes. Yet this I may say, that whatever Vices are found amongst us, have in general both their fource, and encouragement from them.

The Question I shall at present handle is, whether the time an ingenious Gentleman spends in the Company of Women, may justly be said to be misemploy'd, or not? I put the question in general terms; because whoever holds the affirmative must maintain it so, or the Sex is no way concern'd to oppose him. On the other

---

1 Almost certainly William Wotton's *Reflections upon Ancient and Modern Learning* of 1694. Wotton's work was an important intervention in the controversy between the ancients and moderns, begun in France by Fontenelle and transported to England by the statesman Sir William Temple with his essay, *The Gardens of Epicurus,* of 1692. There Englishmen Charles Boyle, Richard Bentley, Wotton, and the Irishman Jonathan Swift, joined in the fray. Swift, Temple's adopted son, whom he used as a go-between with William III (Queen Anne's brother-in-law), later lampooned Fontenelle's position in his famous *Battle of the Books* of 1704, but Wotton, although a formidable classical scholar, took the side of the moderns. As a member of the Royal Society and ardent promoter of its causes, he argued for the superiority of the new science and the sophistication of modern philology that could marshal the wisdom of antiquity and adapt ancient learning to modern causes.

2 Marginal Note. All other text in square brackets are marginal notes by Drake.

3 Intelligent.

4 Conversation.

5 Note that Drake inserts an aspirated "h" from colloquial diction.

side I shall not maintain the Negative, but with some Restricions and Limitations; because I will not be bound to justifie those Women, whose Vices and ill Conduct expose them deservedly to the Censure of the other Sex, as well as of their own. The Question being thus stated, let us consider the end and purposes, for which Conversation was at first instituted, and is yet desirable; and then we shall see, whether they may not all be found in the Company of Women. These Ends, I take it, are the same with those we aim at in all our other Actions, in general only two, Profit or Pleasure.[1] These are divided into those of the Mind and those of the Body. Of the latter I shall take no further Notice, as having no Relation to the present Subject; but shall confine my self wholly to the Mind, the Profit of which is the Improvement of the Understanding, and the Pleasure is the Diversion, and Relaxation of its Cares and Passions. Now if either of these Ends be attainable by the Society of Women, I have gain'd my Point. However, I hope to make it appear, that they are not only both to be met with in the Conversation of Women, but one of them more generally, and in greater measure than in Mens.

Our Company is generally by our Adversaries represented as unprofitable and irksome to Men of Sense, and by some of the more vehement Sticklers against us, as Criminal. These Imputations as they are unjust, especially the latter, so they savour[2] strongly of the Malice, Arrogance, and Sottishness[3] of those, that most frequently urge 'em; who are commonly either conceited Fops,[4] whose success in their Pretences to the favour of our Sex has been no greater than their Merit, and fallen very far short of their Vanity and Presumption, or a sort of morose, ill-bred, unthinking Fellows, who appear to be Men only by their Habit[5] and Beards, and are scarce distinguishable from Brutes but by their Figure[6] and Risibility.[7] But I shall wave these Reflections at pre-

1 Drake clearly follows Hobbes and Locke, who adopted the position of the Hellenistic Stoics and Epicureans in holding that the principal human motivations are pursuit of pleasure and avoidance of pain, a position which later characterized utilitarianism. Astell explicitly rejected such a position.

2 Smack.

3 Foolishness.

4 Fools.

5 Dress.

6 Form, shape.

7 Capacity for laughter.

sent, however just, and come closer to our Argument. If Women are not qualified for the Conversation of ingenious Men, or, to go yet further, their friendship, it must be because they want some one condition, or more, necessarily requisite to either. The necessary conditions of these are Sense, and good nature, to which must be added, for Friendship, Fidelity and Integrity. Now if any of these be wanting to our Sex, it must be either because Nature has not been so liberal as to bestow 'em upon us; or because due care has not been taken to cultivate those Gifts to a competent measure in us.

The first of these Causes is that, which is most generally urg'd against us, whether it be in Raillery, or Spight. I might easily cut this part of the Controversy short by an irrefragable[1] Argument, which is, that the express intent, and reason for which Woman was created, was to be a Companion and help meet[2] to Man; and that consequently those, that deny 'em to be so, must argue a Mistake in Providence, and think themselves wiser than their Creator. But these Gentlemen are generally such passionate Admirers of themselves, and have such a profound value and reverance for their own Parts,[3] that they are ready at any time to sacrifice their Religion to the Reputation of their Wit, and rather than lose their point, deny the truth of the History. There are others, that though they allow the Story yet affirm, that the propagation, and continuance of Mankind, was the only Reason for which we were made; as if the Wisdom that first made Man, cou'd not without trouble have continu'd the Species by the same or any other Method, had not this been most conducive to his happiness, which was the gracious and only end of his Creation. But these superficial Gentlemen wear their Understandings like their Clothes, always set and formal, and wou'd no more Talk than Dress out of Fashion; Beau's that, rather than any part of their outward Figure shou'd be damag'd, wou'd wipe the dirt of their shoes with their Handkercher, and that value themselves infinitely more upon modish Nonsense, than upon the best Sense against the Fashion. But since I do not intend to make this a religious Argument, I shall leave all further Considerations of this Nature to the Divines,[4] whose more immediate Business and

---

1 Irrefutable.

2 Helpmate: Biblical, Gen.ii.18.20 (*OED*).

3 Abilities (obs.).

4 Clerics.

Study it is to assert the Wisdom of Providence in the Order, and distribution of this World, against all that oppose it.

[*No distinction of Sexes in Souls.*] To proceed[1] therefore if we be naturally defective, the Defect must be either in Soul or Body. In the Soul it can't be, if what I have hear'd some learned Men maintain, be true, that all Souls are equal, and alike, and that consequently there is no such distinction, as Male and Female Souls; that there are not innate *Idea's*, but that all the Notions we have, are deriv'd from our External Senses, either immediately, or by Reflection.[2] These Metaphysical Speculations, I must own Madam, require much more Learning and a stronger Head, than I can pretend to be Mistress of, to be consider'd as they ought: Yet so bold I may be, as to undertake the defence of these Opinions, when any of our jingling[3] Opponents think fit to refute 'em.

[*No advantage in the Organization of their Bodies.*] Neither can it be in the Body (if I may credit the Report of learned Physicians) for there is no difference in the Organization of those Parts,[4] which have any relation to, or influence over the Minds; but the Brain, and all other Parts (which I am not Anatomist enough to name) are contriv'd as well for the plentiful conveyance of Spirits,[5] which are held to be the immediate Instruments of Sensation, in Women, as Men. I see therefore no natural Impediment in the structure of our Bodies; nor does Experience, or Observation argue any: We use all our Natural Faculties, as well as Men, nay and our Rational too, deducting only for the advantages before mention'd.

[*Confirm'd from Experience of Brutes*]. Let us appeal yet further to Experience, and observe those Creatures that deviate least from simple Nature, and see if we can find any difference in Sense, or understanding between Males and Females. In these we may see Nature plainest, who lie under no constraint of Custom or Laws, but those of Passion or Appetite, which are Natures, and know no

---

1 Debate (obs.).

2 Drake endorses Locke's theory of sensationalist psychology, as expounded in *An Essay Concerning Human Understanding*, and rejects the doctrine of innate ideas associated with Neoplatonism, which sets her apart from Astell.

3 Affecting the repetition of the same sounds.

4 Body parts.

5 Vital powers.

difference of Education, nor receive any Byass[1] by prejudice.[2] We see great distance in Degrees of Understanding, Wit, Cunning and Docility (call them what you please) between the several Species of Brutes. An Ape, a Dog, a Fox, are by daily Observation found to be more Docile, and more Subtle than an Ox, a Swine, or a Sheep. But a She Ape is as full of, and as ready at Imitation as a He; a Bitch will learn as many Tricks in as short a time as a Dog, a Female Fox has as many Wiles as a Male. A thousand instances of this kind might be produc'd; but I think these are so plain, that to instance more were a superfluous labour; I shall only once more take notice, that in Brutes and other Animals there is no difference betwixt Male and Female in point of Sagacity, notwithstanding there is the same distinction of Sexes, that is between Man and Women. I have read, that some Philosophers have held Brutes to be no more than meer Machines, a sort of Divine Clock-work, that Act only by the force of nice unseen Springs without Sensation, and cry out without feeling Pain, Eat without Hunger, Drink without Thurst, fawn upon their Keepers without seeing 'em, hunt Hares without Smelling, *etc.*[3] Here Madam is cover for our Antagonists against the last Argument so thick, that there is no beatin 'em out. For my part, I shall not envy 'em their refuge, let 'em lie like the wild *Irish* secure within their Boggs;[4] the field is at least ours, so long as they keep to their Fastnesses.[5] But to quit this Topick, I shall only add, that if the learnedest He of 'em all can convince me of the truth of this Opinion, He will very much stagger[6] my Faith; for hitherto I have been able to observe no difference between our Knowledge and theirs, but a gradual one; and depend upon Revelation alone, that our Souls are Immortal, and theirs not.

[*Experience of Mankind.*] But if an Argument from Brutes and other Animals shall not be allow'd as conclusive, (though I can't see,

---

1 Bias.

2 State of Nature argument, more akin to that of Thomas Hobbes in *Leviathan* than John Locke in the *Second Treatise of Government*.

3 This was the view of Descartes.

4 This could be a reference to Jonathan Swift or Richard Steele, the Irish pamphleteers, whom Astell held responsible for satirizing her proposal for a women's academy in the *Tatler*, No.32, June 22, 1709. The "wild Irish," secure in their bogs, was a trope familiar from the time of the Elizabethan settlement of Ireland.

5 Strongholds or fortresses.

6 Shake.

why such an Inference should not be valid, since the parity[1] of Reason is the same on both sides in this Case) I shall desire those, that hold against us to observe the Country People, I mean the inferiour sort of them, such as not having Stocks[2] to follow Husbandry[3] upon their own Score, subsist upon their daily Labour.[4] For amongst these, though not so equal as that of Brutes, yet the Condition of the two Sexes is more level, than amongst Gentlemen, City Traders, or rich Yeomen.[5] Examine them in their several Businesses, and their Capacities will appear equal; but talk to them of things indifferent,[6] and out of the Road of their constant Employment, and the Ballance will fall on our side, the Women will be found the more ready and polite.[7] Let us look a little further, and view our Sex in a state of more improvement, amongst our Neighbours the *Dutch*.[8] There we shall find them managing not only the Domestick Affairs of the Family, but making, and receiving all Payments as well great as small, keeping the Books, ballancing the Accounts, and doing all the Business, even the nicest of Merchants, with as much Dexterity and Exactness as their, or our Men can do. And I have often hear'd some of our considerable Merchants blame the conduct of our Country-Men in this point; that they breed our Women so ignorant of Business; whereas were they taught Arithmetick, and other Arts which require not much bodily strength, they might supply the places of abundance of lusty[9] Men now employ'd in sedentary Business;[10] which would be a mighty profit to the Nation by sending those Men to Employments, where hands and Strength are more requir'd, especially at this time when we are in such a want of People. Beside

---

1 Equality or parallelism: "parity of reason" is an idiomatic expression (*OED*).
2 Capital.
3 Farming.
4 Drake uses Lockean economic language.
5 Gentlemen farmers.
6 Non-specialist issues.
7 Cultivated.
8 Drake is politic in singling out the Dutch, given that the Adressee of the essay, Princess Anne of Denmark, was close to her brother-in-law, the Dutch Protestant, William of Orange, at this time reigning as King William III of England.
9 Active, vigorous (obs.).
10 Occupations requiring sitting.

that it might prevent the ruine of many Families, which is often occasion'd by the Death of Merchants in full Business, and leaving their Accounts perplex'd, and embroil'd[1] to a Widdow and Orphans, who understanding nothing of the Husband or Father's Business occasions the Rending,[2] and oftentimes the utter Confounding[3] a fair Estate; which might be prevented, did the Wife but understand Merchants Accounts, and were made acquainted with the Books.

I have yet another Argument from Nature, which is, that the very Make and Temper of our Remedies shew that we were never design'd for Fatigue; and the Vivacity of our Wits, and the Readiness of our Invention (which are confess'd even by our Adversaries) demonstrate that we were chiefly intended for Thought and the Exercise of the Mind. Whereas on the contrary it is apparent from the strength and size of their Limbs, the Vigour and Hardiness of their Constitutions, that Men were purposely fram'd and contriv'd for Action, and Labour.[4] And herein the Wisdom and Contrivance of Providence is abundantly manifested; for as the one Sex is fortified with Courage and Ability to undergo the necessary Drudgery of providing Materials for the sustenance of Life in both; so the other is furnish'd with Ingenuity and Prudence for the orderly management and distribution of it, for the Relief and Comfort of a Family; and is over and above enrich'd with a peculiar Tenderness and Care requisite to the Cherishing their poor helpless Off-spring. I know our Opposers usually miscall our quickness of Thought, Fancy and Flash, and christen their own heaviness by the specious Names of Judgment and Solidity; but it is easie to retort upon 'em the reproachful Ones of the Dullness and Stupidity with more Justice. I shall pursue this Point no further, but continue firm in my Persuasion, that Nature has not been so Niggardly to us, as our Adversaries would insinuate, till I see better cause to the contrary, then I have hitherto at any time done. Yet I am ready to yield to Conviction, whoever offers it; which I don't suddenly expect.

It remains then for us to enquire, whether the Bounty of Nature be wholly neglected, or stifled by us, or so far as to make us unwor-

1 In a state of confusion or disorder.

2 Surrender.

3 Ruin.

4 Drake turns the argument for women as the weaker sex to advantage by arguing that they are designed for mental pursuits, men for physical.

thy the Company of Men? Or whether our Education (as bad as it is) be not sufficient to make us a useful, nay a necessary part of Society for the greatest part of Mankind. This cause is seldom indeed urg'd against us by the Men, though it be the only one, that gives 'em any advantage over us in understanding. but it does not serve their Pride, there is no Honour to be gain'd by it: For a Man ought no more to value himself upon being Wiser than a Woman, if he owe his Advantage to a better Education, and greater means of Information, then he ought to boast of his Courage, for beating a Man, when his Hands were bound. Nay it would be so far from Honourable to contend for preference upon this Score, that they would thereby at once argue themselves guilty both of Tyranny, and of Fear: I think I need not have mention'd the latter; for none can be Tyrants but Cowards. [*Women industriously kept in Ignorance*] For nothing makes one Party slavishly depress another, but their fear that they may at one time or other become Strong or Courageous enough to make themselves equal to, if not superiour to their Masters. This is our Case; for Men being sensible as well of the Abilities of Mind in our Sex, as of the strength of Body in their own, began to grow Jealous, that we, who in the Infancy of the World were their Equals and Partners in Dominion,[1] might in process of Time, by Subtlety and Stratagem, become their Superiours; and therefore began in good time to make use of Force (the Origine of Power) to compell us to a Subjection, Nature never meant;[2] and made use of Natures liberality to them to take the benefit of her kindness from us. From that time they have endeavour'd to train us up altogether to Ease and Ignorance; as Conquerors use to do to those, they reduce by Force, that so they may disarm 'em, both of Courage and Wit; and consequently make them tamely give up their Liberty, and abjectly submit their Necks to a slavish Yoke. As the world grew more Populous, and Mens Necessities, whetted their Inventions, so it increas'd their Jealousie, and sharpen'd their Tyranny over us, till by degrees, it came to that

---

1 Equal in power or authority. Hobbes, in *Leviathan*, chapter 26, insisted that men and women had equal dominion over their children, arguing against the patriarchalism of Sir Robert Filmer (*Leviathan*, London, 1651, 102-03; ed. Richard Tuck, 1991, 139-40).

2 It is the position of John Locke, that "men" were born free, argued in the opening chapters of the second of his *Two Treatises of Government*, 1690 (ed. Peter Laslett [Cambridge: Cambridge University Press, 1988], 284).

height of Severity, I may say Cruelty, it is now at in all the Eastern parts of the World, where the Women, like our Negroes in our Western Plantations, are born slaves,[1] and live Prisoners all their Lives. Nay, so far has this barbarous Humour prevail'd, and spread in self, that in some parts of *Europe*, which pretend to be most refin'd and civiliz'd, in spite of Christianity, and the Zeal for Religion which they so much affect, our Condition is not very much better. And even in *France*, a Country that treats our Sex with more Respect than most do, We are by the *Salique Law*[2] excluded from Soveraign Power. [*Original of the Salique Law.*] The *French* are an ingenious People, and the Contrivers of that Law knew well enough, that We were no less capable of Reigning, and Governing well, than themselves; but they were suspicious, that if the Regal Power shou'd fall often into the hands of Women, they would favour their own Sex, and might in time restore 'em to their Primitive Liberty and Equality with the Men,[3] and so break the neck of that unreasonable Authority they so much affect over us; and therefore made this Law to prevent it. The Historians indeed tell us other Reasons, but they can't agree among themselves, and as Men are Parties against us, and therefore their Evidence may justly be rejected. To say the truth Madam, I can't tell how to prove all this from Ancient Records; for if any Histories were anciently written

---

1 Drake's position differs significantly from that of Astell, who asked the famous rhetorical question (*Reflections upon Marriage*, 3rd edn, 1706, xi/1996,18):

> *If all Men are born free*, how is it that all Women are born slaves? as they must be if the being subjected to the *inconstant, uncertain, unknown arbitrary Will* of Men, be the *perfect condition of Slavery?*

In answer to a verbal query by John Pocock about the status of Astell's reference to women as slaves, I would answer that it must be ironic. Astell denied Locke's central proposition that we have property in our own persons and cannot voluntarily relinquish it, so she could not technically argue the slavery of women compared with the freedom of men. But Drake's comparison between early modern English married women and "our Negroes in our Western Plantations" took the notion of women's slavery seriously, on the basis of Locke's principle of freedom as an inalienable right.

2 The alleged fundamental law of the French monarchy by which women were excluded from the throne (*OED*).

3 Drake refers to the theories of Hobbes and Locke that men and women were free and equal in the state of nature, and even before marriage, to which Astell did not subscribe.

by Women, Time, and the Malice of Men have effectually conspir'd to suppress 'em; and it is not reasonable to think that Men shou'd transmit, or suffer to be transmitted to Posterity, any thing that might shew the weakness and illegallity of their Title to a Power they still exercise so arbitrarily, and are so fond of. But since daily Experience shews, and their own Histories tell us, how earnestly they endeavour, and what they act, and suffer to put the same Trick upon one another, 'tis natural to suppose they took the same measures with us at first, which now they have effected, like the Rebels in our last Civil Wars, when they had brought the Royal Party under,[1] they fall together by the Ears about the Dividend. [*Amazons; why they rejected the Society of Men.*] The Sacred History takes no notice of any such Authority they had before the Flood, and their Own confesses that whole Nations have rejected it since, and not suffer'd a Man to live amongst them, which cou'd be for no other Reason, than their Tyranny. For upon less provocation the Women wou'd never have been so foolish, as to deprive themselves of the benefit of that Ease and Security, which a good agreement with their Men might have afforded 'em. 'Tis true the famous Histories tell us, that there were whole Countries where were none but Men, which border'd upon 'em. But this makes still for us; for it shews that the Conditions of their Society were not so easie, as to engage their Women to stay amongst 'em; but as liberty presented it self, they withdrew and retired to the *Amazons*: But since our Sex can hardly boast of so great Privileges, and so easie a Servitude any where as in *England*, I cut this ungrateful Digression short in acknowledgment; tho' Fetters of Gold are still Fetters, and the softest Lining can never make 'em so easy, as Liberty.

You will excuse, I know Madam, this short, but necessary Digression. I call it necessary, because it shews a probable Reason, why We are at this time in such subjection to them, without lessening the Opinion of our Sense, or Natural Capacities either at present, or for the time past; beside that it briefly lays open without any Scandal to our Sex, why our Improvements are at present so disproportion'd to those of Men. I would not have any of our little, unthinking Adversaries triumph at my allowing a disproportion between the Improvements of our Sex and theirs; and I am

---

1 Drake refers to the English Civil War (1642-46) and the execution of Charles II, January 30, 1649.

sure those of 'em that are ingenious Men, will see no reason for it from what I have said.

After having granted so great a disparity as I have already done in the customary Education, and advantagious Liberties of the Sexes, 'twere Nonsense to maintain, that our Society is generally and upon all accounts as Beneficial, Improving and Entertaining, as that of Men. He must be a very shallow Fellow, that resorts to, and frequents us in hopes by our means to make himself considerable as a Schollar, a Mathematician, a Philosopher, or a Statesman. These Arts and Sciences are the result only of much Study and great Experience; and without one at least of 'em are no more to be acquir'd by the Company of Men, however celebrated for any or all of them, than by ours. Quallifications, which are as indispensably necessary to a Gentleman, or any Man that wou'd appear to Advantage in the World, which are attainable only by Company, and Conversation, and chiefly by ours. Nor can the greatest part of Mankind, of what Quallity soever, boast much of the use they make, or the benefit they reap from these acknowledg'd Advantages. So that Schollars only, and some few of the more thinking Gentlemen, and Men of Business have any just claim to 'em. And of these the first generally fall short enough some other way to make the Ballance even. [*Character of a Pedant*.] For Schollars, though by their acquaintance with Books and conversing much with Old Authors, they may know perfectly the Sense of the Learned Dead, and be perfect Masters of the Wisdom, be throughly [*sic*] inform'd of the State, and nicely skill'd in the Policies of Ages long since past, yet by their retir'd and unactive Life, their neglect of Business, and constant Conversation with Antiquity, they are such strangers to, and so ignorant of the Domestick Affairs and manners of their own Country and Times, that they appear like the Ghosts of Old Romans rais'd by Magick. Talk to them of the *Assyrian*, or *Perssian* Monarchies, the *Grecians* or *Roman* Common-wealths. They answer like Oracles, they are such finish'd Statemen [*sic*], that we shou'd scarce take 'em to have been less than Confidents of *Semiramis*,[1] Tutours to

---

1 Daughter of a Syrian goddess and wife of the king of Assyria who, upon his death, ruled for many years in her own right. Believed to be one of the founders of Babylon, she is possibly the historical figure Sammuramat (fl. 810-805 BC) (*Oxford English Reference Dictionary*, ed. Judy Pearsall and Bill Trumble [Oxford: Oxford University Press, 1995]).

Cyrus[1] the great, old Cronies of *Solon* and *Lycurgus*,[2] or Privy Councellours at least to the Twelve *Caesars*[3] successively, but engage them in a Discourse that concerns the present Times, and their Native Country, and they heardly speak the Language of it, and know so little of the affairs of it, that as much might reasonably be expected from an animated *Egyptian* Mummy. They are very much disturbed to see a Fold or a Plait amiss in the Picture of an Old *Roman* Gown, yet take no notice that their own are thredbare out at the Elbows, or Ragged, and suffer more if *Prician's*[4] Head be broken then if it were their own. They are excellent Guides, and can direct you to every Ally, and turning in old *Rome*; yet lose their way at home in their own Parish. They are mighty admirers of the Wit and Eloquence of the Ancients; yet had they liv'd in the time of *Cicero*,[5] and *Caesar*[6] wou'd have treated them with as much supercilious Pride, and disrespect as they do now with Reverence. They are great hunters of ancient Manuscripts, and have in great Veneration any thing, that has scap'd the Teeth of Time and Rats, and if Age have obliterated the Characters, 'tis the more valuable for not being legible.[7] But if by chance they can pick out one Word, they rate it higher then the whole Author in Print, and wou'd give more for one Proverb of *Solomons*[8] under his own Hand, then for all his Wisdom. These Superstitious, bigotted Idolaters of time past, are Children in their understanding all their lives; for they hang so incessantly upon the leading Strings of Authority, that their Judgments like the Limbs of

---

1 Cyrus the Great (d. 530 BC), father of Cambyses and king of Persia (559-530 BC) as founder of the Achaemenid dynasty (*Oxford English Reference Dictionary*, ed. Judy Pearsall and Bill Trumble [Oxford: Oxford University Press, 1995]).

2 Spartan lawgiver (9c. BC).

3 Title of the Roman Emperors from Augustus to Hadrian (*Oxford English Reference Dictionary*, ed. Judy Pearsall and Bill Trumble [Oxford: Oxford University Press, 1995]).

4 Priscian (Priscianus Caesariensis) (fl. AD 500), Latin grammarian.

5 Marcus Tullius Cicero (106-43 BC), Roman orator, statesman, and man of letters.

6 Julius Caesar (100-44 BC), Roman general and statesman.

7 Like Astell, Drake is clearly on the side of the Moderns in the debate between the Ancients and the Moderns that raged in her day.

8 King of Israel (*c.* 970-*c.*930 BC), son of David, and traditionally associated with the Song of Solomon, Ecclesiastes, and the book of Proverbs.

some *Indian* Penitents, become altogether crampt and motionless for want of use.

[*Character of a Country Squire.*] But as these Men, will hardly be reckon'd much superiour to us upon the account of their Learning or Improvements, so neither will I suppose another sort diametrically opposite to these in their Humors and Opinions: I mean those whose Ancestors have been wise and provident, and rais'd Estates by their Ingenuity and Industry, and given all their Posterity after 'em Means, and Leisure to be Fools. These are generally sent to School in their Minority, and were they kept there till they came to Years of Discretion, might most of 'em stay, till they cou'd tuck their Beards into their Girdles before they left carrying a Satchel. In conformity to Custom, and the Fashion, they are sent early to serve an Apprenticeship to Letters, and for eight or nine years are whipt up and down through two or three Counties from School to School; when being arriv'd a[1] Sixteen, or Seventeen Years of Age, and having made the usual *Tour* of Latin, and Greek authors, they are call'd Home to be made Gentlemen. As soon as the young Squire has got out of the House of Bondage, shaken off the awe of Birch[2] and begins to feel himself at Liberty, he considers that he is now Learned enough, (and 'tis ten to one but his Friends are wise enough to be of his Opinion) and thinks it high time to shake off the barbarous Acquaintance he contracted, with those crabbed, vexatious, obscure Fellows, that gave him so much trouble and smart at School, Companions by no means fit for a Gentleman, that writ only to torment and perplex poor Boys, and exercise the tyranny of Pedants and School-masters. These prudent resolutions taken, his Conversation for some years succeeding is wholly taken up by his Horses, Dogs and Hawks (especially if his Residence be in the Country) and the more sensless Animals that tend 'em. His Groom, his Huntsman, and his Falconer are his Tutors, and his walk is from the Stable to the Dog-kennel, and the reverse of it. His diversion is drudgery, and he is in highest satisfaction when he is most tir'd. He wearies you in the morning with his Sport, in the Afternoon with the noisie Repetition and Drink, and the whole Day with Fatigue and Confusion. His Entertainment is stale Beer, and the History of his Dogs and Horses, in which he gives you the Pedigree of every one with all

---

1 *Sic.* On this as other occasions Drake appears to lapse into colloquialisms.

2 Drake is probably referring to the practice of caning.

the exactness of a Herald; and if you be very much in his good Graces, 'tis odds, but he makes you the Compliment of a Puppy of one of his favourite Bitches, which you must take with abundance of Acknowledgments of his Civillity, or else he takes you for a stupid, as well as an ill bred Fellow. He is very constant at all Clubs and Meetings of the Country Gentlemen, where he will suffer nothing to be talk'd or hear'd of but his Jades,[1] his Curs,[2] and his Kites.[3] Upon these he rings perpetual Changes, and trespasses as much upon the patience of the Company in the Tavern, as upon their Enclosures in the Field, and is least impertinent, when most drunk.

His grand Business is to make an Assignation for a Horse Race, or a Hunting Match, and nothing discomposes him so much as a Disappointment. Thus accomplish'd, and finish'd for a Gentleman, he enters the Civil Lists,[4] and holds the Scale of Justice with as much Blindness as she is said to do. From hence forward his Worship becomes as formidable to the Ale-Houses, as he was before Familiar; he sizes an Ale Pot, and takes the dimensions of Bread with great Dexterity and Sagacity. He is the terrour of all the Deer and Poultry Stealers in the Neighbourhood, and is so implacable a Persecutor of Poachers, that he keeps a Register of all the Dogs and Guns in the Hundred,[5] and is the Scare-Beggar of the Parish. Short Pots,[6] and unjustifiable Dogs and Nets, furnish him with sufficient matter for Presentments,[7] to carry him once a Quarter to the Sessions;[8] where he says little, Eats and Drinks too much, and after Dinner, Hunts over the last Chace, and so rides Worshipfully Drunk home again. At home he exercises his Authority in granting his Letters, Pattents to Petitioners for erecting Shovel Board, Tables and Ginger Bread Stalls. If he happens to live near any little Borough or Corporation that sends Burgesses to Parliament, he may become ambitious and sue for the Honour of being made

---

1 A contemptuous name for a horse; a draught-horse, or cart horse as opposed to a riding horse; a nag, a hack (*OED*).

2 A contemptuous name for a dog (*OED*).

3 A falcon or hawk (*OED*).

4 Civil service (*OED*).

5 An archaic English administrative district (*OED*).

6 A vessel used in hunting or fishing that does not meet regulations.

7 The statement by a grand jury at assizes or quarter sessions of an indictable offence (*OED*).

8 Quarter sessions, a type of local court.

their Representative. Henceforward he grows Popular, bows to, and treats the Mob all round him; and whether there be any in his Discourse or not, there is good Sense in his Kitchin and his Cellar, which is more agreeable and edifying. If he be so happy as to outtap his Competitour, and Drink his Neighbours into an Opinion of his Sobriety, he is chosen, and up he comes to that Honourable Assembly, where he shews his Wisdom best by his Silence, and serves his Country most in his absence.

I give you these two Characters, *Madam*, as irreconcileable as Water and Oyl, to shew that Men may and do often Baffle and Frustrate the Effects of a liberal Education, as well by Industry as Negligence. 'Tis hard to say, which of these two is the more Sottish; the first is such an Admirer of Letters, that he thinks it a disparagement to his Learning to talk what other Men understand, and will scarce believe that two, and two, make four, under a Demonstration from *Euclid*,[1] or a quotation of *Aristotle*:[2] The latter has such a fear of Pedantry always before his Eyes, that he thinks it a Scandal to his good Breeding, and Gentility to talk Sense, or write true *English*; and has such a contemptible Notion of his past Education, that he thinks the *Roman* Poets good for nothing but to teach Boys to cap Verses. For my Part I think the Learned, and the Unlearned Blockhead pretty equal; for 'tis all one to me, whether a Man talk Nonsense, or Unintelligible Sense, I am diverted and edified alike by either; the one enjoys himself less, but suffers his Friends to do it more; the other enjoys himself and his own Humour enough, but will let no body else do it in his Company. Thus, *Madam*, I have set them before You, and shall leave you to determine a Point, which I cannot.

[*The Education of the Female Sex not so deficient as commonly thought.*] There are others that deserve to be brought into the Company of these upon like Honourable Reasons; but I keep them in reserve for a proper place, where I may perhaps take the Pains to draw their Pictures to the Life at full length.[3] Let us now return to our Argument, from which we have had a long breathing while. Let us look into the manner of our Education, and see

---

1 Greek mathematician (*c.* 300 BC) who taught at Alexandria, author of *Elements of Geometry*.

2 Aristotle (384-322 BC), Greek philosopher and scientist.

3 See the sketches of the Bully (62-64), the Scowter (64-67) the Beau (68-78), the Poetaster (79-87), the Coffee-House Politician (87-96), the Vertuoso (96-108), and the City-Critick (119-24), which follow.

wherein it falls short of the Mens, and how the defects of it may be, and are generally supply'd. In our tender years they are the same, for after Children can Talk, they are promiscuously taught to Read and Write by the same Persons, and at the same time both Boys and Girls. When these are acquir'd, which is generally about the Age of Six or Seven Years, they begin to be separated, the Boys are sent to the *Grammar School*, and the Girls to *Boarding Schools*, or other places, to learn Needle Work, Dancing, Singing, Music, Drawing, Painting, and other Accomplishments, according to the Humour and Ability of the Parents, or Inclination of the Children. Of these, Reading and Writing are the main Instruments of Conversation; though Musick and Painting may be allow'd to contribute something towards it, as they give us an insight into two Arts, that makes up a great Part of the Pleasures and Diversions of Mankind. Here then lies the main Defect, that we are taught only our Mother Tongue, or perhaps *French*, which is now very fashionable, and almost as Familiar amongst Women of Quality as Men; whereas the other Sex by means of a more extensive Education to the knowledge of the *Roman* and *Greek* Languages, have a vaster Field for their Imaginations to rove in, and their Capacities thereby enlarg'd.[1] To see whether this be strictly true or not, I mean in what relates to our debate, I will for once suppose that we were instructed only in our own Tongue, and then enquire whether the disadvantage be so great as is commonly imagin'd. You know very well, *Madam*, that for Conversation, it is not requisite we should be Philologers, Rhetoricians, Philosophers, Historians or Poets; but only that we should think pertinently and express our thoughts properly, on such matters as are the proper Subjects for a mixt Conversation. [*Religion, Etc. no proper subjects for mixt Conversation.*]. The *Italians*, a People as delicate in their Conversation as any in the World, have a Maxim that our selves, our Neighbours, Religion, or Business ought never to be the Subject. There are very substantial Reasons, to be given for these Restrictions for Men are very apt to be vain, and impertinent, when they talk of themselves, besides that others are very jealous, and apt to suspect, that all the good things said, are intended as so many arguments of preference to them. When they speak of their Neighbours, they are apt out of a Principle of Emulation and Envy, natural to all the race

1 Drake concedes here to the ancient languages a value she elsewhere denies.

of *Adam* to lessen, and tarnish their Fame, whether by open Scandal, and Defamatory Stories, and Tales, or by malicious Insinuations, invidious Circumstances, sinister and covert Reflections. This humour springs from an over fondness of our selves, and a mistaken conceit that anothers loss is an addition to our own Reputation, as if like two Buckets, one must necessarily rise as the other goes down. This is the basest and most ungenerous of all our natural Failures, and ought to be corrected as much as possible e'ry where; but more especially in *Italy*, where Resentments are carried so high, and Revenges prosecuted with so much Heat, and Animosity. Religion is likewise very tender there, as in all other places, where the Priests have so much Power and Authority. But even here, where our differences and Disputes have made it more tame, and us'd it to rough handling, it ought carefully to be avoided; for nothing raises unfriendly warmths among Company more than a religious Argument, which therefore ought to be banisht all Society intended only for Conversation and Diversion. Business is too dry and barren to give any Spirit to Conversation, or Pleasure to a Company, and is therefore rather to be reckon'd among the Encumbrances than Comforts of Life, however necessary. Besides these, Points of Learning, abstruse Speculations, and nice Politicks, ought, in my opinion, to be excluded; because being things that require much Reading and Consideration, they are not fit to be canvas'd *ex tempore* in mixt Company, of which 'tis probable the greatest part will have little to say to 'em, and will scarce be content to be silent Hearers only; besides that they are not in their nature gay enough to awaken the good Humour, or raise the Mirth of the Company. Nor need any one to fear, that by these limitations Conversation shou'd be restrain'd to too narrow a compass, there are subjects enough that are in themselves neither insipid, nor offensive; such as Love, Honour, Gallantry, Morality, News, Raillery, and a numberless train of other Things copious and diverting. [*Great Improvements to be made by the help of English Books only.*] Now I can't see the necessity of any other Tongue beside our own to enable us to talk plausibly, or judiciously upon any of these Topicks: Nay, I am very confident that 'tis possible for an ingenious Person to make very considerable progress in most parts of Learning, by the help of English only. For the only reason I can conceive of learning Languages, is to arrive at the Sense, Wit, or Arts, that have been communicated to the World in 'em. Now of those that have taken the pains to make themselves Masters of those Treasures, many have been so generous as to impart a share of 'em to the

Publick, by Translations for the use of the Unlearned; and I flatter my self sometimes, that several of these were more particularly undertaken by Ingenious, good Natur'd Men in Kindness and Compassion to our Sex. But whatever the Motives were, the obliging Humour has so far prevail'd that scarce any thing either Ancient or Modern[1] that might be of general use either for Pleasure, or Instruction is left untouch'd, and most of them are made entirely free of our Tongue. I am no judge either of the Accuracy, or Elegance of such Performances; but if I may credit the report of Learned and Ingenious Gentlemen, (whose Judgment or Sincerity I have no reason to question) many of those excellent Authors have lost nothing by the change of Soil. I can see and admire the Wit and Fancy of *Ovid*[2] in the Translation of his Epistles and Elegies, the softness and Passion of *Tibullus,*[3] the Impetuosity and Fire of *Juvenal,*[4] the Gayety, Spirit and Judgment of *Horace;*[5] who, though he may appear very different from himself through diversity, and inequality of the Hands concern'd in making him speak *English*, yet may easily be guess'd at from the several excellent Pieces render'd by the Earl of *Roscommon,*[6] Mr. *Cowley,*[7] Mr. *Dryden,*[8] Mr. *Congreve,*[9] Mr. *Brown*[10] and other ingenious Gentlemen, who have oblig'd the Nation with their excellent Versions of some

---

1 Drake appears to refer explicitly to this contemporary debate in which Astell too participated.

2 Publius Ovidius Naso (43 BC to AD 17), Roman poet.

3 Albius Tibullus, (*c.* 54-19 BC), Roman elegiac poet.

4 Decimus Junius Juvenalis (*c.* AD 55-140), Roman lawyer and satirist.

5 Quintus Horatius Flaccus (65-8 BC), Roman poet and satirist.

6 The Fourth Earl of Roscommon (1633-85), Irish translator, critic, and poet, who translated Horace's *Art of Poetry* (1680).

7 Abraham Cowley (1618-67), English poet, who translated Horace's Odes in *Essays in Verse and Prose* (1668).

8 John Dryden (1631-1700), English poet, who translated Horace's Odes in *Sylvae* (1685).

9 William Congreve (1670-1729), English dramatist, and poet, noted for his extremely witty comic dialogues. He wrote five plays during the 1690s: *The Old Bachelor* (1693), *The Double Dealer* (1694), *Love for Love* (1695), *The Mourning Bride* (1697), and his masterpiece *The Way of the World* (1700). He was a friend of Swift, Pope, Steele, and members of the Kit Kat Club.

10 Thomas Brown (1663-1704), English satirist, friend of Aphra Behn and author of scurrilous verses, including *Amusements Serious and Comical* (1700).

parts of him. Nor is it possible to be insensible of the sweetness and Majesty of *Virgil*,[1] after having read those little but Divine Samples already made Publick in *English* by Mr. *Dryden*,[2] which gives us so much Impatience to see the whole Work entire by that admirable Hand. I have heard some ingenious Genlemen say, That it was impossible to do Justice in our Tongue to these two last Celebrated Roman Poets, and and[3] I have known others, of whose Judgments I have as high an Opinion, affirm the contrary; my ignorance of Latin disables me from determining whether we are in the right, but the Beauty of what I have already seen by the means of those Gentlemen, has so far prejudic'd me in favour of the latter; that might I have 'em entire from the same hands, I think I shou'd scarce envy those who can tast the pleasure of the Originals. Nor is it to the Poets only, that we stand indebted for the Treasure of Antiquity, we have no less Engagements to those, who have successfully labour'd in Prose, and have made us familiar with *Plutarch*,[4] *Seneca*,[5] *Cicero*, and in general with all the famous Philosophers, Orators and Historians, from whom we may at once learn both the Opinions and Practices of their Times. Assisted by these helps, 'tis impossible for any Woman to be ignorant that is but desirous to be otherwise, though she know no part of Speech out of her Mother Tongue. But these are neither the only, nor the greatest Advantages we have; all that is excellent in *France, Italy*, or any of our neighbouring Nations is now become our own; to one of whom, I may be bold to say, we are beholding for more, and greater Improvements of Conversation, than to all Antiquity, and the learned Languages together. [*The name of Learning unjustly restrained to the knowledge of Latin and Greek only*.] Nor can I imagine for what good Reason a Man skill'd in Latin and Greek, and vers'd in the Authors of Ancient Times shall be call'd Learned; yet another who perfectly understands *Italian, French, Spanish, High Dutch*,[6] and the rest of the *European* Languages, is acquainted with

---

1 Publius Vergilius Maro (70-19 BC), Roman poet.

2 This suggests that Dryden's complete Virgil, *Aeneis*, (1697), was not yet published.

3 Uncorrected error.

4 Plutarch (*c.* AD 46-*c.* 120 AD), Greek historian, biographer, and philosopher.

5 Lucius Annaeus Seneca ("the Younger") (4 BC to AD 65), Spanish-born Roman Stoic philosopher, statesman, and tragedian.

6 I.e., *Hoch Deutsch*, or German.

the Modern History of all those Countries, knows their Policies, has div'd into all the Intrigues of the several Courts, and can tell their mutual Dispositions, Obligations and Ties of Interest one to another, shall after all this be thought Unlearned for want of those two Languages. Nay, though he be never so well vers'd in the Modern Philosophy, Astronomy, Geometry and Algebra, he shall notwithstanding never be allow'd that honourable Title. I can see but one apparent Reason for this unfair Procedure; which is, that when about an Age[1] and an half ago, all the poor Remains of Learning then in Being, were in the hands of the School-men;[2] they wou'd suffer none to pass Muster, that were not deeply engag'd in those intricate, vexatious and unintelligible Trifles, for which themselves contended with so much Noise and Heat; or at least were not acquainted with *Plato*[3] and *Aristotle*, and their Commentators; from whence the Sophistry and Subtleties of the Schools at that time were drawn.[4] This Usurpation was maintain'd by their Successors, the Divines,[5] who to this day pretend almost to the Monopoly of Learning; and though some generous Spirits have in good measure broke the neck of this Arbitrary, Tyrannical Authority; yet can't they prevail to extend the name of Learning beyond the Studies, in which the Divines are more particularly conversant. Thus you shall have 'em allow a Man to be a wise Man, a good Naturalist, a good Mathematician, Politician, or Poet, but not a Scholar, a learned Man, that is no Philologer. For my part I think these Gentlemen have just inverted the use of the Term, and given that to the knowledge of words, which belongs more properly to Things. I take Nature to be the great Book of Universal Learning, which he that reads best in all or any of its Parts, is the greatest Scholar, the most learned Man; and 'tis as ridiculous for a Man to count himself more learned than another, if he have no greater extent of knowledge of things, because he is more vers'd in Languages; as it would be for an Old Fellow to tell a Young One, his Eyes were better than his, because he Reads with Spectacles, the other without.

---

1 Century.

2 Scholastics.

3 Plato (*c.* 428-348 BC), Greek philosopher.

4 Drake displays anti-clerical sentiments and even a lack of reverence for Plato and Aristotle that would not be true of Astell.

5 Clergy. Drake shows very little religiosity compared with Astell, who is deeply religious and the author of significant theological works.

[*English Books the best helps to Conversation.*] Thus, *Madam*, you see we may come in Time to put in for Learning, if we have a mind, without falling under the Correction of Pedants. But I will let Learning alone at present, because I have already banish'd it (though not out of disrespect) from mix'd Conversation; to which we will return, and which the greatest Magazines[1] and Supports[2] are still in Reserve. I mean the many excellent Authors of our own Country, whose Works it were endless to recount. Where is Love, Honour and Bravery more lively presented than in our Tragedies, who has given us Nobler, or juster Pictures of Nature than Mr. *Shakespear*?[3] Where is there a tenderer Passion, than in the Maids Tragedy?[4] Whose Grief is more awful and commanding than Mr. *Otways*?[5] Whose Descriptions more Beautifull, or Thoughts more Gallant than Mr. *Drydens*? When I see any of their Plays acted, my Passions move by their Direction, my Indignation, my Compassion, my Grief are all at their Beck.[6] Nor is our Comedy at all inferiour to our Tragedy; for, not to mention those already nam'd for the other part of the Stage, who are all excellent in this too, Sir *George Etherege*[7] and Sir *Charles Sedley*[8] for neat Raillery and Gallantry are without Rivals, Mr. *Wicherley*[9] for strong Wit, pointed Satyr, sound and useful Observations is beyond Imitation; Mr. *Congreve* for sprightly, gentile, easie Wit falls short of no Man. These are the Masters of the Stage; but there are others who though of an inferiour Class, yet deserve Commendation, were that at present my Business. Nay, even the worst of 'em afford us some diversion; for I find a sort of foolish Pleasure, and can laught at Mr. *D——y's*

---

1 Storehouse or repository valuable goods (rare). (*OED*, 1970 edn.)
2 Spiritual help, assistance.
3 William Shakespeare (1564-1616), English playwright, poet, actor.
4 John Fletcher (1579-1625), author of *The Maid's Tragedy* (*c.* 1610-11).
5 Thomas Otway (1652-85), English tragic dramatist and poet.
6 Beck and call.
7 Sir George Etherege (1635-91), English Restoration dramatist.
8 Sir Charles Sedley (1639-1701), English poet, dramatist, courtier, and wit.
9 William Wycherley (1641-1716), English Restoration dramatist and poet, best known for *The Country Wife* (1675), and *The Plain Dealer* (1676). (See *Of Dramatic Poesy and Other Critical Essays*, ed. George Watson, London, 1962, vol. 1, 199).

Farce,[1] as I do at the Tricks, and Impertinencies of a Monkey; and was pleased to see the humour and delight of the Author in Mr. *H———n's*[2] Eating, and Drinking Play which I fancy'd was written in a Victualling House. In short, were it not for the too great frequency of loose Expressions, and wanton Images, I should take our Theaters for the best Schools in the World of Wit, Humanity and Manners; which they might easily become by retrenching that too great Liberty. Neither have the Poets only, but the Criticks too Endeavour'd to compleat us; Mr. *Dennis*[3] and Mr. *Rimer*[4] have by their Ingenious, and judicious labours taught us to admire the Beauties as we ought, and to know the faults of the former. Nor are we less beholding to these for forming our Judgments, than to those for raising our Fancies.

These are the Sources from whence we draw our gayer part of Conversation; I don't mean in exclusion to the other parts of Poetry, in most of which (as I have heard good Judges say) we equal at least the Ancients, and far surpass all the Moderns. I honour the Names, admire the Writings of *Denham*,[5] *Suckling*,[6] and *D'avenant*,[7] I am ravish'd with the Fancy of *Cowley*, and the Gallantry of *Waller*.[8] I reverence the *Fairy Queen*,[9] am rais'd, and elevated with *Paradise Lost*,[10] *Prince Arthur*[11] composes and reduces me to a State of Yawning indifference; and Mr.

---

1 Thomas Durfey (1653-1723), indefatigable writer of farces, operas, and melodramas, author of some 32 comedies in the service of four monarchs from Charles II to Queen Anne. Best known for *The Fond Husband* (1676), *Madam Fickle* (1677), and *Sir Barnaby Whig* (1681).

2 Henry Higden (*fl.* 1693), who wrote *The Wary Widow* (1693), which played for a night or two and then was thrown off the stage because the actors were all drunk.

3 John Dennis (1657-1734), English critic and playwright.

4 Thomas Rymer (1641-1713), English critic, historiographer to William III, and anthologist.

5 Sir John Denham (1615-69), Irish-born Cavalier poet.

6 Sir John Suckling (1609-42), English Cavalier poet and dramatist.

7 Sir William D'Avenant (1606-68), English Cavalier poet and dramatist.

8 Edmund Waller (1606-87), Cavalier poet and politician.

9 Edmund Spenser (*c.*1552-99), *The Faerie Queene* (1589-96).

10 John Milton (1608-74), *Paradise Lost* (1667).

11 King Arthur, AD fifth or sixth century Romano-British chieftain or general, the subject of tales by Sir Thomas Malory (1400-71), and others.

W——stl—y's[1] *Heroicks* lull me to sleep. Thus all Ranks and Degrees of Poets have their use, and may be serviceable to some body or other from the Prince to the Pastry Cook, or Past-board Box Maker. I should mention our Satyrists, but it would be endless to descend to every particular, of these Mr. *Oldham*[2] is admirable, and to go no further, the inimitable Mr. *Butler*[3] will be an everlasting Testimony, of the Wit of his Age, and Nation, and bid eternal defiance to the Wits of all Countries, and future Ages to follow him in a Path before untrack'd. Our Prose Writers, that are eminent for a gay Style and Iovial Argument, are so many, that it would swell this Letter[4] too much to name 'em, so that I shall only take notice, that whoever can read without Pleasure, or Laughter, *The contempt of the Clergy*,[5] and the following Letters and Dialogues by the same Author, or the facetious Dialogues of Mr. *Brown*[6] *must be more Splenetick than Heraclitus*,[7] or more stupid, than the Ass[8] he laugh'd at.

Nor are we less provided for the serious Part; Morality has generally been the Province of our Clergy who have treated all parts of it very largely with so much Piety, Solidity, and Eloquence, that as I think I may venture to say, they have written more upon it than the Clergy of the rest of the World; so I believe no Body will deny that they have written better. Yet I cou'd wish, that our Ingenious

---

1 Probably William Winstanley (1628?-98), author of *The lives of the most famous English poets* (1687), who, as a man of letters, likely also wrote tedious Heroicks.

2 John Oldham (1653-83), satirical poet, author of *a Satire upon Woman, Who by Her Falsehood and Scorn was the Death of My Friend* (1678).

3 Samuel Butler (1612-80), English satirical poet and one-time secretary to the Duke of Buckingham, author of the long burlesque, *Hudibras* (1663, 1664, 1678).

4 Note that this work is explicitly in the epistolary genre.

5 John Eachard, *The Grounds and Occasions of the Contempt of the Clergy and Religion enquired into … With Mr. Hobb's State of Nature Considered in a Dialogue between Philautus and Timothy* (1672).

6 Tom Brown (1663-1704), famous for his adaptations of Roman satirists, Martial, Petronius, and Lucian, as well as being a translator of Paul Scarron's *Le Roman Comique*, was commonly referred to as "facetious."

7 Tom Brown's *Heraclitus ridens redivisus: or a Dialogue between Henry and Roger, concerning the Times* (1688).

8 Tom Brown also translated Lucian (Lucius Apuleius), the African-born second-century Roman satirist, author of *The Metamorphoses, or The Golden Ass*, which lampooned the priesthood as quackery.

Gentlemen wou'd employ their Pens oftner on these Subjects; because the severity of the other's Profession obliges 'em to write with an Air, and in a Style less agreable, and inviting to Young People. Not that we are without many excellent Pieces of Morality, Humanity and Civil Prudence written by, and like Gentlemen. But it is the Excellence of 'em, and the ability of our Gentlemen, which appears in the Spirit, Wit, and curious Observations in those Pieces, which make me desire more of the same Nature. Who can read the Essays of that Wonderful Man my Lord *Bacon*,[1] or the no less to be admir'd Sir *Walter Raleigh*'s,[2] or Mr. *Osborns* advice to a Son,[3] the *Advice to a Daughter*,[4] Sir *William Temple*'s,[5] or Sir *George Machenzie*'s[6] Essays, Sir *Roger L'Estrange*'s[7] Esop (to which last we are likewise oblig'd for an incomparable Version of *Seneca*)[8] and abundance of others, without wishing for more from the same or the like hands? Our Neighbours the *French*, have written a great deal of this kind, of the best of which we have the benefit in *English*; but more particularly *Sieurs, Montagne*,[9] *Rochefaucant*,[10] and St. *Evermont*[11] deserve to be immortal in all Languages. I need not mention any more, it is apparent from these that Women want not the means of being Wise and Prudent without more Tongues than one; nay, and Learned too, if they have any Ambition to be so.

---

1 Francis Bacon, Baron Verulam of Verulam and Viscount of St. Albans (1561-1626), English philosopher and statesman, author of *Essays* (1625).

2 Sir Walter Raleigh (1552-1618), English courtier, navigator, poet, and essayist.

3 Francis Osborne (1593-1659), *Advice to a Son* ... (1656).

4 George Savile, first Marquis of Halifax (1633-95), an English statesman elevated to viscount in 1668 for his part in the Restoration; author of *Advice to a Daughter* ... (1688).

5 Sir William Temple (1628-99), *Fables of Aesop* (1692).

6 Typographical error, Machenzie, for Sir George MacKenzie of Rosehaugh (1636-91), Scottish lawyer and prolific author.

7 Sir Roger L'Estrange (1616-1704), English journalist and pamphleteer.

8 Roger L'Estrange *Seneca's Morals by way of abstract*. London (1678).

9 Michel Eyquem de Montaigne (1533-92), French author of sceptical *Essayes* (1580, 1588), influential on Shakespeare, Bacon, and others.

10 François, sixth Duc de la Rochefoucauld (1613-80), French writer and courtier.

11 Charles Marguetel de Saint Denis, Seigneur de Saint-Évremond (1610-1703), French writer and wit.

The numberless Treatises of Antiquities, Philosophy, Mathematics Natural, and other History (in which I can't pass silently by, that learned One of Sir *Walter Raleigh*, which the World[1] he writ of can't match) written originally in, or translated to our Tongue are sufficient to lead us a great way into any Science our Curiosity shall prompt us to. The greatest difficulty we struggled with, was the want of a good Art of Reasoning, which we had not, that I know of, till that defect was supply'd by the greatest Master of that Art, Mr. *Locke*,[2] whose Essay on Human Understanding makes large amends for the want of all others in that kind.[3]

Thus Madam I have endeavour'd to obviate all our Adversarie's Objections, by touching upon as great a Variety of things relating to the Subject as I conveniently cou'd. Yet I hope I have troubled you with nothing but what was necessary to make my way clear, and plain before me; and I am apt to think I have made it appear, that nothing but disencouragement or an Idle Uncurious Humour can hinder us from Rivalling most Men in the knowledge of great Variety of things, without the help of more Tongues than our Own; which the Men so often reproachfully tell us is enough. This Idleness is but too frequently to be found among us, but 'tis a Fault equally common to both Sexes. Those that have means to play the Fool all their lives,[4] seldom care for the trouble of being made wise. We are naturally Lovers of our Ease, and have great apprehensions of the difficulty of things untry'd; Especially in matters of Learning, the common Methods of acquiring which are so unpleasant, and uneasie. I doubt not but abundance of noble Wits are stiffled in both Sexes, for want but of suspecting what they were able to do, and with how much facility. Experience shews us every day Blockheads, that arrive at a moderate, nay sometimes a great Reputation by their Confidence, and brisk attempts which they maintain by their Diligence; while great Numbers of Men naturally more Ingenious lye neglected by, for want of Industry to improve, or Courage to exert themselves. No Man certainly but wishes he had the Reputation in, and were Respected and Esteem'd by the World as he sees some Men are for

1 Sir Walter Raleigh's *History of the World* (1614).

2 John Locke (1632-1704), English philosopher, author of the *Essay Concerning Human Understanding* (1689).

3 Clearly Drake does not share Astell's antipathy for Locke.

4 Like Astell, Drake is scathing about the morals and mores of her time, common to both sexes.

the Fruits of their Pens; but they are loth to be at the pains of an Attempt, or doubt their sufficience to perform; or what I believe is most general, never to enquire so far into themselves, and their own Abilities, as to bring such a thought into their Heads. This last I fancy is the true Reason, why our Sex, who are commonly charged with talking too much, are guilty of writing so little. I wish they would shake of this lazy Despondence, and let the noble examples of the deservedly celebrated Mrs. *Philips*,[1] and the incomparable Mrs *Behn*[2] rouse their Courages, and shew Mankind the great injustice of their Contempt. [*Ignorance of Latine etc. no disadvantage.*] I am confident they would find no such need of the assistance of Languages as is generally imagin'd. Those that have of their own need not graft upon Foreign Stocks. I have often thought that the not teaching Women Latin and Greek, was an advantage to them, if it were rightly consider'd, and might be improv'd to a great heigth.[3] For Girles after they can Read and Write (if they be of any Fashion) are taught such things as take not up their whole time, and not being suffer'd to run about at liberty as Boys, are furnish'd among other toys with Books, such as *Romances, Novels, Plays* and *Poems*; which though they read carelessly only for Diversion, yet unawares to them, give 'em very early a considerable Command both of Words and Sense; which are further improv'd by their making and receiving Visits with their Mothers, which gives them betimes the opportunity of imitating, conversing with, and knowing the manner, and address of elder Persons. These I take to be the true Reasons why a Girl of Fifteen is reckon'd as ripe as a Boy of One and Twenty, and not any natural forwardness of Maturity as some People would have it. These advantages the Education of Boys deprives them of, who drudge away the Vigour of their Memories at Words, useless ever after to most of them, and at Seventeen or Eighteen are to begin their Alphabet of Sense, and are but where the Girles were at Nine or Ten. Yet because they have learnt Latin and Greek, reject with Scorn all *English* Books their best helps, and lay aside their Latin ones, as if they were already Masters of all that Learning, and so hoist Sail for the wide World without a Compass to Steer by. Thus

---

1 Katherine Philips, pseud. "Orinda" (1631-64), English author and translator.

2 Aphra Behn (1640-89), English writer and spy.

3 Typographical error.

I have fairly stated the difference between us, and can find no such disparity in Nature or Education as they contend for; but we have a sort of ungenerous Adversaries, that deal more in Scandal than Argument, and when they can't hurt us with their Weapons, endeavour to annoy us with stink Pots. Let us see therefore, *Madam*, whether we can't beat them from their Ammunition, and turn their own Artillery upon them; for I firmly believe there is nothing, which they charge upon us, but may with more Justice be retorted upon themselves.

They tax us with a long List of Faults, and Imperfections, and seem to have taken a Catalogue of their own Follies and Vices, not with design to correct them, but to shift of the Imputation to us. There is no doubt, but particular Women may be found upon whom every charge may be justified; but our Sex is not answerable for them, till they prove there are no such Men, which will not be before Dooms-day. However, like ill Neighbours they bring the Dirt out of their own Homes not out of Neatness, but out of Envy to their Neighbours, at whose Doors they lay it. But let them remove their Follies as oft as they please, they are still as constant to them, as the *Needle* to the *North Pole*, they point them out which way soever they move. Let us see what these Qualities are, they so liberally bestow upon us, and after see how they fit the Donours, and survey 'em in their proper Figures and Colours. The most familiar of these are Vanity, Impertinence, Enviousness, Dissimulation, Inconstancy, etc.

Appendix B: Daniel Defoe, An Essay upon Projects *(London, 1697)*

AN ESSAY UPON PROJECTS, by DANIEL DEFOE. London, Print'd by *R:R*: for *Theo. Cockerill* at the corner of *Warwick-Lane*, near *Pater-Noster Row*, 1697.

Upon this Head of *Academies*, I might bring in a Project for *An Academy for Women*

I have often thought of it as one of the most barbarous Customs in the world, considering us as a Civiliz'd and a Christian Countrey, that we deny the advantages of Learning to Women: We reproach the Sex every day with Folly and Impertinence, while I am confident, had they the advantages of Education equal to us, they wou'd be guilty of less than our selves:

One wou'd wonder inde'd how it shou'd happen that Women are conversible at all, since they are only beholding to Natural Parts for all their Knowledge: Their Youth is spent to teach them to Stitch and Sew, or make Bawbles: They are taught to Read indeed, and perhaps to Write their Names, or so, and, that is the height of a Woman's Education: And I wou'd but ask any who slight the Sex for their Understanding, What is a man (a Gentleman, I mean) good for, that is taught no more?

I ne'd not give Instances, or examine the Character of a Gentleman with a good Estate, and of a good Family, and with tolerable Parts,[1] and examine what Figure he makes for want of Education:

The Soul is plac'd in the Body like a rough Diamond, and must be polish'd, or the Lustre of it will never appear: And 'tis manifest, that as the Rational Soul distinguishes us from Brutes, so Education carries on the distinction, and makes some less brutish than others: This is too evident to ne'd any demonstration: But why then shou'd women be deni'd the benefit of Instruction? If Knowledge and Understanding had been useless additions to the Sex, God Almighty wou'd never have given them Capacities; for he made nothing needless: Besides, I wou'd ask such, What they can

---

1 Abilities, capacities, talents (archaic).

see in Ignorance, that they shou'd think it a necessary Ornament to a Woman? Or how much worse is a Wise Woman than a Fool? Or what has the Woman done to forfeit the Privilege of being taught? Does she plague us with her Pride and Impertinence? Why did we not let her learn, that she might have had more Wit? Shall we upbraid Women with Folly, when 'tis only the Error of this inhuman Custom, that hindred them being made wiser?

The Capacities of Women are suppos'd to be greater, and their Senses quicker than those of the Men; and what they might be capable of being bred to is plain from some Instances of Female-Wit which this age is not without; which upbraids us with Injustice, and looks as if we deni'd Women the advantages of Education, for fear they shou'd vye with the Men in their Improvements:

To remove this Objection, and that Women might have at least a needful Opportunity of Education in all sorts of Useful Learning, I propose the Draught of an Academy for that purpose:

I know 'tis dangerous to make Public Appearances of the Sex; they are not either to be *confin'd* or *expos'd*; the first will disagree with their Inclinations, and the last with their Reputations; and therefore it is somewhat difficult; and I doubt a Method proposed by an ingenious Lady, in a little book called, *Advice to the Ladies*, wou'd be found impracticable.[1] For, saving my Respect to the Sex, the Levity which perhaps is a little peculiar to them, at least in their Youth, will not bear the Restraint; and I am satisfi'd nothing but the heighth of Bigotry can keep up a Nunnery: Woman are extravagantly desirous of going to Heaven, and will punish their *Pretty Bodies* to get hither; but nothing else will do it; and even in that case sometimes it falls out *that Nature will prevail.*

When I talk therefore of an Academy for Women, I mean both the Model, the Teaching, and the Government different from what is propos'd by that Ingenious Lady, for whose Proposal I have a very great Esteem, and also a great Opinion of her Wit; different too from all sorts of Religious Confinement, and, above all, from *Vows of Celibacy*:

Wherefore the academy I propose shou'd differ but little from Publick Schools, wherein such Ladies as were willing to study,

1 From what follows, in particular the references to the Nunnery, the language in terms of which Astell's work was lampooned by Damaris Masham, it is clear that Defoe is referring to Astell's *A Serious Proposal*, which he mistitles.

shou'd have all the advantages of Learning suitable to their Genius.[1]

But since some Severities of Discipline more than ordinary wou'd be absolutely necessary to preserve the Reputation of the House, that Persons of Quality and Fortune might not be afraid to venture their Children thither, I shall venture to make a small Scheme by way of Essay:

The House I wou'd have built in a Form by it self, as well as in a Place by it self.

The Building shou'd be of Three plain Fronts, without any Jettings[2] or Bearing-Work, that the eye might at a glance see from one Coin[3] to the other; the gardens wall'd in the same Triangular Figure, with a large Moat, and but one Entrance.

When thus every part of the Scituation was contriv'd as well as might be for discovery, and to render *Intrieguing* dangerous, I wou'd have no Guards, no Eyes, no Spies set over the Ladies, but shall expect them to be try'd by the Principles of Honour and strict Virtue:

And if I am ask'd *Why*, I must ask Pardon of my own Sex for giving this reason for it:

I am so much in Charity with Women, and so well acquainted with men, that 'tis my opinion, There needs no other Care to prevent Intrieguing, than to keep the men effectually[4] away: For tho' *Inclination*, which we prettily call *Love*, does sometimes move a little too visibly in the Sex, and frailty often Follows; yet I think verily, *Custom*, which we miscall *Modesty*, has so far the Ascendant over the Sex that *Solicitation*[5] always goes before it:

> "Custom with Women 'stead of Virtue rules;
> It leads the Wisest, and commands the Fools:
> For this alone, when Inclination reign,
> Tho' Virtue's fled, will Acts of Vice restrain:
> Only by Custom 'tis that Virtue lives,
> And Love requires to be ask'd before it gives.
> For that which we call *Modesty*, is *Pride*:
> They scorn to ask, and hate to be deni'd:

---

1 Talent, ability, inclination, bent.
2 Projection (obsolete).
3 Corner, angle (obsolete).
4 Effectively.
5 The exertion of a physically attracting influence or force.

'Tis Custom thus prevails upon their want;
They'll never beg, what askt they easily grant.
And when the needless Ceremony's over,
Themselves the Weakness of the Sex discover.
If then Desires are strong, and Nature free,
Keep from her Men and Opportunity.
Else 'twill be vain to curb her by Restraint;
But keep the Question off, you keep the Saint."[1]

In short, let a Woman have never such a Coming-Principle,[2] she will let you ask before she complies — at least, if she be a Woman of any Honour:

Upon this Ground I am persuad'd such measures might be taken, that the Ladies might have all the Freedom in the world within their own Walls, and yet no Intrieguing, no Indecencies, nor Scandalous Affairs happen; and, in order to this, the following Customs and Laws shou'd be observ'd in the Colleges, of which I wou'd propose one at least in every County in *England*, and about Ten for the City of *London*:

After the Regulation of the Form of the Building as before;

(1.) All the Ladies who enter into the House, shou'd set their Hands to the Orders of the House, to signify their Consent to submit to them.
(2.) As no Woman shou'd be receiv'd, but who declared her self willing, and that it was the Act of her Choice to enter herself, so no Person shou'd be confin'd to continue there a Moment longer than the same voluntary Choice inclin'd her.
(3.) The Charges of the House being to be paid by the Ladies, every one that entred shou'd have only this Incumbrance,[3] That she shou'd pay for the whole Year, tho' her mind shou'd change as to her continuance.
(4.) An Act of Parliament shou'd make it a Felony without Clergy,[4] for any Man to enter by Force or Fraud into the House, or to

---

1 The author of this poem is unknown. Defoe gives it in italics, using Roman for emphasis, which I have reversed according to convention.
2 Approach (obsolete).
3 A claim, lien, liability attached to property.
4 Refers to the Old Law, Benefit of clergy, originally the privilege of exemption from trial by a secular court allowed to clergymen arraigned

solicit any Woman, *tho it were to Marry*, while she was in the House: And this law wou'd by no means be severe; because any Woman who was willing to receive the Addresses of a Man, might discharge her self of the House when she pleas'd; and on the contrary, any Woman who had occasion, might discharge herself of the Impertinent Addresses of any Person she had an Aversion to by entering into the house.

In This House

The Persons who Enter, shou'd be taught all sorts of Breeding suitable to both their Genius and their Quality; and in particular, *Musick* and *Dancing*, which it wou'd be cruelty to bar the Sex of, because they are their Darlings:[1] But besides this, they shou'd be taught languages, as particularly French and Italian; and I wou'd venture[2] the injury of giving a woman more tongues than one.

They shou'd, as a particular Study, be taught all the Graces of Speech, and all the necessary Air of Conversation; which our common Education is so defective in, that I need not expose it: They shou'd be brought to read Books, and especially History, and so to read as to make them understand the World, and be able to know and judge of things when they hear of them.

To such whose Genius wou'd lead them to it, I wou'd deny no sort of Learning; but the chief thing in general is to cultivate the Understandings of the Sex, that they may be capable of all sorts of Conversation; that their Parts and Judgments being improved, they may be as Profitable in their conversation as they are Pleasant.

Women, in my little observation, have little or no difference in them, but as they are, or are not distinguish'd by Education. Tempers[3] indeed may in some degree influence them, but the main distinguishing part is their Breeding:

---

on a felony; in later times the privilege of exemption from the sentence, which, in the case of certain offences, might be pleaded on the first conviction by every one who could read. Abolished in 1827 (*OED*, 1970 edn). Defoe is arguing that in this case the privilege should not be allowed.

1 Favourites.

2 Risk.

3 Temperaments.

The whole Sex are generally Quick and Sharp: I believe I may be allow'd to say generally so; for you rarely see them lumpish and heavy when they are Children, as Boys will often be. If a Woman be well-bred, and taught the proper Management of her Natural Wit, she proves generally very sensible and retentive: And without partiality, a Woman of Sense and Manners is the Finest and most Delicate Part of God's Creation; the Glory of her Maker, and the great Instance of His singular regard to Man, his Darling Creature, to whom he gave the best Gift either God cou'd bestow, or Man receive: And 'tis the most sordid Piece of Folly and Ingratitude in the World, to withhold from the Sex the due Lustre which the advantages of Education gives to the Natural Beauty of their Minds.

A Woman well Bred and well Taught, furnish'd with the additional Accomplishments of Knowledge and Behaviour, *is a Creature without comparison*; her Society[1] is the Emblem of sublimer Enjoyments; her Person is Angelick, and her Conversation heavenly; she is all Softness and Sweetness, Peace, Love, Wit, and Delight: She is very way suitable to the sublimest Wish, and the Man that has such a one to his Portion has nothing to do but to rejoice in her, and be thankful:

On the other hand, Suppose her to be the *very same* Woman, and rob her of the Benefit of Education, and it follows thus;

If her Temper be Good, want of Education makes her soft and easy.

Her Wit, for want of Teaching, makes her Impertinent and Talkative.

Her Knowledge, for want of Judgment and Experience, makes her Fanciful and Whimsical.

If her Temper be Bad, want of Breeding makes her worse, and she grows Haughty, Insolent, and Loud.

If she be Passionate, want of Manners makes her Termagant[2] and a Scold,[3] *which is much at one with Lunatick.*

If she be Proud, want of Discretion (which still is Breeding) makes her Conceited, Fantastic, and Ridiculous:

---

1 Company.

2 The name of an imaginary deity held in medieval Christendom to be worshipped by Muslims; in the mystery plays, represented as a violent or overbearing person.

3 A woman, rarely a man, addicted to abusive language.

And from these she degenerates to be Turbulent, Clamorous, Noisy, Nasty, *and the Devil.*

Methinks Mankind for their own sakes, since say what we will of the Women, we all think fit one time or other to be concern'd with 'em, shou'd take some care to breed them up to be *suitable* and *serviceable,* if they expected no such thing as *Delight* from 'em: Bless us! What Care do we take to Breed up a good Horse, and to Break him well! And what a value do we put upon him when it is done, and all because he shou'd be fit for our use! and why not a Woman? Since all her Ornaments and Beauty, without suitable Behaviour, is a Cheat[1] in nature, like the false Tradesman, who puts the best of his Goods uppermost, that the Buyer may think the rest are of the same Goodness:

Beauty of the Body, which is the Womens Glory, seems to be now unequally bestow'd, and Nature or rather, Providence, to lye under some Scandal about it, as if 'twas given to a Woman for a Snare to Men, and so make a kind of *She-Devil* of her: Because, they say, Exquisite Beauty is *rarely* given with Wit; *more rarely* with Goodness of Temper, and *never at all* with Modesty.[2] And some, pretending to justify the Equity of such a Distribution, will tell us 'tis the Effect of the Justice of Providence in dividing particular Excellences among all his Creatures, *share and share alike, as it were,* that all might for something or other be acceptable to one another, else some wou'd be despis'd.

I think both these Notions false; and yet the last, which has the shew[3] of Respect to Providence, is the worst; for it supposes Providence to be Indigent and Empty; as if it had not wherewith to furnish all the Creatures it had made, but was fain to be parcimonious in its Gifts, and distribute them by *piece-meal,* for fear of being exhausted.

If I might venture my Opinion against an almost universal Notion, I wou'd say most men mistake the Proceedings of Providence in this case, and all the world at this day are mistaken in their Practice about it. And because the Assertion is very bold, I desire to explain myself.

That Almighty First Cause which made us all, is certainly the Fountain of Excellence, as it is of Being, and by an Invisible Influ-

---

1 Fraud, trick or deception.

2 Defoe betrays his basic misogyny.

3 Appearance.

ence cou'd have diffused[1] Equal Qualities and Perfections to all the Creatures it has made, as the Sun does its Light, without the least Ebb or Diminution to Himself; and has given inde'd to every individual sufficient to the Figure his Providence had design'd him in the world.

I believe it might be defended, if I shou'd say, That I do suppose God has given to all Mankind Equal Gifts and Capacities, in that He has given them all *Souls* equally capable; and that the whole Difference in Mankind proceeds either from Accidental Difference in the make of their Bodies, or from the *foolish Difference* of Education.

1. *From Accidental Difference in Bodies.* I wou'd avoid discoursing here of the Philosophical Position of the Soul in the Body: but if it be true, as Philosophers do affirm, That the Understanding and Memory is dilated[2] or contracted according to the accidental Dimensions of the organ through which 'tis conveyed; then, tho' God has given a Soul as capable to me as another, yet if I have any Natural Defect in those parts of the Body by which the Soul shou'd act, I may have the same soul infus'd as another man, and yet he be a Wise Man and I a very Fool. *For example*, if a Child naturally have a Defect in the Organ of Hearing, so that he cou'd never distinguish any Sound, that Child shall never be able to speak or read, tho' it have a Soul capable of all the Accomplishments in the World: The Brain is the Centre of the Soul's actings,[3] where all the distinguishing Faculties of it reside; and 'tis observable, a man who has a narrow contract'd Head, in which there is not room for the due and necessary Operations of Nature by the Brain, is never a man of very great Judgment;[4] and that proverb, *A Great Head and Little Wit*, is not meant, by nature, but is a Reproof upon Sloth; as if one shou'd by way of wonder, say, *Fye, fye, you that have a great head but little wit; that's strange! that must certainly be your own fault.* From this Notion I do believe there is a great matter in the Breed of Men and Women; not that Wise Men shall always get Wise Children; but I believe Strong and Healthy Bodies have the Wisest Children; and Sickly, Weakly Bodies affect the Wits as well as the Bodies of their Children: We are easily persuad'd to believe this in

---

1 Pour out, spread.
2 Expand, extend, increase.
3 Actions.
4 Defoe subscribes to now discredited theories about the brain.

the Breeds of Horses, Cocks, Dogs, and other Creatures; and I believe 'tis as visible in Men.

But to come closer to the business; the great distinguishing difference which is seen in the world between Men and Women is in their Education; and this is manifested by comparing it with the difference between one Man or Woman, and another.

And herein it is that I take upon me to make such a bold Assertion, That all the world are mistaken in their Practice about Women: For I cannot think that God Almighty ever made them so delicate, so glorious Creatures, and furnish'd them with such Charms, so Agreeable and so Delightful to Mankind, with Souls capable of the same Accomplishments with Men, and all to be only Stewards of our houses, Cooks, and Slaves.

Not that I am for exalting the Female Government in the least: But, in short, *I wou'd have Men take Women for Companions, and Educate them to be fit for it.* A Woman of Sense and Breeding will scorn as much to encroach upon the Prerogative of the Man, as a Man of Sense will scorn to oppress the *Weakness* of the Woman. But if the Women's Souls were refin'd and improv'd by Teaching, that word wou'd be lost; to say, *The Weakness of the Sex*, as to Judgment, wou'd be Nonsense; for Ignorance and Folly wou'd be no more to be found among Women than Men. I remember a Passage which I heard from a very Fine Woman, she had Wit and Capacity enough, an extraordinary Shape and Face, and a Great Fortune, but had been cloyster'd up all her time, and for fear of being stoll'n,[1] had not had the liberty of being taught the common necessary knowledge of Women's Affairs; and when she came to converse in the world her Natural Wit made her so sensible of the want of Education, that she gave this short Reflection on herself:

I am asham'd to talk with my very maids, says she, *for I don't know when they do right or wrong: I had more need go to School than be Married.*

I need not enlarge on the Loss the Defect of Education is to the Sex, nor argue the Benefit of the contrary Practice; 'tis a thing will be more easily granted than remedied:[2] this Chapter is but an Essay[3] at the thing, and I refer the Practice to those Happy Days, if ever they shall be, when men shall be wise enough to mend it.

---

1 Stolen.

2 I.e., more easily granted in theory than remedied in practice.

3 Attempt.

Appendix C: From The Tatler, *no. 32 (June 23, 1709)*

[From *The Tatler*, 2 vols., London: Printed for Rivington, Marshall and Bye, 1789, vol. 1. Notes marked * are supplied by the anonymous editor of this edition of the *Tatler*.]

THE TATLER. N° 32., Thursday, June 23, 1709. SWIFT AND ADDISON.[1]

Quicquid agunt homines — nostri est farrago libelli.
Juv. Sat. i. 85, 86.

"Whate'er men do, or say, or think, or dream,
Our medley[2] Paper seizes as its theme." P.

---

1 * This humorous Paper probably originated in the licentious imagination of the Dean of St. PATRICK's, whom no laws, divine or human, could either confine to strict truth, or restrain from the exercise of indiscriminating satire, and illaudible ridicule. Even ADDISON corrupted by his company, seems to have been more than merely his *Amanuensis*, so that SWIFT might have said here, in his own way of *refinement*, as truly at least, as in the case of the Examiner, "that he had really no *hand* in this Paper." It came probably with ADDISON's 2d or 3d contribution from Ireland, to the Author and Editor of the TATLER. An humorous compliment to JANUS in the article annexed, seems to disclose, and to ascertain the Author of this Paper, as an eminent *Punster*. The reader will see more proofs, or at least presumptions of the propriety of ascribing this Paper to SWIFT, and ADDISON in No 59; No 63, and *Notes*. What relates to MADONELLA in TAT. No 63, evidently appears to have been written by the Author of this Paper, certainly reprehensible, for having treated so ludicrously, subjects so serious, and characters so respectable. It ought not to be concealed, that this number has been suspected to have been the production of A. HENLEY, Esq; sent to his familiar friend STEELE from Clay-Hill in Middlesex. This suspicion is grounded on the supposition of its being written in a stile of superior elegance and scholarship to most of SWIFT's things; but the argument falls to the ground, from the probability of ADDISON's having been, on this occasion, SWIFT's *amanuensis* and co-adjutor. See TAT. No 11; No 25; No 26; No 44; SPECT. No 494; and *Notes* on ANTHONY HENLEY, *Esq*.

2 In a disparaging sense, a heterogeneous combination or mixture of things (*OED*).

WHITE'S Choclate-house, June 22.

An answer to the following letter being absolutely necessary to be dispatched with all expedition, I must trespass upon all that come with horary[1] questions into my antichamber, to give the gentleman my opinion.

"To ISAAC BICKERSTAFF, Esquire.
June 18, 1709.

Sir

I know not whether you ought to pity or laugh at me; for I am fallen desperately in love with a professed PLATONNE, the most unaccountable creature of her sex. To hear her talk seraphics,[2] and run over NORRIS,[3] and MORE,[4] and MILTON,[5] and the whole

---

1 **Horary questions* are questions relative to an hour to be resolved astrologically. See No 56, and "Lives of ASHMOLE and LILLY, etc. 1774," p. 36, 43, *et passim*.

2 Concerning sublime subjects (obs.) (*OED*).

3 *JOHN NORRIS, a man of great ingenuity, learning, and piety, was born in 1657, and died in 1711, aged 54. He published in 1688 "The Theory and Regulation of Love," in which he considers all virtues and vices as the various modifications and irregularities of LOVE. He maintained this principle, "that the *love* of GOD ought to be entire, and exclusive of all other LOVES." Biog. Brit. *Art.* NORRIS.

4 *HENRY MORE, whose name is perhaps affectedly mispelled Moor in the original Paper, an eminent divine and Platonic philosopher, was born in 1614, and died in 1687, aged 73. He composed many books, which he called "preaching at his finger ends." Mr. CHISHULL, an eminent bookseller, declared, that Dr. MORE's "Mystery of Godliness," and his other works, ruled all the book-sellers of London for twenty years together.

5 *MILTON, the fellow-collegian of Dr. H. MORE, makes up the *trio* of INTELLECTUAL TRIFLERS here mentioned. As he was born in 1608, and died in 1674, it is obvious that these writers are not classed in a chronological order. A complete collection of MILTON's "Works" not having been consulted, it cannot be positively affirmed, that there is no particular tract of his referred to here; but the following fine sentiments were probably sufficient, to procure their author the honour of being thus ranked, and abused in very good company:

> "In loving thou do'st well, in passion not,
> Wherein true LOVE consists not; LOVE refines

set of INTELLECTUAL TRIFLERS, torments me heartily; for, to a lover who understands metaphors, all this pretty prattle of ideas gives very fine views of pleasure, which only the dear declaimer prevents, by understanding them literally: why should she wish to be a cherubim, when it is flesh and blood that makes her adorable? If I speak to her, that is a high breach of the idea of *Intuition*. If I offer at her hand or lip, she shrinks from the touch like a *Sensitive* PLANT, and would contract herself into mere spirit. She calls her chariot, vehicle; her furbelowed[1] scarf, pinions;[2] her blue manteau[3] and petticoat is her azure dress; and her footman goes by the name of OBERON.[4] It is my misfortune to be six feet and a half high,

---

> The thoughts, and heart inlarges, hath his feat
> In reas'n, and is judicious, is the scale
> By which to heav'nly LOVE thou may'st ascend,
> LOVE leads to HEAV'N, is both the way, and guide."
> MILTON's Par. Lost, b.VIII. 588-614

I speak not of the books expressly so called, but as many, indeed most of FENELON's *Oeuvres Spirituelles* must have been known at this time, it might have been expected, that he would have been classed here with his congenial English friends. It might be supposed to imply an unmerited and unintended censure on other equally excellent, and no less meritorious authors, to say that the beautiful lines above quoted, express the *peculiar distinguishing* tenets of the sentimental writers here alluded to; they express however their leading principles; and if, guarding against the wantonness of imagination, good sense and the New Testament be taken as guides in reading their writings, very many things will be found in them, that equally approve themselves to every sound understanding, and every well-disposed heart. Not a few of their books might be mentioned, that seem evidently intended, and not ill-calculated, to do the heart good; that breathe and inspire a spirit of piety; and therefore their luxuriancies claim the veil of candour, and even their very errors are respectable.

1 Ornamented with a furbelow, flounce, or the pleated border of a petticoat or gown. Used also as a contemptuous term for showy ornaments or trimming (*OED*).
2 The distal or terminal segment of a bird's wing (*OED*).
3 A cape or cloak (*OED*).
4 *An allusion to a musical drama of BEN JONSON, intituled, "Oberon the Fairy Prince:" or perhaps to the character of Oberon in "The Midsummer Night's Dream," and in Spenser.

two full spans between the shoulders, thirteen inches diameter in the calves; and, before I was in love, I had a noble stomach, and usually went to bed sober with two bottles. I am not quite six-and-twenty, and my nose is marked truly aquiline. For these reasons, I am in a very particular manner her aversion. What shall I do? Impudence itself cannot reclaim her. If I write miserably, she reckons me among the children of perdition, and discards me her region: if I assume the gross and substantial, she plays the real ghost with me, and vanishes in a moment. I had hopes in the hypocrisy of her sex; but perseverance makes it as bad as fixed aversion. I desire your opinion, whether I may not lawfully play the inquisition upon her, make use of a little force, and put her to the rack and the torture, only to convince her, she has really fine limbs, without spoiling or distorting them. I expect your directions, before I proceed to dwindle and fall away with despair; which at present I do not think adviseable, because, if she should recant, she may then hate me perhaps, in the other extreme, for my tenuity.[1] I am (with impatience) your most humble servant,

CHARLES STURDY.

My patient has put his case with very much warmth, and represented it in so lively a manner, that I see both his torment and tormentor with great perspicuity. This order of Platonic ladies, are to be dealt with in a manner peculiar from all the rest of the sex. Flattery is the general way, and the way in this case; but it is not to be done grossly. Every man that has wit, and humour, and raillery, can make a good flatterer for woman in general: but a PLATONNE is not to be touched with panegyric:[2] she will tell you, it is a sensuality in the soul to be delighted that way. You are not therefore to commend, but silently consent to all she does and says. You are to consider, in her the scorn of you is not humour, but opinion.

There were, some years since, a set of these ladies who were of quality, and gave out, that virginity was to be their state of life during this mortal condition, and therefore resolved to join their fortunes and erect a nunnery. The place of residence was pitched

---

1 Meagreness, slightness, weakness, poverty (*OED*).

2 Laudatory discourse, eulogy (*OED*).

upon; and a pretty situation, full of natural falls and risings of waters, with shady coverts, and flowery arbours, was approved by seven of the founders. There were as many of our sex who took the liberty to visit their mansions of intended severity; and among others,[1] a famous rake[2] of that time, who had the grave way to an excellence. He came in first; but, upon seeing a servant coming towards him, with a design to tell him this was no place for him or his companions, up goes my grave impudence to the maid; "Young woman," said he, "if any of the ladies are in the way on this side of the house, pray carry us on the other side towards the gardens: we are, you must know, gentlemen, that are travelling England; after which we shall go into foreign parts, where some of us have already been." Here he bows in the most humble manner, and kissed the girl, who knew not how to behave to such a sort of carriage.[3] He goes on: "Now you must know we have an ambition to have it to say, that we have a protestant nunnery in England: but pray, Mrs. Betty" — "Sir," she replied, "my name is Susan at your service." "Then I heartily beg your pardon" — "No offence in the least," said she, "for I have a cousin-german,[4] whose name is Betty." "Indeed," said he, "I protest to you, that was more than I knew; I spoke at random: but since it happens that I was near in the right, give me leave to present this gentleman to the favour of a civil salute." His friend advances, and so on, until they have saluted her. By this means the poor girl was in the middle of the crowd of these fellows, at a loss what to do, without courage to pass through them; and the Platonics, at several peep-holes, pale, trembling, and fretting. RAKE perceived they were observed, and therefore took care to keep Sukey[5] in chat with questions concerning

---

1 *A Mr. REPINGTON, a Warwickshire wag, is said to have been the "famous Rake" here alluded to, who might probably have been accompanied with HENLEY, NORTON, etc., See Introd. *Note*.

2 A man of loose habits and immoral character; an idle dissipated man of fashion (*OED*).

3 Conduct or behaviour (*OED*).

4 Closely connected (*OED*).

5 A variant of sook, from suck, indicating infantile behaviour (*OED*); possibly passed off as a diminutive of Susan.

their way of life; when appeared at last MADONELLA,[1] a lady who had writ a fine book concerning the recluse life, and was the projectrix[2] of the foundation. She approaches into the hall; and the RAKE, knowing the dignity of his own mien[3] and aspect, goes deputy from his company. She begins, "Sir, I am obliged to follow the servant, who was sent out to know what affair could make strangers press upon a solitude which we, who

---

1 *The person here grossly misrepresented, under the name of *Madonella*, was, Mrs. MARY ASTELL, a lady of superior understanding, of considerable learning, and singular piety. She was the daughter of a merchant in Newcastle upon Tyne, where she was born about 1668, and lived about twenty years. The remainder of her inoffensive, irreproachable, and exemplary life she spent at London and Chelsea, where she died in 1731. Mr. NORRIS, before-mentioned, published her epistolary correspondence with him on the "*Love* of GOD" IN 1695. The well-written BOOK alluded to is in two parts, and intitled, "A serious Proposal to the Ladies for the Advancement of their true and greatest Interest, etc." She proposed the establishment of a seminary for female education; and the scheme appeared so rational and important to a certain great lady, that she intented to have given 10,000l. towards the erection of a convenient college for this purpose, and as a retreat for ladies who might chuse to lead a single life, in an agreeable retirement from the bustle and distractions of the world. Mr. BALLARD affirms, in his "Memoirs of learned ladies," that Bishop BURNETT industriously frustrated this generous design, by buzzing in the ears of a lady, who was zealously attached to the church of England, and over-apprehensive of innovation, that such an establishment would be reputed, as it is miscalled here, a PROTESTANT *Nunnery*, and might pave the way to the introduction of POPISH *orders*, etc." There is little doubt but that the person here alluded to, was the truly great, and liberal-minded lady ELIZABETH HASTINGS; and it is a pity that she was so far the dupe of a ridiculous argument, as to suffer such a change to be put upon her, where the question was not about the possible reputation, but the real nature of a harmless, and beneficial institution. She continued, however, to the end of Mrs. ASTELL's life, her great friend and benefactress, and is most justly celebrated by CONGREVE, under the name of ASPASIA, "as an illustrious pattern to all who love praise-worthy things." See No 42; No 63; and *Notes*.

2 Female projector, the author of projects, but also used in a pejorative sense for speculators and cheats (*OED*). The specific reference is to Astell as the author of the project for a female academy outlined in *A Serious Proposal*, 1694.

3 Appearance (obs.) (*OED*).

are to inhabit this place, have devoted to heaven and our own thoughts?" "Madam," replies RAKE, with an air of great distance, mixed with a certain indifference, by which he could dissemble dissimulation, "your great intention has made more noise in the world, than you design it should; and we travellers, who have seen many foreign institutions of this kind, have a curiosity to see, in its first rudiments, the feat of primitive piety; for such it must be called by future ages, to the eternal honour of the founders: I have read MADONELLA's excellent and seraphic discourse on this subject." The lady immediately answered, "If what I have said could have contributed to raise any thoughts in you that may make for the advancement of intellectual and divine conversation, I should think myself extremely happy." He immediately fell back with the profoundest veneration; then advancing, "Are you then that admired lady? If I may approach lips which have uttered things so sacred" — He salutes her. His friends followed his example. The devoted within stood in amazement where this would end, to see MADONELLA receive their address, and their company. But the RAKE goes on — "We would not transgress rules; but if we may take the liberty to see the place you have thought fit to choose for ever, we would go into such parts of the gardens as is consistent with the severities you have imposed on yourselves."

To be short, MADONELLA permitted RAKE to lead her into the assembly of Nuns, followed by his friends, and each took his fair-one by the hand, after due explanation, to walk round the gardens. The conversation turned upon the lilies, the flowers, the arbours, and the growing vegetables; and RAKE had the solemn impudence, when the whole company stood round him, to say,"[1] that "he sincerely wished men might rise out of the earth like plants; and that our minds were not of necessity to be sullied with carnivorous appetites for the generation, as well as support, of our species." This was spoken with so easy and fixed an assurance, that MADONELLA answered, "Sir, under the notion of a pious thought, you deceive yourself in wishing an institution foreign to that of Providence. These desires were implanted in us for reverend purposes, in preserving the race of men, and giving oppor-

---

1 *An allusion to Sir T. BROWN's "*Religio Medici*," part II, sect. 9. edit. Lond. 1656; and *ibidem*, p. 287.

tunities for making our chastity more heroic." The conference was continued in this celestial strain, and carried on so well by the managers on both sides, that it created a second, and a third interview; and, without entering into further particulars, there was hardly one of them but was a mother or father that day twelvemonth.[1]

Any unnatural part is long taking up, and as long laying aside; therefore Mr. STURDY may assure himself PLATONICA will fly for ever from a forward behaviour; but if he approaches her according to this model, she will fall in with the necessities of mortal life, and condescend to look with pity on an unhappy man, imprisoned in so much body, and urged by such violent desires.

From my own Apartment, June 22.

The evils of this town increase upon me to so great a degree, that I am half afraid I shall not leave the world much better than I found it. Several worthy gentlemen and critics have applied to me, to give my censure of an enormity which has been revived, after being long suppressed, and is called *Punning*.[2] I have several arguments ready to prove, that he cannot be a man of honour, who is guilty of this abuse of human society. But the way to expose it is, like the expedient of curing drunkenness, shewing a man in that condition: therefore I must give my reader warning, to expect a collection of these offences; without which preparation, I thought it too adventurous to introduce the very mention of it in good company; and I hope, I shall be understood to do it, as a divine mentions oaths and curses, only for their condemnation. I shall dedicate this discourse to a gentleman, my very good

---

1 *This is mere fiction, and unpardonable, as it seems to imply an oblique censure on Mrs. ASTELL, of a nature totally repugnant to her eminently virtuous, and respectable character.

2 *See an apology for *punning*, GUARDIAN, No 36. The affectation of this sort of wit was most general in the reign of king JAMES I. when it was common, and not thought unsuitable even in the pulpit. See Dr. DONNE's "Sermons," *passim*.

There seems here to be an *oblique stroke* at Mr. DENNIS, who held *Punning* in utter abomination.

friend, who is the JANUS[1] of our times, and whom, by his years and wit, you would take to be of the last age; but his dress and morals, of this.

---

1 *Under the fanciful name of JANUS, STEELE clearly alludes to SWIFT as a *Punster*, the author most probably of the preceding part of this Paper, and pays him some compliments in return for his communication. SWIFT's *age* was nearly the same as that of STEELE, who was rather the *senior* of the two. This JANUS had *wit* in abundance, but it was seldom innocuous; it flowed most freely from the *indignation which gnawed at his heart*. See SWIFT's "Works," vol. XII. p. 276. cr. 8vo. If it was more licentious, it was less lascivious than what commonly prevailed in the age of CHARLES II. to which it is referred. His *dress* might be perfectly fash'onable; the compliment on the score of his *morals* is obscure. They might be well adapted to his times, but they were ill suited to his profession; and in general like his writings, not very edifying, or worse. See a compliment to SWIFT somewhat similar, which STEELE acknowledges to have been *intentional*, at the time he published it; No 5, *Art.* from WILL's, April 20, p. 46, and *Note* from STEELE's "Apology," etc. 4to. 1714, p. 49.

Appendix D: From The Tatler, *no. 63 (September 3, 1709)*

[From *The Tatler*, 2 vols., London: Printed for Rivington, Marshall and Bye, 1789, vol. 2. Notes marked * are supplied by the anonymous editor of this edition of the *Tatler*.]

THE TATLER, No. 63. Saturday, September 3, 1709.[1] ADDISON, STEELE, and SWIFT.

From my own Apartment, September 2.
The following letter being a panegyric upon me for a quality which every man may attain, an acknowledgment of his faults; I thought it for the good of my fellow-writers to publish it.

"Sir,

It must be allowed, that Esquire BICKERSTAFF is of all authors the most ingenuous. There are few, very few, that will own themselves in a mistake, though all the world see them to be in downright nonsense. You will be pleased, Sir, to pardon this expression, for the same reason for which you once desired us to excuse you, when you seemed any thing dull. Most writers, like the generality of *Paul*[2] LORRAINE's Saints, seem to place a peculiar vanity in dying hard. But you Sir, to shew a good example to your brethren, have not only confessed, but of your own accord mended the indictment. Nay, you have been so good-natured as to discover beauties in it, which, I will assure you, he that drew it never dreamed of. And, to make your civility the more accomplished,

---

1 Pp. 118-25 and notes have been omitted. The excerpt concerns Mary Astell, and is confidently assigned to Swift by the anonymous editor of the *Tatler*: "as it refers to the sequel of the ridiculous *historiette* of MADONELLA, which might likewise have been intituled, and not improperly, 'A short Supplement to the Memoirs of the New Atlantis.' If it be superior in regard of wit and composition to the very best narratives in that scandalous chronicle, it is certainly on a footing with the very worst of them in respect of its want of veracity and good-nature. See No 177, *Note*."

2 *See SPECT. No 338.

you have honoured him with the title of your kinsman, which though derived by the left-hand, he is not a little proud of. My brother, for such OBADIAH is, being at present very busy about nothing, has ordered me to return you his sincere thanks for all these favours; and as a small token of his gratitude, to communicate to you the following piece of intelligence, which he thinks, belongs more properly to you, than to any others of our modern historians.

MADONELLA,[1] who, as it was thought, had long since taken her flight towards the aetherial mansions, still walks it seems, in the regions of mortality; where she has found, by deep reflections on the revolution mentioned in yours of June the twenty-third, that where early instructions have been wanting to imprint true ideas of things on the tender souls of those of her sex, they are never after able to arrive at such a pitch of perfection, as to be above the laws of matter and motion; laws which are considerably enforced by the principles usually imbibed in nurseries and boarding-schools. To remedy this evil, she has laid the scheme of a college for young damsels; where (instead of scissars, needles and samplers) pens, compasses, quadrants, books, manuscripts, Greek, Latin, and Hebrew, are to take up their whole time. Only on holidays the students will, for moderate exercise, be allowed to divert themselves with the use of some of the lightest and most voluble weapons; and proper care will be taken to give them at least a superficial tincture of the ancient and modern Amazonian tactics. Of these military performances, the direction is undertaken by EPICENE,[2] the

---

1 *See No 32, Note on Mrs *Mary* ASTELL.

2 *EPICENE probably means Mrs. D. MANLEY. This lady, having probably no knowledge or suspicion of the real author of what is said of her here, aimed her resentment at the ostensible editor, whom she took all occasions to *traduce* and *calumniate*. With this view she penned a furious dedication of her "Memoirs of Europe," etc. in 8vo. 1711, to *Captain* STEELE, under the fictitious name of ISAAC BICKERSTAFF, Esq. The letter inserted in that dedication, and the paragraph immediately following, obviously allude to this Paper, and furnish an additional proof that it was not written by STEELE, who denies his being the *author*, in the most unequivocal manner, and is charged by the lady with disingenuousness and falsehood, for so doing. See No 177, *Note*.

Soon after this time, Mrs D. MANLEY had the honour to become SWIFT's *amanuensis* and fellow-labourer in the "Examiner," in the "Narrative of GUISCARDS's Examination," in the "Learned Comment on

writer of 'Memoirs from the Mediterranean,' who, by the help of some artificial poisons conveyed by smells, has within these few weeks brought many persons of both sexes to an untimely fate; and, what is more surprising, has, contrary to her profession, with the same odours, revived others who had long since been drowned in the whirlpools of LETHE. Another of the professors is to be a certain lady, who is now publishing two of the choicest Saxon novels,[1] which are said to have been in as great repute with the ladies of queen EMMA's court, as the 'Memoirs from the New

---

Dr. HARE's Sermon," in the "Vindication of the D. of MARLBOROUGH," etc. etc. etc. She rose very high in the dean's favour, who pleaded her merits with the ministry, solicited their generosity in her behalf, and marked her without a *d* in the number of his grateful beneficiaries. See "*Supplement* to Dr. SWIFT's Work," Vol. I. page xli. and page 2.

Ingenuity has laboured often in vain to explain apparent inconsistencies in SWIFT's character and conduct. In the dissimilar instances abovementioned he acted uniformly, on the principles of party-spirit; having shifted sides in the interval. At the time when this Paper was written, SWIFT was avowedly on the same side with ADDISON and STEELE, and a whig by profession: his notorious desertion from that party did not take place, nor his virulent abuse of it begin, until a full year after this date. In the beginning of September 1710, he was introduced to Mr. HARLEY, doubtless at his own desire, "as one extremely ill used by the last ministry, *after some obligations*, because he would not go certain lengths they would have him, which was in some sort Mr. HARLEY's own case." SWIFT's letters to STELLA, in the way of a journal, commence at this period, and furnish numerous and incontestible proofs that he did not hesitate many days about making this change. By abandoning the whigs, he seems to have been cured of his former squeamishness, as he stuck at nothing to serve his new party, and soon after complains that they did not go the lengths he would have had them.

1 *Mrs. *Elizabeth* ELSTOB, the lady here alluded to, was learned in an extraordinary way, and not only learned but meritorious to a very high degree, for her good dispositions as well as her great acquirements. Her temper and conversation were exceedingly agreeable; and her general deportment, to the advanced age of seventy-three under singular vicissitudes of fortune, was not only inoffensive and irreproachable, but admirable and exemplary. In affluence she was studious, in want industrious; and the meekness, resignation, fortitude, and piety, she manifested

Atlantis' are with those of ours. I shall make it my business to enquire into the progress of this learned institution, and give you the first notice of their 'Philosophical Transactions, and Searches after NATURE.'

Yours, etc.
TOBIAH GREENHAT."

---

conspicuously, in struggling many years for a scanty livelihood in obscurity and with bad health, became the ultimate causes of her elevation to an easy affluent station in the family of the late Duchess of Portland, where she spent the last seventeen years of her life with chearfulness, comfort, and *great approbation*. The words in Italics are added with pleasure, on the express testimony of her illustrious patroness. Mrs. E. died on May 30, 1756, and was buried in St. Margaret's Westminster. Besides a competent knowledge of her own and the Latin tongue, she is said to have been mistress of seven other languages. She was uncommonly skilled in the Anglo-Saxon, of which she wrote a grammar, and in northern antiquities. She published in 1709, an English translation with valuable notes and an excellent preface, of an Anglo-Saxon Homily, anciently used in the English-Saxon Church, and containing a curious account of the conversion of the English to Christianity; which seems to be the book here ridiculed under the fiction of *two Saxon Novels*. On a supposition that what is said here was intended for wit, however incomprehensible, and in the way of banter, however improper, little enquiry has been made; but the annotator believes that no publication under the title of a *Saxon Novel* ever appeared in an English translation, or ever existed in a Saxon original. After all that can be urged in favour of No 32, and the sequel of it in this Paper, surely wit is a poor atonement for such gross misrepresentations of truth, and humour a bad apology for injurious insinuations of falsehood. The narrative of Madonella throughout, with this witty supplement to it, is an instance of the justice of Mr. Sheridan's remark, "SWIFT's power of Ridicule, was like a *flail* in his hand, against which there was no fence." "Life of SWIFT," by T. Sheridan, A.M. 1784, 8vo. p. 67. See also TAT. in 6 Vol. 1786, 12mo. No 63; and Vol. II. p. 397.

Select Bibliography

Primary Texts

Allestree, Richard. *The Gentleman's Calling*. London: Printed for Robert Pawlet at the Bible in Chancery Lane, n.d. [Wing, A1130].

Allestree, Richard. *The Ladies Calling*. [1673] 1705 edn. Oxford: at the Theatre [Wing A1141].

Anon. *A Ladies Religion: In a Letter to the Honourable My Lady Howard*. 2nd edn. London: Printed for A. and J. Churchill at the Black-Swan in Paternoster Row, 1704.

Arnauld, Antoine [and Pierre Nicole]. *Logic, or the Art of Thinking* [1662]. London: Printed by T.B. and to be sold by Randal Taylor near Stationers Hall, 1693 [Wing A3724].

Arnauld, Antoine. *On True and False Ideas* [1683]. Tr. with an intr. by Stephen Gaukroger. New York: St. Martin's Press, 1990.

Astell, Mary. *Bart'lemy Fair, or an Enquiry after Wit in which due Respect is had to a Letter Concerning Enthusiasm. To my Lord XXX by Mr. Wotton* [pseud.]. London, 1709. The 2nd edn, 1722, appeared under the title, *an Enquiry after Wit, wherein the Trifling Arguing and Impious Raillery of the Late Earl of Shaftesbury in his letter concerning Enthusiasm and other Profane Writers are fully answered and justly exposed.*

—. *The Christian Religion as Profess'd by a Daughter of the Church of England in a Letter to the Right Honourable T.L., C.I.* London: Printed by S.H. for R. Wilkin, at the King's Head in St. Paul's Churchyard, 1705.

—. *A Collection of Poems humbly presented and Dedicated to the most Reverend Father in God William [Sancroft] by Divine Providence Lord Archbishop of Canterbury etc.* Rawlinson MSS poet. 154:50. Oxford: The Bodleian Library, 1689. Excerpted in Bridget Hill, *The First English Feminist: "Reflections Upon Marriage" and other Writings by Mary Astell* (Aldershot, Hants.: Gower/Maurice Temple Smith, 1986),183-84. Published in full as "Appendix D" to Ruth Perry's, *The Celebrated Mary Astell: An Early English Feminist* (Chicago, Ill.: University of Chicago Press, 1986), 400-54.

—. *A Fair Way with the Dissenters and their Patrons*. London: Printed for E.P. by R. Wilkin, at the King's Head in St. Paul's Churchyard, 1704.

—. *An Impartial Enquiry into the Causes of Rebellion and Civil War in this Kingdom in an Examination of Dr. Kennett's Sermon, Jan. 31, 1703/4 and Vindication of the Royal Martyr*. London: Printed by E.P. for R. Wilkin, at the King's Head in St. Paul's Churchyard, 1704.

—. *Letters Concerning the Love of God, between the Author of the Proposal to the Ladies and Mr. John Norris*. Published by J. Norris, Rector of Bemerton nr. Sarum, London, printed for Samuel Manship [Wing 1254], 1695.

—. *Moderation truly Stated: or A Review of a Late Pamphlet, Entitul'd, Moderation a Vertue .... With a Prefatory Discourse to Dr. D'Avenant, Concerning His Late Essays on Peace and War*, London: Printed by J.L. for Richard Wilkin, at the King's-Head, in St. Paul's Church-yard, 1704.

—. *A Serious Proposal to the Ladies for the Advancement of their True and Greatest Interest*, London: Printed for R. Wilkin, 1694 [Wing A4063]. 2nd edn corrected, 1695. London: Printed for R. Wilkin [Wing A4063]. 4th edn, 1701. London: Printed by J.R for R. Wilkin [Folger Library, PR3316.A655.S3.Cage].

—. *A Serious Proposal to the Ladies, Part II, Wherein a Method is Offer'd for the Improvement of their Minds*. London: Printed for Richard Wilkin at the King's Head in St. Paul's Church-yard, 1697.

—. *A Serious Proposal to the Ladies for the Advancement of their True and Greatest Interest*. Parts I and II. London: Printed for T.W. and R. Wilkin, at the King's Head in St. Paul's Church-Yard [Part II has a separate title page, "A Serious Proposal..." (entered in Wing as C40654), 1697].

—. *Some Reflections Upon Marriage, Occasion'd by the Duke & Dutchess of Mazarine's Case....* London: Printed for John Nutt [Wing A4067]. 2nd edn (no known copies extant). 3rd edn, *Reflections Upon Marriage, To which is added a Preface in Answer to Some Objections*. London: printed for R. Wilkin, at the King's Head in St Paul's Church Yard, 1700. 4th edn, 1630.

B., F. 1698. *A Free but Modest Censure of the late Controversial Writings and Debates (The Lord Bishop of Worcester and Mr. Locke: Of Mr. Edwards and Mr. Locke: The Hon[ble] Charles Boyle, Esq; and Dr. Bentley. together with Brief Remarks on Monsieur Le Clerc's Ars Critica*. London: Printed for A. Baldwin in Warwick-lane [Wing B59].

Ballard, George. *Memoirs of Several Ladies of Great Britain Who have been Celebrated for their Writings or Skill in the Learned Languages,*

Arts and Sciences (1752), ed. Ruth Perry. Detroit, MI: Wayne State University Press, 1985.

Berkeley, George, *The Ladies Library*, 3 vols, London: Published by Mr. Steele, 1714.

Burnet, Gilbert. *History of his Own Time*. 2 vols. London: Vol. 1 printed for Thomas Ward, 1724; vol. 2, printed for the editor by Joseph Downing, 1734.

Bible, Authorized Version, 1611, reprinted. Oxford University Press, 1911.

Centlivre, S. "Basset Table." *The Works of the Celebrated Mrs. Centlivre*. 3 vols. London: Printed for J. Knapton, *et al.*, 1760.

Defoe, Daniel. "An Academy for Women" *An Essay upon Projects*. London: Printed by R.R. for Theo. Cockerill at the Corner of Warwick-Lane, near Pater-noster Row, 1697. Repr. *The Earlier Life and Chief Earlier Works of Daniel Defoe*. Ed. Henry Morley. London: G. Routledge, 1889.

Descartes, René. *The Passions of the Soul*. London: Printed for A.C. to be sold by J. Martin and J. Ridley, 1650 [Wing, D1134].

Drake, Judith. *An Essay In Defence of the Female Sex*. London: Printed for A. Roper and E. Wilkinson at the Black Boy and R. Clavel at the Peacock, in Fleetstreet, 1696.

Fénelon, François de Salignac de la Mothe de. *De l'Education des filles* (1687). Ed. Emile Faguet. Paris, 1933.

Hickes, George. *Instructions for the Education of a Daughter*. London. [Hickes's translation of Fénelon's *L'Education des Filles*. London: Printed for N. R. and Sold by T. Leigh and D. Midwinter, 1699.] [Wing F474c.]

Hickes, George. *Sermons on Several Subjects*. 2 vols. London, n.p. 1713.

Hobbes, Thomas. *Leviathan* [1651] Ed. Richard Tuck. Cambridge: Cambridge University Press, 1991.

Lamy, Bernard. *The Art of Speaking; written in French by Messieurs du Port Royal, in persuance of a former Treatise Intituled, The Art of Thinking, Rendered into English*. London: Printed by W. Godbid, to be sold by M. Pitt, at the Angel against the little North Door of St. Paul's Church, 1676 [Wing, A372a].

Leslie, Charles. *The New Association. Part II. With farther Improvements .... An Answer to some Objections in the Pretended D. Foe's Explication in "the Reflections upon the Shortest Way" .... with "A Supplement," dated March 25, 1703, entitled, "With a short Account of the*

Original of Government. Compared with the Schemes of the Republicans and Whigs" to The New Association. Part II. With farther Improvements....An Answer to some Objections in the Pretended D. Foe's Explication in "the Reflections upon the Shortest Way...." London and Westminister, 1703 [Folger Library, BX.9180.L3.Cage].

Locke, John. *An Essay Concerning Humane Understanding* [1689]. London: Printed for Awnsham and John Churchill, at the Black Swan in Pater-Noster-Row, 1694 [Wing L2740]. Repr. Vol. 1, *The Works of John Locke.* 4 vols. London: Printed for Thomas Tegg, W. Sharpe and son, *et al.*, 1823.

—. *Two Treatises of Government* [1690]. Ed. Peter Laslett. Cambridge: Cambridge University Press, 1988.

—. "Remarks upon some of Mr. Norris's Books, wherein he asserts P. Malebranche's Opinion of seeing all Things in God" [1693]. *The Works of John Locke.* Vol. 9. London: Printed for Thomas Tegg, W. Sharpe and son, *et al.*, 1823. 247-59.

—. "The Reasonableness of Christianity, as Delivered in the Scriptures" [1695]. *The Works of John Locke.* Vol. 7 London: Printed for Thomas Tegg, W. Sharpe and son, *et al.*, 1823. 1-158.

Makin, Bathsua. *An Essay to Revive the Antient Education of Gentlewomen in Religion, Manners, Arts and Tongues. With an Answer to the Objections against this Way of Education.* London: Printed by J. D. to be sold by Tho. Parkhurst, at the Bible and Crown at the lower end of Cheapside, 1673 [Wing M309]. (Repr. with intr. Paula L. Barbour, The Augustan Reprint Society, William Andrews Clark Memorial Library, University of California, Los Angeles, 1980.)

Malebranche, Nicolas. *De la Recherche de la Vérité, où l'on traitte de la nature de l'esprit de l'homme, & de l'usage qu'il en doit faire pour éviter l'erreur dans les sciences*, 4th edn. Paris: André Pralard, 1678 [Folger Library, B1893.R.3.1678.Cage].

—. *De la Recherche de la Vérité*, in *Oeuvres de Malebranche.* Paris: Charpentier, 1853.

—. *Malebranche's search after truth: or a treatise of the nature of the humane mind.* Vol. 1. London: Printed for J. Dunton and S. Manship 1694 [Wing M315, Folger Library, 147104]. Vol. 2. London: Printed for S. Manship, 1695 [Wing M316, Folger Library, 147103].

Masham, Damaris. *Discourse Concerning the Love of God.* London: Printed for Awnsham and John Churchill, 1696.

Montagu, Lady Mary Wortley. *The Works of the Right Honourable Lady Mary Wortley Montagu*. 5 vols. Ed. J. Dallaway. London, 1817.

—. *The Complete Letters of Lady Mary Wortley Montagu*. 3 vols. Ed. Robert Halsband. Oxford: Oxford University Press, 1965–67.

More, Henry. *An Account of Virtue: or Dr Henry More's abridgment of morals*. London: for Benj. Tooke, 1690 [Wing, M2637].

Norris, John. *Cursory Reflections upon a Book Called, An Essay Concerning Humane Understanding* .... appended to *Christian Blessedness, or Discourses upon the Beatitudes of our Lord and Saviour Jesus Christ*. London, for S. Manship, 1690 [Wing 1246].

—. *Practical Discourses on Some Divine Subjects*. 1st edn. London: Printed for Samuel Manship [Wing 1257], 1691; 2nd edn, 1692 [Wing 1258]; 3rd edn, vol. 1, 1694 [Wing 1259]; 2nd edn, vol. 2, 1693, [Wing 1261]; vol. 3, 1693 [Wing 1263] vol. 4 1698 [Wing 1264, 1264a, 1264b].

—. *Reason and Religion; or, the Grounds and Measures of Devotion, considered from the Nature of God, and the Nature of Man*. Parts I and II. London: for Samuel Manship, 1689 [Wing 1265].

Orrery, Charles Boyle, 4th Earl of. *Dr Bentleys Dissertation on the Epistles of Phalaris and the Fables of Aesop examin'd*.... London: Printed for Thomas Bennet, 1698 [Wing O469].

Richardson, Samuel. *Sir Charles Grandison*. Vol 16. *The Works of Samuel Richardson*. London, 1811.

—. *The History of Sir Charles Grandison*. 3 vols. Ed. Jocelyn Harris. Oxford: Oxford University Press, 1972.

Swift, Jonathan. *Bickerstaff Papers and Pamphlets on the Church*. Ed. Herbert Davis. Oxford: Blackwell, 1957.

Tennyson, Alfred Lord. *The Princess*. *The Works of Alfred, Lord Tennyson*. London: Blackie, 1905.

Secondary Works

Aitken, G. A. "Steele's 'Ladies' Library.'" *The Athenaeum* 2958 (July 5, 1884): 16–17.

Ashcraft, Richard. "The Radical Dimensions of Locke's Political Thought: A Dialogic Essay on Some Problems of Interpretation." *History of Political Thought*, 13, 4 (1992): 703–72.

—. *Revolutionary Politics and Locke's Two Treatises of Government*. Princeton: Princeton University Press, 1986.

—. "Simple Objections and Complex Reality: Theorizing Political Radicalism in Seventeenth-Century England," *Political Studies* 40 (1992): 99-117.

Blanchard, Rae. "Richard Steele and the Status of Women." *Studies in Philology* 26, 3 (1929): 325-55.

Brown, Irene Q. "Domesticity, Feminism, and Friendship: Female Aristocratic Culture and Marriage in England, 1660-1760" *Journal of Family History* 7 (1982): 406-24.

Butler, Melissa. "Early Liberal Roots of Feminism: John Locke and the Attack on Patriarchy." *American Political Science Review* 72, 1 (1978): 135-50.

Cranston, Maurice. *John Locke, A Biography*. New York: Macmillan, 1957.

Cross, F.L. and Livingstone, E.A., eds. *The Oxford Dictionary of the Christian Church*. 2nd edn. London: Oxford University Press, 1974.

Dictionary of National Biography From the Earliest Times to 1900. Ed. Sir Leslie Stephen and Sir Sidney Lee. London: Oxford University Press, 1953.

Eaves, T.C. Duncan, and Ben D. Kimpel. *Samuel Richardson: A Biography*. Oxford: Clarendon Press, 1971.

Encyclopaedia Britannica. 11th edn. 29 vols. Cambridge: Cambridge University Press, 1911.

The Encyclopedia of Philosophy. Ed. Paul Edwards, *et al*. New York: Macmillan, 1967.

Ezell, Margaret J.M. *The Patriarch's Wife: Literary Evidence and the History of the Family*. Chapel Hill, NC: University of North Carolina Press, 1987.

Flynn, Carol Houlihan. *Samuel Richardson: A Man of Letters*. Princeton, NJ: Princeton University Press, 1982.

George, Margaret. "From 'Goodwife' to 'Mistress': The Transformation of the Female in Bourgeois Culture." *Science and Society* 37 (1973): 152-77.

Goldie, Mark "The Revolution of 1689 and the Structure of Political Argument." *Bulletin of Research in the Humanities* 83 (1980): 473-564.

—. "The Roots of True Whiggism, 1688-1694." *History of Political Thought* 1 (1980): 195-236.

—. *Tory Political Thought 1689-1714*. Ph. D. Dissertation. University of Cambridge, 1978.

Harrison, John, and Peter Laslett. *The Library of John Locke*. 2nd edn. Oxford: Clarendon Press, 1971.

Higgins, Patricia. "The Reactions of Women, with Special Reference to Women Petitioners." *Politics, Religion and the English Civil War*. Ed. Brian Manning. London: Edward Arnold, 1973.

Hill, Bridget. *The First English Feminist: "Reflections Upon Marriage" and Other Writings by Mary Astell*. Aldershot, Hants.: Gower Publishing, 1986.

—. "A Refuge from Men: The Idea of a Protestant Nunnery." *Past and Present* 117 (1987): 107-30.

Hollingshead, Greg. "Sources for the Ladies' Library." Berkeley Newsletter 11 (1989-90): 1-9.

Hutton, Sarah. "Damaris Cudworth, Lady Masham: between Platonism and Enlightenment." *British Journal for the History of Philosophy* 1, 1 (1993): 29-54.

James, Regina. "Mary, Mary, Quite Contrary, Or, Mary Astell and Mary Wollstonecraft Compared." *Studies in Eighteenth Century Culture* 5 (1976): 121-39.

Keymer, Tom. *Richardson's "Clarissa" and the Eighteenth Century Reader*. Cambridge: Cambridge University Press, 1992.

Kinnaird, Joan K. "Mary Astell and the Conservative Contribution to English Feminism." *Journal of British Studies* 19 (1979): 53-79.

Lemprière's Classical Dictionary of Proper Names mentioned in Ancient Authors. London, 1948.

Levine, Joseph. *The Battle of the Books*. Ithaca, NY: Cornell University Press, 1991.

Lougee, Carolyn C. *Les Paradis des Femmes: Women, Salons, and Social Stratification in Seventeenth-Century France*. Princeton, NJ: Princeton University Press, 1976.

McCrystal, John William. *An Inadvertant Feminist: Mary Astell (1666-1731)*. M.A. Thesis. Department of Political Studies, Auckland University, New Zealand, 1992.

—. "A Lady's Calling: Mary Astell's Notion of Women." *Political Theory Newsletter* 4 (1992): 56-70.

Mack, Phyllis. "Women as Prophets during the English Civil War." *The Origins of Anglo-American Radicalism*. Ed. Margaret Jacob and James Jacob. London: Routledge. 1984. 214-31.

MacKinnon, Flora Isobel. "The Philosophy of John Norris of Bemerton." *The Philosophical Monographs* 1, 2 (1910).

McNally, David. "Locke, Levellers and Liberty: Property and

Democracy in the Thought of the First Whigs." *History of Political Thought* 10 (1989): 17-40.

Monod, Paul Kléber. "The Politics of Matrimony: Jacobitism and Marriage in Eighteenth Century England." *The Jacobite Challenge*. Ed. Eveline Cruickshanks and Jeremy Black. Edinburgh: John Donald Press, 1988. 31-36.

Moyer, Egin S. *Who Was Who in Church History*. Rev. edn. 1962.

Myers, Mitzi. "Domesticating Minerva: Bathsua Makin's 'Curious' Argument for Women's Education." *Studies in Eighteenth Century Culture* 14 (1985): 173-92.

Needham, Gwendolyn B. "Mary de la Rivière Manley, Tory Defender." *Huntington Library Quarterly* 12, 3 (1949): 253-88.

The New Schaff-Herzog Encyclopedia of Religious Knowledge. 12 vols. New York, London: Funk & Wagnalls, Co., 1908.

Norton, J. E. "Some Uncollected Authors XXVII; Mary Astell, 1666-1731." *The Book Collector* 10, 1 (1961): 58-60.

O'Donnell, Sheryl. "Mr. Locke and the Ladies: The Indelible Words on the Tabula Rasa." *Studies in Eighteenth Century Culture* 8 (1978): 151-64.

—. "'My Idea in Your Mind': John Locke and Damaris Cudworth Masham." *Mothering the Mind*. Ed. Ruth Perry and Martine Brownley. New York: Holmes and Meier, 1984. 26-46.

Oxford Classical Dictionary. Cambridge: Cambridge University Press, 1965.

Oxford Dictionary of Foreign Phrases and Classical Quotations. Ed. Hugh Percy Jones. Edinburgh: John Grant, 1929.

The Oxford Dictionary of the Christian Church. Ed. F.L. Cross and E.A. Livingstone. 2nd edn. London: Oxford University Press, 1974.

Pateman, Carole. *The Sexual Contract*. Cambridge: Polity Press, 1988.

—. "God Hath Ordained to Man a Helper: Hobbes, Patriarchy and Conjugal Right" *British Journal of Political Science* 19 (1989): 445-64.

Perry, Ruth. *The Celebrated Mary Astell: An Early English Feminist*. Chicago: University of Chicago Press, 1986.

—. "Mary Astell's Response to the Enlightenment." *Women in History* 9 (1984): 13-40.

—. "Radical doubt and the Liberation of Women." *Eighteenth Century Studies* 18, 4 (1985): 472-93.

Reynolds, Myra. *The Learned Lady in England 1650-1760*. New York: Houghton Mifflin Co., 1920.

Scaltsas, Patricia Ward. "Women as Ends — Women as Means in the Enlightenment." *Women's Rights and the Rights of Man*. Ed. A.J. Arnaud and E. Kingdom. Aberdeen: Aberdeen University Press, 1990. 138-48.

Schochet, G.J. *Patriarchalism and Political Theory*. Oxford: Blackwells, 1975.

Shanley, Mary Lyndon. "Marriage Contract and Social Contract in Seventeenth Century English Political Thought." *Western Political Quarterly* 32 (1979): 79-91.

Smith, Florence M. *Mary Astell*. New York: Columbia University Press, 1916.

Smith, Hilda. *Reason's Disciples*. Urbana, IL: University of Illinois Press, 1982.

Sommerville, Margaret. *Sex and Subjection: Attitudes to Women in Early-Modern Society*. London: Arnold, 1995.

Springborg, Patricia. "Mary Astell (1666-1731), Critic of the Marriage Contract/Social Contract Analogue." *A Companion to Early Modern Women's Writing*. Ed. Anita Pacheco. Oxford: Blackwell, 2002.

—. "Astell, Masham and Locke." *Women Writers and the Early Modern British Political Tradition*. Ed. Hilda Smith. Cambridge: Cambridge University Press, 1998. 105-25.

—. "Mary Astell and John Locke." *The Cambridge Companion to English Literature, 1650 to 1750*. Ed. Steven Zwicker. Cambridge: Cambridge University Press, 1998. 276-306.

—. "Mary Astell (1666-1731), Critic of Locke." *American Political Science Review* 89, 3 (1995): 621-33.

—, ed. *Mary Astell (1666-1731), Political Writings*. Cambridge: Cambridge University Press, 1996.

Spurr, John. "The Church of England, Comprehension and the Toleration Act of 1689." *English Historical Review* 104, 413 (1989): 927-46.

—. "'Latitudinarianism' and the Restoration Church." *The Historical Journal* 31, 1 (1988): 61-82.

—. "'Rational Religion' in Restoration England." *Journal of the History of Ideas* 49, 4 (1988): 563-85.

Squadrito, K.M. "Mary Astell's Critique of Locke's View of Thinking Matter." *Journal of the History of Philosophy* 25 (1987): 433-40.

Upham, A.H. "English *Femmes Savantes* at the End of the Seventeenth Century." *Journal of English and Germanic Philology* 12 (1913): 262-76.

—. "A Parallel Case for Richardson's Clarissa.," *Modern Language Notes* 28 (1913): 103–05.

Watson, Foster, ed. *Vives and the Renascence Education of Women.* New York: Longmans Green & Co., 1912.

Wing, Donald. *Short Title Catalogue of Books Printed in England, Scotland…1641-1700.* 3 vols. New York: Modern Language Association of America, 1972.

Yolton, Jean S. and John W. Yolton. *John Locke: A Reference Guide.* Boston., MA: G.K. Hall & Co., 1985.